The Byzantine princess Theophano, wh to marry the Ottonian emperor Otto I Ottonian empire in Nijmegen in 991. In event a group of distinguished scholars m Hernen in the Netherlands with the aim of discussing various issues and aspects of Theophano's background in Byzantium, her life in the West, and her impact on society at the turn of the first millennium.

This volume brings together in carefully edited form a group of the papers and proceedings from 1991. Each contribution helps to place Theophano in a broad cultural and historical context. The historical, intellectual and artistic background of her age is described, and there are essays on her education, her surroundings, and the image of noble women in the Middle Ages.

The empress Theophano

The empress Theophano

Byzantium and the West at the turn of the first millennium

Edited by
ADELBERT DAVIDS
University of Nijmegen

CAMBRIDGE
UNIVERSITY PRESS

PUBLISHED BY THE PRESS SYNDICATE OF THE UNIVERSITY OF CAMBRIDGE
The Pitt Building, Trumpington Street, Cambridge, United Kingdom

CAMBRIDGE UNIVERSITY PRESS
The Edinburgh Building, Cambridge CB2 2RU, UK
40 West 20th Street, New York NY 10011–4211, USA
477 Williamstown Road, Port Melbourne, VIC 3207, Australia
Ruiz de Alarcón 13, 28014 Madrid, Spain
Dock House, The Waterfront, Cape Town 8001, South Africa

http://www.cambridge.org

First published 1995
First paperback edition 2002

A catalogue record for this book is available from the British Library

Library of Congress Cataloguing in Publication data
The empress Theophano: Byzantium and the West at the turn of the first
millennium / edited by Adelbert Davids.
p. cm.
Papers presented at a symposium held at the Castle of Hernen
in the Netherlands in May 1991.
Published in association with the A. A. Bredius Foundation
(Hernen, the Netherlands) and the Institute for Eastern Christian Studies
(Nijmegen, the Netherlands).
Includes bibliographical references.
ISBN 0 521 45296 1
1. Theophano, empress, consort of Otto II, Holy Roman Emperor, 955–991 – Congress.
2. Empresses – Holy Roman Empire – Biography – Congress.
3. Holy Roman Empire – Relations – Byzantine Empire – Congress.
4. Byzantine Empire – Relations – Holy Roman Empire – Congresses.
I. Davids, Adelbert.
DD140.T47E48 1995
943'.022'092–dc20 94-5289 CIP

ISBN 0 521 45296 1 hardback
ISBN 0 521 52467 9 paperback

Contents

Illustrations

Contributors

A. J. VAN DER AALST is Emeritus Professor of Eastern Theology, University of Nijmegen, the Netherlands

W. J. AERTS is Emeritus Professor of Byzantine and New Greek Studies, University of Groningen, the Netherlands

P. BANGE is Lecturer in Medieval History, University of Nijmegen, the Netherlands

K. CIGGAAR, Department of Byzantine Studies, Leyden, the Netherlands

ADELBERT DAVIDS is Professor of Patristics and the History of the Early Church, University of Nijmegen, the Netherlands and member of the Institute for Eastern Christian Studies, Nijmegen, the Netherlands

ODILO ENGELS is Professor of Medieval History, University of Cologne, Germany

L. F. GENICOT is Emeritus Professor of Medieval History, University of Louvain-la-Neuve, Belgium

JUDITH HERRIN is Professor of Byzantine History, Princeton University, USA

JACQUELINE LAFONTAINE-DOSOGNE is Professor of Byzantine Art, University of Louvain-la-Neuve; Chef de Département at the Royal Museums of Art and History, Brussels, Belgium

KARL LEYSER was Emeritus Professor of Medieval History in the University of Oxford, and Fellow of All Souls' College, Oxford, England

Contributors

ROSAMOND MCKITTERICK is Reader in Medieval History in the University of Cambridge, and Fellow of Newnham College, Cambridge, England

JONATHAN SHEPARD is Lecturer in Byzantine History in the University of Cambridge, England

BERT THISSEN, Municipal Archives of Cleves, Germany

E. VOORDECKERS is Professor of Byzantine Studies, Universities of Gand and Louvain, Belgium

H. WESTERMANN-ANGERHAUSEN is Director of the Schnütgen Museum, Cologne, Germany

JOHANNA MARIA VAN WINTER is Emeritus Professor of Medieval History, University of Utrecht, the Netherlands

HILTJE F. H. ZOMER is Research Fellow at the University of Leyden, the Netherlands

Preface

For many years the A.A. Bredius Foundation at Hernen in the Netherlands has been interested in the history of the relations between East and West during the Middle Ages. In 1985 it published *Byzantium and the Low Countries in the Tenth Century*, a volume which might be considered a forerunner of the present book. The volume dealt with aspects of art and history in the Ottonian era, and with the empress Theophano, as her name is normally spelt in Greek, in particular. A Byzantine princess, she became the wife of the emperor Otto II in 972, and, after his death in 983, became regent for her three-year-old son Otto III. It was to be expected, then, that the millennium of Theophano's death in Nijmegen in the year 991 would be commemorated. To that effect a group of scholars from different countries met at Hernen Castle, not far from Nijmegen, in May 1991 to discuss Theophano and her times. Most of the contributions to that symposium are published in the present volume.

The historical figure of Theophano is hard to grasp. Her name appears in all books on the Ottonian era, but then only peripherally: as wife of Otto II and mother of Otto III, or in connection with her magnificent marriage charter. Only once has an attempt been made to draw a lively and vivid picture of Theophano, the Byzantine princess who became one of the greatest medieval sovereigns in the West. That was done by Albert H. Rausch, who published his historical novel *Die Kaiserin Theophano* under the pseudonym Henry Benrath in 1940.

On the occasion of the commemoration of Theophano's death, several new studies about Theophano were published in 1991, especially, of course, in Germany, where she was buried in the church of St Pantaleon at Cologne. Most significant are the two prestigious volumes of *Kaiserin Theophanu: Begegnung des Ostens und Westens um die Wende des ersten Jahrtausends*, edited by Anton von Euw and Peter Schreiner (Cologne, 1991). In the Schnütgen-Museum at Cologne an exhibition devoted to book illumination was organized. The catalogue *Vor dem Jahr 1000: abendländische Buchkunst zur Zeit der Kaiserin Theophanu* is a worthy witness to this exhibition. Several studies by Gunther Wolf – who also stimulated a reissue of Benrath's historical novel (Stuttgart, 1991) – and others were collected in the volume *Kaiserin Theophanu: Prinzessin aus der Ferne – des Westreichs grosse Kaiserin*, edited by Gunther Wolf (Cologne, 1991). Finally, the proceedings of an international symposium held in the Schnütgen-Museum in June 1991 appeared at Cologne in 1993: *Kunst im Zeitalter der Kaiserin Theophanu*, edited by Anton von Euw and Peter Schreiner as well as at Sigmaringen those of another conference of medieval scholars on Theophano: *Die Begegnung des Westers mit dem Osten: Kongressakten des 4. Symposions des Mediävistenverbandes in Köln 1991*, edited by Odilo Engels and Peter Schreiner.

The present collection of studies offers alternative points of view and new insights into the development of the European world and the role of the imperial palatinate. Besides the historical background and the phenomenon of Theophano as an individual who influenced her new western world (K. Leyser, O. Engels, K. Ciggaar), other topics and questions are treated such as:

Education, marriage-politics, and the image of noble medieval women in contemporary literature: were medieval women instruments or agents in a men's world? (J. Herrin, J.M. van Winter, A. Davids, J. Shepard, P. Bange).

Cross-currents in art: how original was the West? (J. Lafontaine-Dosogne, E. Voordeckers, H. Westermann-Angerhausen, B. Thissen, H.F.H. Zomer).

The intellectual world Theophano found in the West: which books were available and to what extent was Greek known in the western world? (R. McKitterick, W.J. Aerts).

Theophano's world approached from the economic as well as from the spiritual sides (L.F. Genicot and A.J. van der Aalst).

This book could not have been published without the assistance of the staff of the Institute for Eastern Christian Studies at Nijmegen. Especially, Jan Jonk and Marijke Smits have given their utmost of time and energy during the preparation of the contributions for print. Valuable suggestions and effective help came also from Krijnie Ciggaar, Andrew Palmer and Anne-Marie Palmer. William Davies of the Cambridge University Press, and the copy-editing by Frances Brown, brought the whole project to completion.

The last decade of the second millennium seems a good time to publish the different papers which were read at the colloquium. The protagonist is a woman by whose marriage, in a certain sense, Western Europe became allied with the Byzantine Empire in the East. A millennium later, in the 1990s, new alliances are commonplace and are formed across all international boundaries. Whether Theophano is a suitable symbol for feminism in the 1990s is a matter for debate: she is certainly an intriguing woman.

A NOTE ON SPELLING AND TRANSLITERATION

Greek terms and names are given according to the transliteration used in *The Oxford Dictionary of Byzantium*. For Latin and other western terms and names *The Cambridge Medieval History* is usually followed.

This volume is dedicated
to the memory of
Karl Leyser.

Abbreviations

AQDG Ausgewählte Quellen zur deutschen Geschichte des Mittelalters: Freiherr vom Stein-Gedächtnisausgabe (Darmstadt)

BZ *Byzantinische Zeitschrift* (Leipzig and Munich, 1892 ff)

DA *Deutsches Archiv für die Erforschung des Mittelalters* (Marburg and Cologne, 1951 ff)

DOP *Dumbarton Oaks Papers* (Washington, DC, 1941 ff)

DOT Dumbarton Oaks Texts (Washington, DC)

HZ *Historische Zeitschrift* (Munich, 1859 ff)

JÖB *Jahrbuch der Österreichischen Byzantinistik* (Vienna, 1969 ff)

von Euw and Schreiner, *Kaiserin Theophanu* *Kaiserin Theophanu: Begegnung des Ostens und Westens um die Wende des ersten Jahrtausends: Gedenkschrift des Kölner Schnütgen-Museums zum 1000. Todesjahr der Kaiserin*, ed. A. von Euw and P. Schreiner, 2 vols. (Cologne, 1991)

MGH Monumenta Germaniae historica

- **AA** Auctores antiquissimi, 15 vols.
- **Cap.** MGH Leges: Capitularia regum Francorum, 2 vols.
- **Const.** MGH Leges: Constitutiones et acta publica imperatorum et regum, 9 vols.
- **DD O I; II; III; Th** Diplomas: Die Urkunden Ottos I.; Ottos II.; Ottos III.; Theophano
- **SRG** Scriptores rerum Germanicarum

SRG in us. schol.	Scriptores rerum Germanicarum in usum scholarum
SS	Scriptores, 32 vols.
Schriften	Schriften des Reichsinstituts für ältere deutsche Geschichtskunde
ODB	*The Oxford Dictionary of Byzantium*, ed. A. P. Kazhdan *et al.*, 3 vols. (New York and Oxford, 1991)
PG	Patrologiae cursus completus: series graeca, ed. J.-P. Migne, 161 vols. in 166 parts (Paris, 1857–66)
PL	Patrologiae cursus completus: series latina, ed. J.-P. Migne, 221 vols. in 222 parts (Paris, 1844–55)
SC	Sources Chrétiennes (Paris, 1941 ff)

1

Theophanu divina gratia imperatrix augusta: western and eastern emperorship in the later tenth century*

KARL LEYSER

In the second half of the tenth century the eastern and the Ottonian empires confronted one another at a time when neither lacked aggressiveness and self-assurance, though both qualities still had to be tested against crises and setbacks. Their political cultures differed profoundly, and the difference is not best summed up by calling the Byzantine world and its power structures advanced and those of the Saxon Reich barbaric, to use the Greeks' own word. True, Byzantine emperorship rested on ancient and, it was felt, divinely willed certainties, while there was as yet something provisional, tentative and looking for a content in that of the West. Yet it too wanted to be seen and understood as being directed providentially, by the heavenly architect. As the *arenga* of one of Otto I's diplomas for Hersfeld succinctly expressed it:[1]

> Otto by the ordinance of divine providence august emperor. The power of God advanced us to the pinnacle of the imperial summit so that we should promote the well-being and progress especially of all the places devoted to the service of God, so that by the orisons of his servants, of those who watch and pray there, the prosperity of our empire should be guided in uninterrupted tranquillity and that after the passing away of this

* Karl Leyser left this text, which also appears in his *Communications and Power in Medieval Europe: The Carolingian and Ottonian Centuries*, ed. T. Reuter (London, Hambledon Press, 1993), as an unfootnoted lecture at his death in 1992; I have copy-edited the text lightly and supplied the necessary references to primary sources and the secondary literature. My thanks are due for help with references to Donald Bullough and especially to Jonathan Shepard, who gave me invaluable guidance on matters Byzantine. Timothy Reuter

[1] MGH DD O I, no. 356 (Benevento, 15 February 968); the *arenga* recurs essentially unchanged in MGH DD O I, no. 373 for Casa aurea (Pescara), MGH DD O I, no. 404 for St Sophia, Benevento, and MGH DD O II, no. 17 for Hersfeld.

temporal life, companionship in eternal felicity shall not be denied to us.

Contubernium it was called, like sharing a tent. The historians of the Ottonian Reich and its liturgical practice unceasingly proclaimed it as part of the divine order for the world.

The Byzantine emperor was God's viceroy in this life for the *oikoumene,* and by rights his authority stretched over the whole universe, whatever interlopers *de facto* contested, rejected, ignored or denied his lordship.[2] Ottonian emperorship had as yet no such content. It was but an enhanced kingship: rule over more than one kingdom made manifest and recognized by a rank, a dignity and coronation ritual. When the Italian *dictator* who had drafted the preamble of Otto I's diploma for Hersfeld cited above spoke about the advancement of clerks and monks as the servants of God, he was not only uttering a commonplace repeated in hundreds of such preambles and elsewhere, but he also failed to define a specifically imperial task and duty, for the well-being of churches, their protection and tranquillity, were the first and foremost duty of all kings, not just emperors, and most of them swore to it in their coronation promises.[3] *Arengae* similar to this one also occur in Otto I's diplomas before 2 February 962, when he was crowned emperor by pope John XII in St Peter's, though they were less frequent. Here is an example, the gift of half the city of Chur to its bishop with all appurtenances and rights of justice:[4] 'If we strive zealously to augment church possessions as they were established by our predecessors, we do not doubt to earn the highest reward thereby.'

Our task must therefore be to seek out, if possible, and identify those tasks and activities of Otto I's that were specifically imperial and not just royal, and it will soon be found that it is not at all easy

[2] O. Treitinger, *Die oströmische Kaiser- und Reichsidee nach ihrer Gestaltung im höfischen Zeremoniell* (Jena, 1938), pp. 161–213; F. Dölger, 'Die Familie der Könige im Mittelalter', in Dölger, *Byzanz und die europäische Staatenwelt* (Ettal, 1953), pp. 34–69; A. Toynbee, *Constantine Porphyrogenitus and his World* (London, 1973), pp. 346–51.

[3] For the *arengae* of Ottonian diplomas see the works cited in n. 93; on coronation promises see P.E. Schramm, *Kaiser, Könige und Päpste: gesammelte Aufsätze*, 4 vols. in 5 (Stuttgart, 1968–70), especially II, pp. 140–305 ('Die Krönung im 9. und 10. Jahrhundert'), and III, pp. 33–134 ('Die deutschen Herrscher aus dem sächsischen Hause als Könige (bis 962)'); Janet L. Nelson, *Politics and Ritual in Early Medieval Europe* (London, 1986), especially 'Kingship, law and liturgy in the political thought of Hincmar of Rheims', pp. 133–71.

[4] MGH DD O I, no. 191 (Fritzlar, 16 January 958).

to do so. The Byzantine emperor, the *basileus Romaion*, commanded a machinery of government and a *lex scripta* to which he could add in his own novels as the situation required.[5] Difficult and even fundamental problems, such as the relentless pressure of the *dynatoi* seeking to acquire lands at the expense of the *penetes*, that is of the poor and middling peasant owners,[6] the maintenance of military holdings to keep up the armed forces in so far as they were made up of *stratiotai* as against the regiments of standing troops,[7] all these things could be and were countered by legislation. Even if these laws did not in the long run arrest, let alone reverse the process, they nonetheless slowed it down and prevented the rapid erosion of what was considered to be a vital resource for both defensive and offensive military operations. The landed aristocracy had no cause to bless the reign of Basil II. His novels and their enforcement and his taxation for once hit them hard, not

[5] L. Bréhier, *Le Monde byzantin*, II, *Les institutions byzantines* (Paris, 1949), especially pp. 89–217; W. Ensslin, 'The government and administration of the Byzantine Empire', in *The Cambridge Medieval History*, IV, *The Byzantine Empire*, II, *Government, Church and Civilisation*, ed. J.M. Hussey (Cambridge, 1967), 1–54; H. Ahrweiler, 'Recherches sur l'administration de l'Empire byzantin aux IXe–XIe siècles', in Ahrweiler, *Etudes sur les structures administratives et sociales de Byzance* (London, 1971), ch. 8; reconstructions based on lists of officials in N. Oikonomides, *Listes de préséance byzantines des IXe et Xe siècles* (Paris, 1972), especially pp. 281–363. On law see H.J. Scheltema, 'Byzantine law', in *Government, Church and Civilisation*, ed. J.M. Hussey, pp. 55–78; *ODB*, pp. 1497–8 and P.E. Pieler, 'Rechtsliteratur', in H. Hunger, *Die hochsprachliche profane Literatur der Byzantiner*, II, *Byzantinisches Handbuch*, 5/2 (Munich, 1978), pp. 343–480, at pp. 445–72.

[6] On *dynatoi* and *penetes* see G. Ostrogorsky, 'Agrarian conditions in the Byzantine Empire in the Middle Ages', in *Cambridge Economic History of Europe*, I, *The Agrarian Life of the Middle Ages*, second edn ed. M.M. Postan (Cambridge, 1971), pp. 216–22; Toynbee, *Constantine Porphyrogenitus* (see n. 2), pp. 145–76. The views there expressed have been subject to some debate in recent decades: R. Morris, 'The powerful and the poor in tenth-century Byzantium: law and reality', *Past and Present*, 73 (1976), 3–27, argues that the problem is an artificial one; P. Lemerle, *Agrarian History of Byzantium from the Origins to the Twelfth Century: The Sources and Problems* (Galway, 1979), pp. 90–108, sees the issue as essentially one of taxation; A. Harvey, *Economic Expansion in the Byzantine Empire, 900–1200* (Cambridge, 1989), pp. 37–44, sees the problem as a real one caused by demographic increase and the tenth-century imperial legislation as a response to the strength of the magnates.

[7] Toynbee, *Constantine Porphyrogenitus* (see n. 2), pp. 134–45; Lemerle, *Agrarian History* (see n. 6), pp. 115–65; J. Haldon, *Recruitment and Conscription in the Byzantine Empire: A Study in the Origins of the Stratiotika Ktemata*, Sitzungsberichte der Österreichischen Akademie der Wissenschaften zu Wien, phil.-hist. Klasse 357 (Vienna, 1979), 41–65; *Le Traité sur la guérilla (de velitatione) de l'empéreur Nicéphore Phocas (963–969)*, ed. G. Dagron and H. Mihăescu (Paris, 1986), pp. 266–9, 275–83; D. Gorecki, 'The strateia of Constantine VII: the legal status, administration and historical background', *BZ*, 82 (1989), 157–76.

to mention the punishments for rebellions and the drastic diminution of individual noble fortunes.[8]

It does not follow that the weak, the underdogs, prospered under this regime. They too were taxed, if anything more relentlessly, and governed harshly. The imperial bureaucracy could be directed from the centre. It was literate, it received and could respond to *grammata* and *keleuseis* from the palace, but there was rarely, if ever, any attempt to foster attitudes and an atmosphere of loyalty and attachment lower down and among the governed.[9] Army discipline too was harsh and often enough unjust. This must be set against the technical accomplishments of Byzantine warfare in the tenth century, which so greatly impressed those western observers who came to know them. Westerners, not only Italians, were aware of the fast Greek ships with their well-armed troops on board and above all their deadly weapon, Greek fire.[10] Byzantine land forces knew a chain of command, units and sub-units. They could be marshalled and organized in a way that surpassed the military fluidities of the Ottonians, whose own military capacities were at the same time grossly underrated by Nikephoros Phokas in his conversation with Liutprand of Cremona, if we can trust the bishop's report in the *Legatio*.[11] It is

[8] Lemerle, *Agrarian History* (see n. 6), p. 107; J.-C. Cheynet, *Pouvoir et contestations à Byzance (963–1210)* (Paris, 1990), pp. 331–6, argues that Basil II did not direct his novels against landlords as a 'class', but rather against specific rival families such as the Phokades. The purges and conflicts with leading noble families are still best followed in G. Ostrogorsky, *History of the Byzantine State*, third revised edn (New Brunswick, 1969), pp. 295–340.

[9] Dagron and Mihăescu, *Le Traité* (see n. 7), pp. 284–7; G. Dagron, 'Byzance et le modèle islamique au Xe siècle: à propos des constitutions tactiques de l'empereur Leon VI', *Comptes-rendues des séances de l'Académie des inscriptions et belles-lettres* (1983), pp. 219–42, at pp. 237–42 on Byzantine attempts to adapt and exploit Islamic notions of *jihad*; J. Haldon, '"Blood and Ink": some observations on Byzantine attitudes towards warfare and diplomacy', in *Byzantine Diplomacy: Papers from the Twenty-Fourth Spring Symposium of Byzantine Studies, Cambridge, March 1990*, ed. J. Shepard and S. Franklin (London, 1992), pp. 281–94, at pp. 291–4.

[10] E. Eickhoff, *Seekrieg und Seepolitik zwischen Islam und Abendland bis zum Aufstiege Pisas und Genuas (650–1040)* (Saarbrücken, 1954), pp. 42–98; H. Ahrweiler, *Byzance et la mer: la marine de guerre, la politique et les institutions maritimes de Byzance aux VIIe-XVe siècles*, Bibliothèque Byzantine, Etudes 5 (Paris, 1966), especially pp. 93–135. On Greek fire see J. Haldon and M. Byrnes, 'A possible solution to the problem of Greek fire', *BZ*, 70 (1977), 91–9; E. Pásthory, 'Über das "Griechisches Feuer"', *Zeitschrift für Archäologie und Kunstgeschichte*, 17 (1986), 27–37.

[11] For Byzantine military organization at this time see Toynbee, *Constantine Porphyrogenitus* (see n. 2), pp. 282–7; *Three Byzantine Military Treatises*, ed. G. Dennis,

possible that the Greeks, because they seldom, if ever, met the best of the Latin *miles armatus*, heavily armed, shielded, hauberked and mounted warriors, did not follow the military evolution of the West very closely and were thus taken by surprise when they at last came to see it at close quarters during the First Crusade.[12]

To identify and discover a programme, an overarching *raison d'être* for Otto I's emperorship, other than the vast extent of his overlordship, is something that is much harder to do than it is for Charlemagne's, and this for two reasons. In the first place we read in Widukind that he had already been hailed *imperator* by his warriors after the great victory over the Magyars at the battle of the Lech in 955 just as his father's men, according to Widukind again, had called Henry I 'emperor' in 933 after his victory over the Magyars at Riade.[13] This kind of acclamation of a victorious commander, whatever its classical undertones in so well-schooled a writer as the Corvey monk, was not impossible and even received some support from another source, and that a critical one, the older Life of Otto I's mother, Queen Matilda. The author knew of Otto's Roman coronation, which he believed was by God's command, but he also mentioned and censured what he described as a tumultuous act of Otto I's host, which made him emperor by imposing a diadem that he could not decline or repudiate.[14] Yet the idea of an emperorship that did not owe its beginnings and its rights to a papal coronation had some resonance and appeal, not least, as we saw, for Widukind of Cor-

DOT (Washington, DC, 1985); E. McGeer, 'Infantry versus cavalry: the Byzantine response', *Revue des Etudes Byzantines*, 46 (1988), 135–45. For Nikephoros' views on Ottonian soldiers see Liutprand, *Legatio*, in *Quellen zur Geschichte der sächsischen Kaiserzeit*, ed. A. Bauer and R. Rau, AQDG 8, c. 11, p. 182.

12 Anna Komnene, *Alexiad*, VIII, 3, ed. B. Leib (Paris, 1945), III, p. 115; cf. also the comments in X, 3, 5 (II, p. 197) and XIV, 7, 2 (III, p. 173). T. Kolias, *Byzantinische Waffen: ein Beitrag zur byzantinischen Waffenkunde von den Anfängen bis zur lateinischen Eroberung*, Byzantina Vindobonensia (Vienna, 1988), pp. 200–8, especially p. 208 with nn. 129–30, shows that the Byzantines were recruiting mounted warriors from the West from the mid-eleventh century onwards, but the effectiveness of the Crusaders was evidently still a shock and a surprise.

13 Widukind, *Res gestae Saxonicae*, in *Quellen zur Geschichte der sächsischen Kaiserzeit*, ed. A. Bauer and R. Rau, AQDG 8, III, 49, p. 128 (Lechfeld); I, 39, p. 58 (Riade); see E.E. Stengel, 'Der Heerkaiser (Den Kaiser macht das Heer): Studien zur Geschichte eines politischen Gedankens', in Stengel, *Abhandlungen und Untersuchungen zur Geschichte des Kaisergedankens im Mittelalter* (Cologne, 1965), pp. 1–169, at pp. 56–91.

14 *Vita Mahthildis antiquior*, c. 16, MGH SS X, p. 81; for commentary see Stengel, 'Heerkaiser', in *Abhandlungen* (see n. 13), p. 76.

vey.[15] Nevertheless, it could not prevail against the strength of the Carolingian tradition and the papacy's established hold over the act of coronation. It was precisely the frequent papal coronations of local contenders in the struggles for the Italian kingdom during the later ninth and early tenth century, and the occasional imperial unctions of Carolingians from the north like Charles III and Arnolf, that had given the papacy its indefeasible and incontrovertible sanction of crowning or refusing to crown. Wido, Lambert, Louis the Blind and Berengar I had all sought and held emperorships which gave them some standing in Rome without much easing their desperate and treacherous battles for the Italian kingship and its rich assets in Pavia and the Lombard plain.[16] Berengar I of the margraval house of Friuli, and through his mother a grandson of Louis the Pious, had been the last to be so crowned, by pope John X in 915, shortly after the latter's victory over the Saracens at the Garigliano. Berengar had not taken part in this campaign as befitted a king, but a temporary power vacuum in Tuscany had opened the way to Rome for him.[17] It is revealing that entirely local and regional considerations led to the invitation, just as they were to do in the case of Otto I. The house of Theophylact, with its iron grip on Roman society and its very influential friends outside, not least of all in Constantinople, was able to repel at least three assaults by king Hugh, battling at the walls of Rome for an imperial coronation that eluded him. The regime of Alberic, the *princeps Romanus*, may have wanted to dispense with emperorship altogether.[18] When it was unable to do

[15] For a good recent discussion see E. Karpf, *Herrscherlegitimation und Reichsbegriff in der ottonischen Geschichtsschreibung des 10. Jahrhunderts*, Historische Forschungen, 10 (Stuttgart, 1985), especially pp. 168–75, 196; see also H. Beumann, '*Imperator Romanorum, rex gentium:* zu Widukind III 76', in Beumann, *Ausgewählte Aufsätze aus den Jahren 1966–1986* (Sigmaringen, 1987), pp. 324–40.

[16] G. Fasoli, *I re d'Italia (888–962)* (Florence, 1949), pp. 1–96; Fasoli, 'Re, imperatori e sudditi nell'Italia del secolo X', *Studi Medievali*, serie terza, 4 (1963), 52–74; R. Hiestand, *Byzanz und das Regnum Italicum im 10. Jahrhundert*, Geist und Werk der Zeiten, 9 (Zurich, 1964), pp. 36–137, and, for a brief account in English with a broader overall context, C. Wickham, *Early Medieval Italy, 400–1000* (London, 1981), pp. 168–81.

[17] Fasoli, *I re d'Italia* (see n. 16), pp. 83–7; Hiestand, *Byzanz* (see n. 16), pp. 128–37; see most recently R. Savigni, 'Sacerdozio e regno in età post-Carolingia: l'episcopato di Giovanni X, arcivescovo di Ravenna (905–914) e papa (914–928)', *Rivista di Storia della Chiesa in Italia*, 46 (1992), 1–29, at p. 4, with further literature.

[18] This seems at least a plausible deduction from Alberic's refusal to grant imperial coronation to Hugh in 933 and (probably) to Otto I in 951/2; on the latter event see the references in *Regesta Imperii*, II, 1, *Die Regesten des Kaiserreichs unter Heinrich I. und Otto I. 919–973*, ed. J.F. Böhmer and E. von Ottenthal (Hil-

so it turned to an effective and formidable military protector who had already once, in 951–2, subjected the dynasty of the north in the person of Berengar II of the house of Ivrea, who now himself threatened Rome in order to hold together his own following with the magic or poison of success. Otto I's emperorship thus came about because the papacy, the clan of Alberic, now headed by pope John XII, needed help. It did not need or want what it eventually got, a stark northern military presence, not indeed a permanent occupation but repeated Ottonian expeditions at brief intervals, manned by Saxon, Rhine-Frankish, Bavarian, Swabian and Slav contingents.[19]

Otto I's emperorship stemmed from his victories over 'barbarian' peoples, Hungarians and others, so the opening narrative of pope John XII's privilege authorizing the Saxon ruler's most cherished plans proclaimed. He had come to receive the triumphal crown of victory, 'in inperii culmen' from St Peter, prince of the Apostles 'through us [John XII]'.[20] The formulation of Otto's *arenga* in his diploma for Hersfeld cited above, with its reference to the *imperialis culminis ... apicem*, pinnacle of the imperial summit , now becomes very clear and significant.[21] John's privilege harnesses the emperorship to the forcible conversion of the Slav peoples under Saxon military rule and envisaged the archbishopric of Magdeburg and suffragan sees as the bastions from which it was to be brought about.[22] The papal privilege entitled

desheim, 1967), no. 201a, and in general see Hiestand, *Byzanz* (see n. 16), pp. 158–61, 164–9, 177–9 and J. Shepard, 'Byzantium and the West', in *New Cambridge Medieval History*, III, *900–1024*, ed. T. Reuter (Cambridge, forthcoming).

19 Fasoli, *I re d'Italia* (see n. 16), pp. 171–204, has a good account of the last days of the Alberician regime in Rome. It should be noted, however, that the theme of the pope appealing to a power north of the Alps for help and getting far more help than he wanted was not confined to the late tenth century but was a leitmotiv of papal history from the eighth through to the twelfth century at least.

20 John XII for Magdeburg, Rome, 12 February 962: H. Zimmermann, *Papsturkunden, 896–1046*, I, *896–996*, second edn, Denkschriften der Österreichischen Akademie der Wissenschaften, phil.-hist. Klasse, 174 (Vienna, 1988), pp. 281–4, no. 154, here pp. 282–3: 'Otto, devictis barbaris gentibus, Auaribus scilicet ceterisque quam pluribus, ut ad defensionem sanctę Dei ęcclesię triumphalem victorię in inperii culmen per nos. a beato Petro apostolorum principe susciperet coronam ... Otto, qualiter Sclauos, quos ipse devicit, in catholica fide noviter fundaverat, nostrę paternitati innotuit deprecans et obnixe postulans ... [and receives permission to set up sees at Magdeburg and Merseburg].'

21 See above at n. 1.

22 For an attempt to demonstrate a similar link between Charlemagne's coronation of 800 and Slav mission see H. Löwe, *Die karolingische Reichsgründung und der*

the emperor and his successors to allocate and distribute the tributes and the tithes of those baptised or yet to be baptised to the see of Magdeburg, Merseburg and others, together with the converts. But it took some years before Otto's own son, archbishop William of Mainz, would bow to a diminution of his jurisdiction, and bishop Bernhard of Halberstadt, for whom it meant ceding some of his parish to the new metropolis, refused to yield as long as he lived, nor could Otto coerce him.[23]

Of Charlemagne Einhard had written – in one of his very few anecdotes – that he felt at first so dismayed about his emperorship, the *nomen imperatoris*, that he said he would not have gone to St Peter's, even though it was the holiest of feast days, if he had known what the pope planned to do.[24] In the long debate on the interpretation of this utterance – was it merely a modesty topos or an indignant critique of the coronation's modalities? – we need not here enter.[25] But it is essential to remember that we possess an equally characteristic utterance of Otto I's about his coronation, made just before it. We owe it to Thietmar of Merseburg, who belonged to the Saxon high aristocratic circles where such stories had currency, were remembered and echoed more widespread sentiments. Thietmar, as so often, pauses to recall men whose remembrance he wanted to enjoin on his readers as a pastoral duty, and he lit upon the career of Count Ansfried, late bishop of Utrecht. Ansfried was one of the few nobles who had received both a secular and a clerical education. He had at first been

Südosten: Studien zum Werden des Deutschtums und seiner Auseinandersetzung mit Rom, Forschungen zur Kirchen- und Geistesgeschichte, 13 (Stuttgart, 1937), less *zeitbedingt* than the subtitle might suggest.

[23] The resistance put up by William of Mainz and Bernard of Halberstadt (and by others less clearly visible in the sources) to the new ecclesiastical province is best summarized in D. Claude, *Geschichte des Erzbistums Magdeburg bis in das 12. Jahrhundert*, I, *Die Geschichte der Erzbischöfe bis auf Ruotger (1124)*, Mitteldeutsche Forschungen, 67/1 (Cologne, 1972), pp. 63–95; see also O. Engels, 'Die Gründung der Kirchenprovinz Magdeburg und die Ravennater "Synode" von 968', *Annuarium Historiae Conciliorum*, 7 (1975), 136–58; G. Tellenbach, *The Western Church from the Tenth to the Early Twelfth Century*, trans. T. Reuter (Cambridge, 1993), pp. 52–4, 58, 72.

[24] Einhard, *Vita Karoli*, in *Quellen zur karolingischen Reichsgeschichte*, ed. R. Rau, AQDG 5, c. 28, p. 32: 'Quod primo in tantum aversatus est, ut adfirmaret se eo die, quamvis praecipua festivitas esset, ecclesiam non intraturum, si pontificis consilium praescire potuisset.'

[25] Summarized in P. Classen, *Karl der Grosse, das Papsttum und Byzanz: Die Begründung des karolingischen Kaisertums*, revised edn ed. H. Fuhrmann and C. Märtl, Beiträge zur Geschichte und Quellenkunde des Mittelalters, 9 (Sigmaringen, 1985), pp. 74–7.

instructed in secular and divine law by his uncle, archbishop Robert of Trier, and was then placed under the care of Archbishop Brun of Cologne, Otto I's brother, to be trained as a warrior.[26] On the eve of his Roman expedition, in 961, Otto took him into his personal following and made him his swordbearer. On entering Rome he told Ansfried:

> When I pray today at the holy threshold of the Apostles hold your sword always over my head. I know only too well how often our predecessors had reason to worry about the trustworthiness of the Romans. It is wise to be circumspect and guard against all eventualities lest they should get the better of us. Once we are safely back you can go and pray as much as you wish.[27]

A note of hard down-to-earthness is sounded here. Otto wanted to be crowned emperor but he had few illusions about the setting and the immediate source of his newly won dignity.

An age-old Carolingian tradition had been refurbished with the Saxon ruler's coronation in 962. It was one his aristocratic warrior and native following could learn to share. Not uncommon Saxon nobles' names like Gunthar, Ricdag and Reding appear among the *signa* of Otto's *pactum confirmationis*, the solemn diploma for St Peter and his vicar, pope John XII.[28] Kingship over many peoples,[29] such as Otto now possessed, called for some visible expression and recognition, though it was possible without it. Already in the 950s Constantine Porphyrogennetos called Otto I a *megas rex* of 'Francia or Saxony' when he mentioned the 'Belocroats, that is White Croats', in his treatise *De administrando imperio*.[30] They were subject to him. Later Skylitzes, writing in the eleventh century but using a late tenth-century source,

[26] On Ansfried's pre-episcopal career see R. Grosse, *Das Bistum Utrecht und seine Bischöfe im 10. und frühen 11. Jahrhundert*, Kölner Historische Abhandlungen, 33 (Cologne, 1987), pp. 115–54.

[27] Thietmar, *Chronicon*, ed. W. Trillmich, AQDG 9, IV, 32, pp. 169/71; see on the passage H. Grundmann, 'Betrachtungen zur Kaiserkrönung Ottos I.', in *Otto der Grosse*, ed. H. Zimmermann, Wege der Forschung, 450 (Darmstadt, 1976), pp. 214–17.

[28] MGH DD O I, no. 235 (Rome, 13 February 962).

[29] On this aspect of emperorship see Beumann, '*Imperator Romanorum*', in *Ausgewählte Aufsätze* (see n. 15) and E.E. Stengel, 'Kaisertitel und Suveränitätsidee: Studien und Vorgeschichte des modernen Staatsbegriffs', in *Abhandlungen* (see n. 13), pp. 241–81.

[30] *De administrando imperio*, c. 30, lines 73–4, second edn ed. by Gy. Moravcsik and R. Jenkins, DOT 1 (Washington, DC, 1967), pp. 142–3.

described Otto as *ton phrangon basileus* not only when he referred to the deposition of pope John XII in 963 but also when he reported his execution of the *karchas* Bulksu in 955 after the battle at the Lech.[31] What matters here is that they did not see the year of Otto's imperial coronation at Rome as a marker or to present a special challenge such as Charlemagne's had done. For them it changed nothing and made no difference.

Charlemagne, however much he or his literati may have affected to look askance at the imperial dignity, had at once thought to fill it with meaning and content. Again Einhard is one of our chief guides, though by no means the only significant one: *Post susceptum imperiale nomen* he lists his especially imperial activities, attempts which he thought were unsuccessful, to clarify and amend the *leges* of the Franks and to cause the *leges* of the peoples under his lordship to be collected and written down. This he achieved.[32] Einhard regarded as still more important Charles' efforts to record the *carmina antiquissima*, to have a grammar of the vernacular attempted and to settle the names of the winds and the months again in the vernacular, as imperial acts, and for this he could marshal the classical traditions in which he was formidably well schooled.[33] We know of course that Charlemagne did much more: not only had new oaths to be sworn enhancing the obligations of his *fideles*, but historiography was mobilized as a means to propagate a new imperial presence; even the building of a lighthouse could count as an imperial act.[34] There was a ceaseless,

[31] John Skylitzes, *Synopsis historiarum*, 'Konstantinos palin Autokrator', cc. 5, 12, ed. I. Thurn, Corpus Fontium Historiae Byzantinae: Series Berolinensis, 5 (Berlin, 1973), pp. 239, 245.

[32] Einhard, *Vita Karoli* (see n. 24), c. 29, p. 33, essentially confirmed by modern scholarly work on the *Volksrechte*, summarized most recently by H. Siems, *Handel und Wucher im Spiegel frühmittelalterlicher Rechtsquellen*, Schriften der MGH (Hanover, 1992), pp. 11–157; see also C. Schott, 'Der Stand der Leges-Forschung', *Frühmittelalterliche Studien*, 13 (1979), 29–55.

[33] *Ibid.*, pp. 33–4; see D. Geuenich, 'Die volkssprachige überlieferung der Karolingerzeit aus der Sicht des Historikers', *DA*, 39 (1983), 104–30, at pp. 113–27, for a commentary which significantly relativizes Charles' contribution. On Einhard's literary intentions see above all the classic study by H. Beumann, 'Topos und Gedankengefüge bei Einhard', in Beumann, *Ideengeschichtliche Studien zu Einhard und anderen Geschichtsschreibern des früheren Mittelalters* (Darmstadt, 1962), pp. 1–15, and also H. Löwe, 'Die Entstehungszeit der Vita Karoli Einhards', *DA*, 39 (1983), 85–103.

[34] See F.L. Ganshof, 'Charlemagne's programme of imperial government', in Ganshof, *The Carolingians and Frankish Monarchy*, trans. J. Sondheimer (London, 1971), pp. 55–85. For the lighthouse see *Annales regni Francorum*, s.a. 811, ed. F. Kurze, MGH SRG VI (Hanover, 1895), p. 135: 'ad Bononiam civitatem

almost feverish quest for improvements in all spheres of life, ecclesiastical and lay; a second and almost a third generation of savants and literati were spurred on, and Aachen became a self-consciously imperial centre where Charles could reside and be maintained all the year round, allowing the ageing ruler to break out of the rhythm of itineracy halted only by some months of winter residence which had hitherto dominated his use of time.[35]

No such spate of new activities, the quickened opening of new horizons or the enlargement of older ones stemmed from Otto I's emperorship. The presuppositions were simply not there. As king, it is true, he had done something to mend his own education, learning Latin and to read it after the death of his first wife Edith in 946.[36] During the 950s also, as Fleckenstein has shown, the number of *capellani* serving at his court rose.[37] Among them we note two outstanding historians and men of letters: Liutprand, raised to the see of Cremona in 957;[38] and Adalbert, who became the first archbishop of Magdeburg in 968.[39] The number of *capellani* increased again after 965, the year of archbishop Bruno of Cologne's death. They now numbered fifteen, and were Otto's literate *comitatus*.[40] From this it would seem that the emperorship did not lead to any startling changes in the composition and

maritimam ... accessit farumque ibi ad navigantium cursus dirigendos antiquitus constitutam restauravit'; *restauravit* has unmistakable imperial overtones, especially as the lighthouse had been built by Caligula (Suetonius, *De vita Caesarum*, 'Caligula', c. 46, editio minor M. Ihm (Leipzig and Berlin, 1923), p. 181, 14–17).

35 For this development and its prehistory see D. Bullough, '*Aula Renovata*: the Carolingian court before the Aachen Palace', in Bullough, *Carolingian Renewal* (Manchester, 1992), pp. 123–60, at p. 142 and notes.

36 Widukind, *Res gestae Saxonicae* (see n. 13), II, 36, p. 96, no doubt influenced by Einhard, *Vita Karoli* (see n. 24), cc. 24–6, pp. 29–31.

37 J. Fleckenstein, *Die Hofkapelle der deutschen Könige*, II, *Die Hofkapelle im Rahmen der ottonisch-salischen Reichskirche*, Schriften der MGH, 16/2 (Stuttgart, 1966), pp. 40–58.

38 On Liutprand's career and historical writings see K.J. Leyser, 'Ends and means in Liudprand of Cremona', in *Byzantium and the West c. 850–c. 1200*, ed. J.D. Howard-Johnston (Amsterdam, 1988), pp. 119–43, with full bibliography; see more recently J.N. Sutherland, *Liudprand of Cremona, Bishop, Diplomat, Historian: Studies of the Man and his Age* (Spoleto, 1988 [completed 1977 and published posthumously]).

39 On Adalbert see Karl Hauck, 'Erzbischof Adalbert von Magdeburg als Geschichtsschreiber', in *Festschrift für Walter Schlesinger*, ed. Helmut Beumann (Cologne, 1974), II, pp. 276–344; Karpf, *Herrscherlegitimation und Reichsbegriff* (see n. 15), pp. 47–62. M. Frase, *Friede und Königsherrschaft: Quellenkritik und Interpretation der Continuatio Reginonis* (Frankfurt, 1990), offers nothing new.

40 Fleckenstein, *Hofkapelle* (see n. 37), p. 51.

make-up of Otto's entourage when he returned from his Italian expedition in 965, although the larger number of *capellani* should not be overlooked. One of them for certain and perhaps others became the patrons of outstanding illuminated manuscripts when they were still serving in Otto's entourage before rising to bishoprics, and they also knew where to commission the wonderful luxury diplomas written in gold on purple which Otto I gave to the Roman church in 962 and the young Otto II to Theophano granting her dower to her in 972.[41] Here an imperial note was clearly struck, and Byzantine models and their immense attraction stand behind these magnificently executed and decorated texts. But notaries and *capellani* apart, Otto I did not feel any inner need to foster the cult of letters at his court. He had no programme as emperor to nurture a more expert and homogeneous lay ruling elite side by side with the clerical one. Yet he saw to it that his own son, Otto II, was well taught and he became indeed a book-lover whose visit to their library the monks of St Gallen feared.[42]

Otto the Great was also an exceptionally restless ruler, more of a migrant than most. Even in the confines of his native Saxony he itinerated ceaselessly whatever the season with but brief pauses in his relatively numerous *palatia*, hunting lodges and *curtes* there, some of them in the religious centres he so zealously built up.[43] Only once can he be found staying for half a year on end in the capital of his Italian kingdom, Pavia. Here he resided from September 962 until April 963, taking stock perhaps of its exceptionally sophisticated services, governmental apparatus and inflow

[41] *Ibid.*, p. 49; H. Hoffmann, *Buchkunst und Königtum im ottonischen und frühsalischen Reich*, Schriften der MGH, 30/1 (Stuttgart, 1986), pp. 103–26. Theophano's dowry diploma is discussed in a number of contributions in von Euw and Schreiner, *Kaiserin Theophanu*, notably W. Georgi, 'Ottonianum und Heiratsurkunde 962/972', II, pp. 135–60 and P. Rück, 'Die Urkunde als Kunstwerk', II, pp. 311–33. See also C. Brühl, 'Purpururkunden', in Brühl, *Aus Mittelalter und Diplomatik: gesammelte Aufsätze*, II, *Studien zur Diplomatik* (Hildesheim, 1989), pp. 601–20.

[42] On the differences in this respect between the 'Ottonian' and the 'Carolingian' renaissances see J. Fleckenstein, 'Königshof und Bischofsschule unter Otto dem Großen', in Fleckenstein, *Ordnungen und formende Kräfte des Mittelalters: ausgewählte Beiträge* (Göttingen, 1989), pp. 168–92. For Otto II's education see R. Ahlfeld, *Die Erziehung der sächsischen und salischen Herrscher im Hinblick auf ihre spätere Regierungszeit* (Diss. Greifswald, 1949) [not accessible to me]; Ekkehard IV, *Casus sancti Galli*, c. 147, ed. H.F. Haefele, AQDG 10 (Darmstadt, 1980), p. 284.

[43] Fundamental on this aspect of Ottonian rule is E. Müller-Mertens, *Die Reichsstruktur im Spiegel der Herrschaftspraxis Ottos des Großen: mit historiographischen Prolegomena zur Frage Feudalstaat auf deutschem Boden, seit wann deutscher Feudalstaat?*, Forschungen zur mittelalterlichen Geschichte, 25 (Berlin, 1980).

of revenues.[44] There was another stay there of not quite three months from December 969 to March 970.[45] Otto I legislated sparingly, introducing the judicial duel into Italian legal processes over contested land to curtail perjury.[46] He appointed some *missi* and sent out written mandates, but very few have come down to us, suggesting that it did not become routine.[47] Verbal orders and messages had to do for the most part.

Only in the realm of historiography did his emperorship seek and find the positive expression that it so badly needed to cope with the new tasks that had to be faced. Liutprand of Cremona in his *Historia Ottonis* furnished a justification of Otto's dealings with the papacy and there is no doubt that the need for such a justification was widely felt.[48] For the same years and incidents particularly, the continuation of Regino of Prüm's *Chronicon* was not the least of the services Adalbert of St Maximin rendered to his lord. Yet its resemblance to the *Annales regni Francorum* should not be pressed too far. As the unwilling, plaintive and failed missionary bishop to Kievan Russia, Adalbert pursued at times very personal concerns in his *Chronicon*.[49] His roles and attachments were far too numerous to fit into the year-in year-out routines of the royal chapel. However close he may have been to the Ottonians during the mid-960s, he was not Otto's first choice for the see of Magdeburg, nor was his promotion welcomed by all, as Otto's letter ordering the margraves not to stand in his way shows.[50] Adalbert, moreover, was far from being an unequivocal

[44] *Regesta*, ed. Böhmer and Ottenthal (see n. 18), nos. 329–40a. For the governmental apparatus at Pavia see the *Honorantie Civitatis Papie*, most readily accessible in MGH SS XXX, pp. 1444–60, also edited by C. Brühl and C. Violante, *Die 'Honorantie Civitatis Papie': Transkription, Edition, Kommentar* (Cologne, 1983), with a valuable commentary.

[45] *Regesta*, ed. Böhmer and Ottenthal (see n. 18), nos. 505–14.

[46] MGH Const. 1, p. 37, no. 16 (971).

[47] The dividing line between privilege and mandate is not always easy to draw, but there is no doubt that only a few of Otto I's diplomas from the imperial period could be classified as mandates, perhaps MGH DD O I, nos. 344, 355, 366, 434 (dating uncertain), which represent only a tiny fraction of some 200 surviving diplomas issued between Otto's imperial coronation in 962 and his death in 973. On *missi* see J. Ficker, *Forschungen zur Reichs- und Rechtsgeschichte Italiens*, II (Innsbruck, 1869), pp. 1–6.

[48] Sutherland, *Liudprand* (see n. 38), pp. 86–94; for implicit criticism of Otto's dealings with Benedict V in particular see Thietmar, *Chronicon* (see n. 27), II, 28; IV, 18; VI, 88, pp. 72/74, 152, 378.

[49] See the references given above, n. 39.

[50] Claude, *Erzbistum Magdeburg* (see n. 23), pp. 114–18; the mandate is MGH DD O I, no. 366.

supporter of the emperor. Yet all the same he had a sense of alignment and ended his chronicle with Otto II's ordination as *imperator* by pope John XIII before the *Confessio* of St Peter on Christmas Day 967 'to the great joy of our people (*nostratium*) and of the Romans about the most pleasing togetherness of the two *augusti* and the lord pope'.[51]

It is Adalbert rather than Liutprand of Cremona who opens for us the theme of the new emperor's relations with Byzantium. It is in fact a more complex story than can be pieced together from the *Legatio* and the *Antapodosis* alone. Like Charlemagne's emperorship, Otto I's needed recognition from the much older empire ruled by the *basileus Romaion*, and as in the case of Charlemagne, Otto's insecure and troubled position at Rome forced him southwards towards the Byzantine possessions in Apulia and her clientele in Capua, Naples and Benevento. However, unlike Charlemagne's eastern contemporaries, the Byzantines, or at least the most potent segments of their society, were, whatever the problems of their economic substructure, poised for successful and ongoing offensives both in Asia and, a decade later, also in the north. There was no obvious crisis like the Bulgarian threat of 812 to force them to yield and make concessions over matters of rank and standing.[52] At the same time Ottonian emperorship, just because of its origins and bestowal by the hands of a louche pope from a family of erstwhile Greek clients, urgently needed authentication. There was, as we have said, as yet something provisional about the Ottonian imperial presence. It wanted and was still looking for a larger content, especially south of the Alps where not only its warriors but also its clerics, even its prelates, were predatory and given to plundering cherished relics.[53] The conversion of the heathen Slavs beyond the Elbe as set out in John XII's privilege hung fire and did not altogether suffice.[54]

51 Adalbert, *Continuatio Reginonis*, in *Quellen zur Geschichte der sächsischen Kaiserzeit*, ed. A. Bauer and A. Rau, AQDG 8, 179.

52 For the situation in 812 see Classen, *Karl der Grosse* (see n. 25), pp. 93–7; W. Treadgold, *The Byzantine Revival 780–842* (Stanford, 1988), pp. 163–74, 181–3. For the 960s see Ostrogorsky, *History* (see n. 8), pp. 282–95; H. Grégoire, 'The Amorians and Macedonians, 842–1025', in *The Cambridge Medieval History*, IV, *The Byzantine Empire*, I, *Byzantium and its Neighbours*, ed. J.M. Hussey (Cambridge, 1966), pp. 147–55.

53 E. Dupré-Theseider, 'La "grande rapina dei corpi santi" dall'Italia al tempo di Ottone I', in *Festschrift Percy Ernst Schramm*, ed. P. Classen and P. Scheibert (Wiesbaden, 1964), I, pp. 420–32; T. Reuter, *Germany in the Early Middle Ages, c. 800–1056* (London, 1991), pp. 271–2.

54 See above at n. 3.

There can be no doubt that Otto I, from an early date, wanted his recognition by the rulers of Byzantium to take the form of a marriage alliance for his son, Otto II, who was already king, having been elected by the *populus,* meaning the military following, at Worms in 961 and then again by the Lotharingians at Aachen where he was sacered.[55] We learn of his plans not only from a letter sent from somewhere near Capua to duke Hermann Billung and margrave Dietrich of the northern march, dated 18 January, 968,[56] we know it also from Adalbert's *Chronicon.* In April 967 pope John XIII and Otto I met at Ravenna and here also the emperor's long-cherished wish to see Magdeburg raised to metropolitan status was met by a papal privilege in which the emperor was described as 'omnium augustorum augustissimus' and the third after Constantine; and yet the pope did not quite venture to call him *imperator Romanorum* as he wanted to do.[57] For at Ravenna an embassy from Nikephoros Phokas arrived with presents seeking peace and friendship. So Adalbert, and we know from him also that the envoys were honourably received.[58] He has not told us how they addressed Otto; there is nothing to compare with the celebrated passage from the *Annales regni Francorum* under the year 812, when Greek envoys from the emperor Michael Rangabe called him *basileus* and emperor with *laudes* 'after their fashion', that is to say in Greek.[59] But whatever the protocol in 967, it did not stand in the way of an Ottonian counter-embassy, asking for nothing less than the hand of Romanos II's daughter for his son, Otto II. Most likely Nikephoros Phokas did not at that time deny a non-Roman imperial title to Otto, the *basileus ton phrangon* designation which had by now already gathered age and dust about it. That this is so is to some extent confirmed by a passage in Liutprand's *Legatio* where Nikephoros, after complaining about Otto's invasion of Greek possessions in Apulia and wondering why he was waging offensive war, exclaims: 'We were

[55] *Regesta Imperii*, II, 2, *Die Regesten des Kaiserreiches unter Otto II. 955 (973)-983*, ed. J.F. Böhmer and H.L. Mikoletzky (Graz, 1950), nos. 574e, 574f; Schramm, 'Deutsche Herrscher' (see n. 3), pp. 110–12.

[56] The mandate, MGH DD O I, no. 355, survives only in Widukind, *Res gestae Saxonicae* (see n. 13), III, 70, pp. 146–7, who undoubtedly reworked the text stylistically.

[57] Zimmermann, *Papsturkunden* (see n. 20), pp. 347–9, no. 177. For the question of differences between Otto I and John XIII at this time over 'missionary policy' see most recently the works by Engels and Tellenbach cited above, n. 23.

[58] Adalbert, *Continuatio Reginonis* (see n. 51), p. 178.

[59] *Annales regni Francorum* (see n. 34), p. 136.

friends and had it in mind to conclude an indissoluble alliance through marriage.'[60]

It was in fact Otto's military operations, his attempt to put pressure on the Greeks, not to say blackmail them, rather than Nikephoros' arrogance, so often denounced by modern Byzantinists,[61] which led to a crisis, and not least of all to Liutprand's embassy.[62] Its vicissitudes began when Leo Phokas, the *kouropalates*, now denied Otto the *basileus* title, calling him merely *rex*.[63] The hoped-for marriage alliance was of course discussed when Liutprand had a conference with a committee of high-ranking Byzantine dignitaries, first and foremost the *parakoimomenos* Basil, the only one he named. The price asked for the porphyrogennete Anna was nothing less than 'Rome and Ravenna with all the lands from there as far as us' and it was thus unpayable.[64] The impasse was resolved only with the assassination of Nikephoros and the accession of his murderer, John Tzimiskes. With characteristic self-centredness and self-importance the Saxon authors – Widukind and following him Thietmar – attributed the warrior-emperor's downfall to the minor defeat his troops had suffered at the hands of the Saxon counts Gunthar and Siegfried, Otto's commanders in Apulia. They also knew that Nikephoros' wife Theophano, the mother of the Macedonians, Basil and Constantine, was the instigator of the plot, nor did the usurpation of John Tzimiskes elude them. For them he was simply 'a certain warrior', *quidam miles*, who carried out the coup and benefited from it.[65] With him Otto I could resume negotiations on recognition in the form of a bride for his son, now himself a crowned emperor, a bride he had spent years negotiating for, like Charle-

60 Liutprand, *Legatio* (see n. 11), c. 6, p. 179.

61 E.g. R. Jenkins, *Byzantium: The Imperial Centuries. AD 610–1071* (London, 1966), pp. 279–80; Grégoire, 'Amorians and Macedonians' (see n. 52), pp. 149–51.

62 On the background to this see P. Lamma, 'Il problema dei due imperi e dell'Italia Meridionale nel giudizio delle fonti letterarie nei secoli IX et X', in *Atti del 3. Congresso internazionale di studi sull'alto medioevo* (Spoleto, 1959), pp. 155–254, at pp. 229–46; W. Ohnsorge, 'Die Anerkennung des Kaisertums Ottos I. durch Byzanz', in Ohnsorge, *Konstantinopel und der Okzident* (Darmstadt, 1966), pp. 176–207; J.N. Sutherland, 'The mission to Constantinople in 968 and Liudprand of Cremona', *Traditio*, 31 (1975), 55–82; Leyser, 'Ends and means' (see n. 38), pp. 134–8.

63 Liutprand, *Legatio* (see n. 11), c. 2, p. 176.

64 Liutprand, *Legatio*, c. 15–18, pp. 183–5; on Basil, the *éminence grise* of mid-tenth-century Byzantine politics, see *ODB*, p. 270.

65 Widukind, *Res gestae Saxonicae* (see n. 13), III, 73, pp. 149–50; Thietmar, *Chronicon* (see n. 27), II, 15, p. 56.

magne.[66] These negotiations reached their climax with the mission of archbishop Gero of Cologne and two bishops and allegedly even dukes to Constantinople in 971 in order to come to a conclusion. One of the bishops was most probably Liutprand.[67] To have sent so eminent an embassy was in itself an assurance against failure: the loss of face would have been too much. They brought back Theophano, and who she was is therefore an essential clue in answering the question of how much and to what extent Byzantium, which at this point was still in the grip of an iron military regime, was willing to acknowledge Otto I's emperorship when all the while it resented his presence in Rome and his invasion of Byzantine spheres of influence in Capua and Benevento and the real threat to Apulia. Who then was Theophano?

Thietmar of Merseburg gave the fullest answer to this question. She came indeed with a magnificent escort and a breath-taking treasure but she was not the *virgo desiderata*, the purple-born princess the Ottonians wanted. John Tzimiskes, the usurper, had sent his niece as the bride to be.[68] All the other and nearest contemporary sources, with the exception of Widukind, confirm and strengthen Thietmar's comment. Widukind evaded the issue altogether; he merely called her *puella*.[69] Not only the *Annales Casinatenses*,[70] but more important the great dower charter Otto II gave to his wife, dated on their wedding day and that of her coronation at Rome on 14 April, described her as the niece, the *neptis clarissima*, of John the Constantinopolitan emperor.[71] On the luxury version of the diploma, the only text that has survived,[72] any reference to the Byzantine as the Roman Empire is carefully avoided. If the Greeks saw it, as they may have done, it was an

[66] Classen, *Karl der Große* (see n. 25), pp. 25–42; Treadgold, *Byzantine Revival* (see n. 52), pp. 70–1, 89–91. R. Macrides, 'Dynastic marriages and political kinship', in *Byzantine Diplomacy* (see n. 9), pp. 263–80, is helpful on the Byzantine view of such marriages.

[67] Leyser, 'Ends and means' (see n. 38), pp. 120–1.

[68] Thietmar, *Chronicon* (see n. 27), II, 15, p. 56. For recent discussions of the vexed issue of the identity and the family connections of Theophano see G. Wolf, 'Wer war Theophanu?' and O. Kresten, 'Byzantinische Epilegomena zur Frage: Wer war Theophano?', in von Euw and Schreiner, *Kaiserin Theophanu*, II, pp. 385–96 and 403–10 respectively.

[69] Widukind, *Res gestae Saxonicae* (see n. 13), III, 73, p. 149.

[70] MGH SS III, p. 172.

[71] MGH DD O II, no. 21.

[72] Besides the references given in n. 41 see also the facsimile edition, D. Matthes, *Die Heiratsurkunde der Kaiserin Theophanu: 972 April 14* (Stuttgart, 1980).

insult. This too underlined that Theophano was not a purple-born princess, yet even here a cavil is possible. It has already been mentioned that Widukind and Thietmar fully set out the complicity of the empress Theophano, the wife of Romanos II and Nikephoros Phokas, in her husband's assassination.[73] Had our Theophano been her child by Romanos II, she would have been the daughter of a murderess. The Ottonians were very sensitive about such things. Altogether they can be credited with an enormous sense of family, much more so than the Carolingians. When Otto II died at Rome on 7 December 983, while his wife was with him and his mother was also in Italy, Henry the Wrangler, his Bavarian cousin and rebel, walked free from a kind of detention in Utrecht and very soon not only put forward but fully acted out his claim to the kingship. At this critical moment, moreover, he had possession of the young Otto III.[74] Yet he did not attempt to maim, blind or kill him, and no-one accused him of having harboured such plans. It was by now unthinkable in the Ottonian house. In Byzantium the empress Irene had had no such hesitations and the ninth-century Carolingians had few scruples about blinding nephews and even sons.[75]

Theophano was thus in all likelihood a Byzantine noblewoman, no more, who, if she had any experience of the imperial palace, can only have been there for a relatively short time, after the advent of her uncle John Tzimiskes to the purple. It is noteworthy that no Byzantine narrative or documentary source mentioned her or her marriage. Ottonian emperorship, as we have said, needed authentication. That was Theophano's job and it was for this reason that her imperial descent mattered so much. For this reason also she fulfilled the role for which she was needed in the Ottonian house only in part, being as it were defective in the matter of legitimizing imperial origin. Again the Ottonian ambience was well aware of these shortcomings in her titles, so much so that, as Thietmar again tells us, some advised Otto I not to receive her into his family but send her back.[76] He had been deceived. It is just possible that one

[73] Above, n. 65.

[74] See most recently J. Laudage, 'Das Problem der Vormundschaft über Otto III.', in von Euw and Schreiner, *Kaiserin Theophanu*, II, pp. 261–76, with somewhat controversial conclusions and very full references to the earlier literature.

[75] For Irene's blinding of Constantine VI in 796 see Treadgold, *Byzantine Revival* (see n. 52), pp. 108–9; for Carolingian practice see K.J. Leyser, *Rule and Conflict in an Early Medieval Society: Ottonian Saxony* (London, 1979), pp. 85–6.

[76] Thietmar, *Chronicon* (see n. 27), II, 15, p. 56.

who counselled against the match and sought to prevent it was Liutprand of Cremona, if only with his dying breath. He knew the social values of the Greeks better than anyone. Having been on the bridal embassy, he reached his native Italy but not his city, Cremona, before he died.[77]

Why then did Otto I ignore this advice and accept Theophano all the same as his daughter-in-law? It could be argued that even by her most immediate circumstances she was noble enough. The very Thietmar who had questioned her standing and described her as the woman whom they had not wished for later almost contradicted himself and claimed (wrongly) that he had earlier and briefly set out her immense nobility.[78] But above all her bearing and cultural ambience overbore her critics and there were some quite vocal ones, as we shall see. As for Otto I, the reasons why he made do with her were simple and need not be searched for in the parlance of high politics. He had had enough. It was high time to see his house settled, his heir and successor married and so the future, as far as possible, assured. He had been in Italy now for no less than six years. Rule at home *in absentia* had proved troublesome and in Saxony protests were becoming audible and visible.[79] What Theophano lacked in blood she made up by her sheer presence, nor had she, as has been mentioned, arrived empty-handed. Her enormous treasures, including artefacts of every kind, many of them hitherto unknown in the north, were spells no Saxon king and his following could resist.[80] It enhanced the awe with which they looked up to him and also aroused their greedy expectations, not least of all those of the bishops. As for the 'politics' of the match, she brought with her the *amicitia* of the emperor John Tzimiskes, which Otto I needed for security in Italy. It meant also release for numerous Ottonian prisoners in

77 Leyser, 'Ends and means' (see n. 38), pp. 120–1.

78 Thietmar, *Chronicon* (see n. 27), IV, 14, p. 148.

79 For the incident in Magdeburg in 972, when Hermann Billung, encouraged by archbishop Adelbert, dined at the emperor's table and slept in the emperor's bed, see Thietmar, *Chronicon* (see n. 27), II, 28, p. 74 and the comments of K.J. Leyser, 'Ritual, ceremony and gesture: Ottonian Germany', in Leyser, *Communications* (see first note above).

80 H. Wentzel, 'Das byzantinische Erbe der ottonischen Kaiser: Hypothesen über den Brautschatz der Theophanu', *Aachener Kunstblätter*, 40 (1971), 11–84, and 43 (1972), 15–39; Wentzel, 'Alte und altertümliche Kunstwerke der Kaiserin Theophano', *Pantheon*, 30 (1972), 3–18; H. Westermann-Angerhausen, 'Spuren der Theophanu in der ottonischen Schatzkunst?', in von Euw and Schreiner, *Kaiserin Theophanu*, II, pp. 193–218.

Tzimiskes' hands, most important of all for Pandulf Ironhead, the ruler of Capua and Benevento, Otto's chief ally in the south, whom the Greeks had captured in action near Bovino in 969.[81]

Theophano joined her husband and her new family circle at Rome in April 972. Bishop Dietrich of Metz, a kinsman of the Ottonians, escorted her – he was to be one of her harshest critics later, after the disastrous battle of Cotrone.[82] Here, at Rome, the pope not only joined the pair, he also crowned Theophano and here also she received her dower.[83] The coronation is of the greatest moment: it was a constitutive act and thanks to it Theophano could enter into the fullness of rights that gave her rising influence as long as her husband lived and real power when he died and she survived him to face and to negotiate successfully one of the most critical minorities the Reich had to weather.[84] One of her first duties must have been to learn the languages of her new world, both the Latin of the diplomas in which her interventions counted for so much and the vernaculars, the everyday mode of speech of all but the few personal servants she must have taken with her when she left Byzantium. Theophano also had eulogists amongst the chroniclers and historiographers and one of them described her as *ingenio facundam*.[85] *Facundia* suggests fluency, even eloquence, and was a gift in the vernacular no less than in the languages of literacy.[86] The evidence for her growing influence flows for us mainly out of the sponsorship clauses of imperial diplomas in which she – and it was one of her most habitual functions as empress – intervened. Often we can follow the genesis

[81] For the 'geopolitical' background see the references given above, n. 62, and also J. Gay, *L'Empire byzantin et l'Italie méridionale depuis l'avènement de Basile Ier jusqu'à la prise de Bari par les Normands (867–1071)*, Bibliothèque des écoles françaises d'Athènes et de Rome, 82 (Paris, 1904), pp. 289–323 and most recently B.M. Kreutz, *Before the Normans: Southern Italy in the Ninth and Tenth Centuries* (Philadelphia, 1991).

[82] The escort is noted in Sigebert of Gembloux, *Vita Deoderici I episcopi Mettensis*, c. 4, MGH SS IV, p. 475; the criticism in Alpert of Metz, *Fragmentum de Deoderico primo episcopo Mettensi* c. 2, ed. H. van Rij and A.S. Abulafia (Amsterdam, 1980), p. 110.

[83] N. Gussone, 'Trauung und Krönung: zur Hochzeit der byzantinischen Prinzessin Theophanu mit Kaiser Otto II.', in von Euw and Schreiner, *Kaiserin Theophanu*, II, pp. 161–74.

[84] F.-R. Erkens, 'Die Frau als Herrscherin in ottonisch-frühsalischer Zeit', in von Euw and Schreiner, *Kaiserin Theophanu*, II, pp. 245–59, at p. 252, with good bibliography.

[85] *Annales Magdeburgenses*, s.a. 972, MGH SS XVI, p. 152.

[86] For a fuller discussion of this theme see Leyser, 'Ritual, ceremony and gesture', in Leyser, *Communications*.

and preliminaries of a grant to an abbey or some other beneficiary: how the abbot approached her and how she then raised the matter with her husband until the time was ripe for the favour to be granted and a diploma to be engrossed recording it.[87] Altogether she intervened seventy-six times in Otto II's lifetime, and from the wording of the texts it is often clear that the *petitio* or *rogatio*, the request for the grant, stemmed from her.[88] Not infrequently of course she shared intervention with her mother-in-law, the empress Adelheid, Otto II's mother. That the two women were not in accord temperamentally and over house issues is known, but their collaboration in the years of supreme crisis after Otto II's death must be regarded as more important than their estrangements.[89]

As yet Theophano brought little that can be described as markedly Byzantine to the language of the diplomas, but some striking innovations there were. *Imperatrix augusta* had been rare

[87] It is not clear here which diplomas are being referred to; for a list of possibilities see the following note and n. 109.

[88] She appears as intervening in MGH DD O II, nos. 26, 42*+, 53*, 57*, 66+, 82*, 88, 89+, 90+, 95+, 100, 104, 106+, 107+, 108+, 110+, 122b+, 127, 130, 131*, 139+, 141, 142, 145, 155+, 157+, 159+, 161, 162, 172, 173, 174+, 175, 176, 179, 183+, 185, 186+, 194, 195, 196, 199, 200+, 201, 206, 207+, 212, 214+, 216, 222, 232, 234, 237+, 241, 242, 258+, 259, 265+, 275+, 280+, 283, 287, 289, 299*, 306*, 307*, 309+; joint interventions with Adelheid are marked with an asterisk, joint interventions with other notables with a cross. See R. Schetter, *Die Intervenienz der weltlichen und geistlichen Fürsten in den deutschen Königsurkunden von 911–1056* (Bottrop, 1935), pp. 11–14 (whose figure of 66 differs from the 68 just listed and from the figure in the text) and M. Uhlirz, 'Studien über Theophano', III, 'Die Intervention der Kaiserin Theophano zugunsten der Nonnenklöster während der Regierungszeit Ottos II. und ihre Bedeutung', *DA* 9 (1952), 122–35. The list and the statistics can in any case only be approximate, as the diplomas often make distinctions between *petitio*, *votum*, *rogatus*, *interventus*, etc., which a more detailed investigation might or might not reveal to be significant. At all events it is common for Theophano's *petitio* or similar word to be distinguished from the *interventus* of others.

[89] W. Glocker, *Die Verwandten der Ottonen und ihre Bedeutung in der Politik: Studien zur Familienpolitik und zur Genealogie des sächsischen Kaiserhauses*, Dissertationen zur mittelalterlichen Geschichte, 5 (Cologne, 1989), pp. 91–4. For differences over dower issues see below, n. 107; for the infrequency of their joint interventions in Otto II's lifetime (before the reconciliation between Otto II and Adelheid in 980) see the evidence assembled in the previous note, and for Adelheid's role in the decades following Otto I's death P. Corbet, *Les Saints ottoniens: sainteté dynastique, sainteté royale et sainteté féminine autour de l'an Mil*, Beihefte der Francia, 15 (Sigmaringen, 1986), pp. 59–60, 91–2; M. Uhlirz, 'Die rechtliche Stellung der Kaiserinwitwe Adelheid im deutschen und im italienischen Reiche', *Zeitschrift der Savigny-Stiftung für Rechtsgeschichte*, Germ. Abt., 74 (1957), 85–97.

before her coming but now it appears much more often, and this for Theophano rather than her mother-in-law.[90] Thus we read in a grant to her by Otto II: 'dilectissimae coniugi nostrae Theophanu coimperatrici nec non imperii regnorumque consorti'.[91] *Regnorum* (or *regni*) *consors* had already begun to appear before this, but *coimperatrix* is peculiar to Otto II, sometimes coupled also with the augusta-title, as in the case of a grant to Memleben of 981.[92] Here the two empires shared common classical precepts and nursed imperial exaltation from a common source.

To study emperorship in the later tenth century, whether eastern or western, one should perhaps not look chiefly at major political and military crises, though these were real enough, but at matters of routine, at what was normal and continuous. Here the *prooimia* of Greek novels and chrysobulls and the *arengae* of Latin diplomas invite comparison because it was precisely in these sonorous commonplaces, these ornate features of official utterance that the duties, functions and underlying values of rulership were rehearsed and proclaimed again and again.[93] One feature stands out, however. The *prooimia* headed the texts of legal enactments; they set out the generalities and reasons prompting the legislator, and so are part of the magnificent development of legislative expertise, traditions and practices that remained at the disposal of the *basileus*. It has already been noted that general legislation was a rarity in Ottonian government. Instead the *arengae* served as an introduction, a flourish, expressing the almost uniform sentiment underlying the grant: the hope of salvation or of the merit accumulated towards it, the hope of blessing in the hereafter and stability for the Reich in this life, these are the sentiments usually coupled together by the pious Ottonian grantors. As against this the *prooimion* sets out the sum of the *basileus*' duties and horizons, something almost like a political theory of Byzantine emper-

90 Wolf, 'Theophanu' (see n. 68), in von Euw and Schreiner, *Kaiserin Theophanu*, II, p. 389, n. 65.

91 MGH DD O II, no. 76 (Mühlhausen, 29 April 974).

92 MGH DD O II, no. 196 (Wallhausen, 21 July 981). For the titles and their significance see Erkens, 'Frau' (see n. 84), and Wolf, 'Theophanu' (see n. 68) in von Euw and Schreiner, *Kaiserin Theophanu*, II, pp. 388–9; T. Vogelsang, *Die Frau als Herrscherin im hohen Mittelalter: Studien zur 'consors regni' Formel*, Göttinger Bausteine zur Geschichtswissenschaft, 7 (Göttingen, 1954), pp. 17–39.

93 On these see H. Fichtenau, *Arenga* (Vienna, 1957); F. Hausmann and A. Gawlik, *Arengenverzeichnis zu den Königs- und Kaiserurkunden von den Merowingern bis Heinrich VI*, MGH Hilfsmittel, 9 (Munich, 1987).

orship.[94] There is the imitation of God and his omnipresence. Basil II in a *prooimion* counted the subjugation of the Bulgars as a special gift conferred by God.[95] The emperorship is presented as something almost eternal; the emperor has a special care and foresight for his subjects, a *pronoia*. He is ever watchful, a shepherd; he is the fulfiller of the law, the bringer of measure and harmony, but above all he preaches and dispenses justice. He is the living law, as a *prooimion* of Nikephoros Phokas announced. He, the *basileus*, was also a helper to his subjects, granting grace and favour. He was even a healer. Welfare and philanthropy emanated from him.[96]

Ottonian imperial practice and utterance had nothing so explicit, no such elaborate, permanent and wide-ranging programme. Occasionally the ideas so explicitly set out in a Byzantine *prooimion* occur in the magic that was thought to attend Carolingian and Ottonian kings: that they slept little, were like lions always watchful, had a special penetrating glance, these features hinted at similar cares and values, if only in a far less sophisticated way.[97] Justice stood at the centre here as well, but it was seen mainly as the reward of the good and faithful and the coercion of the wicked and proud. The concept of *dikaiosyne* with its jurisprudential undertones was scarcely there.[98] When Otto I imposed judicial duels in Italy by a written ordinance, he was, paradoxically by latter-day criteria, at one and the same time both advanced in having a text and regressive in what it contained.[99]

Theophano's moment came when, with the help of a combin-

[94] H. Hunger, *Prooimion: Elemente der byzantinischen Kaiseridee in den Arengen der Urkunden*, Wiener Byzantinische Studien, 1 (Vienna, 1964); see also J. Bompaire, 'A propos des préambules des actes byzantines des Xe–XIe siècles', in *Prédication et propaganda au moyen âge* (Paris, 1983), pp. 133–47. H. Ahrweiler, *L'Idéologie politique de l'Empire byzantin* (Paris, 1975), has little to say about imperial *prooimia*.

[95] Hunger, *Prooimion* (see n. 94), p. 72.

[96] Hunger, *Prooimion* (see n. 94), pp. 84–100 (*prontis* and *agrypnia*), 117–21 (living law), 123–54 (*philanthropia*); see also Ahrweiler, *Idéologie* (see n. 94), *passim* on *philanthropia* as a *Herrschertugend*.

[97] For Charlemagne's and Otto I's short sleeping hours and watchfulness see Einhard, *Vita Karoli* (see n. 24), c. 24, p. 29; Widukind, *Res gestae Saxonicae* (see n. 13), II, 36 and III, 75, pp. 96, 153; see K.J. Leyser, 'Some reflections on twelfth-century kings and kingship', in Leyser, *Medieval Germany and its Neighbours, 900–1250* (London, 1982), pp. 245–6 and on the king's glance Leyser, *Rule and Conflict* (see n. 75), p. 83.

[98] For the legislative and judicial content of western diplomas see H. Krause, 'Königtum und Rechtsordnung in der Zeit der sächsischen und salischen Herrscher', *Zeitschrift der Savigny-Stiftung für Rechtsgeschichte*, Germ. Abt., 82 (1965), 1–91. Hunger, *Prooimion* (see n. 94), discusses *dikaiosyne* on pp. 114–17.

[99] See above at n. 46.

ation of forces, headed or held together by archbishop Willigis of Mainz,[100] she regained the person of her son, the very young Otto III and became effective sole regent for him until her untimely early death aged less than forty at Nijmegen on 15 June 991. The situation she had to face was critical. Bad news travelled fast in the tenth century, scarcely less so than today. The report of the battle at Cotrone near Rossano in south Italy in July 982, where Otto II lost the better part of his host, including a good few Saxon nobles,[101] sparked a massive revolt of the Slav tribes east of the Elbe: the Redarii, Wilzi and Liutizi, now all tributaries of the Saxon Reich. The burgwards – the fortresses from which Saxon garrisons dominated tribal areas – and the recently built churches were assaulted, fired and destroyed; the left bank of the river was seriously threatened. The whole work of Henry I's and Otto I's conquest, occupation and mission, reaching well beyond Brandenburg, was destroyed and lost. Only the southern sector of the occupation, the country between Merseburg and Meissen, seems to have held. Archbishop Giselher of Magdeburg with a number of Saxon margraves and counts succeeded in fighting a victorious defensive action by the river Tanger while Otto II still lived, but Theophano inherited the results of this catastrophe which had destroyed an uphill, albeit profitable effort of three generations.[102] The year 984 passed with its struggles for the regency and warding off Henry the Wrangler's attempts on the kingship.[103] From 985 onwards there were annual expeditions across the Elbe into Sclavinia to restore the situation and regain, if possible, some of the ground that had been lost, especially Brandenburg with its bishopric founded in 948.[104] Of Theophano's own attitude towards and experience of war, we do not know much, but we

[100] For the legitimists of 984 see M. Uhlirz, *Jahrbücher des deutschen Reiches unter Otto II. und Otto III.*, II, *Otto III., 983–1002*, Jahrbücher der deutschen Geschichte, 10/2, (Berlin, 1954), pp. 10–40.

[101] *Regesta*, ed. Böhmer and Mikoletzky (see n. 55), no. 874b.

[102] On 983 and its consequences for the Ottonians' 'Eastern policy' in the 980s and 990s see W.H. Fritze, 'Der slawische Aufstand von 983: Eine Schicksalswende in der Geschichte Mitteleuropas', in *Festschrift der Landesgeschichtlichen Vereinigung für die Mark Brandenburg zu ihrem hundertjährigen Bestehen 1884–1984* (Berlin, 1984), pp. 9–55 and J. Fried, 'Theophanu und die Slawen: Bemerkungen zur Ostpolitik der Kaiserin', in von Euw and Schreiner, *Kaiserin Theophanu*, II, pp. 361–70.

[103] Uhlirz, *Otto III.* (see n. 100), pp. 10–40; Laudage, 'Vormundschaft' (see n. 74).

[104] See Uhlirz, *Otto III.* (see n. 100), pp. 64–6, 70, 88, 125–6, and Fried, 'Theophanu' (see n. 102), in von Euw and Schreiner, *Kaiserin Theophanu*, II.

must assume that she stood fully behind the Saxon margraves' efforts to counter-attack. Above all the loyalties of Mieszko of Poland and Boleslas of Bohemia found a focus in her, and Mieszko's armed support in 985 and 986 was of crucial importance. In 986 Otto III himself, 'adhuc puerulus' – he was only six years old – took the field so that Mieszko could join the host and do homage to him. He brought a camel as an exotic present to please and gratify his young overlord.[105] By 987 the Saxon expeditions into Sclavinia had made it possible to begin rebuilding the destroyed castles by the Elbe.[106] Theophano's regency, thanks to the vigorous response of the east Saxon warlords, emerged creditably from this crisis. For Theophano, it might be mentioned, there was no personal interest at stake. Unlike her mother-in-law, Adelheid, she had no direct holdings in the Saxon-Slavonic lands, though the recovery of tribute was also at stake. Her dower, while it included several important Saxon *curtes* like Herford, Tilleda and Nordhausen, included no possessions east of the Elbe. The West and the Rhineland were her favourite regions, not to mention Italy.[107]

The constitutional formalities of the Reich and its society made little or no allowance for a royal or imperial minority.[108] Diplomas were uttered in the infant Otto III's name as if he were fully able to shoulder them as acts of his own will. They were of course grants and gifts made by his mother, whose intervention now became decisive and habitual. There were few diplomas in which episcopal and lay aristocratic sponsors appeared on their own without her. Yet she was usually not the sole intervenient, and above all archbishop Willigis of Mainz, who together with Saxon

105 Thietmar, *Chronicon* (see n. 27), IV, 9, p. 140.

106 *Annales Quedlinburgenses*, MGH SS III, p. 67.

107 For Theophano's dower see MGH DD O II, nos. 21, 76, 171, 202a and b; for Adelheid's see MGH DD O II, no. 109, renewed in MGH DD O III, no. 36 (Allstedt, 21 May 987), in which Theophano appears as intervenor, thus marking a reconciliation between the two women (see above, n. 89). For Theophano's itinerary see G. Wolf, 'Itinerar der Prinzessin Theophano/Kaiserin Theophanu', *Archiv für Diplomatik*, 35 (1989), 237–54.

108 Laudage, 'Vormundschaft' (see n. 74), in von Euw and Schreiner, *Kaiserin Theophanu*, attempts with some new arguments to maintain the traditional legal historians' view that the rules governing the minority of rulers were the same as those applying in any noble family; for a less legalistic and probably more realistic view of medieval minority arrangements see T. Kölzer, 'Das Königtum Minderjähriger im fränkisch-deutschen Mittelalter: eine Skizze', *HZ*, 251 (1990), 291–324, who writes (p. 323) of 'de facto regencies which kept up the fiction that [a child king] ruled in person'.

enemies of Henry the Wrangler and the chancellor, bishop Hildibald of Worms, had really saved the throne for Otto III in 984, appear together as intervenients many times. They, especially Hildibald, must have been her closest advisers. Only at the beginning did the longevitous empress Adelheid share interventions; then she disappeared leaving the field to her superior rival, who now appears regularly as *imperatrix augusta.*[109]

We possess two diplomas which Theophano issued wholly in her own name and not in that of her son, the king. In 989 the affairs of the Reich in the north were sufficiently becalmed, despite the intense struggle between the Capetians and the last Carolingian, duke Charles of lower Lotharingia, during which she was constantly appealed to,[110] for Theophano to be able to cross the Alps and visit Rome. She went for two reasons: to revisit her husband's tomb and to assert her son's rights. In April 990 we find her at Ravenna, where she responded to a complaint of abbot John of Farfa with a gift restoring a church, a daughter house, to the abbey. The diploma duly recorded the plea: how, moved by compassion and for the remedy of her soul and that of her lord Otto, she had reinvested the abbot. It is the sanctions clause that invites special attention. Any inhabitant, great or small, 'of our empire' acting against 'our investiture or *mundeburdium*' would be compelled by 'our imperial command' to make composition with 100 pounds of the best gold. Authentication is announced next, the impression of her ring. But what matter above all are the protocol and the dating clause: 'Theophanius, gratia divina imperator augustus.'[111] She appears in full possession as sole emperor even more in the dating clause where we read: 'anno vero imperii domni Theophanii imperatoris XVIII (octodecimo)'. Otto III is not mentioned at all here; she has created the impression of eighteen years of full emperorship. It was a revealing moment, and one of singular daring perhaps, because in her earlier grant to San Vincenzo on the Volturno she styled herself 'Theo-

[109] She intervenes in MGH DD O III, nos. 2+, 3*, 4+, 6*+, 9*+, 11+, 12+, 14+, 15+, 16, 19+, 20, 23+, 29+, 31+, 32+, 33+, 34*+, 35, 37+, 38+, 39, 40, 43+, 44+, 47+, 48+, 49+, 50, 53, 54, 55+, 58+, 65+, 66+, 67, 68+, 69, 70, 71, 107. For further literature and an explanation of the symbols and caveats see above, n. 88; for Theophano's *intitulatio* see above, n. 90.

[110] This will be discussed more fully in K.J. Leyser, '987: The Ottonian connection', in Leyser, *Communications*. See also B. Schneidmüller, 'Ottonische Familienpolitik und französische Nationsbildung im Zeitalter der Theophanu', in von Euw and Schreiner, *Kaiserin Theophanu*, II, pp. 345–60.

[111] MGH DD Th, no. 2 (Ravenna, 1 April 990).

phanu divina gratia imperatrix augusta' and dated by her son's regnal years.[112]

From these very oddities we may conclude that western emperorship was not as coherent, settled and secure as that of the palace of Constantinople. Even during her regency Theophano had not sought to introduce Byzantine ritual, let alone governmental practice. It was too dangerous, and she depended too much on the loyalties of a heterogeneous group of lay nobles who had already set their seal on the styles and forms of western emperorship. It was after all sporadic, with a good many years when there had been no emperor at all. In the last resort an Ottonian emperor remained what he always had been, long before he became that or even king, the leader of a warrior *comitatus*, with friends and *familiares* with whom he closely shared his daily life and marches. Here the encompassing ritual of the Byzantine court, its luxuries and profound elaborations, created a wholly different setting and atmosphere. The *palatia* of the Ottonians were not built for the secrecy and intrigues that could be housed so adequately in the East. Neither in his hall nor in his chamber did the Ottonian ruler enjoy or even seek privacy. It was here that Theophano's son, Otto III, became the sole exception. He did indeed cultivate Rome and Aachen as if he were in search of a capital, he surrounded himself at one time with new court-offices, dignities and ranks, and he even, to the horror of the onlookers, dined alone.[113] He had moreover the friendship and devotion of some of the most outstanding men of his time. Gerbert of Aurillac was only too anxious to be called for and noticed.[114] As so often in the history of the Reich, Otto did not live long enough for any of this to become permanent. Continuity and endurance in the later tenth century seemed to be on the side of the Byzantines. But let us not forget that the heir to Ottonian emperorship, the Holy Roman Empire of the German Nation, lived on until 1806.

112 MGH DD Th, no. 1 (Rome, 2 January 990).

113 Thietmar, *Chronicon* (see n. 27), IV, 47, p. 184; see for Byzantine parallels P.E. Schramm, *Kaiser, Rom und Renovatio*, I, second edn (Darmstadt, 1957), p. 111 and Schramm, 'Kaiser Otto III. (*980, †1002): seine Persönlichkeit und sein "byzantinischer Hofstaat"', in Schramm, *Kaiser, Könige und Päpste* (see n. 3), III, pp. 277–97 and for comment Leyser, 'Ritual and ceremony' in Leyser, *Communications*.

114 See the letter of Gerbert to the chancellor Heribert, *Die Briefsammlung Gerberts von Rheims*, no. 184, ed. F. Weigle, MGH Die Briefe der deutschen Kaiserzeit, 2 (Weimar, 1966), pp. 217–19, and to Otto III, no. 185, pp. 219–20, both of late 996.

2

Theophano, the western empress from the East*

ODILO ENGELS

The empress Theophano has gained an aura of mystery in western Europe. She, who came from the East, as yet a child, who became a widow after ten years and kept her husband's inheritance for her son with motherly vigilance, not only arouses our compassion but, even more, our admiration. Constantinople in the tenth century was the epitome of civilization and culture. One can imagine what it was like for a girl to have to leave the capital on the Bosporos, realizing that she would hardly have an opportunity to see it again. What must she have felt in these new surroundings, where people were so admiring of her dowry, that for years after her death they applied cups and other crockery to the pulpit of the cathedral of Aachen, a pulpit donated by the emperor Henry II, because they thought this noble material equal to the other gems. Besides, the ruling lady rouses our curiosity: how, in the so-called dark Middle Ages, did a lady cope with a man's world of ruffians and fighters, who looked down on reading and writing as effeminate abilities?

But expectation soon gives way to disappointment. The sources are not so clear that a quick glance would suffice to grasp the outlines. From the moment Theophano left Constantinople, Byzantine sources fail to mention her altogether, which is typical of the Byzantine world-view, according to which a princess who has left the country is no longer of any interest for the imperial court, unless political interests require contact with her far-off

* In 1993 this text appeared in German with notes in *Die Begegnung des Westens mit dem Osten: Kongressakten des 4. Symposions des Mediävistenverbandes in Köln 1991 aus Anlass des 1000. Todesjahres der Kaiserin Theophanu*, ed. O. Engels and P. Schreiner (Sigmaringen, 1993), 13–36.

residence. It is intrinsically likely that the empress was joined in the West by a number of artists whom she encouraged to set, by her own creativity, new artistic standards. Ninth- and tenth-century Byzantium experienced a revival of its art and culture. But that is not our subject here; it is the constitutional questions raised by Theophano which will concern us.

It would not be correct to think that with Theophano the first contact was made between the imperial courts on the Bosporos and in Germany. As early as the 940s there were enough reasons to exchange embassies and, especially from the Byzantine point of view, to keep an eye on the standing of emperor Otto, which could be seen strengthening everywhere. The common interest was focused on the Hungarians, a nomad people of Mongolian origin that had not yet settled completely and had a relatively new centre in the Danube basin between the Alps and the Carpathian Mountains. For decades they had undertaken looting raids ever deeper into northern Italy, had reached out for Gaul across southern Germany and had turned up in lower Saxony after a long ride through Bohemia and the Slav settling grounds between the Elbe and the Oder. And there was not only activity in the West; even in the south-east Byzantium had to ward off their attacks. The Hungarians did not simply plunder aimlessly, but made a systematic attempt to upset their neighbours. Their plan was that these should have a loose dependence secured by means of tribute, so that the Hungarians themselves, the main power, could determine the course of European politics for a long time to come. One should bear in mind that the norms of modern international law were yet unknown. It was unheard of that weaker neighbours should be regarded as equals; to be safe yourself, you had to subjugate your neighbour by whatever means were available to you; there was simply no alternative. To put an end to this predicament the Germans and the Byzantines considered making an alliance against the Hungarians, with a view to gaining full control over them. The natural next step was to seal a political alliance with a marriage between the ruling houses. Otto I thought of his niece Hedwig, the daughter of his brother Henry, who as duke of the Bavarians and neighbour to the Hungarian settling areas was most interested in an effective defence against them. As early as 949 Byzantium sent a eunuch, who was to teach the girl Greek, accompanied by a painter, who should draw a lifelike portrait of the bride-to-be, but the little girl, abhorring the future marriage, knew a way out, and firmly pulled faces, so that the picture was never realized.

Hedwig could feel safe; the marriage was not necessary, because Otto wiped out the Hungarians in the battle on the Lech near Augsburg in 955. The danger of a major Hungarian power was warded off forever, with the result that such power now fell to the German ruler. Thus the way was finally paved for Otto to become the imperial ruler. It would be wrong to see in this a competition with Byzantine emperorship. For the emperor on the Bosporos had the title of *basileus*, which was translated into the Latin *rex*; what mattered was the addition *Romaion*, i.e. of the Romans. Byzantium saw itself as the living remains of the Old Roman Empire. And, whatever the power of a barbarian lord, he was always more than one step lower in the hierarchy. The situation did not become delicate until Otto the Great had himself crowned as emperor, after the Italian king Berengar of Ivrea had been subdued, and Otto tried to link the southern area of what was later to be the church state to his empire, to get more power over the city of Rome and the papacy. It was here, namely, that he entered the Byzantine sphere of interest, for southern Italy still partly belonged to the Byzantine Empire; besides, Nikephoros Phokas definitely wanted also to capture the Lombard principalities of Benevento and Capua.

It was inevitable that the new situation should be clarified some time or other; and a marriage between the families was once again seen as one of several options. In 967 the western imperial court responded to an eastern mission by sending back the Venetian Dominicus. His assignment was to ask on Otto II's behalf for the hand of Anna, the daughter of Romanos II and his wife Theophano. Otto II was Otto's son and heir. In order that Otto II could meet his bride on equal terms, Otto II was hastily crowned emperor at Christmas, disregarding the fact that his father, the emperor, was still alive. Bishop Liutprand of Cremona, who had been Otto's confidant for a long time and who understood Greek–Italian relations better than most, continued the negotiations in 968 and also left a message about his embassy, of which one does not know how much should be attributed to Liutprand's vain exaggeration. Whatever the case may be, the question at issue can be taken as the highest demand Byzantium could make: Otto should return the Roman dukedom and its southern region, as if it had not been Charlemagne but he himself who had conquered central Italy. Liutprand, on the other hand, argued that the emperor had freed Rome from a morally depraved regime, something which had for years been what the *basileus* should have done, had he had the power. In reality the German side was interested in the Benevento-Capua area between Rome and Naples. The negotiations failed, because Adalbert, the son of Berengar of Ivrea, whom Otto had subjected, offered the Greeks to return to Italy and to drive out the Germans with the aid of Greek forces.

Formally the Byzantine side caused the negotiations to break down on a different point. They refused to offer a porphyrogennete as a bride, and Anna was one. It was an outrage to demand a porphyrogennete, because a daughter born in the purple of an emperor born in the purple was simply not given in marriage to foreigners. The grounds given to Liutprand were flimsy, for between 948 and 952 Constantine VII had issued a sort of guideline for his son Romanos II, on how to deal with representatives of foreign powers. The barbarians, it says, often come with the request to give them imperial clothing or the so-called Greek fire; these requests should be declined. It was Constantine the Great's orders that neither the emperors of the Romans – which means, no doubt, the *basileus* – nor their children should enter into marriage with partners from foreign peoples. The only exception – and this proves how hypocritical the Byzantine negotiators were – being the Franks, because Constantine had had his roots in this part of the empire, namely Trier. Close relations with the illustrious Franks had been known to exist for a long time.

This point has to be dealt with more extensively, for the fact that our Theophano was not a porphyrogennete could prompt us to draw certain conclusions. Liutprand had negotiated with Nikephoros Phokas, who as a successful commander-in-chief had been proclaimed emperor after the death of Romanos II, and who not only married his predecessor's widow but also adopted her two purple-born children. His assassination in December 969, instigated by the very widow he had married, brought about a new situation. The usurper John Tzimiskes, a warlord of the same mettle, not only had to cope with the Saracens, but also with the Bulgarians to the north of Constantinople. One just could not accept another centre of turbulence in southern Italy, so the new emperor released from prison the duke of Benevento, Pandulf Ironhead, who brought about an end to the fighting. By the end of 971, the time had come for the archbishop of Cologne, Gero, to start on his journey to Constantinople as a match-maker.

Gero probably set out on his journey in the hope of winning Anna's hand. But, when the bride came to Germany, many were disappointed because it was not the *porphyrogenita* who had arrived. There was even pressure exerted on Otto I to send the bride back again, because people felt that their pride had been wounded, but Otto did not give in. Apparently Gero had had so much authority that he could also negotiate about another bride in case the one he had negotiated about for several years would not be given. But who in fact was Theophano? John Tzimiskes did not have any children of his own, and must therefore have offered his niece, who on her mother's side was a Phokas, offspring of an ancient line of magnates in Asia Minor, closely related to the fallen emperor Nikephoros Phokas. The use of Theophano as a bargaining point may have been based on political grounds. If the marriage were to be a guarantee for new peace agreements, then the bride should originate from those circles in Byzantium that were in power at the time. This was not the case with either son of the deceased Romanos II; they were in fact born in the purple, but still under age, and their mother Theophano had been chased by the patriarch from the imperial court as an instigator of murder. But all that was also true of Anna. The last word rested with John Tzimiskes, who was then only a usurper on the imperial throne, but whose word was decisive. For the West a substantial condition of peace must have been that the Benevento and Capua areas remain in Otto's hands; which, through her uncle, only Theophano could guarantee. It was done, however, in a very clever way, which helped Byzantium save its face. Although in this case the confirmation comes only in a later source, according to Byzantine law a bride should be given a substantial dowry by the bride's father. It would not be going too far to state that the dowry consisted of the Benevento and Capua areas; for archbishop Gero also had to negotiate the place where the bride was to be handed over, which was usually somewhere on the border or at a reasonably large town near it. And, indeed, it was in Benevento that bishop Theoderich of Metz received Theophano in the spring of 972.

This leads us to the conclusion that Theophano was not prepared for her new life at all. Whether or not she knew any other language than her native tongue is unknown, and the West did not really know very much Greek. When, on 14 April 972, she was married to Otto II by pope John XIII in Saint Peter's in Rome, and at the same time crowned empress, she was a *puella*, as Widukind of Corvey says. And that corresponds to an age of twelve rather than of fourteen. So she does not seem to have been of age, nor able to bear children yet. She must have had maid-servants, but who they were is unknown. Straight after their marriage Otto and Theophano were presented with the magnificent marriage charter, which tried to copy the court models of the East; it was certainly not drawn up in Byzantium, for it dealt with the wedding gift, which the bridegroom used to present to his bride in case she should be widowed. The charter also proves the marriage to be a state affair, for it not only mentions the young bridegroom, but also the father, Otto the Great, as the signatory of the charter, without whose consent the whole procedure could not have taken place.

Theophano bore her husband five children, only one of whom was a son, later to become emperor Otto III. The name or the sex of the fifth child is not known; but there was an endowment for an annual memorial service for a deceased child. It would be wrong to think that Theophano should have been able to care intensively for the upbringing of her children. At that time the German imperial court did not yet have a fixed residence, but managed rule during constant journeys from place to place. For their education the children were sent to monastic institutions. The third daughter, Matilda, for example, was entered into the convent at Essen, where her aunt on her father's side, Matilda, was abbess. Theophano accompanied her husband on almost all his journeys. What influence she had on state affairs cannot be remotely assessed, because the charters normally only mention the emperor. The veil of obscurity can only be removed by indirect means.

It is worth looking back. The last of three uprisings against Otto in the empire was a consequence of his first journey to Italy in 951. Adelheid, the widow of king Lothar of Italy, had been deposed and imprisoned by her rival Berengar of Ivrea. Otto wanted to release and later marry her, and therefore Liudolf of Swabia, Otto's elder son from his first marriage, who was worried about the succession, hastened out before the imperial army, hoping to upset the marriage at Pavia. But Otto's younger brother, duke Henry I of Bavaria, arrived before his nephew, made the marriage possible and thus also the incorporation of Italy into the eastern Frankish realm. When Adelheid bore her son Otto II, Liudolf unexpectedly started the unrest in which Henry of Bavaria was his most bitter enemy. Adelheid never forgot Henry's help against Liudolf, and even passed on her thanks to his son Henry, who was nicknamed 'The Wrangler' and who succeeded his father as duke of the Bavarians. When one realizes that Adelheid was the sister of king Conrad of Upper Burgundy, whose daughter Gisela was to marry Henry the Wrangler, and that Adelheid's daughter from her first marriage, Emma, married the French king Lothar, one can assess Adelheid's wide influence, which extended right across the Frankish realm. But one can also observe that the feeling at Otto the Great's court hardened against Adelheid, as he grew older. Otto I reluctantly accepted the choice of Gero as archbishop of Cologne, because his family had been on Liudolf's side; but Gero was assigned to match-making in Byzantium shortly afterwards. How much the tide had turned at court was clear after 974. It is wrong to see the tribal dukes only as agents of the king. They rather considered themselves as powers of a kingly nature, who had pushed themselves with unrestricted power between king and nobility, who forced the king to tolerate them, and who had now to fend off nobility ever pressing upward from the second line. In the case of Henry the Wrangler this is evident from the almost raid-like occupation of the Augsburg episcopal see in cooperation with duke Burchard III of the Swabians, his sister Hedwig's husband; and also, shortly after, from the imprisonment of the Wrangler by the emperor without judicial sentence, after the Wrangler – together with the duke of Bohemia and the duke of Poland – had tried to weaken the count of Schweinfurt, notwithstanding that this count had received orders to guard the borders against the Slavs – in this particular case against the Bohemians. The same can be deduced from the emperor's reaction to the death of Burchard III, in the year 973: whether his widow Hedwig thought to rule on alone with ducal power, or whether she had to share the ducal rights given to her and guaranteed till her death by the royal chancellery in her title of duchess, yet in 973 Otto II joined with Otto I in making one of Liudolf's sons the new duke, who considered his rulership to be no less than hereditary.

When Theophano, therefore, tried to make herself feel at home at the new court, she entered Liudolf-friendly waters. Whether she liked it or not, loyalty to her husband forced her into an enmity to Henry the Wrangler, and thus into strained relations with her mother-in-law. In his *Epitaphium* Odilo of Cluny says about Adelheid that she suffered very much as a result of the estrangement from her son, the emperor. And, indeed, since the summer of 974, at the very time the argument started between the court and Henry the Wrangler, the interventions of Adelheid in the charters decrease conspicuously, while those of Theophano proportionally increase, until in 978 Adelheid temporarily had to leave the imperial court and to flee to Italy, because her son-in-law, Lothar of France, had invaded the western German area and had for some time occupied the *palatium* at Aachen.

When Otto II travelled to Italy in 980, a new chapter was opened for Theophano, in which her influence on her husband became more distinct. As early as 976 the regime in Constantinople of her uncle John Tzimiskes was overthrown by that of Basil II, one of two purple-born sons of Romanos II, now of age, who had had imperial dignity for a long time, but had always been in the shadow of the soldier emperors. One can understand that Basil II did not care much about Theophano and her dowry in southern Italy. And the south of Italy should have taken priority with him at that time: in 976 the forces of the Fatimid caliphate in Cairo had conquered Sicily and in 977 had partly occupied Calabria, and since then their raids threatened Apulia. But there was very little prospect that Byzantium would organize effective defensive measures. The western imperial court had trusted in the skilful prince Pandulf Ironhead, the ruler of Spoleto and Benevento, and of Capua and Salerno, but he died in 981, and this seemed to leave not only Theophano's dowry open to attacks from the Saracens, but also the city of Rome. Otto ordered new military forces from Germany; and in July 982 the battle of Cape Colonne near Cotrone took place, with heavy casualties on both sides.

The battle-ground was clearly on Byzantine soil, and military actions against the Saracens would in the long run only make sense if the Saracens were driven at least from the mainland, which meant that this military action was to conquer Byzantine territory. This consideration and the need to legitimize the plan led to an innovation that heralded a completely new orientation. From now on Otto II no longer called himself in his charters *imperator augustus*, but *Romanorum imperator augustus*. Till then the western imperial dignity had only meant a supremacy in Western Europe sanctioned by the pope; from now on it had to have new foundations. The new associative reference was the Old Roman Empire; what till then had only been remotely thought of, was now promoted as the new conviction, namely that they should carry on the Roman Empire. This meant that they faced a new rivalry with the Byzantine Empire. The consequences were drawn immediately: for at Whitsun of the next year the emperor had his son Otto III elected his successor in Verona by German and Italian rulers and appointed the archbishop of Ravenna as *coronator* in Aachen alongside the archbishop Willigis of Mainz. Until that time Germany and Italy had had one common ruler, but they had been two separate kingdoms, and each ruler had to have himself crowned twice, once north and then south of the Alps. But from now on Germany and Italy were to form one single realm. The different structure of both realms should no longer be taken into consideration, nor the different tribes that had formed Germany, nor the special position that Italy had held as early as the Frankish Empire. This sweeping levelling out might have been taken from the eastern Roman example, something Theophano cannot but have had a hand in.

This policy could not last long, because Otto II suddenly died on 7 December 983, and was buried in Rome. At Christmas, according to the rules, his three-year-old son was crowned king before the message of his death reached Aachen. The situation was a complete disaster. The child, who was under age, possessed all rights and duties of a king, but everyone knew that he was in fact unable to carry them out; the only thing that mattered now was who would act as regent. Theophano and her mother-in-law stayed at Pavia until the end of April 984 and only arrived at Mainz by the middle of June; they could hardly influence the events in Germany before the summer. Henry the Wrangler was in custody at Utrecht, but was immediately set free by the bishop there, Folkmar, and in Cologne archbishop Warin handed over the imperial child to the Wrangler. The deposed duke of the Bavarians hurried to Saxony with the child, and had himself proclaimed king there. These almost revolutionary events draw a picture of the Wrangler as an unscrupulous usurper greedy for power, a picture which is confirmed by various sources.

As we cannot simply follow this judgement uncritically, we should first realize that nobody could have foreseen Otto's sudden death, or could have made provisions against such an eventuality. The fact that the bishop of Utrecht was quick to release the Wrangler, and that the bishop of Cologne not only gave him the child he was in charge of, but even joined the Wrangler going to Saxony, shows the extent of Adelheid's influence. The court must have known the nature of the loyalty of both clergymen. To give the rebellious duke and the child into their custody must have been the wish of a considerable number of powerful people who did not agree with Otto II's policy. Theophano was not popular everywhere in the western empire. People probably feared a continuation of imperial actions in southern Italy on her initiative.

And then there is the question of the legality of the Wrangler's actions. In most studies the question is raised as to whether a woman was allowed to be a guardian of a child that was under age, and it is stated that the Wrangler was the only possible guardian, as the cousin of the deceased father. No doubt, he seized the opportunity in Quedlinburg at Easter 984 and had himself proclaimed king instead of his ward. King Lothar of France was another possible guardian. The Wrangler had indeed promised him Lotharingia, roughly the territory west of the river Rhine, if he accepted him as the new king. It is necessary to point out that guardianship did not mean education of the child, but rather the outward protection of him; it had its roots in tribal law and it included the widow, the child's mother, as well. Even Thietmar of Merseburg calls the Wrangler Otto's *patronus legalis*, and the Quedlinburg Annals condemn the Bavarian duke's ambition to the throne, but not his *tutela* over the child *ob ius propinquitatis*. There is no point in looking back at tenth-century examples, like Theophano, the emperor Romanos II's widow, who managed the rule of the empire for half a year for her two sons; or like Gerberga and Hedwig, Otto the Great's sisters, of whom one managed the inheritance of Louis IV of France and the other the dukedom of Hugh the Great of Francia. The examples of Judith, Henry the Wrangler's mother, and also of Cunegunde, his future daughter-in-law, show that a widow needed a male guardian for legal transactions. During the imperial diet at Rohr near Meiningen in Thuringia, Henry the Wrangler put the royal child in his mother's and grandmother's care and renounced every obligation of loyalty that was promised to him by the empire. The two ladies promised him the restitution of the Bavarian dukedom and, besides that, took care of the restoration of the *ius propinqui-*

tatis. In Rohr, and a year later at the imperial diet in Frankfurt, when the Wrangler got back the Bavarian dukedom, it was decided that everything he was entitled to according to the court should definitively remain in his hands, including the guardianship, i.e. a right closely connected to the membership of a clan.

Henry the Wrangler could not make much use of his right, because Theophano had regency over the empire mainly in cooperation with Willigis, archbishop of Mainz, and Hildebald, bishop of Worms, but without the noticeable participation of the Wrangler. On what legality did she base her claim to do this? Quite often in the diplomas of her husband and even more often in those of her son, who as the nominal king was the only drawer, she was called *consors regni*, co-ruler of the empire. This title had its origins in late Roman antiquity and did not completely fall into disuse in the Byzantine Empire. Occasionally it found its way to the West with the later Carolingians. Adelheid used it every now and then after her coronation as empress. In 972 and 974 Otto II called his wife *coimperatrix*, probably to intensify the eastern idea of co-rulership. Since the period of Adelheid's rule, her interventions in the diplomas of her husband increased rapidly, especially in the Frankish-German Empire.

Critics could have objections to this and could argue that this is not evident proof but only a patch-up explanation. The two often quoted diplomas of Theophano, drawn up in the year 990 for Italian addressees, do not help either. In the first she calls herself *imperatrix*, in the second *Theophanius gratia divina imperator augustus*, as if she were a man. The first diploma is dated according to the years of her son's rule, and only in the second diploma does she count from her own coronation on. But before we draw a conclusion from this, we should remember that Otto III did not accompany his mother on her journey to Italy. This could explain the uncommon wording. Before and after this date it was not unusual in the chancellery of the empire to give a male title to a duchess, although the female form was not unknown. We cannot exclude the Byzantine precedent for the regency of Theophano, but we should not ignore the unusually long stay of both ladies in Italy after Otto II's death. Their presence in Germany would have been urgent if their main task had been to impose Byzantine norms. Anyhow, around 984, a female regency with ducal rights was not unknown north of the Alps. This gave room to risk the regency of the empress in a power struggle. The *consors regni* or *coimperatrix* formula seems to be the consequence rather than the basis of an idea that gave women more rights to participate than we usually assume.

What was the real success of Theophano's rule after she had become a widow? We could think of secondary results such as the clever prevention of a French invasion in the west of the empire. In any case, it was her task to preserve the inheritance of her husband and to pass it on without loss to her son the moment he came of age. This included the stabilization of the border in the east of the empire. In 983, after they had heard of Otto II's disastrous defeat at Cape Colonne, the Liutizes east of the river Elbe revolted; the situation at the border would be unstable up to the twelfth century.

This shows how Theophano combined this task with new concepts, which she may have brought with her to the West and imparted to her son, if only by initiating them. Otto I had proclaimed Magdeburg as the metropolis of a new archdiocese and at the same time as a centre of mission for the Slav East. He also decided that he should be buried there. As a regent, Theophano was not very interested in Magdeburg, but she favoured to an unusual degree the abbey of Memleben on the river Unstrut, which had been founded by herself and her husband. It should have been Adelheid's purpose to honour the memory of her ancestors at the very place where Otto I and his father Henry I had died, though they had not been buried there. But she was not very interested in Memleben. As early as 984 Theophano appointed the abbot of Memleben, Unger, bishop of Poland, as if Memleben were to serve as a bridgehead to Poland. As soon as Adelheid had taken the place of Theophano as regent, Unger had to give way to Reginald, who was appointed abbot, and the abbey had to adapt to Magdeburg. In 1015 emperor Henry II even demoted the abbey to a deanery dependent on the imperial abbey of Hersfeld. All these events reveal Theophano's political theory, and other facts provide further evidence. Archbishop Giselher, who owed his transfer from Merseburg to Magdeburg to Otto II, defected to Henry the Wrangler immediately after his ambitions for the throne became clear. Until Theophano's death he maintained close relations with the Saxon counts who fought for Boleslav, duke of the Bohemians, against Mieszko, duke of Poland. The Bohemians, who had had a coalition with Henry, duke of Bavaria, as early as the seventies, invaded eastern Saxony and conquered Meissen temporarily as soon as they knew the results of the imperial diet of Rohr; this meant a decision in favour of Theophano. Since 985 Theophano herself had been fighting against the Bohemians and Liutizes almost every year, which is an indication of open support of Mieszko, whose offensive politics against the Přemyslids in Bohemia led to the conquests in Silesia and of Cracow. We have to consider that Vladimir of Kiev helped the Byzantine emperor Basil II decisively with armed forces in 988. As a reward he was to marry a sister of the emperor, the purple-born Anna, who originally was to marry Otto, if he had been willing to have himself and his people baptized. Now we get an impression of the numerous aspects which as a regent Theophano was willing to include in a long-term calculation. The conversion to Christianity of the empire of Kiev had obviously been planned for some time. Officially Poland was a Christian country, but its church had only rudimentary organization. As the Poles were not inclined to become part of the metropolitan church of Magdeburg and as the rivalry between the Piasts in Poland and the Přemyslids in Bohemia increased, Poland was in danger of being influenced by the East in the long run. After all, the Byzantine Empire aimed at expansion. In order to resist this danger, Christianity in Poland needed support from the Latin side. An abbey such as Memleben offered adequate contacts without questioning the independence of the Polish church, which was probably inspired by the principle of autocephaly, then prevalent in the eastern church. Otto III realized this by founding the archdiocese of Gnesen around the turn of the millennium. Control of Bohemian politics by binding Bohemia closer to the eastern Frankish-German Empire could only serve his aim.

This also explains the difficult relationship of Theophano with her mother-in-law. It cannot only be reduced to different views on the use of Adelheid's widow-property. Theophano's measures, taken in the autumn of 988, to rule Italy on her own (until then Adelheid ruled Italy), were probably a consequence of the assurance made in the diploma of 987, which guaranteed Adelheid the unrestricted use of her widow-property. This would presuppose that a total use of the widow's property excluded any form of co-rule by Adelheid. Nevertheless, Theophano's policy in the East, which we have described in a few words, shows that two incompatible concepts clashed and poisoned the atmosphere. Odilo of Cluny may have exaggerated, but a power struggle does become clear. 'If I live another full year, Adelheid will not be able to rule in the whole world more than what one hand can grasp', Theophano is said to have uttered. Adelheid showed herself just as implacable. Adelheid survived her daughter-in-law and succeeded her as regent. She prohibited annual memorial services for Theophano, even at her grave in the monastery of St Pantaleon in Cologne. For this reason Otto III expelled his grandmother from court when he came of age in 994.

A closer look at the government of both Otto III, after he had gained majority, and of Henry II can clarify this. Otto's teacher of Greek was John Philagathos from Calabria, Otto II's former chancellor in Italy, at least until 988 when he became bishop of Piacenza and *magister camerae* in Italy. He called his disciple *Graeca scientia non ineruditum*. In 996/7 Otto III himself wanted Gerbert of Aurillac's help to raise himself from *Saxonica rusticitas* to *Graecisca subtilitas*. In Otto III's theory of rule the essential element was the antique example as it still seemed to exist in Byzantium. Otto tried to put an end to the continual travelling; he intended to raise Rome to a permanent residence and wanted to introduce elements of the Byzantine imperial ceremonial. It is well known that Henry II, the son of Henry the Wrangler, rejected this Italian policy. He also put an end to the pro-Polish policy that had been introduced by Theophano and further developed by her son.

The differing legal maxims are also especially confirmed by Henry the Wrangler. It was probably due to the appointment to the bishopric of Augsburg, which took place without imperial influence, or perhaps even as a reaction to the appointment of Luitpold as margrave of the Eastmarch, who was a close relative of Berthold, margrave of Schweinfurt, that in 974 the Wrangler prepared a revolt in coalition with Mieszko, duke of Poland, and Boleslav, duke of Bohemia. The plot was discovered by Otto II, before it was fully shaped. The Wrangler accompanied the imperial envoys, who were sent to take him to the emperor, immediately and of his own free will, which shows that he was not aware of having done anything wrong. Henry the Wrangler was imprisoned, but managed to escape in 976 and found allies in Bavaria and Saxony. The emperor managed to conquer Regensburg, but he could not arrest the Wrangler, who had fled to Bohemia. Only after two attempts to force the duke of Bohemia to surrender and after the subsequent conquest of Passau could he get hold of the duke, and send him to prison in Utrecht in 978.

There is evidence for the Wrangler's idea that his co-rule in the kingdom was legitimate. Therefore we should not simply regard his attempt to be crowned king at Easter 984 as usurpation.

Recent studies have shown that Henry I's house rule of 929 prepared the line of succession of one son, but that this rule did not finally decree it. In 929 and in 936, when Otto I was crowned king, Henry I's younger son Henry, the future duke of Bavaria and father of the Wrangler, was still under age and therefore without allocated inheritance. Just of age, he initiated a revolt against his brother intending to overthrow him, because he was convinced that he had a right to participate in the kingship. When he became duke of Bavaria and got the March of Verona, an area that extended beyond the territory of the tribal dukedom, he was satisfied. He saw his wishes of co-rule fulfilled and remained a loyal supporter of his brother. Ruotger, the biographer of Brun, archbishop of Cologne and Otto's younger brother, says that during the revolt against his brother the rebels hated him in particular. And Brun was not the representative of the so-called imperial church system, but acted as the king's brother, whose power was much greater than that of a duke or an archbishop. Ruotger reports that he not only cared for Lotharingia but also for the whole empire, so that one brother could pride himself on the deeds of the other. The poet Hrotsvit of Gandersheim praises the three brothers Otto, Henry and Brun as the persons who ruled the empire together. Even the imperial court on the Bosporos must have heard that in Germany the idea of a *corpus fratrum*, a kingdom seen as a community of brothers, was still alive. Otherwise, Henry, the younger of the two, would never have been called *rex* in a letter that was addressed to both Otto and Henry.

But in the second half of the tenth century there was an increasing tendency towards exclusive individual succession. The later *Vita* of Matilda, initiated in the beginning of the eleventh century by the Wrangler's son, emperor Henry II, to support his claim to the inheritance of the kingdom, maintained that in 936 Otto's brother Henry should actually have been proclaimed king, because he was, unlike his brother, not born until his father was king. This explanation, which follows the example of the Byzantine idea of being born in the purple, was only possible because the idea of the *corpus fratrum* had not been completely forgotten. This is particularly true of other sources, for example Richer, who, because of the royal child's incompetence, considered the Wrangler the right candidate, but also saw him clearly as a robber of the throne, eager for power. But in the West they knew better. In 984 archbishop Adalbero of Rheims, archchancellor of the French king, wrote in satirical words to Egbert, metropolitan of Trier, to win him over to Theophano's side. He hints that Egbert thinks of the little Otto III as a Greek and therefore, *more Grecorum*, might be willing to put a co-ruler at his side. He expressed himself in the same way to bishop Notger of Liège. It was not only the church of Rheims that suggested that the Wrangler intended to be a co-ruler. Bishop Theoderich of Metz, an ally of the Bavarian duke, must also have made a similar remark to Charles of Lotharingia. Yet, we cannot easily deny Richer's statement that Henry the Wrangler wanted royal power exclusively for himself. Though he is said to have acquired and desired the sceptre and the crown, he was not anointed king. He hurried from Cologne via Corvey to Magdeburg, where he called a convention on Palm Sunday that was to discuss his elevation to the position of king. He celebrated Easter in Quedlinburg at the grave of his grandfather king Henry I. Here he was openly called king, lauds were sung for him, oaths that befit a king were sworn and benefits were distributed. From Quedlinburg he went to Werla intending to gain the loyalty of the opponents who had gathered around duke Bernhard.

The act of the elevation to the kingship cannot be reconstructed satisfactorily. Thietmar of Merseburg hints at a possible solution, which reduces the act to the acclamation of the magnates, the singing of the lauds and the oath of allegiance. The Annals of Quedlinburg maintain that the Wrangler wanted a church coronation ceremony, but that this was refused. Who prevented this? 'Multi ex his fidem violare ob timorem Dei non presumentes paululum evaserunt', writes Thietmar, and the Annals of Quedlinburg add that those who did not want to swear the oath explained that they first had to be released from the one they had given to the person who had been king up till then. All others who had stayed at the place of election obviously agreed with the Wrangler's line of action. It was probably Henry the Wrangler himself who did not intend more than what actually happened. Those who refused the oath thought that they could only swear it to one single king. This view did not allow for a co-king. The pictures of that time could lead to the conclusion that the Wrangler saw himself as the only king, to the exclusion of the infant Otto. But it is also possible that all these facts simply prove that on both sides the idea of *conregnans* no longer existed. We are, indeed, in a grey area. Even if the Wrangler did not intend more than what happened after the last revolt against Otto I, the events cannot be fully compared. Henry I of Bavaria and especially Brun of Cologne had been proclaimed co-rulers by a king with legal power in a perilous situation, whereas the Wrangler was at best commissioned by an assembly of magnates. But, as the allies of Theophano accepted her regency on the basis of her dignity as empress – she had never been commissioned to her regency by the magnates – the Wrangler had to obtain a similar legal basis, at least to be more than, for example, Conrad of Franconia at the side of Louis IV the Child. Quedlinburg, as the place where his grandfather was buried, shows the importance of his royal origin. An admittedly distorted remnant of the idea of *corpus fratrum* can be found in the *Vita Mahthildis posterior*. This *Vita* is a result of the need of king Henry II, the Wrangler's son, to prove his right to the crown. According to the king's widow, Matilda, Otto I's brother Henry had claims to the throne in 936, because, in contrast to his elder brother, he was born after his father had ascended the throne. It was also said that Otto's son and Henry's son had played together when they were children. Both are described as *regales pueri* of the same rank. This is emphasized by the considerations of Adelheid and her mother-in-law Matilda as to whether the Wrangler's reputation could be enhanced if they betrothed him to Adelheid's daughter Emma. Theophano's argument with Adelheid over the widow's portion points to the unclear final stage of the transition from *Samtherrschaft* to individual succession. The special case of Matilda's widow's portion was an important element of Henry I's house rules, introduced in 929 in Quedlinburg. These rules introduced the individual succession into the Saxon kingdom. The widow's portion guaranteed that the female ruler should be provided for after the death of her husband, but excluded her definitely from any form of co-rule. Adelheid had her widow's portion at her disposal and looked after imperial interests in Italy at the same time. This was understandable as long as the king was under age, but it also gave legal grounds to Theophano to keep her mother-in-law away from power by reconfirming Adelheid's widow's portion.

The fact that Theophano concluded this process in favour of individual succession is yet another merit of hers, and also a long-term one. However, she benefited not only from the Ottonian tradition but also from several provisional decisions taken in the year 984. Archbishop Willigis of Mainz, a leading figure, opposed the policies of Henry the Wrangler even before Theophano returned from Italy. He managed to set up a coalition between opponents of the Wrangler in eastern Saxony and in the West. As Otto's chancellor he was familiar with the empress. As there was no need to change the personnel of the chancellery, the important persons at court were Willigis, archchaplain and archchancellor, and Hildebald, bishop of Worms and chancellor. Together with Theophano they formed a regency council and had to advise Otto III, who theoretically took his own decisions. As this body was not institutionalized (in the sources there is not even an adequate term for the modern word regency-council) and as there was no delimitation of its number of members, we have no idea how the competences were divided. Obviously Theophano held a major position, but the interventions show that Henry the Wrangler also took part in it, but certainly with far less influence than Willigis and Hildebald. In 986 the empress gave a demonstration of her power in Quedlinburg, where she celebrated Easter with great ceremony. Just as in 936, during the crowning banquet at Aachen, four dukes had to serve at table. One of them was Henry the Wrangler as Lord High Steward (*Truchsess*).

The support the empress found in the two clergymen led to a new relation between the ruler and the imperial church. For the last decade it has been doubted whether Otto I developed the so-called Ottonian imperial church system after his bad experiences with the ducal power. The theory was that this system intended to weaken secular powers by giving countships and sovereign rights to the churches, which thus became true supporters of the king. This new system developed over a long period of time into the eras of Otto III and Henry II. Only then can we speak of a comprehensive effort to come to a close institutional link between the king and the church. If we take as a standard the transference of whole countships instead of single rights to the imperial churches, we see that this practice began when Theophano became regent. We can draw the conclusion that Theophano had considerable influence on the nature of the eleventh century with its characteristic close relationship between the bishop and the king. Thietmar of Merseburg, an imperial bishop in the early eleventh century, could not yet understand this. In his chronicle he characterizes the empress differently and draws the following conclusion about her work: 'Though she was of the weak sex she possessed moderation, trustworthiness and – which is not often found in Greece – very good manners. In this way she protected with male vigilance the royal power for her son, friendly against all those who were honest, but with terrifying superiority against rebels.'

These words might form a fine conclusion, but they constituted a *topos* – at least as to the 'weak sex' and the 'male' vigilance – given to many women who had to do 'a man's work' in the Middle Ages. On 15 January 991, Theophano died in the imperial palace at Nijmegen. According to her will she was buried in St Pantaleon in Cologne. She chose this church, because here were buried the relics of the popular martyr Pantaleon from Asia Minor, which had been brought to the West by the match-maker, archbishop Gero. For Theophano this was a little memento of her home.

Select bibliography

PRIMARY SOURCES

The diplomas of Otto II and Otto III, including those few diplomas of Theophano, are published completely in MGH DD O II and MGH DD O III, ed. Th. Sickel.

The most important source for the late tenth century is Thietmar of Merseburg's *Chronicon*, ed. R. Holtzmann, MGH SRG IX.

See for Henry the Wrangler especially Richer's *Historiae*, ed. R. Latouche (Paris, 1937); furthermore the *Annales Quedlinburgenses*, MGH SS III, and the *Annales Hildesheimenses*, ed. G. Waitz, MGH SRG in us. schol. VIII.

Evidence for faint, but still existing claims to co-rule can be found in Ruotger's *Vita Brunonis*, ed. I. Ott, MGH SRG X (1951), in Hrotsvit's *Gesta Ottonis*, ed. P. von Winterfeld, MGH SRG XXXIV (1902), and especially in Gerbert of Rheims's letter collection, ed. F. Weigle, MGH Die Briefe der deutschen Kaiserzeit, 2 (1966).

The most important source for the first attempt to win the hand of a bride is Liutprand's *Legatio ad imperatorem Constantinopolitanum*, ed. J. Becker, MGH SRG XLI in us. schol. (3rd edn, 1915).

There is only one source, the *Brunwilarensis monasterii fundatorum actus*, ed. G. Waitz, MGH SS XIV (1883), which proves – even in its distorted form – that the dowry caused the military expedition of 982. This is a relatively late authority, but, as Theophano's daughter

Matilda founded this monastery, the unknown author was also interested in the empress.

Odilo of Cluny offers information in his *Epitaphium Adelheidae*, ed. H. Paulhart, *Die Lebensbeschreibung der Kaiserin Adelheid von Abt Odilo von Cluny*, Mitteilungen des Instituts für Österreichische Geschichtsforschung, Supplement 20, 2 (1962), about the empress Adelheid, though he treats the subject one-sidedly.

SECONDARY WORKS

There are no learned well-founded biographies of Theophano, Adelheid, Otto II, Otto III and Henry the Wrangler. A very detailed compilation of the facts can be found in *Jahrbücher des Deutschen Reiches unter Otto II. und Otto III.*, I, *Otto II. 973–983*, by K. Uhlirz (Leipzig, 1902), II, *Otto III. 983–1002*, by M. Uhlirz (Berlin, 1954).

A shorter representation of the imperial rules can be found in H. Beumann, *Die Ottonen* (Stuttgart, 1987, 2nd edn 1991).

The approaching thousandth anniversary of Theophano's death was heralded by the acta of the symposium *Byzantium and the Low Countries in the Tenth Century*, ed. V.D. van Aalst and K.N. Ciggaar (Hernen, 1985). The most important publication for the millennium is von Euw and Schreiner, *Kaiserin Theophanu*, including fifty-three essays.

On East–West relations in the tenth century see W. Ohnsorge, *Konstantinopel und der Okzident: gesammelte Aufsätze zur Geschichte der byzantinisch-abendländischen Beziehungen und des Kaisertums* (Darmstadt, 1966).

For the various attempts to realize a marriage see R. Hiestand, *Byzanz und das Regnum Italicum in 10. Jahrhundert* (Zurich, 1964) and J. Koder and Th. Weber, *Liutprand von Cremona in Konstantinopel* (Vienna, 1980).

For the dowry (Capua and Benevento) see W. Georgi, in von Euw and Schreiner, *Kaiserin Theophanu*, II, pp. 135–61; for the endangerment of the dowry as the reason for Otto II's military expedition to Calabria see V. von Falkenhausen, *Untersuchungen über die byzantinische Herrschaft in Süditalien vom 9. bis ins 10. Jahrhundert* (Wiesbaden, 1967); U. Rizzitano, 'Gli Arabi in Italia', *Settimane di studio del Centro Italiano dei studi sull'alto medioevo*, 13 (1965), 93–114; P. Lamma, 'Il problema dei due Imperi e dell'Italia Meridionale nel giudizio delle fonte letterarie dei secoli IX e X', in *Atti del 3° Congresso internazionale di studi sull'alto medioevo* (1959), pp. 155–253.

Concerning the relationships of the Saxon dynasty see the practical compilation by W. Glockner, *Die Verwandten der Ottonen und ihre Bedeutung in der Politik* (Cologne and Vienna, 1989).

On the relation between the eastern and western Frankish realms in the tenth century see the extensive summary by C. Brühl, *Deutschland-Frankreich: die Geburt zweier Völker* (Cologne and Vienna, 1990), and F. Lot, *Les Derniers Carolingiens: Lothaire, Louis V, Charles de Lorraine (954–991)* (Paris, 1891), especially on the last western Frankish Carolingians.

For the structure of the eastern Frankish realm in those days see H. Keller, 'Reichsstruktur und Herrschaftsauffassung in ottonisch-frühsalischer Zeit', *Frühmittelalterliche Studien*, 16 (1982), 74–128, and for the two southern German dukedoms H. Maurer, *Der Herzog von Schwaben* (Sigmaringen, 1978) and S. Weinfurter, 'Die Zentralisierung der Herrschaftsgewalt im Reich unter Kaiser Heinrich II.', *Historisches Jahrbuch*, 106 (1986), 241–97.

For Theophano's co-rule see von Euw and Schreiner, *Kaiserin Theophanu*, I; J. Laudage, 'Überlegungen zur Königserhebung Ottos des Grossen und zu den Aufständen Tankmars, Heinrichs und Liudolfs', *Historisches Jahrbuch*, 112 (1992), 23–71.

On regencies for minor rulers see Th. Kölzer, 'Das Königtum Minderjähriger im fränkisch-deutschen Mittelalter', *HZ*, 250 (1990), 291–304 (Theophano's regency for Otto III is not discussed here).

3

Theophano: an empress reconsidered

K. CIGGAAR

Illa imperatrix Greca (Odilo of Cluny)[1]

On a wall-painting in the monastery of San Salvator Maggiore in Rieti (some 90 km north-east of Rome) the emperor Otto II and his wife Theophano were pictured as saints, i.e. with haloes around their heads. The fresco was unfortunately lost during this century, and only the portrait of the emperor had been published. The painting has been dated to 975. At a superficial glance one might think that the couple had died and been canonized by the time their effigies were painted on the wall of the monastery.

However, a small number of other rulers in the Holy Roman Empire were pictured in the same way during their lifetime: Henry the Wrangler, duke of Bavaria (955–76; 985–95; anti-king in 984), the emperor Henry II (1002–24) and Frederick Barbarossa (1152–90). What was the significance of such representations, exceptional as they were in the western Middle Ages?[2]

From an early date the Ottonian dynasty, as emperors of the West, tried to imitate the 'regalia' of the Byzantine emperors. The *Zweikaiser* problem expressed itself in all sorts of competitiveness. The marriage of Otto II to the Byzantine princess Theophano in 972 was another stimulus to introduce Eastern customs and thus enhance the prestige of the western rulers. It is in this context that we should consider the mural paintings of Rieti, so close to the Byzantine cultural world of southern Italy.

[1] H. Paulhart, *Die Lebensbeschreibung der Kaiserin Adelheid von Abt Odilo von Cluny* (Graz, etc., 1962), p. 35 (PL 142, c. 974).

[2] P.E. Schramm, *Die deutschen Kaiser und Könige in Bildern ihrer Zeit, 751–1190*, new edn ed. F. Mütherich *et al.* (Munich, 1983), pp. 195–6, no. 94, p. 198, no. 95, pp. 268–9, no. 218.

Emperors with a halo occur in contemporary liturgical manuscripts in southern Italy, in the so-called Exultet-Rolls where Byzantine influence is seen clearly. They were used during the Paschal Liturgy and showed portraits. One of them represents the Byzantine emperors Basil II (976–1025) and his brother Constantine VIII (1025–28) being crowned as emperors by their father Romanos II (959–63). In mosaics in Hagia Sophia in Constantinople, this old tradition was continued in portraits of several emperors. The tradition of depicting emperors with a nimbus seems to go back to at least the sixth century. Unfortunately Iconoclasm destroyed many pictures in the Byzantine Empire and especially in Constantinople where they must have been abundant. In Italy, in the churches of San Vitale and San Apollinare Nuovo in Ravenna, such portraits of the emperor Justinian I (527–65) and his wife Theodora have been preserved. During Justinian's reign Italy was still part of the Byzantine Empire even if the emperor had his residence in Constantinople.[3]

The nimbus was part of the imperial 'outfit' and was not necessarily the symbol of a saintly life. Otto II and Theophano were pictured as emperors in the Byzantine style and were not necessarily regarded as people living saintly lives, nor were they canonized in later times. But does the opposite hold true: was Theophano doomed to hell, as some scholars want us to believe? (See below.)

The appreciation of historical persons is often a matter of subjective criteria and of personal taste. This is true for contemporary and later commentators, historians and non-historians alike. Contemporary writers, often anonymous, of a saint's *Life* often express feelings of sympathy for or disapproval of people involved in the life of their hero or heroine. The same can be said of the chroniclers and official historians of a ruling family. Until the present this has not changed.

The selective use of sources by scholars is another factor to take into account. Sometimes the accessibility or inaccessibility of sources, linguistically and/or physically, can be of decisive influence. Unexploited and unknown material provides another complicating factor in the process.

[3] G. Cavallo, *Rotoli di Exultet dell' Italia Meridionale* (Bari, 1973), p. 55 and ill. 10. For the mosaics in Ravenna and in Hagia Sophia, Constantinople, see e.g. J. Beckwith, *Early Christian and Byzantine Art* (Harmondsworth, 1979), ills. 92, 93, 221.

The empress Theophano is one of the 'victims' of vicissitudes among historians and scholars from various countries. They have often seen her as a dominant and over-ambitious person who imbued her son with Greek ideas. A tradition of hostility towards the Greek empress is discernible. Closely related is the problem of the so-called *Byzantinische Frage*, i.e. the influence of Byzantium on Western Europe. Xenophobia, historical and of recent date, may be part of such an attitude, sometimes resulting in a negative judgement. The story told by a German nun who, in a vision, saw the former empress after her death, lamenting her *tormentum* and regretting her sins, seems to have influenced the sometimes negative image of this Greek princess, a judgement that has persisted until recently. To quote just one modern historian: 'the ambitious Theophano turned her son's head with Byzantine ideas of imperial power and glory, and it became young Otto's dream to reunite the eastern and western empires into one great Roman Empire'.[4]

It will always be difficult to judge a historical person whose life often remains obscure and more or less hidden. A thorough examination of all available sources or a more balanced and impartial use of these sources may cast a clearer light on the person in question. This is especially the case with a person of foreign extraction who was in a position to exert power. Theophano was of Greek origin and thus had an 'exotic' background, which might have created specific frustrations.[5] In Western Europe there were certain prejudices about the Greeks, current among large groups living in Western Europe, including the German *Reich*. Whereas the *sapientia* of the Greeks was praised, their *fallatia*, *invidia* and *arrogantia* were denounced.[6] Theophano's real identity (porphyrogennete, princess, aristocratic lady or simply a niece of a ruling emperor; curiously enough she is not mentioned in any Byzantine source), discussed until very recently, will not concern us here. It cannot be denied, however, that there was some

[4] Otloh of St Emmeran, *Liber visionum*, PL 146, cc. 372–3 (MGH SS XI, p. 385); D.J. Geanakoplos, *Medieval Western Civilization and the Byzantine and Islamic Worlds* (Lexington, Mass., 1979), p. 206.

[5] M. Rentschler, 'Griechische Kultur und Byzanz im Urteil westlicher Autoren des 10. Jahrhunderts', *Saeculum*, 29 (1978), 324–55 (p. 343 and n. 145: 'Eine Geschichte des Urteils über Theophanu bis in die jüngste Zeit wäre ein lohnendes Unterfangen').

[6] *De proprietatibus gentium*, ed. T. Mommsen, MGH AA XI (Berlin, 1894), pp. 389–90.

disappointment that she was not the 'purple-born' princess the German missions had been asking for. It is not important to know her family background as long as the West saw her as a member of the upper class in Byzantium.[7]

The purpose of this article is to take a closer look at a few sources that have not yet been sufficiently exploited and which reflect the reactions of society to the presence of this foreign lady, who had such an important position in political life, especially after her husband's death. Lack of space prevents me from commenting fully on the way the empress was described by contemporary writers and their immediate successors. By using positive and negative comments a more balanced view of her personality may emerge. The negative image which several historians have given of Theophano may thus be corrected and be replaced by a more positive judgement.

In the late tenth and early eleventh century learning and writing were limited to ecclesiastical circles, and thus the majority of western authors belonged to the church. This was in contrast to Byzantium, where lay people were not only educated and active as writers, but even had their own libraries. It goes without saying that western authors with a clerical background would be inclined to condemn luxury and especially the person who introduced luxury into their society.

The western appreciation of Byzantine culture and Byzantine artefacts should be included in the discussion but it is again lack of space which prevents their inclusion. Even if Theophano led a more sober life than she was accustomed to in Constantinople, her lifestyle must have undoubtedly played a role in the appreciation of her person by the society in which she lived.

Some negative judgements

1. Odilo of Cluny (*c.* 962–1048) was a contemporary who was on good terms with the empress Adelheid, Theophano's mother-in-law. Adelheid outlived her son's wife, who died in 991. After Adelheid's death in 999 Odilo of Cluny composed an *epitaphium* in which he glorified the deceased empress who came from Burgundy. She was the daughter of Rudolph II of Burgundy. In 1097 she was canonized. In the *epitaphium* Odilo heavily criticized Theophano whom he does not even call by her proper name. At

[7] G. Wolf, 'Nochmals zur Frage: Wer war Theophano?', *BZ*, 81 (1988), 272–83.

times the relationship between the two women was rather tense. Theophano took care of her own interests and continually frustrated her mother-in-law, who, according to the abbot of Cluny, was very happy when her daughter-in-law died. Elsewhere, when speaking of Otto II, Odilo refers to her as 'that Greek woman whom Otto II had married'. Badly advised by his wife, Otto had felt tempted to conquer the Byzantine Empire, by which the Byzantine territories in southern Italy must have been meant, where, indeed, a military confrontation took place. The expedition was not going to be a success for Otto II. It is clear that Odilo and Adelheid were on friendly terms. Generous donations to Cluny and other religious houses must have played a role in the maintenance of good relations. No sympathy existed between Adelheid and Theophano, at least during certain periods after the death of Otto II. Theophano died in 991 which enabled Odilo to express freely the relationship between the two women without fearing revenge. The question remains whether such an *epitaphium* was widely known or even read by outsiders.[8]

2. The hostilities which took place in southern Italy, a confrontation with the Greek army, eventually ended with Otto's defeat by the Saracens. These events are referred to by Albert of Metz who wrote his *Fragmentum de Deoderico primo episcopo Mettensi* some time before 1017. He describes the Greek princess as an unpleasant talkative woman and calls her, in an apparently deprecatory way, *regina*. According to him she was the exponent of Greek mentality when, after her husband's defeat, she trumpeted the virtues of her compatriots, who were now her husband's adversaries. The context of this passage is proof of the existence of stereotyped ideas among westerners about Greeks, and about women in general. Theophano was both Greek and a woman.[9]

[8] Paulhart (see n. 1), pp. 35, 46–7: 'cui successit tertius ex Greca genitus Otto. . . Licet illa imperatrix Greca sibi et aliis fuisset satis utilis et optima, socrui tamen auguste fuit ex parte contraria. . .', 'Greca imperatrix ab hac luce discessit, augusta Adalheida superstes felixque remansit'. . .'illam Grecam in thalami consortium suscepisset.' The terms *ex Greca natus*, *illa imperatrix Greca*, *Greca imperatrix* and *illa Greca* sound very negative (PL 142, cc. 974, 984). See also M. Rentschler, 'Griechische Kultur und Byzanz im Urteil westlicher Autoren des 11. Jahrhunderts', *Saeculum*, 31 (1980), 112–56, at pp. 112–13.

[9] MGH SS IV, p. 698: 'statim procaci locutione, ut fert levitas mulierum, conterrales suos – erat enim de Grecia – ad celum extollere exitumque adversi prelii cum summo probro ad derogationem imperatoris intorquere, qui tanta frequenter virtute laudatus, a suis tam facile sit superatus'; new edition by H. van Rij and A. Sapir Abulafia, *Alpertus van Metz: De diversitate temporum & Fragmentum de Deoderico primo episcopo Mettensi* (Amsterdam, 1980), pp. 110–11.

3. There seem to have been women as well who did not like the foreign empress. One of the most spectacular texts describing Theophano is the story told by a German nun who saw her in a vision. The text was written around 1050 by the monk Otloh of St Emmeran (Regensburg), who lived from 1010 to 1070, in his *Liber visionum*. The story had been told to him by the nun. She had been approached by the empress who was greatly tormented after her death ('in maximo tormento posita sum'). She said to the nun that she deserved eternal damnation ('merui aeternam dampnationem') because she had introduced luxurious garments and decorations (presumably jewelry) into France and Germany. The empress implores the nun to pray for her and deliver her from her torments.[10] For some unknown reason this vision, in a shortened form, was added to the *Vita* of St Bernward of Hildesheim (*c.* 960–1022), in a fifteenth-century manuscript. In no way, however, is the *Vita* a pamphlet against Theophano. Thangmar of Hildesheim, the author of the *Vita* (945/50–before 1013), speaks of her as the 'venerabilis et sapientissima mater domna Theuphanu augusta'. And even if the expression *sapientissima* belongs to the category of stereotyped ideas, it expresses admiration in this context.[11]

Some interpretations of the Visio

Several western medievalists and Byzantinists, S. Runciman, D.J. Geanakoplos, K. Leyser and D.M. Nicol, came to the conclusion that the empress Theophano ended up in hell, contributing to the negative image of the empress.[12] Others, E. Kubach, V. Elbern, H. Wentzel and P. Corbet, speak of a *Jenseits* and an *au-delà*.

[10] Otloh of St Emmeran (see n. 4), cc. 372–3, 'Ego sum Theophanu, quae olim de Graecia veniens in Franciam conjuncta fueram connubio Caesaris Ottonis. . .quia videlicet multa superflua et luxuriosa mulierum ornamenta, quibus Graecia uti solet, sed eatenus in Germaniae Franciaeque provinciis erant incognita, huc primo detuli memeque eisdem plus quam humanae naturae conveniret, circumdans et in hujusmodi habitu nocivo incedens alias mulieres similia appetentes peccari feci'; cf. MGH SS IV, p. 888.

[11] Thangmar, *Vita Bernwardi*, MGH SS IV, p. 759; new edn ed. H. Kallfelz, AQDG XXII (Darmstadt, 1973), pp. 278–9, with German translation.

[12] S. Runciman, *Byzantine Civilization* (London, 1933), p. 296; D.J. Geanakoplos, *Byzantine East and Latin West* (Oxford, 1966), p. 39; K. Leyser, 'The tenth century in Byzantine–Western relationships', in *Relations between East and West in the Middle Ages*, ed. D. Baker (Edinburgh, 1973), pp. 29–63, at p. 45; D.M. Nicol, *Byzantium and Venice* (Cambridge, 1988), p. 47.

Seeing things in the perspective of xenophobia, noticeably where the difference of culture between East and West was concerned, they suggested that her torments took place in a more neutral *au-delà*.[13] So far few scholars, for example F.J. Tschan and G. Cames, 'saw' Theophano in purgatory, but their views seem to have gone almost unnoticed.[14] Such opinions and verdicts have contributed to the negative image of the Byzantine princess who did not, or did not want to adapt to western life. True Theophano was a foreigner, someone with a different religious background, who had been raised as a member of the Orthodox faith. Curiously enough, when imploring the nun to say prayers for her, she refers to her 'Catholic' faith, a difficult term to appreciate at a time when East and West were growing apart. In Byzantine theology, however, there was no purgatory.

In his book *La naissance du purgatoire*, J. Le Goff gives a fragment of the vision without discussing it in detail. He says that we see here the cultural gap between East and West, saying that it was 'un bel exemple d'utilisation de l'au-delà pour exprimer le fossé culturel entre l'Occident et l'Orient'. J. Le Goff was convinced that the idea of purgatory, a sort of flaming hell from which one could be redeemed or released by prayers and good works, was born in the twelfth century. He may therefore have somewhat neglected Otloh's testimony.[15]

The nineteenth-century editor of the *Liber visionum* in the *Patrologia Latina* interpreted the text as the description of Theophano's torments in purgatory when he gave the title: *Theophaniae imperatricis ob luxum vestium in purgatorio poenae*. I think that he was right in assuming that the empress' 'hell' was rather a purgatory, since she implores the nun to pray for her so that she may be delivered from her eternal damnation, if only prayers could be constantly said for her: 'si aliqui servi Dei pro me constanter orare vellent, de dampnatione perpetua me liberare possent'. Otloh ends with an exhortation to his readers or audi-

[13] E. Kubach and V.H. Elbern, *Das frühmittelalterliche Imperium* (Baden-Baden, 1968), pp. 220–2; H. Wentzel, 'Das byzantinische Erbe der ottonischen Kaiser: Hypothesen über den Brautschatz der Theophano', *Aachener Kunstblätter*, 43 (1972), 11–96, at p. 86, n. 40; P. Corbet, *Les Saints ottoniens* (Sigmaringen, 1986), p. 71, n. 8.

[14] F.J. Tschan, *Saint Bernward of Hildesheim: His Life and Times*, 3 vols. (Notre Dame, 1942), I, p. 440; G. Cames, *Byzance et la peinture romane de Germanie* (Paris, 1966), p. 11.

[15] J. Le Goff, *La naissance du purgatoire* (Paris, 1981), pp. 499–500.

ence to pray for the empress in order that she may receive absolution. Did he try to slightly readjust the negative feelings about the empress that existed, persisted perhaps, among his contemporaries?

It is clear that the terms purgatory and middle place deserve more attention from medievalists. In visions, in miracle stories and in wills they received a connotation different from the ideas developed in the early centuries of Christendom.[16]

4. Xenophobia is also seen as the impetus for Peter Damian's inculpation of Theophano of having had a love-affair with John Philagathos, or at least to have been very intimate with him. He was a Greek monk from southern Italy who succeeded in seizing the papal throne for a while and who acted as anti-pope. Peter Damian wrote about John Philagathos as a person who had had immoral contacts with the then reigning empress: 'qui etiam cum imperatrice, quae tunc erat [i.e. Theophano], obscoeni negotii dicebatur habere mysterium'. There may have been feelings of hostility for a foreigner, a Greek, who acted as anti-pope. Peter Damian (*c.* 1007–72), contemporary of Otloh of St Emmeran, was an influential theologian and church leader in eleventh-century Italy. The cultural gap between East and West during his lifetime, especially when the schism of 1054 became more and more clear, may have played a role in such rumours and his severe judgement. Elsewhere Peter Damian blames the Greek princess Maria Argyropoula for introducing to Venice a luxurious life-style, unknown in Italy, for which she was eventually punished by an early death during the plague. Here, too, we find criticism of the lifestyle of Byzantine ladies. There are indications that the Italian prelate detested high-born Greek women.[17]

Some positive judgements

1. We shall return to some contemporary writers who were more positive about the Greek-born empress. We have seen how

[16] See e.g. M. Bull, *Knightly Piety and the Lay Response to the First Crusade: The Limousin and Gascony c. 970–c. 1130* (Oxford, 1993), s.v. purgatory, pp. 168, 194, 202, and s.v. middle place, pp. 19, 168, 187–8, 189–90, 192–6, 198, 201, 202, 286.

[17] PL 144, c. 253 (K. Reindel, *Die Briefe des Petrus Damianus*, 2 vols. (Munich, 1988), II, p. 539, no. 89); PL 145, *Institutio Monialis*, c. 744; cf. J. Leclercq, 'S. Pierre Damien et les femmes', *Studia monastica*, 15 (1973), 43–53. John Philagathos had been introduced into the imperial household by Theophano, *Annales Quedlinburgenses*, MGH SS III, p. 74. According to a Greek envoy to the Ottonian court he

the German nun saw the empress being tortured after her death. During her lifetime the empress was preoccupied with life after death and the Last Judgement. This does not imply that she led a holy life. Thietmar of Merseburg, a well-known and widely used chronicler (975–1018), who was educated at Magdeburg, says that after her husband's death in 983 she worried about his fate. St Lawrence appeared to her in a dream and advised her to let her son repair her husband's sins by restoring the bishopric of Magdeburg. The chronicler may not have been entirely impartial where the bishopric of Magdeburg was concerned and Theophano's good works. He praises the excellent behaviour of the empress and her way of life, although as he says, 'this was exceptional for Greeks, and although, being a woman, she had certain weaknesses'. He also praises her for having paid her tithe to the church by sending her daughters to convents to live saintly lives. Elsewhere Thietmar of Merseburg mentions her good relationship with her mother-in-law, the empress Adelheid, after the death of her husband. This is in contrast to the *epitaphium* of Odilo of Cluny who may, however, exclusively refer to a later period in her life.[18]

2. Theophano was on good terms with a number of highly placed persons in the *Reich*, amongst them Adalbert, bishop of Prague. In the *Vita* of St Adalbert, written by Bruno of Querfurt (974–1009), the empress' role in society is described expressing the author's admiration for her. Bruno stayed in Rome for some years where he seems to have written the *Vita*, of which two versions exist. After the death of her husband Theophano also spent some time in Rome where she cared for the poor, to whom she distributed money, and had prayers and masses said for her husband's soul. She was generous towards Adalbert when he came to Rome and was planning a pilgrimage to the Holy Land. She sent for him in secret and gave him a large amount of money which

had been intimate with a number of women, *The Correspondence of Leo, Metropolitan of Synada and Syncellus*, Greek text, English trans. and commentary ed. by M.P. Vinson (Washington, DC, 1985), pp. 20, 21, 101.

[18] Thietmar of Merseburg, *Chronicon*, ed. W. Trillmich, AQDG 9 (Darmstadt, 1957), pp. 114–15, 124–6, 130–1, 'Haec, quamvis sexu fragilis, modestae tamen fiduciae et, quod in Grecia rarum est, egregiae conversationis fuit regnumque filii eius custodia servabat virili, demulcens in omnibus pios terrensque ac superans erectos. De fructo vero ventris sui decimas Deo obtulit filias suas, I. ad Quidilingeburg Aethelheidam nomine, alteram ad Gonnesheim, quae Sophia dicitur', with German translation.

Adalbert, in his turn, secretly gave away to the poor.[19] Theophano hoped to save her husband from the fire ('ut peccatorem regem ab incendio liberaret') by doing good works. It seems as if the author of the *Vita* explicitly heard the words of the empress. The other version of the *Vita* of St Adalbert, published by Bielowski in an edition which is not easily accessible, gives the same passage.[20]

3. During her lifetime the empress conversed with all sorts of pious men, bishops, monks and hermits. In Rome she could remain in contact with Greek spirituality. Southern Italian rulers sent St Sabas to her to solve political problems. When the saint died in Rome in 990 the empress paid her respects to him, according to the Greek *Vita* written by Orestes: 'At the time of his death an immense crowd gathered together, which was composed not only of fellow-monks, but of eminent laymen, and of many nobles with their wives and children: and indeed the wife of the king [the Byzantines only regarded their own *basileus* as the emperor], when she heard the remarkable news of this great event, came to prostrate herself before the body of the holy man.' The Greek text continues that it was an extraordinary scene.[21]

4. We have seen that Theophano was generous towards the church and its institutions. Magdeburg was one of the beneficiaries and so were the chapel of St Salvator in Frankfurt and many more religious institutions.[22] According to the *Vita* of St Gregory of Burtscheid, another Greek from southern Italy, she took the initiative to sponsor new religious foundations. In Rome she built the small monastery of San Salvator, in Aachen an oratory dedicated to St Nicholas. Gregory was another Greek friend of the empress. The *Vita* also reports donations to the church of the

[19] *S. Adalberti Pragensis episcopi et martyris vita altera auctore Brunone Querfurtensi*, ed. H. Karwasínska, Monumenta Poloniae Historica, n.s. IV (Warsaw, 1969), pp. 13, 15, 'Ibi tunc pulchrum luctum Greca imperatrix augusta, que iam longos dies mortuum flevit, sepulti coniugis memoriam reparat, dulcem Ottonem elemosinis et orationibus celo commendat. Sed peccatum quod vivens neglexit, mortuo marito emendare uxor superstes instabat; legatos mittit elemosinas et orationes multorum, per quos propicium Redemptorem appellaret, ut peccatorem regem ab incendio liberaret' (MGH SS IV, pp. 586–7).

[20] *Passio sancti Adalberti*, ed. H. Bielowski, Monumenta Poloniae Historica, I (Lvov, 1864), pp. 190, 198, 199.

[21] *Historia et Laudes SS. Sabae et Macarii iuniorum e Sicilia, auctore Oreste, patriarcha Hierosolymitano*, ed. G. Cozza Luzi (Rome, 1893), p. 67 (inaccessible); cf. G. da Costa-Louillet, 'Saints de Sicile et d'Italie méridionale aux VIIIe, IXe et Xe siècles', *Byzantion*, 29/30 (1959–60), 89–173, at pp. 138–9.

[22] Wolf (see n. 7), p. 283.

Virgin in Cologne. The anonymous author of the *Vita* calls her a 'matrona religiosa et Deo devota imperatrix'.[23] Such donations and foundations were of course part of the imperial status. The same may be said of translations of relics. The church of St Pantaleon in Cologne, apparently one of her favourite places, also benefited from the generosity of the *diva augusta*, as we learn from the *Translatio S. Albini*. The church of St Pantaleon had been founded by bishop Bruno of Cologne, brother of Otto I. He had brought the body of the saint from Nicomedia. After her death Theophano was buried in the church of St Pantaleon, named after the popular eastern medical St Panteleemon.[24]

Other eastern saints may have been introduced by the Greek empress or by near relatives, such as St Nicholas, St Demetrios and St Dionysios. Reliquaries with relics of these saints may have formed part of her dowry. Later such saints became patron saints of churches and chapels. It is possible that, as far as dedications are concerned, a number of sources remain unexploited. This may also be true of sources which refer to her presence in Italy during longer periods. Italian sources may be hiding certain aspects of her life in the West and her politics.[25]

So much for churches, saints and relics. More important seems to have been the import of Byzantine religious artefacts with pictures of the Virgin, alone or in scenes from the New Testament. The Crucifixion was a popular theme and so was the Deesis, a picture of the Virgin and St John who stand on either side of Christ and implore His intercession. The exact impact of these images on western European religious art has still to be determined. The same can be said of dedications of sanctuaries to the Virgin or to Christ. An almost unknown tenth-century ivory

[23] *Vita Gregorii abbatis Porcetensis posterior*, MGH SS XV, pp. 1195–8.

[24] MGH SS XV, pp. 686–8, 'Quae diva augusta Sancti Pantaleonis monasterium summo honore coluit et regali munificentia sublimavit sanctorumque reliquiis permunivit'. Hugo of Flavigny, *Chronicon*, MGH SS VIII, p. 374, says that the body of St Panteleemon had been brought to the West, but many of his relics were still venerated in the Byzantine Empire, K.N. Ciggaar, 'Une description de Constantinople traduite par un pèlerin anglais', *Revue des Etudes Byzantines*, 34 (1976), 211–67, at p. 267.

[25] See e.g. A. Krickelberg-Pütz, 'Die Mosaikikone der Hl. Nikolaus in Aachen-Burtscheid', *Aachener Kunstblätter*, 50 (1982), 9–141; H. Wentzel, 'Byzantinische Kleinkunstwerke aus dem Umkreis der Kaiserin Theophano', *Aachener Kunstblätter*, 44 (1973), 43–86, and ills. 14–9c; J. Flemming, *Byzantinische Schatzkunst* (Berlin, 1979), pp. 66–7, ills. 19–24; St Dionysios was one of the patron saints of Quedlinburg.

1. The Crucifixion. Byzantine ivory, tenth century (Gemeentemuseum Arnhem, The Netherlands).

with the Crucifixion has been preserved in the Netherlands, now in the Gemeentemuseum of Arnhem (Fig. 1).[26]

Scholars are now convinced that Theophano's arrival in the West made an important contribution to the development of the cult and iconography of the Virgin there. In Byzantium the Virgin played a prominent role in the church and in the daily life of the Byzantines. Iconographical types, such as the Hodigitria (she who shows the way), appear in western art in these times. An ancient ivory of this type is now kept in the Rijksmuseum Het Catharijneconvent, Utrecht. The iconography of the apocryphal Death of the Virgin in Ottonian art seems clearly influenced by the presence of Byzantine religious objects, such as the ivory which decorated the Evangeliary of Otto III. The *Vita* of St Adalbert called the Virgin 'bona angelorum imperatrix augusta', an imitation of the Greek *basilissa*, the Greek empress. In Byzantium she was considered as the Divine mother of Christ, the supernatural defender of Constantinople, and was often depicted enthroned. Theophano was raised in a religious ambiance where the Virgin was venerated daily. By bringing images of the Virgin to the West and by venerating these she contributed to the popularity of the Virgin Mary in the West. Images were important in the Middle Ages because they carried a message and so the Virgin became a carrier of culture, of Byzantine culture, to the West.[27]

Conclusion

In spite of her good works and her 'saintly behaviour' when she tried to repair her husband's sins, and the introduction of new religious ideas and new saints, Theophano was never canonized like other members of the Ottonian dynasty. Matilda, wife of

[26] A. Goldschmidt and K. Weitzmann, *Die byzantinische Elfenbeinskulpturen des X.-XIII. Jahrhunderts*, 2 vols. (Berlin, 1934), II, p. 67 (no. 160), and pl. LV, which decorated a manuscript of the monastery of Bethlehem, near Doetinchem. For another rather unknown Byzantine ivory in the Netherlands, a Virgin with Child, in the parochial church of Ommel, A.M. Ammann, 'Ein unbekanntes Elfenbein aus dem 11. Jahrhundert', *Orientalia Christiana Periodica*, 26 (1960), 415–17, with illustration.

[27] H. Jantzen, *Ottonische Kunst* (Munich, 1959), pp. 77–80, 139; K. Weitzmann, 'Various aspects of Byzantine influence on the Latin countries from the sixth to the twelfth centuries', *DOP*, 20 (1966), 3–24, at pp. 15–16; H. Appuhn, *Einführung in die Ikonographie der mittelalterlichen Kunst in Deutschland*, 3rd edn (Darmstadt, 1985), 126–30.

Henry I (father of Otto I, whose *Vita* was ordered by Otto II in 972), and the two wives of Otto I, Edith and Adelheid, have survived in *Vitae*, and so has Cunegunda, wife of Henry II, cousin and successor of Otto III. Theophano's life was not recorded in a *Vita* or in an *epitaphium*. Even her name, an exotic sounding name, in occurrence in Byzantine imperial and princely circles, has hardly left a trace in Germany. The only Theophano one finds in written sources (the name has often been preserved in a distorted form), is her granddaughter, abbess of Essen (1039–54).

Theophano's portrait was not included in the genealogical tree which we find in the *Chronicle* of St Pantaleon, now in Wolfenbüttel, Herzog August Bibliothek (cod. Guelf 74.3 Aug. 2°, fol. 226). The only painted portrait preserved until the present day seems to be a small miniature in an Evangeliary from around 1000.[28]

Her foreign background may have formed an obstacle to her being fully integrated into western life, even if she was surrounded by saints and future saints, Latin and Greek alike, like St Gregory, St Neilos, St Sabas, St Bruno, St Romuald, St Adalbert and others. Her dealings with Greeks, especially when in Rome, may have given 'uneasy feelings'. In fact she led a sort of dual life, engaged in western political life and interested in the Greek society of southern Italy. Jealousy of her luxurious lifestyle, which was considered a bad example for other women, was another factor as we have seen. If we consider the sources used in this article, it seems rather unfair to 'condemn her to hell' as later historians have done. Some of her contemporaries saw her in purgatory from which she had a chance to be saved, where she had a future, this 'imperatrix devota'. Saint among the saints? Her luxurious lifestyle and her foreign background were the most likely obstacles for her canonization in the West. A woman in hell or in purgatory would be a better question, but the question has to remain in suspense. Like every human being she had her good and her bad points, accentuated by friends and enemies. The two questions can both be answered negatively: she was not a saint, at least not in the opinion of the westerners of her time even if she was depicted in an Italian monastery as a saintly person, nor was

[28] Corbet, *Les Saints ottoniens* (see n. 13), frontispiece; R. Kahsnitz, 'Ein Bildnis der Theophanu?: zur Tradition der Münzen und Medaillon-Bildnisse in der karolingischen und ottonischen Buchmalerei', in von Euw and Schreiner, *Kaiserin Theophanu*, II, pp. 101–34, and ill. 1.

she in hell if we carefully read the vision written by Otloh of St Emmeran. Negative and positive comments on her person kept the judgement in balance, and that may have been the very reason why the eleventh-century German nun saw her in purgatory, from where she could still be redeemed by devout believers. However, a more elaborate study of all contemporary sources involved and of the judgement of later historians may reveal other interesting aspects of the life of this Greek princess in the West and contribute to a rehabilitation of her person and her politics.

4

Theophano: considerations on the education of a Byzantine princess

JUDITH HERRIN

When Theophano arrived in Rome in 972 to marry the young German prince, Otto II, she was presented as a Byzantine princess. While there may have been some doubt as to her precise relationship to the ruling emperor, her clothing and demeanour, her retinue and her extravagant gifts confirmed a close imperial connection. Not only did she bring with her the luxurious silks and jewels that fascinated western commentators on the marriage, but also in some way she embodied a prestige associated with brides from Constantinople, qualities that made these Greek princesses especially desirable.

This particular marriage had been pursued for a long time by the bridegroom's father Otto I; it was part of an ongoing effort to build a diplomatic alliance with Byzantium. And as in all medieval diplomacy, political considerations and goals were of paramount importance. Within this process, successful marriages could seal an alliance and ensure friendly relations probably better than any written agreement. So the younger members of ruling dynasties across Europe were constantly pressed into diplomatic service. Like others before and after her, Theophano played a significant role in the foreign relations of the Byzantine Empire. During the second half of the tenth century, her contribution was similarly subjected to diplomatic needs and political ends. To that extent, all Byzantine princesses were expected to represent something over and above their own family's interests, something quintessentially imperial. They had to perform their appointed roles in the empire's developed system of diplomacy.[1]

[1] For a recent survey, see *Byzantine Diplomacy*, ed. Jonathan Shepard and Simon Franklin, Society for the Promotion of Byzantine Studies, Publications 1 (Variorum, Aldershot, 1992).

Theophano: the education of a Byzantine princess

Although Theophano's family background and early life have been the subject of a great number of studies, all the evidence is derived from western sources. She is simply absent from the Byzantine documents. However, the fact that she performed her diplomatic role in the West with apparent skill suggests a novel method of investigation. Rather than imagine what her life might have been like, I propose to investigate the education of Byzantine princesses in general. This chapter will therefore examine the preparation they received in order to fulfil their specific tasks, in addition to acting as ambassadors for Byzantium, and thus securing the alliances of cooperation or at least peace, which was the aim of formal diplomacy. Clearly, no two Byzantine princesses were ever the same. But within the formal diplomatic requirements of the term, they had to conform to certain expectations, to meet certain criteria, to fit a preconceived model. So in this chapter I will investigate the parameters of this model and then try to discover how well Theophano fitted them.[2]

By the mid-tenth century the term 'Byzantine princess' could designate at least two different types, which have to be distinguished. First, those born in the Purple Chamber of the Great Palace, the *porphyrogennetoi*,[3] daughters of reigning emperors or co-emperors, designated heirs to the throne. Thanks to Psellos we have vivid descriptions of two famous examples, Zoe and Theodora, daughters of Constantine VIII, the last representatives of the Macedonian dynasty.[4] But there are many others: in the tenth century, Anna and Theodora, sisters of Romanos II. These are purple-born princesses, without peers, the ones so much desired by foreign rulers. Theophano was not of this elite.

Second, in a slightly lower category are those Byzantine princesses related to the ruling family, who were not born in the

[2] During revision of this chapter in May and June 1993, the marriage of the heir to Japan's Chrysanthemum Throne took place amid ceremonies that appeared to an outsider highly reminiscent of Byzantine court ritual. In some respects crown-princess Masako has to fulfil a role comparable to that in Byzantium of incoming foreign brides, who entered the imperial court to be trained as future empresses. This is different from Theophano, who represents rather the outgoing bride, leaving the empire to perform the role of princess in a new context. But both have had to conform to established roles in imperial courts.

[3] Literally, 'born in the Purple (Chamber)', a birthing room that was evidently lined with porphyry (purple marble) or hung with purple silk. The term was transliterated as *Porphyrogenitus/porphyrogenita*, in the Latin West.

[4] See, for instance, Ernest Gamillscheg, 'Zoe und Theodora als Träger dynastischer Vorstellungen in den Geschichtsquellen ihrer Epoche', in von Euw and Schreiner, *Kaiserin Theophanu*, II, pp. 397–401.

Porphyry Chamber. Some of these had important connections to those in power and probably had considerable familiarity with the imperial court, for instance Maria Lekapena, granddaughter of Romanos I, who was married to Peter of Bulgaria.[5] Theophano may have been among their number.

Third, in a separate category altogether are those who became princesses by marrying into the ruling family from quite different backgrounds. Here, there are three distinct methods of recruitment.

1. By foreign alliance: these foreigners became princesses through political decisions taken in Constantinople with regard to diplomatic relations with external powers. The Khazars provide an interesting example from the seventh century on. Because of their formidable military power and geographic position, Herakleios was interested in a Khazar alliance; later, the exiled Justinian II sought refuge with the Khagan and married his sister, and in the 730s a Khazar bride was chosen for Leo III's son, Constantine. These arrangements stemmed from foreign policy and had nothing to do with the suitability of the bride apart from age. However, once the alliance had been agreed and the betrothal settled, pictures of the future bride and groom were exchanged. In a later eighth-century instance, Constantine VI is said to have been so attached to the picture he received of his fiancée that he wept when the engagement was broken off by his mother Irene.[6]

2. By internal alliance: princesses selected as suitable brides from among aristocratic families of the empire because they brought political support and useful alliances. In this way, Irene, daughter of the important Sarandapechys family in central Greece, was chosen in the mid-eighth century to become the wife of Leo IV. After his early death in 775, she eventually ruled as emperor, using the masculine denomination, *basileus*, in place of her son Constantine VI. Such alliances also developed from diplomatic concerns.

3. By beauty-competition, bride-show, a process documented from the *Lives* of some of the individuals so chosen as well as from narrative sources. In the eighth and ninth centuries these Byzan-

[5] J. Shepard, 'A marriage too far?: Maria Lekapena and Peter of Bulgaria', chapter 7 in this volume.

[6] Theophanes, *Theophanis Chronographia*, A.M. 6281, ed. C. de Boor (Leipzig, 1889), I, p. 463; cf. English trans., Harry Turtledove, *The Chronicle of Theophanes* (Philadelphia, 1982), p. 147.

tine 'Judgements of Paris' provide such circumstantial detail that it seems difficult to doubt the existence of the bride-show altogether, though recent studies have emphasized its literary character.[7] Commissioners were sent throughout the empire to find the most beautiful young ladies, and a prototype of such beauty in the form of an official portrait, the *lauraton*, was circulated. In this way Irene found Maria of Amnia as a bride for Constantine VI, after breaking off his first engagement; Euphrosyne did the same for Theophilos, who chose Theodora over Kassia, and so on. Five instances are documented between 788 and 882.[8]

Nonetheless, these contests left little to chance: notions of suitability, while not made explicit, must have existed; questions of family alliance and regional loyalty played a part. In every case the empress-mother engineered the choice and probably undertook the subsequent training of the successful candidate. For in all cases the incoming bride would become a Byzantine princess and therefore had to be prepared for her new duties, especially if she was to fulfil the role of a future empress.

In addition, from the tenth century onwards 'Byzantine princesses' were sent abroad to marry important allies, for instance by Leo VI. In about 900, he sent his daughter Anna to marry Louis III, the German, later blinded, and she bore him a son aptly named Charles Constantine, who survived to the 960s as count of Vienne.[9] Anna was an illegitimate daughter, born to Leo's mistress Zoe during his first marriage to Theophano the Elder. But the child's status had been regularized by the subsequent second marriage of Leo to Zoe, and indeed Anna had performed certain important functions at court, as we shall see. She was probably the first of these new female ambassadors for Byzantium; our Theophano is certainly one of the most celebrated.

7 For example, L. Rydén, 'The bride-shows at the Byzantine court: history or fiction?', *Eranos*, 83 (1985), 175–91.

8 W. Treadgold, 'The bride-shows of the Byzantine emperors', *Byzantion*, 49 (1979), 395–413; H. Hunger, 'Die Schönheitskonkurrenz in "Belthandros und Chrysantza" und die Brautschau am byzantinischen Kaiserhof', *Byzantion*, 35 (1965), 150–8. Recently, L.-M. Hans, 'Der Kaiser als Märchenprinz: Brautschau und Heiratspolitik in Konstantinopel', *JÖB*, 38 (1988), 33–52, has re-emphasized the credibility of this method of 'choosing' a suitable bride, citing the long tradition preserved in Hellenistic romances, cf. C. Cupane, 'Il "concorso di bellezza" in Beltrando e Crisanza sulla via fra Bisanzio e l'occidente medievale', *JÖB*, 33 (1983), 221–48.

9 C. W. Previté Orton, 'Charles, Count of Vienne', *English Historical Review*, 29 (1914), 703–6.

This practice, however, was in flagrant violation of established Byzantine traditions. For in the middle of the tenth century Constantine VII recorded the diplomatic principle that purple-born princesses should on no account be married to foreigners. The only exception that might be made to this rule, according to this emperor, was in the case of the Franks. In chapter 13 of his *De administrando imperio*, he reports that it was specifically permitted by Constantine I, 'because he himself drew his origin from those parts . . . [and] because of the fame of those lands and the nobility of those tribes'.[10] The Romans (meaning Byzantines) were, therefore, allowed to intermarry with the Franks (meaning Christians from the western parts of Europe, identified as Francia, *Phrangia*).[11] In contrast, Constantine VII sharply criticizes his father-in-law Romanos I for sending Maria Lekapena to marry Peter of Bulgaria.

As ruler, Constantine VII himself used this special pleading to justify the choice of a Frankish bride for his son Romanos II. In 944 the six-year-old Bertha, daughter of Hugh of Arles, was betrothed to Romanos with the properly Greek name of Eudokia. There seems little doubt that she would have become empress had she not died five years later, before the marriage could be celebrated and consummated. Constantine VII then negotiated an agreement with Hedwig of Bavaria, niece of Otto I, which never came to fruition. In due course Romanos was married to a Byzantine bride, another Theophano, not the subject of this book.[12]

Even though the alliance with Otto I had come to nothing, the same western ruler later sent Liutprand, bishop of Cremona, with a similar mission, to find a bride for his son. He had in mind Romanos II's daughter, Anna, a true *porphyrogennetos*. This was the embassy of 968, so coldly received by Nikephoros Phokas, to

[10] Constantine VII Porphyrogennetos, *De administrando imperio*, ed. G. Moravcsik, with English trans. by R.J.H. Jenkins, I (Budapest, 1949), pp. 70–2; II, *Commentary* (London, 1962), pp. 63, 67. On this crucial text, see now R. Macrides, 'Dynastic marriages and political kinship', in *Byzantine Diplomacy* (see n. 1), pp. 263–80, at pp. 266–70.

[11] J. Shepard, 'Aspects of Byzantine attitudes towards the West in the tenth and eleventh centuries', *Byzantinische Forschungen*, 13 (1988), 67–118, at pp. 87–94.

[12] In *c.* 955, when he was fourteen and she about the same age. From this fact it seems unlikely that the young prince, co-emperor with his father Constantine VII, had any freedom of choice in the matter. His bride was an internal candidate, who would need to be trained for her position.

Liutprand's great displeasure.[13] But his successor, John Tzimiskes, who reigned from 969 to 976, was willing to comply with the request, which is where our Theophano comes in.

Before turning to Theophano, however, it is necessary to follow Anna's ultimate fate, as this illustrates one important development of tenth-century diplomatic practice. After Romanos II had rejected Otto I's request, it was the turn of Hugh Capet of France, who wanted Anna as a bride for his son, Robert.[14] In fact, Gerbert's letter about the proposal, though written, was never sent because in the meantime Hugh had learned that the ruling emperor, Basil II, had promised his sister to Vladimir of Kiev. After Russian assistance to Basil during the civil war, Anna was sent to Kiev in the summer of 988. Her large retinue included bishop Theophylaktos, appointed as the first metropolitan of the capital of the *Rus'*. Anna herself undertook an evangelizing role there and was responsible for building many churches in the 990s.[15] She may have been the mother of Boris and Gleb, later recognized as patron saints of Russia.

So in Anna's case we know that this particular Byzantine princess had been courted before, that is, she was an established prize, and exercised a truly ambassadorial role in Kiev. Although the marriage was forced upon Basil II, he managed to insist that Vladimir convert to Christianity. This preserved at least the notion that Byzantine princesses should never be married to pagan rulers, though the Christian faith was barely established in Russia at the time. But the break with tradition is perhaps reflected in Anna's initial unwillingness, recorded in the Russian sources.[16] Subsequent alliances, however, regularly followed this new pattern, subordinating Constantine VII's diplomatic principle to expediency.

From this brief overview it is clear that 'Byzantine princesses'

[13] Liutprand of Cremona, *Legatio*, MGH SRG in us. schol. XLII (Hanover, 1839), pp. 347–63; English trans., F.A. Wright (London, 1930), reprinted with an introduction by J.J. Norwich (London, 1993), pp. 177–210.

[14] A.A. Vasiliev, 'Hugh Capet of France and Byzantium', *DOP*, 6 (1951), 227–51.

[15] *The Russian Primary Chronicle*, trans. S. H. Cross and O. P. Sherbowitz-Wetzor (Cambridge, Mass., 1953), 112; Macrides, 'Dynastic marriages' (see n. 10), 273; cf. D. Obolensky, *The Byzantine Commonwealth* (London, 1971), pp. 253–8.

[16] The fact that 'all contemporary Byzantine writers are strangely silent' about the marriage (Obolensky, *ibid.*, p. 254) might be interpreted as disapproval of Basil II's break with imperial tradition. Yet since the same silence shrouds the marriage of Theophano to Otto II, it seems more likely to reflect an indifference among Byzantine chroniclers as to the fate of such princesses.

came in many guises. Still, certain characteristics were associated with the term itself and these must now be examined. In the first place, imperial women were obviously aware of the duties of princesses, and their role in court ceremonial. Those who had been participating as *porphyrogennetoi* since their youth had taken an active part in imperial functions; the more distantly related had less exposure to them and must have needed coaching.

Secondly, for those foreigners coming into the empire to marry the heir apparent, those who would become empress, a certain amount of education in Greek and introduction to Byzantine culture was required. This is evident from the training provided for Rotrud, Charlemagne's daughter, during the 780s when she was officially betrothed to Constantine VI. Empress Irene sent a court official, Elissaios the eunuch, from Constantinople to instruct Rotrud, who was known in the East by the name Erythro, i.e. a translation of her Germanic name, meaning red.[17] Had the marriage gone ahead, instead of being broken off, she would have been collected from the West and brought ceremonially to Byzantium for the arranged marriage, with at least a modicum of preparation for her new life.[18] A similar attention is documented in the case of Çiçek, the Khazar princess selected as the bride of Constantine V. Her name meant Flower (*Anthousa* in Greek) though she was renamed Irene (Peace) at her baptism in Byzantium. In connection with this preparation for imperial status, one iconophile source claims that Irene became eminent for her piety and condemned the iconoclasm of her husband and father-in-law.[19] If so, this was a subversion of the marriage alliance, which had surely intended her to support her new family in every way. The name Anthousa was later used by the ruling family, but probably under the influence of St Anthousa of Mantineon, who predicted the safe birth of twins to Eudokia, Constantine's third wife.[20]

[17] Theophanes, *Chronographia* (see n. 6), A.M. 6279, I, p. 455; English trans., p. 141.

[18] See n. 6 above.

[19] Theophanes, *Chronographia*, A.M. 6224, I, pp. 409–10; English trans. p. 101; cf. Nikephoros Patriarch of Constantinople, *Short History*, ed. and trans. C. Mango, DOT, 10 (Washington, DC, 1990), ch. 63, p. 130. Since Constantine was about twelve years old in 730, Çiçek-Irene must have been a young girl at the time of the marriage.

[20] See C. Mango, 'Saint Anthusa of Mantineon and the family of Constantine V', *Analecta Bollandiana*, 100 (1982), 401–9. I am grateful to Nick Constas for discussions on these saints, who regularly get confused, and for allowing me to consult his translation of the brief *Vita* of Anthousa, the emperor's daughter.

This basic training for Byzantine court-life can also be observed in the proposed marriage of Romanos II to Hedwig of Bavaria and later matches.[21] Again, Byzantine eunuchs were dispatched to give the bride instruction in Greek culture, probably oral and unwritten. The engagement came to nothing, however, and Hedwig later married Burchard II of Swabia. But in the mid-twelfth century this style of teaching prepared Bertha of Sulzbach for her marriage to Manuel I in 1142. Later Bertha not only acquired the necessary knowledge of Greek but also commissioned paraphrases of difficult ancient Greek texts, patronizing writers who used the vernacular or demotic (spoken) Greek of the time.[22] It is difficult to judge whether such patronage sprang from a desire to become more fully aware of the Byzantine literary heritage. But evidently the young empress gathered a group of scholars around her, including John Tzetzes, who prepared versions of the classics in a less daunting form. In her case, the education required of a foreign-born imperial bride encouraged further learning.

Apart from some familiarity with Greek, all brides also had to acquire quite an extensive knowledge of court-ceremonial. Although these rituals and traditions were written down in the *Book of Ceremonies*, documented at the insistence of Constantine VII in the middle of the tenth century, court officials had preserved them by word of mouth from generation to generation. It was probably in this verbal form that they were communicated to strangers to Byzantium, who had to learn how to participate in special receptions and dinners. Although the master of ceremonies gave constant spoken instructions during these long theatrical events, it was very important for everything to proceed according to tradition. The order, execution and significance of each gesture, act and acclamation had to be mastered by those taking part.[23]

From the cases cited above, it is evident that in the East

21 On Hedwig of Bavaria, niece of Otto I, and the Byzantine embassy of 952, see W. Ohnsorge, 'Drei *deperdita* der byzantinischen Kaiserkanzlei und die Frankenadressen im Zeremonienbuch des Konstantinos Porphyrogennetos', *BZ*, 45 (1952), 320–39, at pp. 325–6; cf. G. Wolf, 'Die byzantinisch-abendländischen Heirats- und Verlobungspläne', *Archiv für Diplomatik*, 37 (1991), 15–32.

22 E. Jeffreys, 'The Comnenian background to the "Romans d'Antiquité"', *Byzantion*, 50 (1980), 455–86, at pp. 472–4, reprinted in *Popular Literature in Late Byzantium* (Variorum, 1983); cf. now P. Magdalino, *The Empire of Manuel I Komnenos 1147–80* (Cambridge, 1992) on this marriage of 1146, pp. 42–3.

23 On the formal aspect of the *Book of Ceremonies*, see my article, 'Byzance: le palais et la ville', *Byzantion*, 41 (1991), 213–30, at p. 218.

instruction in both Greek and court ceremonial was considered an important element in the training of foreign brides. This training was entrusted to high-ranking officials, whose primary responsibility was to attend upon the emperor and empress in their private apartments, and to guard the women's quarters of the imperial palace.[24] Within the Byzantine court eunuchs formed a separate and quite distinct hierarchy, reserved for 'beardless men', who were considered reliable with female members of the imperial family. Owing to their close proximity to the highest circles of the ruling class they often became trusted personal servants and confidants of emperors. As guardians of imperial tradition, they also played an active part in ensuring the smooth performance of palace-ceremonial. Such officials were well qualified to communicate knowledge both of Greek and of Byzantine court-procedures, and were regularly employed to do so.

At the highest level of the court, the empress was involved in an entire calendar of rites performed throughout the year as well as particular ceremonies adapted for special occasions. The Byzantine court required a female figurehead and entourage to balance the male hierarchy attending on the emperor, to receive the wives of visiting dignitaries, and to provide a female counterpart to specifically male ceremonies. The empress also directed and looked after the women's quarters in the palace, attending to the education of imperial children and to the household activities of what was a very large and important establishment.[25] Her presence at court was fundamental to Byzantine protocol; even a female child might be crowned empress, in order that the position might be filled.[26]

[24] On eunuchs in Byzantium, see R. Guilland, 'Les eunuques dans l'Empire byzantin', *Etudes Byzantines*, 1 (1943), 196 ff; 'Fonctions et dignités des eunuques', *ibid.*, 2 (1944), 185 ff; 3 (1945), 179 ff; 'Etudes de titulature byzantine: les titres auliques réservés aux eunuques', *Revue des Etudes Byzantines*, 13 (1955), 50 ff; 14 (1956), 122 ff; 'Etudes sur l'histoire administrative de Byzance: les titres auliques des eunuques', *Byzantion*, 25/27 (1955/57), 649 ff. Cf. K.M. Ringrose, 'The eunuchs of Byzantium: language, image and gender', unpublished paper.

[25] See most recently D. Missiou, 'Über die institutionelle Rolle der byzantinischen Kaiserin', *JÖB*, 32.5 (1982), 489–98; S. Maslev, 'Die staatsrechtliche Stellung der byzantinischen Kaiserinnen', *Byzantinoslavica*, 27 (1966), 308–43.

[26] Emperor Herakleios, for instance, elevated his fifteen-month-old daughter, Epiphaneia, to the role of empress on 4 October 612, see *Chronicon paschale*, ed. L. Dindorf, Corpus scriptorum historiae byzantinae (Bonn, 1832), 702; trans. Michael Whitby and Mary Whitby (Liverpool, 1989), p. 154. On the titles of the empress, see E. Bensammer, 'La titulature de l'impératrice et sa signification:

In the very last years of the ninth century, as his second wife died, Leo VI enunciated this principle in unmistakable fashion: 'not having an empress, it was impossible to celebrate the banquets according to the prescribed tradition and custom'.[27] He therefore crowned his daughter Anna as *augousta*, and she served in this capacity until his third marriage. On other occasions emperors took similar steps: e.g. after the death of his wife, Theodora, Romanos I crowned his daughter-in-law Sophia as empress - she had been married to his son Christopher, and was the daughter of Niketas the Slav.[28] There were already other *augoustai* at court, Romanos' own daughter Helen and his other daughter-in-law Anna, but he needed one who would perform the imperial role.

Why was the figure of the empress so vital? Certain ceremonies, including the complex banquets, could only take place with the empress present. Others involved the promotion of officials to positions in which their wives would also attain a new dignity. As an instance of the ceremonies in which the empress might participate, one could cite a great number of receptions described in the *Book of Ceremonies*, and I have chosen to analyse the reception of one foreign embassy, that of Olga, the Russian princess.[29]

The Russian delegation met the emperor and empress twice, probably in the year 958. On the first occasion, 9 September, the ceremonial must have taken up the best part of a day. It began with the formal reception of Olga by Constantine VII and his court in the Magnaura Palace. Her noble female relations, her elite female attendants, the ambassadors and merchants from Russia, in short, her entire entourage was in attendance.

recherches sur les sources byzantines de la fin du VIIIe à la fin du XIIe siècle', *Byzantion*, 46 (1976), 243–91.

27 Ohnsorge, 'Drei *deperdita*' (see n. 21), pp. 325–6.

28 *Theophanes Continuatus*, ed. I. Bekker, Corpus scriptorum historiae byzantinae (Bonn, 1828), 402; cf. S. Runciman, *The Emperor Romanus Lecapenus and his Reign* (Cambridge, 1929 and reprinted 1963), p. 67.

29 Constantine VII Porphyrogennetos, *De ceremoniis aulae byzantinae*, book 2, ch. 15, ed. I. Bekker, Corpus scriptorum historiae byzantinae, I, 594–8; trans. J. Featherstone, in 'Olga's visit to Constantinople', *Adelphotes: A Tribute to Omeljan Pritsak by His Students*, *Harvard Ukrainian Studies*, 14 (1990), 293–312. The passage occurs in the chapter on receptions held in the Great Triclinium of the Magnaura, when the emperors sit on the throne of Solomon. It follows receptions for the emir of Tarsos (946), who sent an embassy seeking the exchange of prisoners and a peace-treaty; the Hippodrome celebration organized by the demes to celebrate

It continued in the Triclinium of Justinian where the great throne of Theophilos was set up with another one on a platform covered with reddish purple silk. The empress (Helen) and her daughter-in-law (Theophano) received seven separate groups of court-wives; then Olga entered with her entourage and female attendants and talked with the empress, through the intermediary of the *praepositus*. Next, the emperor and empress and their children born in the purple had private conversations with Olga in the empress' bedchamber.

Later the same day, the empress Helen gave a grand banquet in the Triclinium of Justinian for all the female Russians, while the emperor received the males in the Chrysotriclinium and distributed sums of money to each of them. Olga dined with the empress, who stood as godmother to her in her Constantinopolitan baptism and gave her the Christian name Helen. Olga stood beside the empress and Theophano, the daughter-in-law of Helen, on the raised platform; and in this position she received reverence in the form of prostrations made by *archontissai* (wives of the leading men, *archontes*) who attended the banquet. Her own relations and wives of court officials also participated.

Afterwards Olga took her place at a separate table with the *zostai*, according to the prescribed order. This means that she had been admitted to the rank of *zoste patrikia*, the highest court rank for women, marked by a costume with a particular girdle (*zoste*). Although one early Byzantine instance is recorded, this title in its medieval form was created by the emperor Theophilos for his mother-in-law Theoktiste in the ninth century.[30] Promotion to the rank of *zoste* involved a special ceremony documented from the *Book of Ceremonies* (though not mentioned here by Constantine VII). When Olga received this high honour, the empress hosted a special dinner for her as a female head-of-state after a court-ceremony in which the imperial couple had acted together. At the banquet choristers from two major churches sang the imperial praises and the theatrical dances were staged by the factions.

the peace; and the reception for the emir of Amida, at which the Arabs of Tarsos are described as friends.

[30] R. Guilland, 'Contribution à l'histoire administrative de l'Empire byzantin: la patricienne à la ceinture, *e zoste patrikia*', *Byzantinoslavica*, 32 (1971), 269–75, reprinted in *Titres et fonctions de l'Empire byzantin* (London, 1976), pt XXVI; cf. P.G. Sayre, 'The Mistress of the Robes: who was she?', *Byzantine Studies/Etudes*

Finally, a dessert was served in the Aristeterion, and Olga sat with the emperors, Constantine VII and Romanos, with their children and with the daughter-in-law, Theophano. Constantine had five daughters (including a Theophano); Romanos and Theophano had only one child, Basil II.[31] On this occasion Olga was given 500 *miliaresia*, silver coins, in a golden bowl encrusted with precious stones. And her six relations and eighteen attendants received equivalent sums.

On the second occasion, 8 October, another banquet was given by the empress Helen for Olga in the Pentakouboukleion of St Paul, while in the Chrysotriclinium the other *Rus*' dined with the emperor. Again the purple-born children and the imperial daughter-in-law Theophano attended, and the dinner was marked by the distribution of more coin to the princess, her female relations and her ladies-in-waiting. In such receptions the younger generations of the imperial family performed their roles and observed what the reigning empress did under the guidance of the *atriklines* (master of ceremonies), who stage-managed such events. Similarly, the staff of each imperial lady's bedchamber and the wives of senators and other court officials in attendance participated in particular ways that had to be learned.

In these two receptions given for Olga, the empress Helen played a particularly important role precisely because the foreign embassy was headed by a woman. Her daughter-in-law, Theophano, aged about fifteen, was also present, an instance of the heir presumptive's wife 'learning on the job'. She had to observe and follow the whole ceremony, with her infant son Basil, the future emperor. The participation of wives of officials is clear, and again their movements are complex and involve different parts of the Great Palace.[32]

While this tenth-century ceremony may have been especially lavish, the participation of the empress in numerous public events was always required. During a reception for the envoys of the Umayyad Caliphate of Cordoba, one of them remarked on the beauty of the empress Theodora and the unusual fact of her being

Byzantines, 13 (1986), 229–39, who omits Olga from the list of women who held the title.

31 Basil was one year old when Constantine VII died in 959, so he must have been born in 958, but curiously the precise date is not recorded, see P. Grierson, *Catalogue of the Byzantine Coins in the Dumbarton Oaks Collection*, III, 2 (Washington, DC, 1973), p. 574.

32 See, for instance, the evidence cited by Guilland, 'Contribution' (see n. 30).

unveiled at court.[33] Similarly, Marwazi in his account of the imperial couple expressed amazement that the empress accompanied the emperor on campaign and attended particular games in the Hippodrome, when her men took on the emperor's in fights and competitions.[34] The military side of an empress' life is another regular aspect – like Martina in the seventh century, so Irene Doukaina went on campaign with her husband in the twelfth, though there were times in between when empresses did not.

By now it should be obvious that the prominence of the empress, her retinue and the wives of senators at court-ceremonies is modelled on the emperor's role. The feminine side constitutes an essential element. So any incoming princesses, whether of Byzantine or foreign origin, had to be instructed in their roles. They all needed to master a whole cycle of Byzantine traditions and court-ceremonials in order to participate correctly. While this learning may have been of a purely unwritten sort that required only memorization, the symbolic significance of each ceremony was also important. Arguably, this aspect of court-ritual was given special emphasis if the princess was being sent abroad as an ambassador of Byzantine culture.

To turn now to the other more formal aspect of their education, what do we know about their book-learning? Did Byzantine princesses receive any training in reading and writing? Current scholarship on levels of literacy in Byzantine society at large is rather divided.[35] But there is general agreement that most women, the vast majority, were illiterate. Only in certain aristocratic households or nunneries could girls acquire a basic knowledge of reading and writing.[36] This may be illustrated by the *Life* of St Theophano, who later became the pious empress and first

[33] W. Treadgold, *The Byzantine Revival 780–842* (Stanford, Ca., 1988), p. 322.

[34] V. Minorsky, 'Marwazi on the Byzantines', *Mélanges H. Grégoire*, II (Brussels, 1950), pp. 1–69.

[35] R. Browning, 'Literacy in the Byzantine world', *Byzantine and Modern Greek Studies*, 4 (1978), 39–54 (a rather optimistic view); cf. A. Laiou, 'The role of women in Byzantine society', *JÖB*, 31 (1981), 233–60, at p. 254 (stressing female illiteracy). See most recently, M. Mullett, 'Writing in early medieval Byzantium', in *The Uses of Literacy in Early Medieval Europe*, ed. R. McKitterick (Cambridge, 1990), pp. 156–85, at pp. 156–7 (with an emphasis on the dominant oral traditions in Byzantium).

[36] See, for example, E.C. Topping, 'Women hymnographers in Byzantium', *Diptycha*, 3 (1982–3), 98–111. Three particularly impressive women authors, Theodosia, Thekla and Kassia, who all lived in the ninth century, possessed erudition, *logia*, i.e. greater skill than mere literacy and piety, which is attributed to their aristocratic backgrounds and home education.

wife of Leo VI. At the age of six, her father got her a tutor so that she could learn Holy Scripture. Soon she knew the Psalter and hymns by heart and then she devoted herself to reading and prayer.[37] Deeply religious, she had no secular education deemed worthy of record by her hagiographer, but clearly she was literate and well educated in religious matters.

At court there may have been more emphasis on literacy, even for girls. And this was especially likely when no sons were born to an imperial family. The education of Theophilos' daughters, five of whom were born before Michael, or of Constantine VII's, who similarly preceded Romanos, reveals an attention to their potential future roles.[38] If no male child were to be born to an imperial couple, the eldest girl would normally have played a crucial role as wife of the emperor-designate. This was the role assumed by Anna Komnene in the early twelfth century, even after the birth of her brother John. And since emperors died unexpectedly and were occasionally killed in battle, these women might yet wield considerable power as widowed empresses. Several seem to have aspired to full imperial authority; and Irene succeeded in this aim. So the education and preparation of female children for an imperial role became accepted as a necessity.

Of course, at the court there was never a shortage of educated servants, who could act as *amanuensis* for emperors and empresses alike. But rulers and their families were occasionally famous for their literate skills. In the mid-tenth century an interesting example of such education is preserved in the story of Constantine VII's reliance on his daughter Agatha. When he fell ill, she assisted him with chancellery work, not just as a secretary but because she understood it and was well informed about official governmental matters.[39] This is a rare reference to a Byzantine princess having a

[37] *Zwei Griechische Texte über die Hl. Theophano, die Gemahlin Kaisers Leo VI.*, ed. E. Kurtz, Zapiski imperatorskoj Akademii Nauk, VIII, istor.-filol. otdel. III, 2 (St Petersburg, 1898), 6, p. 3.

[38] Psellos, however, accuses Basil II and Constantine VIII of ignoring the needs of their three female heirs (daughters of the latter). The eldest, Eudokia, followed the religious calling and was dedicated to the church. Zoe and Theodora were neither prepared for the role of ruler nor suitably married, although they received their education in the palace, see *Chronographia*, book 2, 4–5, ed. E. Renauld (Paris, 1967), I, pp. 27–8; cf. Michael Psellus, *Fourteen Byzantine Rulers*, trans. E.R.A. Sewter (London, 1953 and reprinted 1979), pp. 55–6.

[39] U.V. Bosch, 'Einige Bemerkungen zum Kanzleiwesen der byzantinischen Kaiserin', *Rivista di Studi Slavi e Bizantini*, 1 (Paris, 1979) = *Mélanges I. Dujčev*, pp. 83–102. In the late eleventh century, Anna Dalassene, mother of Alexios I

command of official state affairs and being allowed to exercise it. But it may be rare partly because our sources do not document such expertise except in most unusual circumstances. The fact that Agatha could help her father, who was one of the most intellectual and scholarly emperors, implies a greater scope for literacy among imperial daughters than is often supposed. It may also reflect this emperor's concern to educate his many daughters, who were born before his only surviving son, Romanos.

To meet the requirements of her high rank and to fulfil the duties of potential future positions, therefore, every Byzantine princess was expected to meet certain criteria. It was necessary for her to understand something of the ideology of empire, as this was represented in court ceremonial and diplomatic activity. She had to master not only her own place in the ceremonies that took up so much of the court's time, but also the roles performed by the others involved. While much of this training might be communicated orally and learnt by imitation (and there are clear instances when a young princess would acquire such expertise by participating at the lower levels of the hierarchy), the reception of foreign embassies, the promotion of office-holders, attendance at special liturgies or distribution of charity involved background knowledge about the diplomatic, political, ecclesiastical and philanthropic considerations behind such functions. A princess who had the capacity to understand more than the basics of reading and writing would have been encouraged to broaden and deepen that knowledge by studying the documents that preserved imperial traditions. The best teachers available would have been employed as tutors and the library of the Great Palace put at the disposal of children of both sexes. They might also receive a specific training in court-protocol and etiquette from the palace eunuchs, who acted as guardians of ceremonial traditions.

A Byzantine princess might well have witnessed some of the emperor's business activities, the work of officials charged with executing imperial policy, or the reports of those who returned from military campaigns or commercial ventures abroad. Other less elevated activities within the palace could instruct a princess about the amount of time and energy required to maintain the furnishings, equipment and official costumes used by the court.

Komnenos, provides a different example: as an older woman and a widow she exercised considerable authority, which was made explicit when her son established her as regent in his absence.

She might also observe the work of craftsmen, who constantly added to the luxury items displayed to impress visitors. So through a combination of regular participation in the calendar of events, attention to the symbolic values attached to ceremonies, and study of imperial political traditions, Byzantine princesses could become familiar with a wide spectrum of the ideological underpinnings of the empire. That they should do so was obviously desirable. When they failed to do so, male historians took pleasure in recording their 'feminine weaknesses'.

This pattern of training makes it possible to enquire into Theophano's education and preparation in a more informed and less personal fashion. To begin with, it is necessary to elucidate her background and the tenth-century world into which she was born.[40] Recent prosopographical work on the established dynastic families of the time has confirmed that she was the daughter of two high-born members of the aristocracy, Constantine Skleros and Sophia Phokas.[41] Her mother was a niece of the emperor Nikephoros II Phokas and she was thus his great niece.[42] It has also been suggested that she was a god-daughter of the empress Theophano, wife of Romanos II and Nikephoros Phokas in turn, and was brought up in the palace. In the West this association with

[40] On the Byzantine background in general, see P. Schreiner, 'Die byzantinische Geisteswelt vom 9. bis zum 11. Jahrhunderts', in von Euw and Schreiner, *Kaiserin Theophanu*, I, pp. 9–24; R. Jenkins, *Byzantium: The Imperial Centuries A.D. 610–1071* (London, 1966), pp. 256–300. For the most useful survey of what can be said about the early life of Theophano, see F. Tinnefeld, 'Die Braut aus Byzanz: Fragen zu Theophanos Umfeld und Gesellschaftlicher Stellung vor ihrer abendländischen Heirat', in *Kaiserin Theophanu, Prinzessin aus der Fremde – des Westreichs Grosse Kaiserin*, ed. G. Wolf (Cologne, 1991), pp. 247–61.

[41] G. Wolf, 'Nochmals zur Frage: Wer war Theophanu?', *BZ*, 81 (1988), 272–83 (with much earlier bibliography on this developed subject); Wolf, 'Die "Grosse Frage": Wer war Theophanu?', in *Kaiserin Theophanu*, ed. Wolf, pp. 223–36; cf. O. Kresten, 'Byzantinische Epilegomena zur Frage: Wer war Theophano?', in von Euw and Schreiner, *Kaiserin Theophanu*, II, pp. 403–10.

[42] On the Phokas family, see I. Djurić, 'Porodica Foka', *Zbornik Radova Vizantološkog Instituta*, 17 (1976), 189–296 (family tree, p. 292, French résumé, pp. 293–6); cf. J.-C. Cheynet, 'Les Phocas', Appendix to *Le Traité sur la Guérilla (De Velitatione) de l'empereur Nicéphore Phocas*, ed. G. Dagron and H. Mihăescu (Paris, 1986), pp. 289–315. On the Skleros side, see W. Seibt, *Die Skleroi: eine prosopographisch-sigillographische Studie*, Byzantina Vindobonensia, 9 (Vienna, 1976). None of these studies, however, notes the possible offspring of the marriage of Sophia and Constantine. In contrast, the novelist Henry Benrath had very accurately worked out this genealogy in the 1930s, as emphasized by G. Wolf ('Nochmals zur Frage', p. 279) and O. Kresten ('Byzantinische Epilegomena', p. 403).

the Great Palace of Constantinople, where the emperors held court, was known.[43]

The most convincing aspect of this identification stems from the naming of Theophano's children: the first daughter was named after her paternal grandmother, Adelheid/Adelaide; the second after her maternal grandmother, Sophia, and the third after her paternal great-grandmother, Matilda. The fourth daughter, twin to Otto, died shortly after birth, but the logical name would have been that of her maternal great-grandmother, Sophia's mother. The fact that Theophano and Otto named their children in precisely this fashion suggests that the correct identification has been made.

As a member of the Phokas family, she had been close to ruling circles from a very young age (Nikephoros II reigned from 963 until 969). Her father Constantine Skleros was a firm ally of John Tzimiskes and would have ensured contact with the court after 969. It is, therefore, unnecessary to argue that she was named after Theophano, empress and wife of Romanos II, who acted as her godmother and brought her up in the court. In fact, Theophano was quite a common name in the tenth century, particularly among the Macedonian dynasty, which produced a saint in the first wife of Leo VI, whose relics were treasured in the palace.

When Otto I sent Liutprand to Constantinople to seek a bride, Nikephoros II Phokas had no children: his wife Theophano had four by Romanos, real *porphyrogennetoi*, including two daughters, Anna and Theodora, but the reigning emperor had no wish to permit either of these legitimate members of the previous ruling dynasty to crown an alliance. After his murder in 969, the widowed empress Theophano was banished with her children, and the new ruler, John Tzimiskes, married another Theodora, a daughter of Constantine VII. The situation was then as follows: the emperor had no children from his first marriage to Maria Skleraina; his second wife gave him a certain legitimacy but he had no children of his own.

[43] The theory of her being named after the empress Theophano the Elder was developed by P. Schramm and accepted as possible by Wolf ('Nochmals zur Frage', p. 276). On the connection with the palace, see *Vita Mahthildis reginae antiquior*, 16, MGH SS X (Hanover, 1852), p. 581. The attempt to identify a particular part of the palace, or even a different palace in Constantinople, seems to me impossibly ambitious, see G. Wolf, 'Vom Kaiserpalast in Byzanz zum Valkhof in Nimwegen', *Kaiserin Theophanu*, ed. Wolf (see n. 40), pp. 19–26, at pp. 22–3.

However, his brother-in-law Constantine Skleros, who was married to Sophia Phokas, a great-niece of the previous emperor, had a daughter Theophano, a girl (*puella*) of the right age to marry Otto's son.[44] It is important to note that all the calculations about Theophano's date of birth and age at marriage turn on this fact. Otto II was born in 955 and thus was sixteen/seventeen years old in 972; his bride had to be of a suitable age. Following Wolf, the current consensus is that Theophano was about twelve years old – twelve was then the minimum age for a girl to marry.[45] The problem of a Byzantine bride had been outstanding since Nikephoros broke off negotiations, and John Tzimiskes wanted peace in Italy in order to concentrate on eastern and northern campaigns.

At this point we have to surmise what might have occurred, given that there is no direct evidence for the emperor's thinking. But it seems quite possible that he would have brought Theophano into the Great Palace in order to prepare her for her new role.[46] Her connection with the new dynasty provided her with imperial credentials as a Byzantine princess and she was a blood-relative of the successful general who had become emperor. But she was not a *porphyrogennetos*, in the same way as Anna and

[44] She is so identified by a contemporary western author, Widukind of Corvey, see *Res gestae Saxonicae, Continuatio*, 74, MGH SS III (Hanover, 1839), p. 465 (cf. *ibid.*, 71). The term *puella* could be used of quite a wide range in age. So from this reference it is only possible to deduce that the bride and groom were considered well matched, i.e. Theophano may have been about the same age as Otto, who was then sixteen or seventeen years old.

[45] Wolf, 'Nochmals zur Frage' (see n. 41), p. 273. The other pointer to Theophano's youth is derived from the birth of her first child in 977. From the five-year gap between marriage and delivery some historians have deduced that she was even younger than twelve in 972 and could not have conceived prior to 976, when she would have reached puberty.

[46] Tinnefeld, 'Die Braut aus Byzanz' (see n. 40), rightly emphasizes that the participation of young girls is not mentioned in court-ceremonies recorded in the *Book of Ceremonies*, and that they were normally kept at home secluded from public view (p. 257). He concludes that Theophano may have witnessed just one ceremonial event put on for her uncle, the emperor, namely the triumph he celebrated through the city of Constantinople in 971 (p. 258). But he overlooks the fact that newly established rulers regularly invited their close relatives into the palace and individuals appointed to high court-offices such as *kouropalates* and *logothetes tou dromou*, positions held by Theophano's grandfather, could gain access. While there is no direct evidence that Theophano and her parents shared in the good fortune of John Tzimiskes, it is quite likely that they moved into the Great Palace at his request and that Theophano witnessed imperial procedure and court-ceremonies as one of the many ladies-in-waiting who attended all high-ranking female office-holders.

Theodora. In this sense, Thietmar of Merseburg may have correctly recorded a certain disappointment, even outright hostility, because Theophano was not the imperial daughter desired by Otto I, merely the emperor's niece.[47]

For this is what the western sources claim: Theophano was a most noble niece, *neptim clarissimam*, of John Tzimiskes.[48] In the *Vita Mahthildis reginae antiquior*, commissioned by Otto II, she is identified as follows: '. . .augusti de palatio, regalis fuisset data coniunx praeclara dicta nomine Theophanu'[49] ('From the palace of the emperor, a most noble regal wife had been given, by name Theophano'). Moreover, the noble niece, who came from the imperial palace of Constantinople, appears to have been well schooled in the role of a real Byzantine princess.

As in all the other cases Theophano had to learn what was expected of a Byzantine princess who would be sent to serve as ambassador to a foreign country. In about two years' exposure to court-life, she had to study the relevant language and culture of her future husband, and to master the correct style of dress, deportment and manners. If she had not been taught to read and write at home, she now had to acquire those literate skills she would need in her new role. This she clearly did with some success because in the West her expertise was appreciated as something typically Byzantine.[50]

To her background is attributed her determination to reign as empress and later as regent for her son.[51] This Byzantine practice had been exemplified by Theophano the Younger, whom Theo-

[47] Thietmar of Merseburg, *Chronicon*, II, 15, ed. R. Holtzmann, MGH SRG (Berlin, 2nd edn, 1935), p. 56.

[48] MGH DD O II, ed. Th. Sickel (Hanover, 1884), no. 21, pp. 28–30, at p. 29. This is the bridegroom's wedding-contract, listing the gifts equivalent to Theophano's dowry, drawn up by Otto II in Rome and dated 14 April 972 (on the day of the marriage).

[49] *Vita Mahthildis* (see n. 43), 16, p. 581, lines 44–6.

[50] K.N. Ciggaar, 'The Empress Theophano (972–991): political and cultural implications of her presence in Western Europe for the Low Countries, in particular for the county of Holland', in *Byzantium and the Low Countries in the Tenth Century: Aspects of Art and History in the Ottonian Era* (Hernen, 1985), pp. 33–76; cf. J. Fleckenstein, 'Hofkapelle und Kanzlei unter der Kaiserin Theophanu', in von Euw and Schreiner, *Kaiserin Theophanu*, II, pp. 305–10.

[51] Ciggaar, 'The Empress Theophano', especially pp. 35–7; but note the developed western tradition of widowed mothers acting as regent, as documented by F.-R. Erkens, 'Die Frau als Herrscherin in ottonisch-frühsalischer Zeit', in von Euw and Schreiner, *Kaiserin Theophanu*, II, pp. 245–59 (and articles by J. Laudage and G. Althoff, in the same volume); R. McKitterick, 'Ottonian intellectual culture in the tenth century and the role of Theophano', chapter 9 in this volume.

phano may have known personally, and also by two famous empresses of the ninth and eighth centuries, Theodora and Irene. Both were celebrated in Byzantium as Orthodox rulers who insisted on restoring the veneration of icons after long periods of destruction. This iconophile tradition, commemorated in their *Lives*, ensured their prominence; they were both recognized as saints of the eastern church. Through the premature deaths of their husbands, they had become *de facto* regents for their young sons, and ruled in the name of these minors. In Constantinople, however much court-officials deplored the fact in private, it was sometimes unavoidable for women to be in control. As heads of state, even if only for brief periods, they wielded supreme authority and established an image of the female ruler that ran counter to the general seclusion of women. So it would hardly be surprising if Theophano had become familiar with stories of their personal rule at court.[52]

In this context it is important to remember that young girls were expected to learn fast. Princesses must have matured quickly, under pressure, for they were expected to cope with important affairs of state, and clearly some of them did. They were married at the inception of puberty, and were expected to bear children as soon as possible. Theophano gave birth four times between November/December 977 and June/July 980, the last being a delivery of twins (Otto III's twin sister died before 8 October 980), and she herself died 'before her time' on 15 June 991. For her age, Theophano seems even more remarkable than other ruling queens and empresses. And it seems very likely that some of her stamina and skill must be derived from her Byzantine background and training.

From her mature life in the West, it seems clear that Theophano had acquired in Constantinople a certain basic preparation for the role of a Byzantine princess, and conformed to an established model. Like others before her, she had been exposed to developed cultural standards and traditions that set Byzantium apart from the West. These extended beyond the glamour of court-ceremonial, official costume and state-occasions, to some

[52] In this context, Theophano's use of the male form of the term for emperor, 'Theophanius imperator', as well as the more familiar 'imperatrix', empress, might suggest a parallel with Irene, who signed her documents as emperor, *basileus*, rather than empress, *basilissa*, see most recently Ciggaar, 'The Empress Theophano' (see n. 50), p. 36, n. 17.

acquaintance with the Byzantine style of government: the rhetoric of universal authority used in every imperial document, methods of diplomacy, dispensation of justice, appointment of officials, reception of foreign delegations and so on. It included familiarity with imperial responsibilities (of philanthropy, for instance) and with ecclesiastical practices, liturgy, festivals and moral judgements. At the court, Theophano might have observed some aspects of tenth-century political life and her uncle's style of government, not least her own role in it. All this helped her to train her son and to establish patterns of government in her own territories in the West. Yet despite it all, she could still become identified with 'luxury from Greece'.[53]

In the process of assimilation, she was probably helped by her mother-in-law, Adelheid, and her sister-in-law, Matilda, who became her spiritual sister.[54] Among her entourage from Constantinople she must have had advisers who wanted to see her successfully perform the expected role of a Byzantine princess in the West. Although we know very little about the Greek servants who accompanied her, it is possible that they resembled those sent with Anna to Kiev. Theophano probably took her own priest; she certainly had her own ladies-in-waiting who attended her at official ceremonies in the West. There must have been a whole team of assistants to look after her wardrobe, personal clothes, jewels, linens, rugs and so on. Her appreciation of Byzantine silks is documented in the gifts she later made to western churches; indeed, her marriage-contract was even drawn up on parchment painted to resemble one of these imperial purple silks.[55] So Byzantine influences surrounded her as she sailed to Benevento, where she was met by bishop Dietrich of Metz who escorted her to Rome.

All this finery was part of what made Byzantine princesses desirable and much sought after in the West.[56] Another crucial

[53] See Thangmar, *Vita beati Bernwardi episcopi et confessoris*, MGH SS IV (Hanover, 1841), addendum, p. 888, describing a vision, in which Theophano appeared mourning the vanities that she had introduced to Germany and France, which seduced many women. These are identified as 'superflua et luxuriosa mulierum ornamenta quibus Grecia uti solet'. Cf. W. Georgi, 'Ottonianum und Heiratsurkunde 962/972', in von Euw and Schreiner, *Kaiserin Theophanu*, II, pp. 135–60, at pp. 159–60.

[54] McKitterick, 'Ottonian intellectual culture', p. 184 in the present volume.

[55] See W. Georgi, 'Ottonianum' (see n. 53).

[56] It is also this association that traditionally connected Theophano and her dowry with a number of de luxe objects found in western cathedral treasuries and collections. But see now chapter 13 by H. Westermann-Angerhausen in this volume.

part was their standard of education and knowledge of imperial traditions. Despite her status as a close imperial relative rather than a purple-born princess, Theophano appears to have executed the expected role with success. Judged by her adult life in the West, she conformed to and embodied in her own way the archetypal character of a Byzantine princess. That she produced children, including a son and heir, is not exceptional. But she also undertook their education and supervised their learning in a thorough and masterful way. She brought distinction to the court of the western emperor and inspired her son Otto III with visions beyond his father's ambitions. Had he not died at a young age, the history of Europe might have been changed. As it was, Theophano ensured that his short life inspired others and introduced novel ideas into the West. In this respect, she performed the task of Byzantine ambassador to an unprecedented degree. This was precisely what Otto I had wanted and had he witnessed her activity he would probably have been well pleased.[57]

[57] I would like to thank Dr Arnoud-Jan Bijsteveld for his helpful discussion and careful reading of the text, which permitted the correction of several errors. Any that remain are mine alone.

5

The education of the daughters of the nobility in the Ottonian Empire

JOHANNA MARIA VAN WINTER

About the education of princesses and other noble ladies we hear only occasionally in the chronicles, for the writers of these records (most of whom were male) were not interested in this aspect of history. Only when such a girl was betrothed or married did she become interesting; her next great moment was as a widow, when she appeared again on the marriage-market or became the abbess of a monastery.

Take for example Liutprand of Cremona, whose *Antapodosis* is largely devoted to occurrences in northern Italy and Burgundy, which were the regions of provenance of queen Adelheid, king Otto I's second wife. About Adelheid herself he cannot tell anything bad and therefore he hardly shows any interest in her, let alone in her youth; she only becomes important for him when, after the death of her first husband, king Lothar of Italy, in 950, she gets molested and imprisoned by the usurper Berengar of Ivrea. For bad people Liutprand has the keener eye, and this includes bad women; and so we are informed elaborately about the fornication of Berengar's wife Willa with a squalid priest, to whom she had trusted her two daughters Gisela and Gerberga for education, giving him dainty meals and beautiful clothes, although normally she was a model of avarice. What that priest really taught these girls is referred to in a subordinate clause: 'ut eas litterarum scientia epotaret', which the translators in the Freiherr vom Stein edition render as 'um ihnen das Lesen und Schreiben beizubringen'[1] (to teach them reading and writing).

This Willa was the daughter of another no less niggardly Willa,

[1] Liutprand, *Antapodosis*, V, c. 32, *Quellen zur Geschichte der sächsischen Kaiserzeit*, ed. A. Bauer and R. Rau, AQDG 8 (Darmstadt, 1971), pp. 480–1.

of whose avarice Liutprand gives a nice example,[2] and of Boso, margrave of Tuscany. Boso in his turn was the unloving brother of Hugh king of Italy, king Lothar's father, and this Hugh was a sitting duck for Liutprand's satire because of his many concubines, from whom he had delightful daughters. After having described this situation Liutprand incidentally gives us a revealing insight into the difference between Greeks and Romans regarding the value they set upon the legitimate birth of nobles. The Byzantine emperor Romanos wanted to negotiate with king Hugh about a marriage between his grandson and a daughter of Hugh's; and when Hugh made it clear that he had no daughters from his legitimate wife but only from his concubines, Romanos gladly accepted the offer, because, as Liutprand writes, the Greeks only ask about the father and not about the mother.[3]

With the Romans, the Franks and the Saxons it was quite different; for notwithstanding the lack of explicit interest in the chronicles there are clear signs that in Western Europe great value was set upon the female descent, which should be legitimate.

Daughters were cherished and watched over as precious family pawns on the political chess-board. They might be the future brides of political allies or the instruments of reconciliation with an adversary, and also the guardians of the community of prayer and of the memory of the ancestors. The latter role they played as virgins in a noble lady's chapter or as widows at such a place, more often than not with the rank of abbess.

The genealogical tree (Fig. 2) shows the tight network of such institutions, which might date from the eighth or the first half of the ninth century. Susteren for example, in the now Dutch province of Limburg, was founded in 714 by Pippin II and his wife Plectrude; other examples are St Mary in the Capitol in Cologne (where Plectrude was interred in 717), Vreden (founded by Waltbert, a descendant of the Saxon duke Widukind), Herford (founded by Adelhard and Wala, kindred of Charlemagne, who were both founders of Corvey at the river Weser as well), and Essen (*c.* 852 by Altfried bishop of Hildesheim). Others were founded by ancestors or members of the royal family itself in the ninth, tenth or eleventh centuries, such as Gandersheim, founded by Liudolf and Oda shortly after 850; Quedlinburg, founded by queen Matilda as the widow of king Henry I in 937; Gernrode,

[2] *Ibid.*, IV, c. 12, pp. 414–17. [3] *Ibid.*, V, c. 14, pp. 460–1.

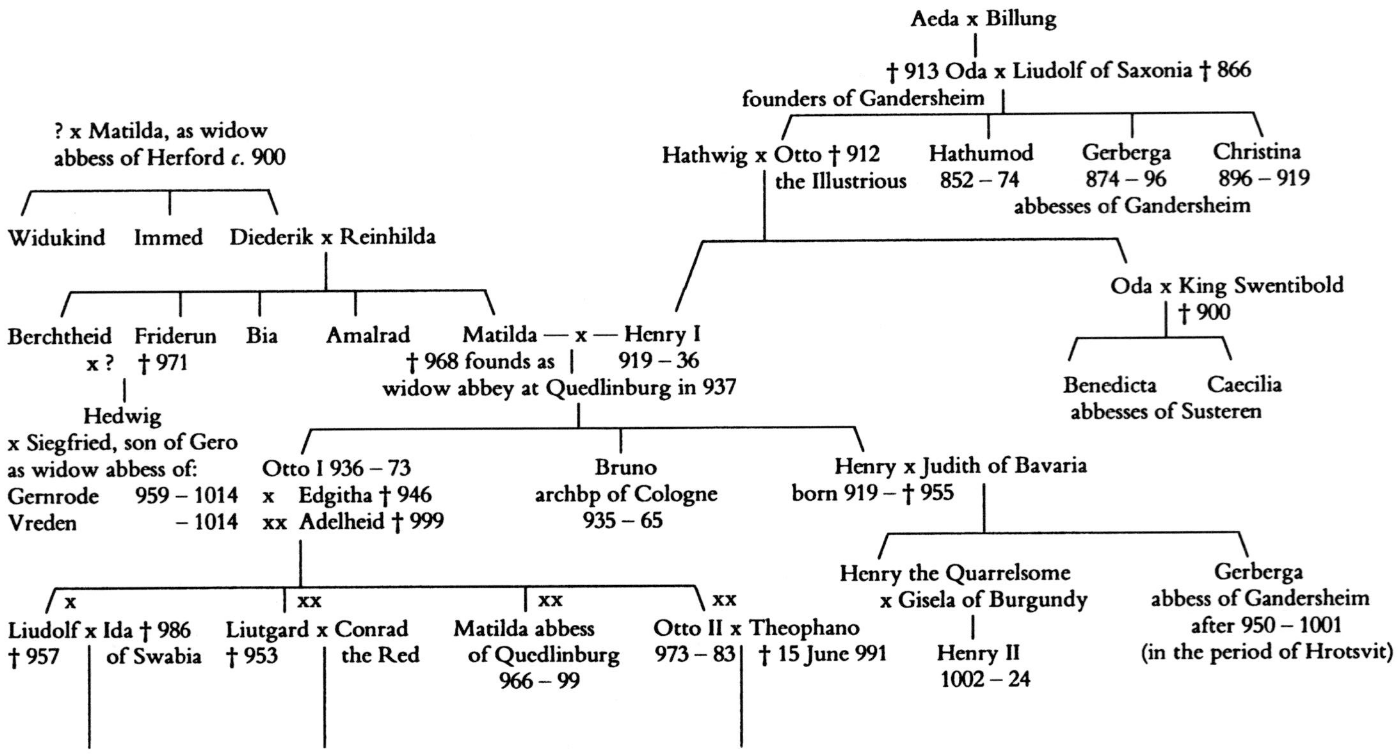
Aeda x Billung
† 913 Oda x Liudolf of Saxonia † 866
founders of Gandersheim
? x Matilda, as widow
abbess of Herford c. 900
Hathwig x Otto † 912
the Illustrious
Hathumod
852 – 74
Gerberga
874 – 96
Christina
896 – 919
abbesses of Gandersheim
Widukind
Immed
Diederik x Reinhilda
Oda x King Swentibold
† 900
Berchtheid
x ?
Friderun
† 971
Bia
Amalrad
Matilda — x — Henry I
† 968 founds as
919 – 36
widow abbey at Quedlinburg in 937
Benedicta
Caecilia
abbesses of Susteren
Hedwig
x Siegfried, son of Gero
as widow abbess of:
Gernrode 959 – 1014
Vreden – 1014
Otto I 936 – 73
x Edgitha † 946
xx Adelheid † 999
Bruno
archbp of Cologne
935 – 65
Henry x Judith of Bavaria
born 919 – † 955
Henry the Quarrelsome
x Gisela of Burgundy
Gerberga
abbess of Gandersheim
after 950 – 1001
(in the period of Hrotsvit)
x
xx
xx
xx
Liudolf x Ida † 986
† 957
of Swabia
Liutgard x Conrad
† 953
the Red
Matilda abbess
of Quedlinburg
966 – 99
Otto II x Theophano
973 – 83
† 15 June 991
Henry II
1002 – 24

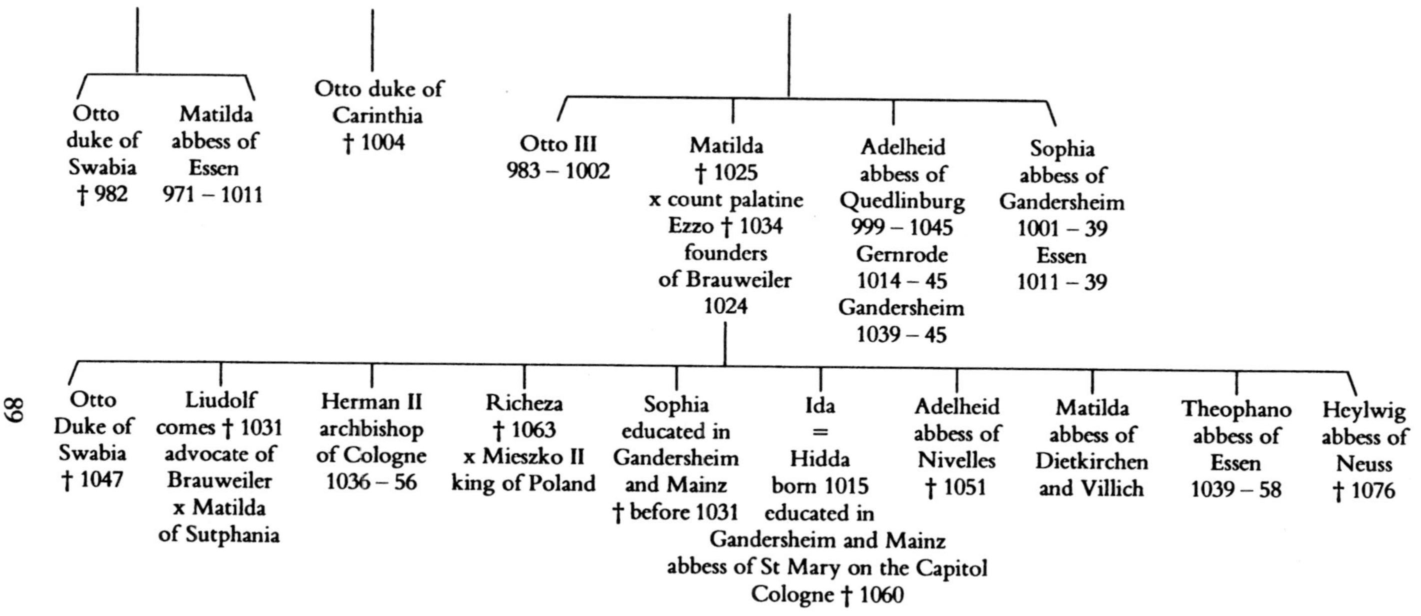

2. Abbesses of royal abbeys: a genealogy (after E.K. Kam)

founded in 959 by margrave Gero of Meissen and his daughter-in-law Hedwig, a niece of queen Matilda – already under royal protection in 961; and Brauweiler, founded in 1024 by the count palatine Ezzo and his wife Matilda, a daughter of the emperor Otto II and Theophano. In St Mary in the Capitol in Cologne, Benedictine nuns from Remiremont were established in the middle of the tenth century by Bruno, archbishop of Cologne, king/emperor Otto I's brother, after he had removed its male canons to the church of St Andrew.

It is noteworthy that these convents, after having been placed under royal protection, were always guided by abbesses from the royal family. These abbesses sometimes governed more than one convent if no other princess was available. After the death of Matilda, abbess of Quedlinburg, in 999, at the request of her mother, the queen-grandmother Adelheid, Otto III entrusted the abbey to his sister and her granddaughter Adelheid, the daughter of Otto II and Theophano,[4] who governed it until 1045. In 1014 she also became head of Gernrode, where the abbess Hathwig had just died, who had also been abbess of Vreden. After Gernrode, Gandersheim was also placed under the guidance of the abbess Adelheid in 1039; her sister Sophia had been abbess of Gandersheim since 1001 and since the death of Matilda of Swabia in 1011, of Essen as well. Essen was entrusted in 1039 to the abbess Theophano, one of the daughters of the count palatine Ezzo and princess Matilda, sister to the abbesses Adelheid and Sophia, who also was abbess of Gerresheim. Evidently only royal blood was good enough to rule these preserves of birth and wealth.

In such places only the daughters of noble families were admitted as canonesses, though not in all cases for life: if it turned out to be better for their family for them to marry after all, they were permitted to leave. Girls destined for marriage were often educated in such houses until the day of their wedding.

To what extent these two groups were kept separate in a convent for noble ladies is difficult to tell, but such a separation would have been almost impossible to maintain. Take the case of Liutgard, the eldest daughter of margrave Ekkehard of Meissen and Swanahild Billung. Betrothed as a child to Werner, the eldest son of margrave Liuthar of the Northmarch and Godila (who was

[4] Thietmar of Merseburg, *Chronicon*, IV, c. 43, ed. R. Holtzmann and W. Trillmich, neu übertragen und erläutert von W.Trillmich, AQDG 9 (Darmstadt, 1957), pp. 158–9.

only thirteen years old when she gave birth to Werner!), she was educated under the abbess Matilda in Quedlinburg. Now Matilda left the abbey in 998 to be regent for Otto III during his stay in Italy, whereupon Werner, who had heard that the margrave Ekkehard might break his promise and betroth his daughter to another man, violently abducted Liutgard with the help of some armed friends, among whom were the brothers of Thietmar of Merseburg (who relates this story). On being informed of this, the abbess Matilda in tears called upon the assembled princes to recover the kidnapped girl, but the abductors had already reached the safety of Walbeck Castle. Liuthar, Werner's father, inquired after the feelings of Liutgard herself, who preferred to stay where she was. But Matilda thought otherwise; and she achieved her object. Barefoot and begging for mercy the abductor brought his 'wife' to an assembly in Magdeburg; by this time the young couple is referred to as 'sponsum cum contectali', the bridegroom with his bedmate, by Thietmar. Liutgard was taken back to Quedlinburg, not as a prisoner, but to teach her the fear of God, as Thietmar tells us.[5] How much longer she stayed there, he does not say; he only tells us that the abbess Matilda died soon afterwards and that she was succeeded by the abbess Adelheid.

Not only girls, however, but also boys were educated in Quedlinburg. Thietmar for example received early lessons there from his father's aunt Emnilda.[6] His father took him away from there in 987, 'primo litteris bene adhuc instructum', i.e. for the time being well instructed in literacy; at that time Thietmar was twelve years old. For higher education he was to be sent to Magdeburg.

The presence of boys in Quedlinburg may also be inferred from a remark made by Widukind of Corvey, who describes how queen Matilda lived as a widow in a cell near the church and proceeded every night from there to the church for a vigil of prayer, passing by a series of male and female singers. Those singers were stationed at three different places: within her cell, outside its door, and along the way to the church.[7] Who could the

[5] *Ibid.*, IV, cc. 39–42, pp. 154–9. [6] *Ibid.*, IV, c. 16, pp. 132–3.

[7] Widukind, *Res gestae Saxonicae*, III, c. 74, *Quellen zur Geschichte der sächsischen Kaiserzeit*, ed. A. Bauer and R. Rau, AQDG 8 (Darmstadt, 1971), p. 178: 'Erat enim ei cellula ecclesiae proxima, in qua modice requiescebat, de qua omnibus noctibus consurgens intrat ecclesiam, nichilominus cantoribus et cantatricibus intra cellulam et pro foribus et in via triformiter constitutis, qui divinam clementiam laudarent atque benedicerent.'

male singers have been? Were they all adult men, mostly clerics? It seems more likely that they were choir-boys, boys like Thietmar, who were educated there. The female singers were nuns and young girl-boarders.

Such a one was Liutgard; but even with girls destined to take the veil, the abbess might have considerable trouble, as we see from the history of Sophia and Ida, daughters of count palatine Ezzo and princess Matilda, who ran away from Gandersheim to take refuge with archbishop Aribo of Mainz. In the oldest *Vita* of bishop Godehard of Hildesheim, written shortly before his death in 1038, we read that these two young girls were educated in the imperial abbey of Gandersheim under the direction of their aunt, the abbess Sophia, and according to the capacity of their tender age were imbued with the study of literacy 'as befits freewomen' (*liberaliter*);[8] but because of their high descent they enjoyed more liberties than their comrades of the same age. They were allowed to travel, with the consent of the abbess, who suspected nothing when, in 1026, they were invited to stay with archbishop Aribo. But once in Mainz they refused to go back again; three other girls from Gandersheim, under the cover of a family visit, received permission to travel from the abbess and joined them there. Archbishop Aribo, less naive than abbess Sophia, placed these five girls in a monastery with discipline under the guidance of his own sister. At the behest of a synod they were brought back to Gandersheim in 1027, not to the imperial abbey but to St Mary's. However, after a few months, during which they allegedly lived 'more according to their pleasure than to their duty' ('plusque pro libitu quam pro debito viventes'), they were abducted to Mainz, again to the monastery of Aribo's choice.[9] Only after the death of Aribo in 1031 could a settlement be reached with his successor: two of the girls stayed in Mainz and the third girl, together with Ida, came back to St Mary's in Gandersheim, Ida's elder sister Sophia having died already.[10]

Before 1038 Ida became abbess of St Mary's in Gandersheim and also – but we do not know when – of St Mary in the Capitol in Cologne. She turned out to be an active builder and an art-loving ruler, who presented other abbeys with works of art.

[8] Wulfhere, *Vita Godehardi episcopi, vita prior*, c. 29, MGH SS XI, pp. 188–9: '...studiisque litteralibus iuxta tenellae etatis capacitatem sunt liberaliter imbutae...' The whole story is to be found there.

[9] *Ibid.*, c. 34, pp. 192–3. [10] *Ibid.*, c. 36, p. 194.

Probably the column of Ida in Essen, the Hitda-codex at Meschede and the Hidda-Gospels at Gerresheim were all commissioned by her between *c.* 1040 and her death in 1060. Her brother, archbishop Herman II of Cologne (1036–56), and her sister Theophanu, abbess of Essen and Gerresheim (1039–58), supported her energetically and their rule was as glorious as her own.[11]

Ida was born in 1015, so she must have been ten or eleven when she first went to Mainz in 1026; at the same age, Thietmar 'was instructed in literacy' by his aunt Emnilda at Quedlinburg. Primary education was described in such terms: 'imbued with' *studiis litteralibus* (Sophia and Ida), 'nourished with *litterarum scientia*' (Willa's daughters, Gisela and Gerberga); 'educated with *literalis studio disciplinae*'[12] (queen Matilda, who was educated by her grandmother in the monastery of Herford; the young Matilda, we are explicitly told, was not counted among the nuns, but 'was trained with books and works for useful things' instead).[13] As a girl of about ten years old her hand was sought in marriage by the future king Henry I, who removed her from the convent as soon as he had obtained her grandmother's consent. Only as a widow in Quedlinburg did she really take up literary studies again, and then she learned so well that she could teach her own servants.[14]

Herford had, in the ninth and at the beginning of the tenth centuries, a high reputation for educating girls. Hathumod, too, was trained there, before becoming, at the age of twelve, the first abbess of Gandersheim in 852. According to her *Vita* she was an unusual girl, totally uninterested in and even terrified of beautiful dresses and female frills. But the *litteras* ('letters'), 'to which others had to be driven by whip-lash, she approached with extra-

[11] See especially Gerhard Weilandt, 'Wer stiftete den Hitda-Codex (Darmstadt, Hess. Landes- und Hochschulbibliothek, Cod. 1640)?: ein Beitrag zur Entwicklung der ottonischen Kölner Buchmalerei', in *Annalen des historischen Vereins für den Niederrhein*, Heft 190 (1987), 49–83. Weilandt proposes to date the Hitda-Codex to after *c.* 1040 instead of to *c.* 1000–20: this accords with the lives and works of the Ezzonen children, Ida, Theophano and Herman.

[12] *Vita Mahthildis reginae*, c. 1, MGH SS X, p. 575.

[13] *Ibid.*, c. 2, p. 575: 'Hanc eandem, ut diximus, virginem, Herevordensi quae inerat monasterio, non inter sanctimoniales numeranda, sed ad quaeque utilia libris operibusque nutrienda cum sui matre genitoris . . .'

[14] Widukind, *Res gestae Saxonicae*, III, c. 74 (see n. 7), pp. 178–9: 'Domesticos omnes famulos et ancillas variis artibus, litteris quoque instituit; nam et ipsa litteras novit, quas post mortem regis lucide satis didicit.'

ordinary zeal and was addicted to with indefatigable meditation'.[15]

What did this study of letters actually entail? Did girls learn only reading and writing, or did they strive for higher goals? We are lucky to have the testimony of a highly gifted canoness, Hrotsvit of Gandersheim, who sheds some light upon these questions in her work. Hrotsvit lived in the abbey of Gandersheim in the mid-tenth century. She wrote in Latin, partly verse and partly dramatic dialogue, stylistically inspired by the comedies of the Roman playwright P. Terentius Afer (second century BC). Of course, her legends and dramas were moralistic: repentance, penance for sin and constancy in the face of martyrdom were the virtues that she impressed upon her readers, or more probably her listeners. Her stories may have been read in the refectory or the study-room, or even performed as drama by the monastic ladies, to which they would lend themselves very well. Besides, she also wrote chronicles in verse: *Gesta Ottonis* and *Primordia coenobii Gandeshemensis*, 'The deeds of Otto I' and 'The origins of the monastery of Gandersheim'.[16]

The moralistic tendency of Hrotsvit's work has been attributed to the sincere bigotry of an isolated boarding-school for girls. Tenth-century convent girls are indeed comparable with boarding-school girls, but life held fewer mysteries for them than one might think. Hrotsvit's plays tell us a surprising amount about life and education in her time.

First of all she evidently envisaged a youthful public, able to identify itself with the heroines of the legend or the drama, most of whom are young. Faith, Hope and Charity, the daughters of Wisdom, prepare for martyrdom at the ages of twelve, ten and eight respectively;[17] Agnes, who not only refuses the advances of

[15] Agius, *Vita Hathumodae*, c. 2, MGH SS IV, p. 167: 'Litteras vero, ad quas alii discendas et verberibus coguntur, ipsa ultroneo studio appetiit, infatigabunda meditatione addidicit.'

[16] Hrotsvit, *Opera* (hereafter *Opera*), mit Einleitungen und Kommentar von H. Homeyer (Munich, Paderborn, etc., 1970); German translation in: Hrotsvitha von Gandersheim, *Werke in deutscher Übertragung* (hereafter *Werke*), mit einem Beitrag zur frühmittelalterlichen Dichtung von H. Homeyer (Munich, Paderborn, etc., 1973).

[17] *Opera*, p. 361, Sapientia, III, v. 11, *Werke*, p. 267:

> SAPIENTIA. Karitas duas olimpiades iam volvit, Spes duo lustra, Fides tres olympiades.

the prefect's son but manages to convert father and son to the Christian faith, is thirteen years old;[18] Maria, the niece of the hermit Abraham, is an orphan of seven when her uncle takes her with him to devote her life to Christ;[19] the virgins Agape, Chionia and Irene ('Love', 'Snowwhite', i.e. 'Purity', and 'Peace') must be very young, especially Irene who is only a child, when they resist the lustful advances of Diocletian's governor Dulcitius and die as martyrs.[20] This accords with what we know from the chronicles about the age of the girls who inhabited such abbeys as Gandersheim.

Another characteristic of these tales is the self-possession and pride with which Hrotsvit's heroines meet menacing males, who think of them as members of the weaker sex. Take the following instances:

> The prefect, whose son is desperately in love with the thirteen-year-old Agnes, wants to make her indulge him by threatening to put her in a brothel, but she, fearless and bold, replies that Christ is her Bridegroom and that He will protect her.[21]

[18] *Opera*, p. 211, Agnes, vs. 41–2, *Werke*, p. 160:

> Ast ubi lustra duo celeri cursu revoluta
> Insuper et ternos aetatis transiit annos . . .

[19] *Opera*, p. 304, Abraham, I, v. 4, *Werke*, p. 225:

> EFFREM. Cuius est aetatis?
> ABRAHAM. Si unius rotatus mansurni apponeretur, duas olympiades vitali aura vesceretur.

[20] *Opera*, p. 270, Dulcitius, II, v. 1, *Werke*, p. 203:

> DULCITIUS. Producite, milites, producite, quas tenetis in carcere!
> MILITES. Ecce, quas vocasti!
> DULCITIUS. Papae! quam pulchrae, quam venustae, quam egregiae puellulae!

Opera, p. 273, Dulcitius, X, *Werke*, p. 206:

> SISINNIUS. O milites, ubi sunt lascivae, quae torqueri debent, puellae?
> MILITES. Affliguntur in carcere.
> SISINNIUS. Hirenam reservate et reliquas producite.
> MILITES. Cur unam excipis?
> SISINNIUS. Parcens infantiae. Forte facilius convertetur, si sororum praesentia non terrebitur.
> MILITES. Ita.

[21] *Opera*, p. 217, Agnes, vs. 193–205, *Werke*, p. 164:

> At sacra virgo, minis nimium trepidans super istis,
> Audacter mox praefecto dedit ista responsa. . .

Irene, still a child and likewise threatened with the brothel, challenges and derides the soldiers and their captain who are about to torture her, after her sisters have already died as martyrs;[22] in an earlier scene the three girls have made fun of the governor Dulcitius, 'that fool', who has had them enclosed in the cook's pantry, hoping to make love with them during the night, but who instead kisses and embraces the soot-black pans.[23]

Wisdom uses the same phrase, 'this fool', of the emperor Hadrianus, when he asks how old her daughters are; she goes on to reveal their ages in a learned discourse on arithmetic;[24] with flattery he tries to convert her to idolatry, believing that the feminine sex in its fragility will be mollified more easily by that means, but this just makes him even more foolish in her eyes.[25]

22 *Opera*, pp. 274–5, 277, Dulcitius, XII, vs. 1–5, XIV, v. 3, *Werke*, pp. 207–9.

23 *Opera*, p. 271, Dulcitius, IV, vs. 1–3, *Werke*, p. 204:

> AGAPES. Quid strepat pro foribus?
> HIRENA. Infelix Dulcitius ingreditur.
> CHIONIA. Deus nos tueatur!
> AGAPES. Amen.
> CHIONIA. Quid sibi vult collisio ollarum, caccaborum et sartaginum?
> HIRENA. Lustrabo. Accedite, quaeso, per rimulas perspicite!
> AGAPES. Quid est?
> HIRENA. Ecce, iste stultus, mente alienatus, aestimat se nostris uti amplexibus.
> AGAPES. Quid facit?
> HIRENA. Nunc ollas molli fovet gremio, nunc sartagines et caccabos amplectitur, mitia libans oscula.
> CHIONIA. Ridiculum.
> HIRENA. Nam facies, manus ac vestimenta adeo sordidata, adeo coinquinata, ut nigredo, quae inhaesit, similitudinem Aethiopis exprimit.
> AGAPES. Decet, ut talis appareat corpore, qualis a diabolo possidetur in mente.

24 *Opera*, p. 360, Sapientia, III, v. 8, *Werke*, p. 266:

> ADRIANUS. Quot annos aetatis volverunt?
> SAPIENTIA. Placetne vobis, o filiae, ut hunc stultum aritmetica fatigem disputatione?
> FIDES. Placet, mater, nosque auditum praebemus libenter.

25 *Opera*, p. 359, Sapientia, III, v. 3, *Werke*, p. 266:

> ADRIANUS. Quid, si illas primule aggrediar blanda alloquutione, si forte velint cedere?
> ANTIOCHUS. Melius est; nam fragilitas sexus feminei facilius potest blandimentis molliri.

The girls at Gandersheim may have learned the fear of God, but they evidently were not educated as submissive simpletons. To a pagan, Hrotsvit taught them, no respect is due at all, although he be the emperor of Rome.

To understand these texts the audience needed more than an education in reading and writing alone; grammar and the rhetorical subjects taught in the *trivium* were needed, followed by the four disciplines taught in the *quadrivium* (arithmetic, geometry, astronomy and music) in order to appreciate them in all their stylistic refinement. Probably most people were not able to do this and simply submitted to the force of a tale well told. In the plays the characters converse in short sentences. But Hrotsvit uses just such dialogues to introduce difficult subjects, such as the learned discourse on arithmetic already mentioned,[26] or the discussion of harmony and musical theory in the history of the hermit Pafnutius and the whore Thais.[27] It is rewarding to study the latter in some detail.

Pafnutius feels concerned about the salvation of Thais, a prostitute in the neighbouring town, who lures many men to their ruin. To explain to his pupils what troubles him, he speaks to them of the Universe as a macrocosm (*maior mundus*, i.e. the larger, cosmic world) and of man as a microcosm (*minor mundus*, i.e. the smaller world, which reflects and interacts with the cosmic forces, the elements, the seasons, the sun, the moon and the planets), with a mortal body and an immortal soul; these two, opposed as they are, yet must remain in harmony with each other and with the

[26] *Opera*, pp. 360–3, Sapientia, III, vs. 9–22, *Werke*, pp. 267–8.

[27] *Opera*, pp. 328–34, Pafnutius, I, vs. 2–21, *Werke*, pp. 242–5. Thais is an interesting name, because it refers to the Greek courtesan who challenged Alexander the Great after the conquest of Persepolis to burn down that royal city, as we are told in the 'vulgate' tradition of Diodorus Siculus (first century BC) and Quintus Curtius Rufus (first century AD), although not in the shorter and less romanticized version of Arrian (second century AD); cf. A.B. Bosworth, *A Historical Commentary on Arrian's History of Alexander*, Commentary on books I–III (Oxford, 1980), pp. 24, 331. The *Res gestae Alexandri Magni* of Quintus Curtius Rufus were well known in the Middle Ages; cf. D.J.A. Ross, *Alexander Historiatus: A Guide to Medieval Illustrated Alexander Literature*, Warburg Institute Surveys (London, 1963), I, p. 67. So Hrotsvit may have known them, in which case Homeyer's remark in her introduction to the *Werke*, p. 31, should be revised: 'Spuren irgendwelcher historischer Autoren fehlen bezeichnenderweise ganz; Geschichtsschreibung galt nicht als Fach.' My attention was drawn to Thais, the Greek courtesan, thanks to Heleen Sancisi-Weerdenburg, *'Den wereltvorst een vuyle streek aan sijn eercleet': Alexander en Persepolis*, Oratie 10 oktober 1991, Faculteit der Letteren Rijksuniversiteit Utrecht, p. 9.

Creator. After this exposition he goes out; disguised as a customer, he gains access to Thais and manages to bring her to introspection and repentance. After having burnt, to the horror of her lovers, all her jewels and other valuables in the marketplace, she follows Pafnutius to a women's cloister, where she is immured in a cell, with the foul smell of her own excrement, until she gets remission from her penance after three years, and then dies.

In his discussion of the theory of harmony Pafnutius explicitly calls music one of the four disciplines of the *quadrivium*, one that builds on the method of dialectic from the *trivium*. But he refuses to call himself a philosopher; at the most he is someone who has caught a drop from the scales of wisdom in passing and is handing this on to his pupils.[28] By this *topos* Hrotsvit probably also depicts herself in all humility, not as a philosopher but only a passer-on of learning. Like Pafnutius, she must have been surrounded by a circle of pupils, who tried to understand the complicated subject-matter she put before them in verse and drama. She was fortunate in enjoying the support of her abbess, Gerberga of Bavaria, who did not spurn the dedication of her works.

Most chronicles are silent as to the age of the daughters of princes and nobles, who were educated in convents. But in the works of Hrotsvit of Gandersheim we possess a source that can deepen our understanding of such circles. These girls, who as children were already betrothed or desired by men, were proud and self-possessed in their behaviour, sometimes to the despair of their abbess; probably they were also appreciative of art, musical and eager to learn. The imperial abbeys that were ruled by members of the royal family, such as Gandersheim, Quedlinburg, Gernrode and Essen, provided a protected environment in which such young and cultivated females could mature.

[28] *Opera*, pp. 333–4, Pafnutius, I, v. 19, *Werke*, p. 245:

> PAFNUTIUS. Tenuem scientiae guttulam, quam de plenis sciorum pateris effluentem, non ad colligendum residens, sed casu praeteriens, repertam elambi, vobiscum communicare studui.

6

Marriage negotiations between Byzantium and the West and the name of Theophano in Byzantium (eighth to tenth centuries)

ADELBERT DAVIDS

Liutprand of Cremona and his delegation met with stubborn opposition at the court of Constantinople in 968, when they asked for a purple-born (*porphyrogennetos*) bride for the son of the emperor Otto I.[1] 'It is unheard of that a daughter born in the purple of an emperor born in the purple should contract a foreign marriage. Still, great as is your demand, you shall have what you want if you give what is proper: Ravenna, namely, and Rome with all the adjoining territories from thence to our possessions.'[2]

[1] Abbreviations used in footnotes
Dölger, *Regesten*: *Regesten der Kaiserurkunden des oströmischen Reiches von 565–1453*, I, 1, *von 565–1025*, I, 2, *von 1025–1204*, ed. F. Dölger (Munich and Berlin, 1924–5 and reprinted Hildesheim, 1976).
Nikephoros Gregoras, *Logos*: Nikephoros Gregoras' life of St Theophano, in *Zwei griechische Texte über die Hl. Theophano, die Gemahlin Kaisers Leo VI.*, ed. E. Kurtz, Zapiski imperatorskoj Akademii Nauk, VIII, Istor.-filol. otdel., III, 2 (St Petersburg, 1898), pp. 25–45.
Skylitzes, *Synopsis*: John Skylitzes, *Synopsis historiarum*, ed. I. Thurn (Berlin, 1973).
Theophanes, *Chronographia*: Theophanes, *Chronographia*, ed. C. de Boor, 2 vols. (Leipzig, 1883–5, and reprinted Hildesheim 1980).
Theophanes Continuatus: Theophanes Continuatus, *Chronographia*, ed. I. Bekker (Bonn, 1838).
Vita Theoph.: The anonymous life of St Theophano, in *Zwei griechische Texte*, pp. 1–24.

[2] Liutprand of Cremona, *Legatio ad imperatorem Constantinopolitanum Nicephorum Phocam*, ed. A. Bauer and R. Rau, AQDG 8 (Darmstadt, 2nd edn, 1977), 15, p. 538, 7 ff: 'inaudita res est, ut porphyrogeniti porphyrogenita, hoc est in purpura nati filia in purpura nata, gentibus misceatur'; for a translation see *The Works of Liudprand of Cremona*, trans. F.A. Wright (London, 1930), p. 239. On Liutprand see J. Koder and Th. Weber, *Liutprand von Cremona in Konstantinopel: Untersuchungen zum griechischen Sprachschatz und zu realkundlichen Aussagen in seinen Werken*, Byzantina Vindobonensia, 13 (Vienna, 1980); M. Rentschler, *Liudprand von Cremona: eine Studie zum ost-westlichen Kulturgefälle im Mittelalter*, Frankfurter

The term *porphyrogennetos* dates from the ninth century and became current in the tenth through the works of Constantine VII Porphyrogennetos, although the special status of a son or daughter born to a ruling emperor goes back to at least the sixth century.[3] Purple was the imperial colour and the sign of the legitimation of hereditary rulership.[4] In his draft of a letter to be sent by the emperor Michael VII Dukas to the duke of the Normans, Robert Guiscard (1072/3), in which one of Robert's daughters is sought as a bride for the porphyrogennete brother of the emperor, Michael Psellos gives the following definition: 'having been born to my father not before his emperorship (*basileia*), but having been both conceived and born after he became emperor ... Those born like that, we Romans call "purple-born" emperors.'[5] And Anna Komnene, porphyrogennete herself, explains the name further in her *Alexiad* in the chapter about her own birth (in 1083): the part of the palace or the room (*oikema*) reserved for imperial deliveries has been called, since Antiquity, the Porphyra; whoever is born there, is 'porphyrogennete'.[6] This tradition is already known to Liutprand, who mentions it in his *Antapodosis*: Leo VI, father of Constantine VII Porphyrogennetos, is not called porphyrogennete because he was born in the purple, but because he was born in the house (*domus* = *oikos*), built by Constantine the Great, who also gave it the name of 'Porphyra'. It is not known where this part of the palace was

Wissenschaftliche Beiträge, kulturwiss. Reihe, 14 (Frankfurt am Main, 1981); J.N. Sutherland, *Liudprand of Cremona, Bishop, Diplomat, Historian: Studies of the Man and his Age*, Biblioteca degli 'Studi medievali', 14 (Spoleto, 1988); K.J. Leyser, 'Ends and means in Liudprand of Cremona', *Byzantinische Forschungen*, 13 (1988), 119–43; and R. Levine, 'Liudprand of Cremona: history and debasement in the tenth century', *Mittellateinisches Jahrbuch*, 26 (1991), 70–84.

3 Du Cange, *Glossarium ad scriptores mediae et infimae Graecitatis* (Lyons, 1688 and reprinted Graz, 1958), c. 1206 f. See also *ODB*, p. 1701. The term *porphyrogennetoi* is also mentioned in an inscription from 906–11; see the text in W. Ohnsorge, 'Zur Frage der Töchter Kaiser Leons VI.', in Ohnsorge, *Konstantinopel und der Okzident: gesammelte Aufsätze zur Geschichte der byzantinisch-abendländischen Beziehungen und des Kaisertums* (Darmstadt, 1966), pp. 171–5, especially p. 171. In *De ceremoniis*, I, 51 (42), ed. A. Vogt (Paris, 1967), II, 24–5, and II, 21, PG 112, cc. 1148–52, Constantine VII Porphyrogennetos discusses the ceremonial at the birth of a porphyrogennete prince.

4 O. Treitinger, *Die oströmische Kaiser- und Reichsidee nach ihrer Gestaltung im höfischen Zeremoniell* (Darmstadt, 1956), pp. 61–2.

5 Michael Psellos, Ep. 144, *Mesaionike Bibliotheke*, ed. C.N. Sathas, vol. V (Venice and Paris, 1876 and reprinted Hildesheim, 1972), p. 390. In acclamations the 'divine name' of the porphyrogennete follows that of the *basileus*.

6 Anna Komnene, *Alexias*, VI, 8, ed. B. Leib (Paris, 1967), II, 60, 27 ff.

located.[7] But from the words quoted at the beginning of this article, it is clear that he, also, had heard, in Constantinople, the explanation of *porphyrogennetos* as 'born in the purple' (*in purpura natus*).

Marriage negotiations between Byzantium and the West (from the eighth till the eleventh century)[8]

The possibility of obtaining a porphyrogennete princess as the bride of a foreign ruler had been demonstrated by Peter of Bulgaria, successor to his father, Symeon, who had married in 927 the purple-born Maria/Irene, daughter of the emperor Christopher, son of Romanos I Lekapenos and co-emperor from 912 to 931. The Byzantine diplomats answered that Christopher himself was not a porphyrogennete. As to the status of Rome, Liutprand urged that Rome had been liberated by Otto I, whom he called *dominus meus imperator augustus*. According to Roman privileges – by which is meant the *Donation of Constantine* – Otto had given all lands belonging to the Roman church to the pope, in imitation of Constantine the Great. But the Byzantine court insisted on its superiority over Rome and the Roman church.[9]

Constantine VII's 'francophilism'[10] had revealed a different attitude towards the West. In his *De administrando imperio* he summarizes his guidelines in discussing requests for marriages from the northern 'barbarians' (Khazars, Turks, Russians, Pechenegs and Slavs):

> For if any nation of these infidel and dishonourable tribes of the north shall ever demand a marriage-alliance with the emperor

[7] Liutprand, *Liber antapodoseos*, I, 6–7, ed. A. Bauer and R. Rau (see n. 2), p. 254, 15 ff; see also III, 30, p. 380, 3 ff. On the Porphyra see R. Janin, *Constantinople byzantine: développement urbain et répertoire topographique* (Paris, 1950), pp. 121–2.

[8] On marriage-negotiations see also G. Wolf, 'Die byzantinisch-abendländischen Heirats- und Verlobungspläne zwischen 750 und 1250', *Archiv für Diplomatik*, 37 (1991), 15–32, and F. Tinnefeld, 'Byzantinische auswärtige Heiratspolitik vom 9. zum 12. Jahrhundert: Kontinuität und Wandel der Prinzipien und der praktischen Ziele', *Byzantinoslavica*, 54 (1993), 21–8. These two papers were not yet available when the present chapter was written.

[9] Liutprand, *Legatio* (see n. 2), 17–19, p. 538, 20 ff. See P.E. Schramm, *Kaiser, Rom und Renovatio: Studien zur Geschichte des römischen Erneuerungsgedankens vom Ende des karolingischen Reiches bis zum Investiturstreit* (Darmstadt, 1962), pp. 71–4. In fact, the very name of Constantine the Great appears to be a stumbling-block between East and West.

[10] A. Toynbee, *Constantine Porphyrogenitus and His World* (London, 1973), p. 18, n. 4.

> of the Romans, and either to take his daughter to wife, or to give a daughter of their own to be wife to the emperor or to the emperor's son, this monstrous demand of theirs also you shall rebut with these words, saying: 'Concerning this matter also a dread and authentic charge and ordinance of the great and holy Constantine is engraved upon the sacred table of the universal church of the Christians in Hagia Sophia, that never shall an emperor of the Romans ally himself in marriage with a nation of customs differing from and alien to those of the Roman order, especially with one that is infidel and unbaptized, unless it be with the Franks alone; for they alone were excepted by that great man, the holy Constantine, because he himself drew his origin from those parts; for there is much relationship (*syngeneia*) and converse (*epimiksia*) between Franks and Romans. And why did he order that with them alone the emperors of the Romans should intermarry? Because of the traditional fame and nobility of those lands and races. But with any other nation whatsoever it was not to be in their power to do this, and he who dared to do it was to be condemned as an alien (*allotrios*) from the ranks of the Christians and subject to the anathema, as a transgressor of ancestral laws and imperial ordinances.'[11]

Constantine VII goes on to discuss two marriages which he thinks very disputable: that of Constantine V to a Khazar princess and that of the granddaughter of Romanos I Lekapenos to the khan of Bulgaria. The marriage of the co-emperor Constantine V – erroneously written as Leo (IV) – in 732 had been arranged by Constantine's father Leo III. But this Constantine was a disgrace to the empire of the Romans and his behaviour defied all rules; besides, as an enemy of the icons, he was a 'heretic'. In Constantine VII's view, an iconoclast (*eikonomachos*) is the same as an unbeliever (*apistos*). As we know from the *Chronicle* of Theophanes, the Khazar princess Çiçek converted from Judaism to Christianity before her marriage and took the name Irene at baptism; she knew Holy Scripture very well and was able to refute the iconoclastic theory of her husband and of her father-in-

[11] Constantine VII Porphyrogennetos, *De administrando imperio*, ed. G. Moravcsik (Washington, DC, 1967), 13, 106 ff, pp. 70–1; trans. R.J.M. Jenkins, *ibid.*, pp. 71–3. By 'law' is meant canon 72 of the Trullo council (*Syntagma ton theion kai hieron kanonon*, ed. G.A. Rhalles and M. Potles, II (Athens, 1852 and reprinted 1966), pp. 471 ff), which forbids marriages between the Orthodox and heretics; see Constantine VII Porphyrogennetos, *De administrando imperio*, II, *Commentary*, ed. R.J.M. Jenkins (London, 1962), p. 68.

law.[12] As to the other marriage, that of Maria/Irene, granddaughter of Romanos I Lekapenos, with Peter of Bulgaria in 927, Constantine stresses that it was against all traditions, but had served political and diplomatic aims by ransoming Christian prisoners; besides, the Bulgarians were (Orthodox) Christians, the Bulgarian patriarchate having been recognized in 927; also, Maria was 'not daughter of the chief and lawful emperor, but of the third and most junior one [Christopher], who was still subordinate and had no share of authority in matters of government'. Besides, here and elsewhere Constantine VII speaks of 'the ladies of the imperial family', relatives of the imperial house and marriageable princesses.[13]

If one considers the diplomatic traffic between Byzantium and the countries abroad, one is struck by the importance of noble ladies as eminent articles for export to gain mutual political advantage. Whatever the women's personal choice, they were made subordinate to the ideology of the 'family of Christian nations' and the *confraternitas*, when it was convenient in a given situation,[14] particularly when the country was threatened by

[12] Theophanes, *Chronographia*, I, p. 409, 30 ff. Leo IV was called 'the Khazar', see *Vita Theophanis*, in Theophanes, *Chronographia*, II, p. 4, 28. Constantine VII Porphyrogennetos does not mention the marriage, in a foreign country, of the mutilated Justinian II (his nose was cut) with the sister of the Khazar khan, who took the Christian name of Theodora (Theophanes, *Chronographia*, I, p. 373, 1). After Justinian had regained the throne in 705, Theodora became empress and their son Tiberius co-emperor; see G. Ostrogorsky, *Geschichte des byzantinischen Staates* (Munich, 3rd edn, 1963), 121; D.M. Dunlop, *The History of the Jewish Khazars* (New York, 1954), pp. 171–5.

[13] Constantine VII Porphyrogennetos, *De administrando imperio* (see n. 11), 13, 163 ff, p. 74. See Dölger, *Regesten*, no. 612; S. Runciman, *The Emperor Romanus Lecapenus and his Reign: A Study of Tenth-Century Byzantium* (Cambridge, 1929 and reprinted 1988), pp. 66–7, 97–101. Romanos I had made his son Christopher co-emperor in 921 and had given him precedence over Constantine VII, who came after Romanos and Christopher in processions. Liutprand, who had seen Constantine VII at the court of Constantinople in 949, voices Constantine's feelings in his *Antapodosis* (see n. 7), III, 37, p. 382, 13 ff: Christopher was born before his father became emperor, and therefore was not a *porphyrogennetos*; and with a Latin word play: 'Christophoron *primogenitum* domino suo imperatori Constantino *Porphyrogenito* praeposuit.' On the Bulgarian autocephaly see H.-D. Döpmann, 'Zum Streit mit Byzanz um das erste bulgarische Patriarchat', *Byzantinische Forschungen*, 18 (1992), 101–10.

[14] See various studies by F. Dölger, especially in Dölger, *Byzanz und die europäische Staatenwelt: ausgewählte Vorträge und Aufsätze* (Darmstadt, 1964); K. Leyser, 'The tenth century in Byzantine-western relationships', in *Relations between East and West in the Middle Ages*, ed. D. Baker (Edinburgh, 1973), pp. 29–63; J. Shepard, 'Aspects of Byzantine attitudes and policy towards the West in the tenth and eleventh centuries', *Byzantinische Forschungen*, 13 (1988), 67–118.

neighbouring enemies and when diplomacy was needed. Sometimes western diplomats used the existing affinity between western ruling houses as an argument in negotiations to obtain a bride from Byzantium.

Before Liutprand's mission

There had been negotiations for marriages between members of the Byzantine and Frankish nobility before Liutprand's mission in 968. In order to isolate the papacy and the Lombards, Constantine V had approached Pippin in *c.* 765 about a marriage between Pippin's daughter Gisela and Constantine's son and successor Leo (IV); but Pippin, who died in 768, did not agree.[15] As regent for her ten-year-old son Constantine VI, Irene had agreed to the betrothal of her son to Charlemagne's daughter Erythro/Rotrud. In 782, according to Theophanes, she sent the *sakellarios* Konstaes and the *primikerios* Mamalos to the Frankish king. After the betrothal the eunuch and *notarios* Elissaios remained in the West to teach the princess the Greek language and to give her instructions on how to behave in Byzantine court-ceremonial.[16] The betrothal was broken off after the iconophile Council of Nicaea (787), and Constantine, much against his will, had to marry Maria from Amnia in the Armeniakon.[17] But according to Theophanes' *Chronicle* another attempt was made later, in 801/2, when delegates from Charlemagne and pope Leo came to Constantinople with the request that Irene (who in the meantime had had her son Constantine blinded and had become sole empress) marry the Frankish emperor 'in order to unite East and West'.[18] However, a palace revolution put an unexpected end to the negotiations; Irene

[15] Dölger, *Regesten*, no. 325; W. Ohnsorge, 'Das Kaisertum der Eirene und die Kaiserkrönung Karls des Grossen', in *Konstantinopel* (see n. 3), pp. 49–92, at p. 70.

[16] Dölger, *Regesten*, no. 339; Theophanes, *Chronographia*, I, p. 455, 19 ff.

[17] Theophanes, *Chronographia*, I, p. 463, 21 ff. According to Frankish sources, Charlemagne sent the Byzantine delegation of 787 back home without Rotrud, see W. Ohnsorge, '*Orthodoxus imperator*: vom religiösen Motiv für das Kaisertum Karls des Grossen', in Ohnsorge, *Abendland und Byzanz: gesammelte Aufsätze zur Geschichte der byzantinisch-abendländischen Beziehungen und des Kaisertums* (Darmstadt, 1963), pp. 64–78, at pp. 65–6; cf. Dölger, *Regesten*, no. 345. On Charlemagne's marriage politics see P. Speck, *Kaiser Konstantin VI.: die Legitimation einer fremden und der Versuch einer eigenen Herrschaft*, I (Munich, 1978), pp. 119–21, 167–70, 208 (Romuald, son of Arichis of Benevento, marries a sister of Constantine's wife Maria between 788 and 791).

[18] Theophanes, *Chronographia*, I, p. 475, 29 f. Speck, *Konstantin VI.*, pp. 326–33, discusses the background of Theophanes' statement.

was exiled from Constantinople.[19] After Charlemagne had received the title of *imperator* and *basileus* in exchange for Byzantine territory previously conquered by the Franks, the emperor Michael I Rangabe (811–13) suggested that his eldest son and co-emperor Theophylaktos should marry a Frankish princess. When the Frankish delegation arrived at Constantinople, they found Leo V (813–20) on the throne; and before their arrival back home, Charlemagne had passed away.[20]

When the East badly needed assistance against the Arab attacks and was calling for a common 'crusade' against the Saracens, emperor Theophilos (829–42) offered a Byzantine princess as a bride for Lothar I's son, Louis II, at diplomatic negotiations (838–42) between the Constantinopolitan court and Louis I 'the Pious' (who died in 840) and his son Lothar I.[21] This is known from the so-called *Continuatio Constantinopolitana*: 'hic [the emperor Theophilos] etiam dum adviveret legatos suos ad imperatorem Lotharium mittens filiam suam filio eius Ludovico regi dare promisit.'[22] Theophilos died in 842; the marriage was not realized and nothing is heard of further plans. Finally, in 851, Louis II was engaged to Angilberga, which provoked a reaction in

19 Dölger, *Regesten*, no. 357; F. Dölger, 'Europas Gestaltung im Spiegel der fränkisch-byzantinischen Auseinandersetzung des 9. Jahrhunderts', in Dölger, *Byzanz* (see n. 14), pp. 282–369, at pp. 301–2.

20 Dölger, *Regesten*, no. 385; see Dölger, 'Europas Gestaltung', pp. 306–8; P. Classen, *Karl der Grosse, das Papsttum und Byzanz: die Begründung des karolingischen Kaisertums*, Beiträge zur Geschichte und Quellenkunde des Mittelalters, 9 (Sigmaringen, 1985), pp. 82–7; T.S. Brown, 'The background of Byzantine relations with Italy in the ninth century: legacies, attachments and antagonisms', *Byzantinische Forschungen*, 13 (1988), 27–45.

21 Dölger, *Regesten*, no. 443. For the 'crusade' see the famous 'Kaiserbrief' from St Denis, a unique document of Byzantine diplomacy: W. Ohnsorge, 'Das Kaiserbündnis von 842–844 gegen die Sarazenen: Datum, Inhalt und politische Bedeutung des "Kaiserbriefes aus St. Denis"', in *Abendland* (see n. 17), pp. 131–83, at p. 136. The marriage proposal is not mentioned in the papyrus fragment; such a proposal formed a mere 'Begleiterscheinung' to the formal negotiations.

22 *Chronica minora saec. IV. V. VI. VII*, ed. Th. Mommsen, MGH AA XIII, 3 (Berlin, 1898 and reprinted 1961), p. 343. Dölger, 'Europas Gestaltung' (see n. 19), p. 331: it may have been Theophilos' daughter Thecla, as for example (after J.B. Bury) also in L. Bréhier, *Le monde byzantin*, II, *Les institutions de l'empire byzantin* (Paris, 1949), p. 38. Theophilos, who was at war continuously with the caliph al-Ma'mūn, used marriage diplomacy with regard to the Khurramite refugees after their defeat in 833. *Theophanes Continuatus*, 112, 10 ff, and Skylitzes, *Synopsis*, 67, 3 ff, speak of the marriage of the hero Theophobos (Nasr in Arabic and Syriac sources) with Theophilos' sister Helena; according to J.B. Bury (*ODB*, p. 2067) it could also have been the sister of Theophilos' wife Theodora.

the East, according to the *Annales Bertiniani*: 'Greci vero non minus contra Hludowicum filium Lotharii, regem Italiae, concitantur propter filiam imperatoris Constantinopolitani ab eo desponsatam sed ad eius nuptias venire differentem.'[23]

Once again it was a tense situation, in southern Italy, that induced the new Byzantine emperor Basil I (867–86) to resume relations with pope Hadrian II and the Franks, after having dismissed the anti-Roman patriarch Photios. Louis II's help was needed against the Arab occupation of Sicily and the attacks on southern Italy. At Constantinople a delegation dealt with the proposed marriage between Basil's eldest son and co-emperor Constantine and Louis' daughter Irmengard. But, in 871, Louis occupied Bari and called himself not only 'imperator (Francorum)', but even 'imperator Romanorum', which provoked a violent protest from Basil. Diplomatic relations between them were severed.[24]

The marriages that were in fact realized took place in the first half of the tenth century. In *c.* 901, Anna, daughter of Leo VI and half-sister of Constantine VII Porphyrogennetos, was married to Louis III 'the Blind', the candidate for the Italian emperorship;[25] and, in 944, Romanos II, born in 959 to Constantine VII Porphyrogennetos, was married to Bertha/Eudokia, the illegitimate daughter of Hugh of Italy.[26] After Bertha/Eudokia's early death in 949 negotiations were started in order to arrange a marriage between the still young Romanos and Hedwig, daughter of Otto I's brother Henry of Bavaria, but in 954 Hedwig was married to

[23] *Annales Bertiniani*, s.a. 853, MGH SS I, p. 448.

[24] Dölger, *Regesten*, no. 480, on the projected marriage; Dölger, 'Europas Gestaltung' (see n. 19), pp. 316–20, 336–8; Dölger, *Regesten*, no. 487, on Basil's lost letter to Louis II, which can be reconstructed from Louis' reply: MGH Epistolae VII, pp. 385–94, at p. 389, 2 ff. Nothing more is said about the marriage, but the western envoy Anastasius Bibliothecarius mentions it in his letter to pope Hadrian II: 'causa nuptialis commercii . . . ab utraque parte sperabatur simul et parabatur', MGH Epistolae VII, p. 410. Irmengard was married to Boso in 876, see Hincmar of Rheims, *Annales*, MGH SS I, p. 499.

[25] Anna was the daughter, born out of wedlock, of Leo VI and Zoe (daughter of Stylianos Zaoutzes); when she was born (*c.* 890), Leo was still married to Theophano (see below). See, for a survey of Leo VI's marriages and his children, Ohnsorge, 'Zur Frage' (see n. 3), p. 175.

[26] Dölger, *Regesten*, no. 643. After 930 attempts to arrange marriage alliances with Byzantium were also made by the Roman aristocracy, see V. von Falkenhausen, *Untersuchungen über die byzantinische Herrschaft in Süditalien vom 9. bis ins 11. Jahrhundert*, Schriften zur Geistesgeschichte des östlichen Europa, 1 (Wiesbaden, 1967), pp. 43–4.

Burchard II of Swabia, and Romanos married Theophano (on which more below).[27]

After Liutprand's mission

In 968 it was Liutprand of Cremona's duty to negotiate with Nikephoros II Phokas at the court of Constantinople on behalf of Otto I, who had marched towards southern Italy and had crowned his son Otto II as his co-emperor in Rome in 967. The possession of Rome and southern Italy was at stake and the region needed defence against the Arabs. The eastern court had offered Otto I a Byzantine princess for his son Otto in return for his collaboration.[28] When Liutprand asked for the purple-born 'filia Romani imperatoris et Theophanae imperatricis' as a bride,[29] the reaction was harsh and precise. The Byzantine chronicles do not mention these negotiations. Most authors agree that Otto had in mind Romanos II's daughter Anna (born in 963), the granddaughter of Constantine VII – a '*porphyrogeniti porphyrogenita*' – who was later to marry Vladimir of Kiev. Nikephoros was killed in 969. After another embassy to the new emperor John Tzimiskes it was finally a Theophano, hitherto unknown, who arrived in Italy and was married to Otto II and crowned Ottonian empress in St Peter's at Rome in 972. This Theophano was not a porphyrogennete. In the marriage charter (14 April 972) she is called 'neptis clarissima' of the emperor;[30] it is only in later western sources that she is known as 'daughter of the emperor'. There had

[27] Cf. Dölger, *Regesten*, no. 658; W. Ohnsorge, 'Drei *deperdita* der byzantinischen Kaiserkanzlei und die Frankenadressen im Zeremonienbuch des Konstantinos Porphyrogennetos', in *Abendland* (see n. 17), pp. 227–54, at p. 235; J. Fleckenstein, 'Das Reich der Ottonen im 10. Jahrhundert', in *Handbuch der deutschen Geschichte*, ed. H. Grundmann (Munich, 9th edn, 1975), I, 3, p. 59. Liutprand of Cremona was a member of the delegation to Constantinople in 949.

[28] Cf. Dölger, *Regesten*, no. 713.

[29] Liutprand, *Legatio* (see n. 2), 7, p. 530, 25 f.

[30] MGH DD O II, pp. 28–30, at p. 29, 28: 'Theophanu, Iohannis Constantinopolitani imperatoris neptim clarissimam'. *Neptis* is the rendering of the Greek *anepsia*. In the *Vita Mathildis reginae antiquior*, 16, MGH SS X, p. 581, 44 ff, Theophano is said to be 'de partibus Graeciae, augusti de palatio, regalis ... coniunx praeclara dicta nomine Theophanu'. Widukind, *Res gestae Saxonicae*, III, 74, MGH SS III, p. 465, 28 has 'puella'. According to A. Poppe, 'The political background to the baptism of Rus': Byzantine-Russian relations between 986–89', *DOP*, 30 (1976), 195–244, at p. 230, n. 114, Otto may have wanted an elder daughter of Romanos II, called Helena (born *c.* 954/5); this Helena is not attested in the Greek sources.

been much discussion about her identity until Gunther Wolf[31] firmly established that she belonged to the family of the Skleroi through her father Constantine, brother-in-law of John Tzimiskes, and to the family of the Phokades through her mother Sophia; Maria Skleraina, sister of Theophano's father, had been the first wife of John Tzimiskes; Theophano's grandfather on her mother's side was a brother of the emperor Nikephoros II Phokas.[32] Eventually, in a last attempt to improve relations with the Bulgarians, this Nikephoros, the same emperor Liutprand had to deal with in 968, had tried to arrange marriages for the two sons of Romanos II, Basil and Constantine, with Bulgarian princesses.[33]

Not until the reign of Basil II (976–1025) did the Byzantine court give away a porphyrogennete princess for a foreign marriage – in eastern Europe. In 989, on condition of being baptized, the Kievan prince Vladimir was offered the porphyrogennete

[31] See, also for the earlier literature about Theophano, G. Wolf, 'Nochmals zur Frage: wer war Theophano?', *BZ*, 81 (1988), 272–83; this same article with some alterations and an excursus, in *Kaiserin Theophanu: Prinzessin aus der Fremde - des Westreichs grosse Kaiserin*, ed. G. Wolf (Cologne, 1991), pp. 59–78; Wolf, 'Wer war Theophanu?', in von Euw and Schreiner, *Kaiserin Theophanu*, II, pp. 385–96; O. Kresten, 'Byzantinistische Epilegomena zur Frage: Wer war Theophano?', in *ibid.*, pp. 403–10; F. Tinnefeld, 'Die Braut aus Byzanz: Fragen zu Theophanos Umfeld und gesellschaftlicher Stellung vor ihrer abendländischen Heirat', in *Kaiserin Theophanu*, ed. G. Wolf, pp. 247–61. Earlier literature has to be corrected, such as Bréhier, *Monde byzantin* (see n. 22), II, p. 38, who assumes that Romanos II had three daughters: Theophano (bride of Otto II), Anna (wife of Vladimir of Kiev), and a third daughter, married to a count of Holland. As tradition has it, this last one, Liutgard, wife of Arnulf of West Frisia, was a sister of the Ottonian empress Theophano, see A.A. Vasiliev, 'Hugh Capet of France and Byzantium', *DOP*, 6 (1951), 227–51, at pp. 246–51; J.M. van Winter, 'The imperial aristocracy in the tenth and the beginning of the eleventh centuries', in *Byzantium and the Low Countries in the Tenth Century: Aspects of Art and History in the Ottonian Era* (Hernen, 1985), pp. 13–32; see also K.N. Ciggaar, 'The empress Theophano (972–991): political and cultural implications of her presence in Western Europe, in particular for the county of Holland', in *ibid.*, pp. 33–76.

[32] Theophano belonged to the 'relatives of the court', known from Constantine VII Porphyrogennetos' *De administrando imperio* (see n. 11), 13, 165, p. 74: 'ton basilikon syngenidon'; and 43, 154, p. 196: 'apo ton basilikon syngenidon'. On the great Byzantine families see W. Seibt, *Die Skleroi: eine prosopographisch-sigillographische Studie*, Byzantina Vindobonensia, 9 (Vienna, 1976), pp. 58–60 (Konstantinos Skleros *c.* 930–991), and J.-C. Cheynet, 'Les Phocas', appendix to *Le Traité sur la guérilla (De velitatione) de l'empereur Nicéphore Phocas (963–969)*, ed. and trans. G. Dagron and H. Mihăescu (Paris, 1986), pp. 289–315 (genealogical table between pp. 317 and 318).

[33] Dölger, *Regesten*, no. 718, according to Leo the Deacon, *Historiae libri decem*, ed. C.B. Hase (Bonn, 1828), V, 3, p. 74, 14 ff; R. Jenkins, *Byzantium: The Imperial Centuries AD 610–1071* (London, 1966), pp. 295–6.

Anna, sister of the emperors Basil II and Constantine VIII; this is what finally brought Russia within the sphere of Orthodox Christianity. Not without great reluctance did Byzantium give her away; but it had been with Vladimir's help that Basil's throne had been saved from the usurper Bardas Phokas.[34]

It was also in these years that Hugh Capet, who had been proclaimed king in 987, asked Constantinople for a 'filia sancti imperii' for his son Robert, at the same time promising his help against any German aggression[35] (by which we must assume that Ottonian aggression is meant, in spite of the fact that Theophano herself was regent at this time). But as early as 988 Robert married Suzanne, the elderly widow of Arnulf II, count of Flanders (†988). This marriage would last one year.

The West had to wait until January 1002, when finally, after several years of negotiations and more than a decade after the death of the empress Theophano (991), a porphyrogennete arrived at Bari as a bride for Theophano's son Otto III.[36] But even this marriage was never consummated; Otto III had died earlier that same month at the age of twenty-one. With his death the idea

[34] Dölger, *Regesten*, no. 778; on the events as described in the Old Russian chronicle *Povest' vremennych let*, see D. Obolensky, *The Byzantine Commonwealth: Eastern Europe, 500–1553* (London, 1974), pp. 254–6, and G. Podskalsky, *Christentum und theologische Literatur in der Kiever Rus' (988–1237)* (Munich, 1982), pp. 17–24. According to G.G. Litavrin ('Die Kiever Rus' und Byzanz im 9. und 10. Jahrhundert', *Byzantinische Forschungen*, 18 (1992), 43–59, at p. 57), Olga, Igor's widow, possibly discussed a marriage of her son Svjatoslav (then five or six years old) with one of the five daughters of Constantine VII Porphyrogennetos at Constantinople as early as 946. On this topic in general see A. Kazhdan, 'Rus'–Byzantine princely marriages in the eleventh and twelfth centuries', *Harvard Ukrainian Studies*, 12/13 (1988/89), 414–29.

[35] Vasiliev, 'Hugh Capet' (see n. 31), pp. 227–51. Gerbert of Rheims, who would later become one of Otto III's advisers, wrote the letter, Ep. 111, PL 139, cc. 229–30.

[36] Dölger, *Regesten*, no. 784 and no. 787. See W. Ohnsorge, 'Otto III. Legation an Basileios II. vom Jahre 998: ein Beitrag zur Frage des byzantinischen Einflusses auf die Metallsiegelpraxis des Westens', in *Abendland* (see n. 17), pp. 288–99; P.E. Schramm, 'Kaiser, Basileus und Papst in der Zeit der Ottonen', in Schramm, *Kaiser, Könige und Päpste: gesammelte Aufsätze zur Geschichte des Mittelalters*, III (Stuttgart, 1969), pp. 200–45, at pp. 218–28; on the important letters of the delegate Leo of Synada, see Schramm, 'Zwölf Briefe des byzantinischen Gesandten Leon von seiner Reise zu Otto III. aus den Jahren 997–998', in *ibid.*, pp. 246–76 (Greek text with translation); and *The Correspondence of Leo, Metropolitan of Synada and Syncellus*, ed. and trans. M.P. Vinson (Washington, DC, 1985). Usually Zoe, daughter of Constantine VIII, is thought to be the bride, see for example Jenkins, *Byzantium* (see n. 33), p. 324, p. 339. G. Wolf, 'Zoe oder Theodora: die Braut Kaiser Ottos III.? (1001/1002)', in *Kaiserin Theophanu*, ed. Wolf (see n. 31), pp. 212–22, argues in favour of Zoe's younger sister Theodora.

of a 'renovatio imperii Romani' had come to an end. The dream of reuniting 'both East and West in one empire in the manner of Justinian' was over.[37]

In 1028, after Basil's death (1025), the German emperor Conrad II asked for a porphyrogennete princess for his son Henry III, but Constantinople offered him the sister of Romanos III Argyros instead.[38]

'Byzantine luxury' in the West

The West had a vivid, though quite biased idea of the way of life of a Byzantine princess. The doge Peter II Orseolo, a good friend of Otto III's, had freed the Adriatic coasts from the fear of the Arabs. After the defeat of the Arabs at Bari in 1004, his son John was invited by emperor Basil II (together with his other son Otto) to Constantinople, in order to marry Maria Argyropoulina, a sister of Romanos III (according to Skylitzes). At the arrival of the couple in Venice, Maria was believed to be a member of the imperial family (a niece or sister of Basil II).[39] It was probably she the ascetical Peter Damian had in mind when he poured contempt on a Greek dogaressa for her excessive and luxurious style of living, for which she was punished 'rightly' by God. Maria, her husband and their child died in the plague which followed the famine of 1006:

> Such was the luxury of her habits that she scorned even to wash herself in common water, obliging her servants instead to collect the dew that fell from the heavens for her to bathe in.

[37] D.J. Geanakoplos, *Byzantine East and Latin West: Two Worlds of Christendom in Middle Ages and Renaissance* (New York, 1966), p. 19; but the possession of Rome and Italy is the particular objective of Byzantine diplomacy: see K. Leyser, 'Tenth century' (see n. 14), p. 37. Cf. J. Fleckenstein, 'Reich der Ottonen' (see n. 27), p. 111.

[38] According to Wolf, 'Zoe' (see n. 36), pp. 219–20. Cf. Dölger, *Regesten*, no. 830. Romanos III Argyros showed matrimonial interests also towards the Caucasian lands, where the Byzantine position had to be secured: one of his nieces (Helena) was married to Bagrat IV of Georgia (see Dölger, *Regesten*, no. 833; Skylitzes, *Synopsis*, p. 377, 23 f), and another niece to John Smbat III (see *ibid.*, p. 385, 37 ff).

[39] Dölger, *Regesten*, no. 794; cf. Skylitzes, *Synopsis*, p. 343, 76 ff ('to submit' Venice !); Johannes Diaconus, *Chronicon Venetum*, s.a. 1004, MGH SS VII, p. 36, 5 f: 'cuiusdam nobilissimi patricii filiam Argiropoli nomine, imperiali editam stirpe'; and p. 36, 17: 'imperatorum videlicet neptis'. On Maria Argyropoulina (*c.* 985–*c.* 1007) see J.-F. Vannier, *Familles byzantines: les Argyroi (IXe–XIIe siècles)*, Byzantina, 1 (Paris, 1975), pp. 43–4, and D.M. Nicol, *Byzantium and Venice: A Study in Diplomatic and Cultural Relations* (Cambridge, 1988), pp. 45–7.

> Nor did she deign to touch her food with her fingers, but would command her eunuchs to cut it up into small pieces, which she would impale on a certain golden instrument with two prongs and thus carry to her mouth. Her rooms, too, were so heavy with incense and various perfumes that it is nauseating for me to speak of them, nor would my readers readily believe it. But this woman's vanity was hateful to Almighty God; and so, unmistakably, did He take his revenge.[40]

After her death, the Ottonian empress Theophano was also accused of lavish luxury,[41] which had everything to do with the virulent anti-Byzantine attitude of western ecclesiastical reformers.

The name of Theophano in Byzantine sources from the ninth to the tenth century

Theophano, the Ottonian empress, is not mentioned in Greek sources. Her name ('divinely shining') is not common. In Greek the name was known as *Theophane* from mythology (daughter of Bisaltes) and as the proper name *Theophania*. The form *Theophano*, a feminine diminutive form (-/ó/),[42] was not used before

[40] Petrus Damianus, *Institutio monialis*, 11, PL 145, c. 744 C; trans. taken from J.J. Norwich, *A History of Venice* (Harmondsworth, 1983), p. 60.

[41] For the divine retribution of Theophano see Leyser, 'Tenth century' (see n. 14), pp. 45–6; P. Corbet, *Les Saints ottoniens: sainteté dynastique, sainteté royale et sainteté féminine autour de l'an Mil*, Beihefte der Francia, 15 (Sigmaringen, 1986), p. 71; M. Stratmann, 'Die Kaiserin Theophanu in den erzählenden Quellen des 11. und 12. Jahrhunderts', in von Euw and Schreiner, *Kaiserin Theophanu*, II, pp. 413–18.

[42] Cf. A.N. Jannaris, *An Historical Greek Grammer Chiefly of the Attic Dialect* (London, 1897), p. 132; cf. E. Schwyzer, *Griechische Grammatik*, I, Handbuch der Altertumswissenschaft, II, I, 1 (Munich, 1953 and reprinted 1968), p. 478. J.R. Martindale, *The Prosopography of the Later Roman Empire*, III B (Cambridge, 1992), 1307, lists one Theophano on a lead seal (Zacos 2932) from the seventh century, but the ending –/oi/ (dative) is a conjecture. For the form *Theophanou* – which reflects the normal Latin rendering of Theophanu – see G.S. Henrich, 'Theophanu oder Theophano? Zur Geschichte eines "gespaltenen" griechischen Frauennamensuffixes', in von Euw and Schreiner, *Kaiserin Theophanu*, II, pp. 89–99; and for the spelling in medieval Greek an inscription from *c.* 965 in Cappadocia (Çavuşin): **ΤΟΥΣ ΑΙΨΕΒΕΙΣ ΗΜΟΝ ΒΑΣΕΙΛΗΣ / ΔΗΑΦΟΙΛΑΞΟΝ ΚΕ ΠΑΝΤΩΤΑΙ / ΔΕΣΠΥΝΗΣ ΗΜΟΝ / ΝΗΚΗΦΟΡΟΝ ΚΕ ΘΑΙΦΑΝΟΥΣ**, published by M. Restle, *Byzantine Wall Painting in Asia Minor* (Shannon, 1969), I, p. 138, and III, pl. 327; N. Thierry, 'Un portrait de Jean Tzimiskès en Cappadoce', *Travaux et Mémoires*, 9 (1985), 477–84, at p. 482, corrects the name into Θεοφανοῦς and corrects δεσπύνης into δέσποιναν. A trisyllable Θεοφουνô is attested in G. Morgan, 'A Byzantine satirical song?', *BZ*, 47 (1954), 292–7, at p. 292, v. 3.

the ninth century; it is not attested in inscriptions, papyri or in literary texts. The Macedonian dynasty (867–1056) includes two Byzantine empresses named Theophano.[43]

Theophano (1). Staurakios, son of the emperor Nikephoros I (802–11), married a Theophano from Athens, a relative of the iconophile empress Irene (†802). Theophanes narrates that she was chosen as a bride for Staurakios at a bride-show and was consequently separated from her fiancé. At the wedding in 807 Staurakios behaved badly with two other girls from the competition. When his father was killed in 811 in pursuit of the Bulgarian khan Krum, Staurakios was heavily wounded, but was brought back to Constantinople, where he tried, together with Theophano, to save the throne. Theophano, who was childless, was to become empress, like the widowed Irene before her. After the revolt and the crowning of Staurakios' brother-in-law Michael Rangabe in 811, Staurakios and Theophano both took the monastic habit. Theophano was given a monastery, called 'Ta Hebraika' by Theophanes, where Staurakios, who died soon afterwards, was buried. Constantine VII Porphyrogennetos knew of a tomb of white marble containing the remains of Staurakios and Theophano in the chapel of the Prodromos in the monastery of the Holy Trinity, called 'Ta Staurakiou'.[44]

Theophano (2). Michael I Rangabe and Prokopia were married before 794. Prokopia was a daughter of Nikephoros I and a sister of Staurakios. According to the *Vita Ignatii* by Niketas David they had five children: two daughters, called Georgo and Theophano, and three sons, called Theophylaktos, Staurakios, who died young, and Niketas. This Niketas, who had been appointed *domestikos ton hikanoton* at the age of ten, was exiled in 813, after

[43] On the prosopography of the era see especially F. Winkelmann, 'Probleme einer byzantinischen Prosopographie des 8. und 9. Jahrhunderts', *Studien zum 8. und 9. Jahrhundert in Byzanz*, ed. H. Köpstein and F. Winkelmann, Berliner Byzantinische Arbeiten, 51 (Berlin, 1983), pp. 121–9, and Winkelmann, *Quellenstudien zur herrschenden Klasse von Byzanz im 8. und 9. Jahrhundert*, Berliner Byzantinische Arbeiten, 54 (Berlin, 1987); see also E. Patlagean, 'Les débuts d'une aristocratie byzantine et le témoignage de l'historiographie: système des noms et liens de parenté aux IXe–Xe siècles', in *The Byzantine Aristocracy IX to XIII Centuries*, ed. M. Angold (Oxford, 1984), pp. 23–43, and D. Nicol, 'The prosopography of the Byzantine aristocracy', in *ibid.*, pp. 79–91.

[44] Theophanes, *Chronographia*, p. 483, 15 ff, p. 492, 24 ff, p. 494, 4 ff; see W. Treadgold, *The Byzantine Revival 780–842* (Stanford, 1988), pp. 152–3. R. Janin, *La Géographie ecclésiastique de l'empire byzantin*, I, 3 (Paris, 2nd edn, 1969), p. 470, on the different names of Ta Hebraika.

the deposition of his father, to the Princes' Islands – together with his father and his brother Theophylaktos; where, after having been castrated, he took the monastic name of Ignatios. He would later become the famous patriarch (847–58; 867–77) who rivalled Photios.[45]

Theophano (3). Theophano, first wife of Leo VI, is venerated as a saint and a miracle-worker in the Byzantine church.[46] She was born (*c.* 875) of 'royal blood' and of the family of the Martinakioi through her father Constantine; her mother Anna was of oriental (i.e. Armenian?) origin. The chronicles mention her marriage with Leo in 881/2, her saintly life and the place of her tomb.[47] An anonymous contemporary *Vita*,[48] written by an aristocratic supporter of the imperial family, extravagantly depicts her many virtues, her holy character and her care for the sick and the poor. At the bride-show for Leo she was chosen by his mother Eudokia Ingerina. In this *Vita* her life at court seems to be in perfect

[45] *Vita Ignatii*, PG 105, 492 A–B.

[46] *Synaxarium ecclesiae Constantinopolitanae*, Propylaeum ad Acta sanctorum Novembris, ed. H. Delehaye (Brussels 1902 and reprinted 1954), cc. 313–16; for the veneration as early as the middle of the tenth century, see *Le Typicon de la Grande Eglise*, I, ed. and trans. J. Mateos, Orientalia Christiana Analecta, 165 (Rome, 1962), p. 132, 25 ff: synaxis in the Church of the Holy Apostles. For other MSS of synaxaries with the life of Theophano see 'Catalogus codicum hagiographicorum graecorum Regii Monasterii S. Laurentii Scorialensis', *Analecta Bollandiana*, 28 (1909), 353–98, at p. 387, and F. Halkin, *Manuscrits grecs de Paris: inventaire hagiographique*, Subsidia Hagiographica, 44 (Brussels, 1968), pp. 214, 216, 217.

[47] For example, *Theophanes Continuatus*, p. 361, 13 ff, p. 364, 20 ff; Skylitzes, *Synopsis*, p. 172, 91 ff, p. 179, 66 ff, p. 180, 14 ff. On the marriage, 'almost certainly' in 882, see R.J.H. Jenkins, 'The chronological accuracy of the "Logothete" for the years A.D. 867–913', *DOP*, 19 (1965) 89–112, at p. 101. On the family of the Martinakioi see Winkelmann, *Quellenstudien* (see n. 43), pp. 186–7.

[48] *Zwei griechische Texte über die Hl. Theophano, die Gemahlin Kaisers Leo VI.*, ed. E. Kurtz, Zapiski imperatorskoj Akademii Nauk, VIII, Istor.-filol. otdel., III, 2 (Saint Petersburg, 1898), *Vita Theoph.*, pp. 1–24; a résumé in French: G. da Costa-Louillet, 'Saints de Constantinople aux VIIIe, IXe et Xe siècles', *Byzantion*, 25–7 (1955–7), 783–852, at pp. 823–36. The *Vita Theoph.*, composed before 812 (da Costa-Louillet, p. 824), occurs in only one manuscript of lives of female saints, Florence, Conventi Soppressi, B. 1, Camaldoli 1214; on this MS see 'Vita sanctae Olympiadis et narratio Sergiae de eiusdem translatione', *Analecta Bollandiana*, 15 (1896), 400–23, at pp. 406–8. The historian Nikephoros Gregoras also wrote, in 1328/9 (Kurtz, *Zwei griechische Texte*, p. VIII), a life of Theophano, which was partly published, with a Latin translation, by J. Hergenröther, in his *Monumenta Graeca ad Photium eiusque historiam pertinentia* (Regensburg, 1869 and reprinted Farnborough, 1969), pp. 72–83, from cod. Monac. gr. 10; Kurtz, *Zwei griechische Texte*, edited the entire text, making use also of cod. Vindob. theol. gr. Nessel 279. Nikephoros depends heavily upon the anonymous *Vita* of Theophano.

harmony with her husband. Theophano sustains and consoles Leo, when he is isolated by his father Basil I.[49] But another document (from *c.* 930), the *Vita Euthymii*,[50] shows a more realistic side of the empress. Both Leo and Theophano had a great esteem for the holy 'hesychastic' monk Euthymios, their *pater pneumatikos*, who was made *synkellos* and a member of the senate, and who, much later (from 907 until 912), would reign as patriarch.[51] According to the *Vita Euthymii* Theophano wanted a divorce after the death of her child and because of 'the many griefs inflicted on her'. Besides, she was ill and wanted to retire to the sanctuary of the Holy Casket (Soros) at Blachernai. The holy man Euthymios tried to mediate in the conflict, telling Leo, disingenuously, that his wife had merely tested him by threatening to leave. But Leo replied that Theophano had done him great harm by telling his father about his relationship with Zoe, daughter of the *basileopator* Stylianos Zaoutzes, after which he had been badly beaten by his father, who had forced Zoe to marry someone else. Leo stressed the fact that he had been compelled by his father to marry Theophano much against his own will. Theophano left the court, retired to the Soros and died soon afterwards, exhausted by her illness and her asceticism, having reigned as empress for

[49] *Vita Theoph.*, 12, p. 8, 4, about the imprisonment of Leo in a *koiton*, that is, according to *Theophanes Continuatus*, p. 350, 10, the part of the Great Palace called Margarites ; see R. Janin, *Constantinople byzantine* (see n. 7), p. 115. Only his wife Theophano and their daughter had access to Leo. On the imprisonment see A. Vogt, 'La jeunesse de Léon le Sage', *Revue Historique*, 59 (1934), 389–428, at pp. 423–4. In connection with this isolation the *Vita Theoph.* does not mention the child, who was called Eudokia (according to Constantine VII, see n. 54); Nikephoros Gregoras, *Logos*, corrects this omission, 17, p. 36, 15 f. On the detention of Leo from 883 until 886 see Jenkins, 'Chronological accuracy' (see n. 47), p. 102, and P. Magdalino, 'Saint Demetrios and Leo VI', *Byzantinoslavica*, 51 (1990), 198–201.

[50] The manuscript, found in 1874 in Turkey, had been edited by De Boor in 1888, before it got lost; see the new edition with English translation: *Vita S. Euthymii*, ed. P. Karlin-Hayter, *Byzantion*, 25–7 (1955–7), 1–172, at pp. 8–153, and B. Flusin, 'Un fragment inédit de la Vie d'Euthyme le Patriarche?', *Travaux et Mémoires*, 9 (1985), 119–31. The *Vita S. Euthymii* dates from *c.* 930 (Karlin-Hayter, p. 3).

[51] *Vita S. Euthymii*, 4, p. 26, 28; 5, p. 36, 30. Besides the vivid language, especially in the dialogues, the 'hesychastic' terminology is interesting; see for example Stylianos Zaoutzes' (*basileopator* of Leo VI and father of Leo's beloved Zoe) sarcasm towards Euthymios, whom he did not like at all: 'But you, since you are a monk, and according to the emperor, a holy one, keep quiet (*hesychaze*) in your cell, attend to yourself (*proseche seauto*), and do not meddle further', *Vita S. Euthymii*, 3, p. 20, 3. Euthymios is called *philesychos* in 2, p. 14, 3. *Hesychazein* is here synonymous with 'living the monastic life'.

twelve years. It was rumoured that Zoe, Leo's lover, contributed to her death, as well as to that of her own husband Theodore Gouzouniates.[52] Theophano was buried, in miraculous meteorological conditions, in the Church of the Holy Apostles. After forty days miracles began to happen in the family of the author of the *Life*. People were healed through her *maphorion* and embroideries, her ring, and her apparition in imperial dress together with the Holy Virgin and the mother of the author, as well as by the oil of the lamps near her tomb.[53] Nikephoros Gregoras adds that the emperor Leo took up the plan to transfer her relics either to the monastery of the Holy Constantine, built by Theophano herself, or to a church to be constructed in her honour. This church, which he built at the eastern side of that of the Holy Apostles, was to be called 'Holy Theophano', but strong objection from the bishops forced him not to use that name; instead, he called the church 'All Saints'. Theophano's relics were transferred to the monastery of Holy Constantine.[54] Allegedly,

[52] *Vita S. Euthymii*, 6–7, p. 42, 26 ff. Theophano was ill because of her excessive ascetical practices, *Vita Theoph.*, 22, p. 15, 13 ff. The girdle of the Holy Virgin was preserved in the casket, see *Vita S. Euthymii*, p. 43, n. 2; *ODB*, p. 280. – *Theophanes Continuatus*, p. 361, 13 ff, mentions her death. F. Halkin, *Novum auctarium Bibliothecae hagiographicae Graecae*, Subsidia hagiographica, 65 (Brussels, 1984), p. 207, gives as the year of Theophano's death 893 or 895–6 or 897; see especially V. Grumel, 'Chronologie des événements du règne de Léon VI (886–912)', *Echos d'Orient*, 35 (1936), 5–42, at pp. 22–9, and P. Karlin-Hayter, 'La mort de Théophano (10.11.896 ou 895)', *BZ*, 62 (1969), 13–19. Suspicion about Zoe's part in the death of Theophano: *Vita S. Euthymii*, 7, p. 50, 33 ff. Leo VI would soon marry Zoe.

[53] *Vita Theoph.*, 24 ff, p. 16 ff; Nikephoros Gregoras, *Logos*, 26, p. 44, 8 ff, speaks of miracles only in a general way, but he expresses his desire to write a special work on the topic.

[54] Nikephoros Gregoras, *Logos*, 24, p. 43, 1 ff. Janin, *Géographie ecclésiastique* (see n. 44), p. 245, is confusing; it is not the *Vita Theoph.* that mentions two sanctuaries, but Nikephoros Gregoras' *Logos*, 24, p. 43, 1 ff. As for the transfer of Theophano's relics forty days after her death (Janin, *ibid.*, p. 389): in Nikephoros Gregoras, *Logos* no mention is made of a period of forty days; it is a confusion with the *Vita Theoph.*, 24, p. 17, 4, according to which the miracles started forty days after Theophano's burial. Constantine VII Porphyrogennetos, *De ceremoniis*, II, 7, PG 112, cc. 1004–5, mentions the Church of All Saints and its function in imperial processions, and (II, 42, PG 112, c. 1196 A) the tomb of green marble from Thessaly with the remains of Theophano and her daughter Eudokia among the other imperial tombs in the Church of All Saints. On the later traditions concerning Theophano's tomb see Kurtz, *Zwei griechische Texte* (see n. 48), pp. 63–5; Janin, *Géographie ecclésiastique*, pp. 389 f; G. Downey, 'The Church of All Saints (Church of St Theophano) near the Church of the Holy Apostles at Constantinople', *DOP*, 9–10 (1956), 301–5: and, following Downey, G.P. Majeska, 'The body of St Theophano, the Empress, and the Convent of St

the transport of materials for Leo's pious constructions meant that insufficient Byzantine vessels could be committed to the defence of Sicily: Taormina was conquered by the Arabs in 902.[55]

Theophano (4). After the death of his eldest son Christopher in 931 Romanos I Lekapenos (920–44) wanted his two other sons, Stephen and Constantine, brothers-in-law of Constantine VII Porphyrogennetos, to marry. Constantine married (in 939?) the Armenian Helena and, after her early death, a Theophano from the Mamas family.[56]

Theophano (5). Constantine VII Porphyrogennetos and Helena, Romanos I's daughter, whom he had married in 919, had one son (Romanos) and five daughters (Zoe, Theodora, Agathe, Theophano and Anna).[57] After Romanos II, Theophano's husband (see below), had become emperor in 959, his five sisters were confined to the cloister or palace of Kanikleion – under heavy protest from their mother Helena and against their will – where also Sophia, widow of Romanos I's son Christopher, lived as a nun. Soon Zoe, Theodora and Theophano (and Anna?) were transferred to the monastery of Antiochos, whereas Agathe was sent to the convent (*phrontisterion*) of Myrelaion, founded by Romanos I. The princesses received a royal pension.[58]

Constantine', *Byzantinoslavica*, 38 (1977), 14–21, at pp. 19–20, with the interesting suggestion that St Constantine, to whom the convent was dedicated by Theophano, might be St Constantine of Synada, who had arranged the reconciliation between Leo VI and his father (cf. n. 49). On the unfinished church of St Theophano see the fragment, published by Flusin, 'Un fragment inédit' (see n. 50), 30, p. 131, 118 f; and on the social activities of Theophano and of the imperial house in general in the tenth century see D.J. Constantelos, *Byzantine Philanthropy and Social Welfare* (New Brunswick, 1968), pp. 114–22.

55 *Theophanes Continuatus*, p. 364, 20 ff; Georgios Monachos, *Vitae recentiorum imperatorum*, ed. I. Bekker (Bonn, 1838), p. 860, 12 ff, with more information; Skylitzes, *Synopsis*, p. 181, 19 ff. Cf. A.A. Vasiliev, *Byzance et les Arabes*, II, 1, *La dynastie macédonienne (867–959)*, ed. M. Canard (Brussels, 1968), p. 146.

56 *Theophanes Continuatus*, p. 423, 8 ff; Skylitzes, *Synopsis*, p. 228, 85 ff; cf. Runciman, *The Emperor Romanus Lecapenus* (see n. 13), p. 78.

57 The name of Theophano should be added to the genealogical table in *The Cambridge Medieval History*, IV, *The Byzantine Empire*, I, *Byzantium and its neighbours*, ed. J.M. Hussey (Cambridge, 1966), 792. Theodore Skutariotes (thirteenth century), *Synopsis Chronike*, in *Mesaionike Bibliotheke*, ed. C.N. Sathas, VII (Venice and Paris, 1894 and reprinted Hildesheim, 1972), p. 153, 20 f, confuses the situation by calling the five women daughters of Romanos II and Theophano, see F. Dölger, 'Nochmals wer war Theophano?', *BZ*, 43 (1950), 338–9.

58 *Theophanes Continuatus*, p. 471, 11 ff. Skylitzes, *Synopsis*, p. 252, 8 ff, says that Helena had to leave, too, and that it was all at the instigation of Romanos' wife Theophano. For the Kanikleion and the Myrelaion (cf. *Theophanes Continuatus*, p. 473, 16), the burial place of the Lekapenoi, see Janin, *Géographie ecclésiastique*

Theophano (6). Symeon the (New) Theologian (949–1022) was of a good and wealthy family from Galate in Paphlagonia; his parents were called Basil and Theophano. As he grew up in court circles at Constantinople, he may have been one of the *eugeneis*, with whom Constantine VII Porphyrogennetos surrounded himself, according to a contemporary source.[59]

Theophano (7). The ambitious and extremely beautiful second wife of Romanos II is, no doubt, the best-known Byzantine woman named Theophano, not least thanks to the portrait drawn of her by Charles Diehl in his *Figures byzantines*.[60] In 944, Romanos had been engaged at the age of five to Bertha/Eudokia, daughter of Hugh of Italy. Five years later, before the marriage could be consummated, the young girl[61] had died; some time between 954 and 957, Romanos had married Anastaso[62] (born at Constantinople after 940), whose fiancé had died. She was of low birth and the daughter of a wine-merchant. As empress she was to play an important role in court events for almost fifteen years. After the death of Romanos II (perhaps by poisoning) in 963, she became the wife of the successful general Nikephoros Phokas – not without the resistance of patriarch Polyeuktos on grounds of their 'spiritual affinity'. She had secret encounters with the widowed general John Tzimiskes, Nikephoros' nephew, and played an important role in the murder of her husband Nike-

(see n. 44), pp. 277, 351–4. As to Janin, *ibid.*, 365: according to *Theophanes Continuatus*, p. 471, 21, it is Agathe, and not Anna, who is sent to Myrelaion. In the manuscript tradition there is some confusion between Agathe and Anna, see *ibid.*, p. 471, 21, app., and Symeon Magistros, *Annales*, ed. I. Bekker (Bonn, 1838), p. 757, 15 f. Skylitzes, *Synopsis*, p. 252, 8 ff, does not give names and mentions a confinement only at the palace of Antiochos (Janin, *Constantinople byzantine* (see n. 7), p. 291, where Romanos III should be corrected to Romanos II), but adds that the sisters soon threw off their monastic habits and ate meat.

59 See Niketas Stethatos, *Vie de Syméon le Nouveau Théologien (949–1022)*, ed. and trans. I. Hausherr and G. Horn, Orientalia Christiana, 12 (Rome, 1928), 2, 5, p. 2: Symeon's parents were 'eugeneis kai plousioi'; and 3, p. 4 on Symeon's life at court. On the *eugeneis* at court see *Theophanes Continuatus*, p. 456, 14 ff.

60 Ch. Diehl, *Figures byzantines*, I (Paris, 3rd edn, 1908), pp. 217–43, quoting on p. 218, with some reservations, G. Schlumberger: 'cette grande pécheresse, dont les charmes devaient avoir une influence si fatale et qui devait successivement se faire aimer de trois empereurs'.

61 For engagements at a very early age see E. Patlagean, 'Byzance Xe–XIe siècle', in *Histoire de la vie privée*, ed. Ph. Ariès and G. Duby, I, ed. P. Veyne (Paris, 1985), pp. 531–614, at pp. 575–6.

62 Both forms, *Anastaso* and *Anastasia*, have been transmitted: Skylitzes, *Synopsis*, p. 240, 85 (*Anastaso*; in the edition of Kedrenos, *Synopsis*, II, ed. I. Bekker (Bonn, 1839), p. 329, 9: *Anastasia*; app.: *Anastaso*); *Theophanes Continuatus*, p. 458, 10 (*Anastasia*).

phoros in 969. The unlucky emperor's epitaph, by John Geometres, says: 'O Nicephorus, well-named indeed, since thou wast / Conqueror of all thine enemies, except thy wife.'[63]

After the murder, John Tzimiskes had to banish Theophano to the island of Prote or to Prokonnesos on the orders of the patriarch; she managed to escape from there to Constantinople, tried to obtain the protection of the church, but was only sent further away, to the Armeniakon Theme. John Tzimiskes married Theodora, sister of Romanos II. After his death in 976, when her sons Basil II and Constantine VIII succeeded to the throne, Theophano reappeared in Constantinople, but nothing more was heard of her.[64]

It was in these years of troubled court life and successful fighting against the Bulgarians and the Arabs, that the Ottonian empress Theophano, niece of John Tzimiskes, grew up in Constantinople.

Whereas in the West the name Theophanu (which is the Latin rendering of Theophano) occurs only once in later times (one of the granddaughters of the Ottonian empress Theophano, received

[63] Skylitzes, *Synopsis*, p. 283, 89 f. Translation in H. Grégoire, 'The Amorians and Macedonians 842–1025', in *Cambridge Medieval History* (see n. 57), pp. 105–92 at p. 151. See also G. Morgan, 'Byzantine satirical song?' (see n. 42), 292–7, and H.-G. Beck, *Geschichte der byzantinischen Volksliteratur*, Byzantinisches Handbuch, II, 3 (Munich, 1971), p. 27.

[64] *Les régestes des actes du patriarcat de Constantinople*, I, 2, *Les régestes de 715 à 1043*, ed. V. Grumel (Socii assumptionistae chalcedonenses, 1936), no. 793, on the order of patriarch Polyeuktos against Theophano and against Nikephoros' 'anti-ecclesiastical' policy; *Theophanes Continuatus*, p. 458, 8 ff, is still positive about Theophano (his chronicle ends in 961): she is of well-born parents; Constantine VII Porphyrogennetos calls her 'rightly' Theophano, because 'divinely shining and elected'. Leo the Deacon, *Historiae* (see n. 33), V, 6, p. 85, 6 ff, knows more about her and tells for example about her secret relationship with John Tzimiskes and her participation in the murder of Nikephoros. Skylitzes hated her; in *Synopsis*, p. 240, 84 ff (about her marriage): she was not *ton apophanon*, but of low birth (Kedrenos, *Synopsis* (see n. 62), p. 329, 8, reads: *ton epiphanon*). On the date of her marriage with Romanos II see Tinnefeld, 'Braut aus Byzanz' (see n. 31), p. 251, n. 21: between 954 and 957, with a preference for 955. On her dismissal see Leo the Deacon, *Historiae*, VI, 4, p. 99, 6: to Proti; Skylitzes, *Synopsis*, p. 285, 35: to Prokonnesos; see R. Janin, *Les Eglises et les monastères des grands centres byzantins* (Paris, 1975), pp. 71 and 211. There is a portrait of Nikephoros and Theophano from *c.* 965 at Çavuşin in Cappadocia (not mentioned in *ODB*, p. 1479): Restle, *Wall Paintings* (see n. 42), III, pl. 328. During his campaign against the Arabs Nikephoros spent the winter of 964–5 in Cappadocia, see Leo the Deacon, *Historiae*, III, 11, p. 53, 22.

the name of her grandmother and died as abbess of Essen in 1056 at the age of about 45[65]), in Byzantium the name Theophano became more common in later times. A quick survey produces the following persons: Theophano Mouzalonissa, wife of the Russian prince Oleg/Michael (†1115), known from the Synodikon of Ljubeč; a Theophano 'doukissa Opsikiou', known from a seal;[66] a Theophano, wife of Michael Kakabas and mother of George, Theodore and Leo (1232); a Theophano, wife of George Gounaropoulos (1250);[67] the Armenian princess Theophano, younger sister of Michael IX (1294–1320) Palaiologos' wife Rita/Maria (on Rhodes this Theophano changed her name into Theodora, and she died on her way to Thessalonike in 1295, where she was due to marry to the *sebastokrator* Angelos Theodore); a Theophano, wife of the *paroikos* Kelliotes John at Stomion, Chalkidike (1300–20); and, finally, from Anatolikon, a Theophano, *paroikos* at Hierissos (1341).[68] A more systematic survey would probably produce even more Theophanos in later times.

Conclusion

A quick survey of marriage negotiations between Byzantium and the West shows that several marriages were planned from the times of Pippin (*c.* 765) onwards, but that the first marriage to be realized took place only in *c.* 901: Louis III married Anna, the illegitimate daughter of Leo VI.

In 968 Liutprand of Cremona asked for a porphyrogennete princess as a bride for Otto II. It was not until 972 that Theophano finally arrived in Italy and was crowned Ottonian empress. She was, however, not a porphyrogennete.

65 G. Wolf, 'Könige und Kaiser als leibliche Nachkommenschaft der Kaiserin Theophanu', in *Kaiserin Theophano*, ed. G. Wolf (see n. 31), pp. 180–211, at pp. 185–6.

66 A.V. Soloviev, 'Domination byzantine ou russe au Nord de la Mer Noire à l'époque des Comnènes?', *Akten des XI. Internationalen Byzantinistenkongresses München 1958*, ed. F. Dölger and H.-G. Beck (Munich, 1960), pp. 569–80, at pp. 570–1, 578.

67 *Acta et diplomata Graeca medii aevi*, ed. F. Miklosich and J. Müller (Vienna, 1871 and reprinted Aalen, 1968), IV, pp. 77, 200; see N. Henkelmann and A. Ludat, *Namenregister zu Miklosich-Müller, Acta et diplomata graeca medii aevi Vol. IV und V*, Glossar zur frühmittelalterlichen Geschichte im östlichen Europa, Beiheft 3 (Stuttgart, 1986), p. 60.

68 E. Trapp, *Prosopographisches Lexikon der Palaiologenzeit*, I, 1–8 Add. (Vienna, 1988), nos. 92028 and 92029 on p. 106; and I, 1 (Vienna, 1976), no. 881 on p. 84.

Only in the times of Basil II (976–1025) were porphyrogennete princesses given as brides abroad, the first being the daughter of the emperor Romanos II Lekapenos and his wife Theophano: Anna, who was married to Vladimir of Kiev in 989. The West had to wait until 1002, when a porphyrogennete bride, a daughter of Basil II (was it Zoe or Theodora?), arrived in Italy in order to be married to Otto III.

As for the name of Theophano (cf. also names like Anastaso and Georgo), Byzantine historiographical and hagiographical sources of the ninth and tenth centuries show that the name occurs in the first half of the ninth century. At the time of the Macedonian dynasty (867–1056), the name was more common at court and in high circles; this may reflect the fame of the Holy Theophano, first wife of the emperor Leo VI. Around the middle of the tenth century we know of four women bearing the name of Theophano.

As it is quite common in Byzantium for a girl to change her name when she is to be married, the Ottonian empress Theophano, who is not mentioned in the Byzantine sources, might not have had that name at birth.

7

A marriage too far? Maria Lekapena and Peter of Bulgaria*

JONATHAN SHEPARD

The marriage of Maria Lekapena to tsar Peter of Bulgaria in 927 may seem incongruous in a volume dedicated to Theophano. However the marriages of these two ladies have some bearing on one another, seeing that Maria's was virtually the only foreign marriage to have been contracted by a member of a ruling house in Byzantium before that of Theophano to Otto II, and the only such marriage to a non-'Frank' since the mid-eighth century.[1] It was therefore a departure from Byzantine diplomatic custom, and Byzantine statesmen were well aware that it might be cited as a precedent by other foreigners desirous of a marriage-tie with the imperial family. Constantine VII expressed apprehensions concerning the northern 'barbarians' in this respect. Writing in his *De administrando imperio c.* 950, he tried to equip his son and heir with counter-arguments in order to demonstrate to the 'Scythian' suitors that the Bulgarian marriage was a special case and highly reprehensible, 'an unworthy and unseemly innovation into the noble polity of the Romans'.[2] Byzantine expectations of the

* This represents the text of a paper only lightly retouched and with minimal annotation. No attempt is made to provide a full survey of tenth-century Byzantino-Bulgarian relations, or full bibliography. That it appears at all is due to the patience and persistence of Professor A. Davids and to the labours of Victoria van Aalst, who word-processed the text from my handwritten text with remarkable accuracy and insight. I am most grateful to them both.

1 W. Ohnsorge, 'Drei Deperdita der byzantinischen Kaiserkanzlei und die Frankenadressen im Zeremonienbuch des Konstantinos Porphyrogennetos', reprinted in Ohnsorge, *Abendland und Byzanz* (Darmstadt, 1958), pp. 227–54, at pp. 229–32; R. Macrides, 'Dynastic marriages and political kinship', in *Byzantine Diplomacy*, ed. J. Shepard and S. Franklin (Aldershot, 1992), pp. 263–80, at pp. 267–8.

2 Constantine VII Porphyrogennetos, *De administrando imperio*, ch. 13, 174–5 ed. G. Moravcsik and R.J.H. Jenkins, DOT 1 (Washington, DC, 1967), pp. 74–5.

wide-ranging repercussions of the Bulgarian marriage were not ill founded, judging by the case of Liutprand of Cremona. For he represents himself as invoking the marriage of Maria Lekapena to Peter in support of his request for a porphyrogennete bride for Otto II; 'My lord rules over Slav [princes] who are [themselves] more powerful than Peter', he supposedly told Byzantine officials during his mission to Constantinople in 968.[3] In fact, as the officials immediately pointed out to him, the precedent was spurious, seeing that Maria Lekapena was not the daughter of a *porphyrogennetos*, let alone a porphyrogennete herself; the match was therefore of lower status than the one which Otto was seeking for his son and could not be deemed a precedent. Even so, this reported exchange suggests that the Bulgarian marriage was a potential embarrassment for mid- and later tenth-century Byzantine statesmen. It left the way open for diverse western – 'Frankish' – potentates to claim higher status than Peter possessed, and thus the right to a bride 'born in the purple'. This could pose problems for a Byzantine imperial regime even though Constantine VII had expressly, in fact enthusiastically, exempted the Franks from his general strictures on matches between emperors or their children raised in the palace and foreign potentates or their offspring.[4]

The Bulgarian marriage was, then, quite well known to members of ruling elites among Byzantium's northern and western neighbours, and this alone might earn it a mention in a study of Theophano. But there are also some noteworthy analogies in the background to the two marriages. They were both contracted after a period of conflict. Three years of campaigning

[3] Liutprand of Cremona, *Legatio*, ch. 16, in *Opera*, ed. J. Becker, MGH SRG in us. schol. (Leipzig, 1915), p. 184; ed. and trans. B. Scott (Bristol, 1993), pp. 6, 34. My translation takes account of, but is not identical to, Scott's.

[4] Constantine VII, *De administrando imperio* (see n. 2), ch. 13, 116–22, pp. 70–3. Constantine had personal, dynastic, reasons for extolling the legitimacy of imperial marriage-ties with Frankish ruling houses, since the first wife of his son Romanos had been Bertha, daughter of Hugh of Arles, and about the time of compilation of the *De administrando imperio* Constantine was seeking for his newly bereaved son the hand of Hadwig, the daughter of Duke Henry of Bavaria: Ekkehard IV, *Casus sancti Galli*, MGH SS II, pp. 122–3; Ohnsorge, *Abendland und Byzanz* (see n. 1), p. 235 and n. 39; J. Shepard, 'Aspects of Byzantine attitudes and policy towards the West in the tenth and eleventh centuries', in *Byzantium and the West c. 850–c. 1200*, ed. J.D. Howard-Johnston (Amsterdam, 1988), pp. 67–118, at pp. 87–9. The latter démarche was wholly of Constantine's making, and this suggests that he was disposed to regard the Franks as worthy partners of imperial 'Romans'.

by Otto and his vassals in southern Italy preceded the negotiations leading to Theophano's marriage, and there are undeniable elements of emulation, even rivalry, in Otto's approach to the Greek emperors. For example, Otto's recourse to Byzantine models for the design, from 962 onwards, of seals portraying him *en buste* need not have been conceived as a deliberate, frontal challenge to Byzantine imperial authority, but it is most unlikely that prior permission was sought.[5] And in Liutprand he had an articulate proponent of the view that the Greek emperors had forfeited any right they might once have had to rule over Rome through their neglect and that they were 'Roman' emperors 'only in name'. The Saxons are upheld as the mirror-opposites of the Greeks: pious, brave and committed to defending the city of Rome from 'the yoke of. . .tyrants' and restoring 'full honour and power to the vicars of the Holy Apostles'.[6] The line advocated by Liutprand's *Legatio* essentially represents an attempt to justify his conduct of his embassy and to persuade his Saxon masters and their leading counsellors to press on with warfare against the Greeks. It does not constitute a carefully formulated and widely propagated self-portrayal of the Ottonian regime. Even so, Liutprand was expressing the actuality that another ruler with an arguable right to style himself 'emperor' had emerged in the Christian West, a partner of, if not a rival to, the Greek *basileus*.

Armed conflict had also preceded the marriage of Maria Lekapena to Peter of Bulgaria, and although the periods of active hostilities were probably briefer than is commonly supposed,[7] there had been tension between Peter's father, Symeon, and Byzantium for a generation. Rivalry and Symeon's pretensions to imperial status played a part in this. Whatever may have been the exact crowning ritual which patriarch Nicholas Mystikos performed on Symeon outside the walls of Constantinople in 913, it

[5] For Otto's seals from the time of his imperial coronation, see P. Schramm, *Die deutschen Kaiser und Könige in Bildern ihrer Zeit*, I (Leipzig and Berlin, 1928), p. 77; *ibid.*, II, *Tafeln*, 59 (b); W. Messerer, 'Zur byzantinischen Frage in der ottonischen Kunst', *BZ*, 52 (1959), 32–60, at pp. 41–2 and 44–5; Tafel IV, Abb. 15, Abb. 18 (second imperial seal-type of Otto).

[6] Liutprand, *Legatio* (see n. 3), chs. 5, 22, 54, ed. Becker, pp. 178, 187, 204; ed. and trans. Scott, pp. 2–3, 8–9, 20, 29, 36, 50. The views expressed in Liutprand's polemic were not necessarily identical to those of Otto. Cf. J. Sutherland, 'The mission to Constantinople in 968 and Liudprand of Cremona', *Traditio*, 31 (1975), 55–81, at pp. 80–1; K.J. Leyser, 'Ends and means in Liudprand of Cremona', in Howard-Johnston, *Byzantium and the West* (see n. 4), pp. 119–43, at p. 135.

[7] See J. Shepard, 'Bulgaria: the other Balkan "empire"', *New Cambridge Medieval History*, III, ed. T. Reuter (forthcoming).

clearly involved some act of legitimization or recognition of imperial status which Symeon prized and which the Byzantine government subsequently sought to disavow. It was probably from this time that he began to style himself *basileus*, 'emperor', on his lead seals.[8] And in the last years of his life Symeon began formally to style himself 'emperor of the Romans' or 'emperor of the Bulgarians and Romans'. He was ridiculed and rebuked by emperor Romanos Lekapenos for appropriating the latter title.[9] Hostilities between Byzantium and Bulgaria were not immediately terminated with the death of Symeon in May 927. The Bulgarians launched a major incursion into the theme of Macedonia. Then the Thracian towns which had been under Bulgarian occupation for several years were evacuated and razed to the ground. Thus acts of war continued up to within a few months of the contraction of the marriage between Peter and Maria.[10]

A comparison such as this at once shows up significant differences between the Saxon and the Bulgarian marriage pacts. The Bulgarian ruler's principal residence at Preslav lay only about 250 kilometres from Constantinople, and his boundaries marched with those of the Byzantine emperor for hundreds of kilometres, with inevitable uncertainties or disagreements over particular points in the borderlands. The Bulgarians were anyway, in imperial Byzantine eyes, ultimately intruders on what was rightfully their own, 'Roman', soil. Romanos I reminded Symeon as much in one of his letters to him.[11] Such disparagement of the legitimacy of the Bulgarian presence south of the Danube was mitigated, but not dispelled, by the notional status of the Bulgarian ruler as 'spiritual son' of the Byzantine *basileus*. This was held to be the consequence of khan Boris' acceptance of Christianity from Michael III in the mid-860s, and was formally expressed in diplomatic communications between the emperor and the khan, and in court receptions at Constantinople.[12] But

[8] *Theophanes Continuatus*, ed. I. Bekker (Bonn, 1838), p. 385; V. Beševliev, *Die protobulgarischen Inschriften* (Berlin, 1963), pp. 331–2, Abb. 152.

[9] Theodore Daphnopates, *Correspondance*, ed. J. Darrouzès and L. Westerink (Paris, 1978), pp. 58–9, 72–3.

[10] *Theophanes Continuatus* (see n. 8), p. 412; *Vita Mariae Junioris, Acta Sanctorum*, Novembr., IV, p. 702.

[11] Theodore Daphnopates, *Correspondance* (see n. 9), pp. 64–5.

[12] Constantine VII Porphyrogennetos, *De ceremoniis*, II, 47, ed. J.J. Reiske, vol. I (Bonn, 1829), pp. 681–2, 690; F. Dölger, 'Der Bulgarenherrscher als geistlicher Sohn des byzantinischen Kaisers', reprinted in Dölger, *Byzanz und die europäische Staatenwelt* (Darmstadt, 1976), pp. 183–96, at pp. 188–93.

neither emperor Romanos' aspersions nor the niceties of court ceremonial could alter the fact that orthodox Christian Bulgaria constituted a rival in the Balkans to Byzantium. This was the case in terms both of ideology – the claim of Symeon to be an 'emperor', which Peter presumably expected to inherit – and of military power. Symeon had proved capable of occupying significant portions of Byzantine Thrace, garrisoning and provisioning towns and colluding with the Slavs already living on Byzantine territory.

In contrast to the close proximity of Bulgaria and Byzantium to one another, the roots of Saxon kingly power lay far away and even Liutprand of Cremona's most strident injunctions in his *Legatio* fall short of calling for an invasion of the Byzantine Balkans. There were real disputes over territorial possessions and spheres of influence in Italy, but in the last analysis, central and southern Italy lay on the fringes of the realms of Byzantine and early Saxon rulers alike. The Saxons' incursions into the Byzantine-held south were of quite short duration and, it could be argued, were essentially a means to the end of extracting a Byzantine imperial bride for Otto I's son and heir.[13] Moreover, the marriage negotiations which were to culminate in Theophano's wedding to Otto II were clearly initiated by the Saxons. In contrast, the marriage of Maria Lekapena to Peter seems essentially to have been the development of a proposal made by emperor Romanos Lekapenos to Peter's father several years earlier – that there should be a marriage-tie between their two families.[14]

But it is at this point, when the contrasts between the backgrounds of the two marriages appear at their starkest, that certain similarities come back into view. For neither marriage actually involved a *porphyrogennetos*, a boy or girl born in the Purple Chamber to a reigning emperor. To that extent, each match represented a climb-down from the respective foreign ruler's original demand. Symeon of Bulgaria had rebuffed Romanos Lekapenos' proposal, his earlier desire for a marriage tie with Constantine Porphyrogennetos having been thwarted by Con-

[13] Cf. J. Gay, *L'Italie méridionale et l'empire byzantin (867–1071)* (Paris, 1904), pp. 304, 310–12, 315.

[14] Nicholas I, patriarch of Constantinople, *Letters*, ed. R. J. H. Jenkins and L. Westerink (Washington, DC, 1973), pp. 108–9; V. N. Zlatarski, *Istorija na părvoto bălgarsko carstvo*, I,2 (Sofia, 1927), pp. 416–19.

stantine's marriage to Helena Lekapena in 919. And in 967–8 Otto I had been quite specific in seeking a porphyrogennete 'the step-daughter of Nikephoros himself, namely a daughter of emperor Romanos'.[15] By implication, he was not at that time interested in a marriage to the kin of the dominant figure at Byzantium, Nikephoros II Phokas. Peter of Bulgaria was making do with what had earlier been rejected, in accepting Maria, the daughter of the eldest son of Romanos Lekapenos, while it is as good as certain that Theophano was not a porphyrogennete – in fact she was 'non virginem desideratam', according to Thietmar of Merseburg.[16] The two marriages had in common a background of military stalemate, in which the Byzantines looked set to endure renewed enemy pressure on their networks of bases, while remaining in a position to threaten offensives of their own from them – as in Italy in late 969, where they mounted a far-reaching counter-offensive, only to come to grief subsequently.[17] The two girls were, in that sense, the decorous means of translating the stalemate into a somewhat more positive condition of stability. To Liutprand, the purpose of the marriage agreement between Peter and Byzantium was clear: 'the girl's name was changed and she was called "Irene", "Peace", so that through her a most solid peace might be established between the Bulgarians and the Greeks'.[18] Liutprand wrote these words in the 960s when the peace had lasted some thirty-five years, and it is fair to speculate that he had the apparent success of this marriage treaty in mind when in 968 he travelled to Constantinople 'from love of peace',[19] albeit in

[15] *Continuator Reginonis Trevirensis*, s.a. 967, MGH SS I, p. 629.

[16] Thietmar of Merseburg, *Chronicon*, ed. R. Holtzmann, MGH SS n.s. IX (Berlin, 1935), p. 56. That Theophano was the daughter of Constantine Skleros and the niece of John Tzimiskes through Tzimiskes' marriage to her aunt Maria Skleraina was convincingly proposed by G. Wolf, 'Wer war Theophanu?', in von Euw and Schreiner, *Kaiserin Theophanu*, II, pp. 385–96, at pp. 385–6; cf. O. Kresten, 'Byzantinische Epilegomena zur Frage: Wer war Theophano?', in von Euw and Schreiner, *Kaiserin Theophanu*, II, pp. 403–10, at pp. 406–7; F. Tinnefeld, 'Die Braut aus Byzanz – Fragen zu Theophanos Umfeld und gesellschaftlicher Stellung vor ihrer abendländischen Heirat', in *Kaiserin Theophanu: Prinzessin aus der Fremde – des Westreichs Grosse Kaiserin*, ed. G. Wolf (Cologne, Weimar etc., 1991), pp. 247–61, at pp. 252–3.

[17] Gay, *L'Italie méridionale* (see n. 13), pp. 313–15.

[18] Liutprand, *Antapodosis*, III, 38, in *Opera*, ed. J. Becker, MGH SRG in us. schol. (Leipzig, 1915), p. 92; trans. F.A. Wright, *The Works of Liudprand of Cremona* (London, 1930), p. 128.

[19] Liutprand, *Legatio* (see n. 3), chs. 7, 57, ed. Becker, pp. 180, 206; ed. and trans. Scott, pp. 4, 21, 30, 52.

quest of a porphyrogennete rather than a mere relative of the dominant emperor.

After this sketch of the similarities – and contrasts – between the backgrounds to the two marriages, we shall focus on three main questions arising from Maria Lekapena's marriage. First, why is so much attention paid to it in Byzantine sources? Secondly, what qualities and skills (if any) did Maria bring to Bulgaria? Thirdly, is there any evidence that her presence in Bulgaria had any impact on Byzantino-Bulgarian relations or on Bulgaria itself?

That Maria's wedding received massive publicity at the time is clear, and in this respect it stands in sharp contrast with Theophano's match, which does not receive a word of mention in extant Byzantine sources. The obvious reason is that Maria's wedding was celebrated at Constantinople, in the church of the Mother of God at Pege, and the patriarch of Constantinople himself 'placed the wedding-crowns on their heads'.[20] Theophano's wedding to Otto II, in contrast, was celebrated in Rome, far beyond the compass of Byzantine narrative sources' normal interests. But this begs the question of why Constantinople should have been chosen as the venue: one might have expected the bride to have travelled to the land of her husband-to-be as Theophano did, and also, *c.* 988, Anna, the bride of Vladimir of Kiev.[21] One might perhaps cite practical grounds: the facts that the regent for Peter, George Soursouboullos, negotiated a peace agreement at Constantinople in person; and that there were still powerful persons in Bulgaria who wanted to carry on the war against Byzantium, and who might have tried to disrupt a wedding ceremony in the Bulgarian capital, Preslav. There is also the plain fact that the journey from Preslav to Constantinople was far less arduous than that from Italy or Kiev. But the route was as manageable for Maria as it was for Peter, and the foregoing considerations do not explain why the progress of the negotiations (which were, at least in their earlier stages, secret) and of the wedding festivities receives such full treatment in the principal narrative source, Symeon the Logo-

[20] *Theophanes Continuatus* (see n. 8), p. 414.

[21] Anna was probably wedded to Vladimir in Cherson: *Povest' vremennych let*, s.a. 988, ed. V.P. Adrianova-Peretc and D.S. Lichačev, I (Moscow and Leningrad, 1950), 77; *Russian Primary Chronicle*, trans. S.H. Cross and O.P. Sherbowitz-Wetzor (Cambridge, Mass., 1953), p. 113; J. Shepard, 'Some remarks on the sources for the conversion of Rus'', in *Le origini e lo sviluppo della cristianità slavo-bizantina*, Nuovi studi storici, 17 (Rome, 1992), pp. 59–95, at pp. 69, 95.

thete's chronicle, transmitted to us through such works as Theophanes Continuatus. This chronicle is on the whole not unsympathetic to the government of Romanos Lekapenos and draws on detailed information about the negotiations which can only have emanated from a 'source close to the emperor', maybe an official bulletin issued from the palace soon afterwards, or the Byzantines' chief negotiator, the *protovestiarios* Theophanes.[22] Theophanes' negotiating and martial skills are repeatedly praised in chronicle entries between 927 and 943. In other words, the chronicle at this point is probably relaying Lekapenan propaganda and it is depicting the marriage procedure with a degree of detail and explicit sympathy for the bride and her parents unique in Byzantine accounts of imperial marriages to foreigners. The chronicle purports to enter into the feelings of the principal Byzantine actors in the event:

> When [Maria] was about to depart, [her parents] gathered round their daughter and weeping many tears, as befitted the loss of their most dear heart, they embraced their son-in-law and entrusted her into his hands ... Maria, given over to Bulgarian hands, departed for Bulgaria, joyous yet also grieving: grieving at being bereft of her most dear parents and her palace-home and the company of the members of her family; but delighted at being united with an emperor for a husband and at being addressed as 'mistress' (*despoina*) of the Bulgarians.[23]

It seems to me that both the choice of Constantinople as the venue for the wedding and this discursive chronicle account are facets of a government decision to ensure maximum publicity and to present the marriage as a positive achievement, rather than as an unfortunate necessity. The chronicle points out that Maria's husband was himself an 'emperor', while Maria was to be known as 'mistress of the Bulgarians', presumably in accord with the

22 This section of Theophanes Continuatus (see n. 8) is characterized as being relatively 'reserved' towards Romanos by H. Hunger (*Die hochsprachliche profane Literatur der Byzantiner*, I (Berlin, 1978), p. 343). It is undeniable that, as Hunger indicates (p. 343, n. 73), Romanos' 'perjury' in mounting the senior throne is explicitly condemned (*Theophanes Continuatus*, pp. 400–1). Even so, an ostensibly neutral tone prevails and several passages relate the actions of Romanos or the qualities of his family in a favourable light, e.g., *ibid.*, pp. 406–9, 422, 429–30. Theophanes Continuatus' treatment of Romanos' reign is not, in reality, markedly less sympathetic than that of George Monachus Continuatus and other works deriving from the lost Chronicle of the Logothete.

23 *Theophanes Continuatus* (see n. 8), pp. 414–15.

peace treaty. In other words, this was to be seen as 'a good marriage', not only because it would bring about peace – symbolized by Maria's change of name to 'Irene' – but also because it involved a bridegroom who, although a foreigner, was of imperial status. And the chronicle's details suggest that an effort was made to make a public spectacle of the last stage of the negotiations and of the wedding.

Emperor Romanos greeted Peter at Blachernae, where fourteen years earlier (in 913) two sons of Symeon, one of them perhaps Peter himself, had been treated to a feast in the palace.[24] Peter and his entourage were not admitted inside the city walls, but 'all the senate' – in other words, the senior office-holders and other worthies of the City – went with the patriarch to the wedding church. The church was that of 'the most Holy Mother of God at Pege', a church which, according to the same chronicle, Symeon had 'burnt ... together with all the district round it, making plain from this that he did not want peace', three years earlier, in 924.[25] Presumably the venue was chosen at least partly for its symbolism: the Bulgarians were being reminded of the impiety of their late ruler, while emperor Romanos' ability to bring about unhoped-for peace was demonstrated to the Bulgarians and Byzantine dignitaries alike. Three days after the wedding Romanos 'gave a sumptuous feast on the wharf of Pegai, having decorated it with silken cloths, and with the imperial *dromon* moored to the wharf'.[26] This open-air spectacle on the water's edge would have been visible to onlookers from the other side of the Golden Horn and thus was accessible to far more ordinary Byzantines than a feast or ceremony inside the palace walls would have been. And again, the choice of locale may well

[24] *Ibid.*, p. 385; Zlatarski, *Istorija* (see n. 14), p. 367, and n. 3.

[25] *Theophanes Continuatus* (see n. 8), p. 406.

[26] *Ibid.*, p. 414. The church of the Mother of God at Pege, beyond the Theodosian walls, is emphatically distinguished from 'the wharf of Pegai' on the north side of the Golden Horn by R. Janin, *Constantinople byzantine* (Paris, 1950), pp. 142, 225, 413, 423; cf. Janin, *La Géographie ecclésiastique de l'empire byzantin*, I, 3, *Le Siège de Constantinople et le patriarchat œcuménique: les églises et les monastères* (Paris, 1969), pp. 224–5. This distinction requires that the celebrants should have travelled from the south side of the city to the north of the Golden Horn for the feast at Pegai, and the newly-weds are subsequently described as setting out for Bulgaria via the Hebdomon, to the south of the city (*Theophanes Continuatus* (see n. 8), p. 414). This might invite some attempt at emending the text, if one takes such toing and froing through or round the city to be implausible. However, this sort of activity would have been quite compatible with a desire on Romanos' part for maximum publicity for the wedding and the celebrations.

have been intended to evoke the meeting between Romanos and Symeon three years earlier: that, too, had been on the Golden Horn. We seem, here, to have an answer to the question why the wedding ceremony was staged at Constantinople and why the government of Romanos Lekapenos wished to draw attention to its achievement in making a pact with Bulgaria.

Concessions of a generous nature were made in the treaty accompanying the marriage – the formal recognition of Bulgaria's ruler as an emperor and, most probably, acceptance that the Bulgarian church should retain a patriarch at its head.[27] But with the marriage settlement and ceremonies, Romanos Lekapenos was able to demonstrate to the citizens of Constantinople that they would no longer have to fear Bulgarian raids and the devastation of the suburbs. The government could benefit from the gratitude of the populace at the sudden recession of the Bulgarian threat. That the Bulgarians were still able and willing to fight had been shown only a few months earlier, when they had devastated towns nearby in Thrace before withdrawing.

One other official celebration of the peace-treaty survives, the oration 'On the treaty of the Bulgarians', which was delivered in the presence of Romanos at some sort of ceremony in late 927. The orator hails him, 'the author of the triumphs we celebrate', 'our emperor and bulwark and champion and peacemaker',[28] and goes on, 'Who of those that know how fair a thing is peace will praise these things as they should be praised? Who will worthily extol our present blessings, the unhoped-for transformation, the unexpected change, the inexpressible alteration, this unbelievable union?'[29] The oration does not make any reference to the marriage beyond the ambiguous term 'union' (*enoteta*),[30] possibly

[27] The terms have to be inferred from subsequent Byzantine diplomatic usage; Liutprand's statement that through the 'written agreement' the Bulgarian envoys were given precedence over all other diplomatic visitors to Constantinople and other circumstantial evidence: Liutprand, *Legatio* (see n. 3), ch. 19, ed. Becker, pp. 185–6; ed. and trans. Scott, pp. 7, 35; Constantine VII, *De ceremoniis* (see n. 12), II, 48, p. 690; G. Bakalov, 'Carskata promulgacija na Petăr i negovite priemnici', *Istoričeski Pregled*, 39 (1983), no. 6, pp. 35–44, at pp. 36–7; Bakalov, *Sredno-vekovnijat bălgarski vladetel (titulatura i insignii)* (Sofia, 1985), pp. 119–20; J. Fine, *The Early Medieval Balkans* (Ann Arbor, 1991), p. 161; Shepard, 'Bulgaria' (see n. 7).

[28] I. Dujčev, 'On the Treaty of 927 with the Bulgarians', *DOP*, 32 (1978), 217–95, at pp. 258–9, 266–7.

[29] *Ibid.*, pp. 266–7.

[30] *Ibid.*, pp. 266–7. 'Concord' (*homonoia*) is a commoner motif: *ibid.*, pp. 278–9, 280–1, 286–7.

because this might have been a distraction from the theme of emperor Romanos as the instrument of divine Providence, a new 'Jonah' and a new 'Moses'. And it was, of course, proclaiming what the listening emperor wanted to hear.

But a similar sense of relief is expressed in a private document *not* intended for wide circulation, a short letter of Arethas of Caesarea addressed to Romanos and accompanying a gift of top-quality incense inside a container of silver and gold alloy. Arethas, too, is writing to please, but one may accept at face value his thanks to God at 'the great accomplishment of the world peace now being brought about, which none of mankind hoped for'.[31] No less suggestive is Arethas' explanation of the meaning of the gift of incense: it is in supplication that

> the world peace settlement now established may bring forth a sweet savour to God and to mankind and that through the giving out as an indissoluble bond of peace of the noble offshoot from the imperial loins in a marriage producing fair and numerous children, matters may progress to the point where not only the rule and empire ... of the Romans may be adorned through your autocratic splendour, but even the barbarian nations may be domesticated through the grafting on of your kindred, and may be refashioned and transformed to the virtuous life of human kind.[32]

The incense thus celebrates the achievement of what had seemed impossible, and expresses a prayer for the future.

This fairly perfunctory letter accompanying a gift suggests that the government's celebrations of the treaty and the marriage fell on receptive ears – not only the citizens of Constantinople and the inhabitants of the European provinces raided or overrun by the Bulgarians, but also those in Asia Minor whom the Byzantine army would henceforth be able to protect without being sidetracked by the Bulgarian peril. 'Only the sons of Hagar [i.e. the Saracens] mourn and shall mourn ... at the mere echo of our concord!', exclaims the court orator delivering his speech on the treaty.[33] And this alone could explain the conspicuous celebrating of the treaty and the marriage in Constantinople, before the eyes of a truly grateful populace.

But I think a further consideration underlay Romanos Lekape-

[31] Arethas, *Scripta minora*, ed. L. G. Westerink, I (Leipzig, 1968), p. 265.
[32] *Ibid.*, I, pp. 265–6.
[33] Dujčev, 'Treaty of 927' (see n. 28), pp. 280–1.

nos' stage-management, one which Arethas' high-flown words about 'barbarian nations' would not lead us to suspect: an internal political manœuvre, serving to raise his son Christopher to be his senior co-emperor, and next in line for the throne, demoting Constantine Porphyrogennetos from that position. It is well known that Romanos tried through the 920s to lever aside the purple-born Constantine, and already in 921 he had Christopher, his eldest son, crowned a co-emperor. He had Christopher portrayed beside himself, and to the exclusion of Constantine, on the commonest class of gold coins during the 920s, while the order of emperors on one class of his silver coins – handled and seen by more citizens than was the gold – was Romanos, Christopher, Constantine.[34] But the generally accepted sequence remained: Romanos, Constantine, Christopher. It is expressed in an inscription commemorating the repair of the walls of Cavalla in northern Greece, in 925–6. This names Constantine before Christopher in its list of 'the five felicitous emperors' of the day.[35] It seems in fact to have been the marriage celebrations of 927 which provided an opportunity for the setting of Christopher ahead of Constantine. We are told by the chronicle recounting the celebrations that at the open-air feast on the wharf of the Golden Horn 'the Bulgarians vehemently insisted that Christopher should be acclaimed first, and then Constantine; the emperor acceded to their request, and what they had asked for was carried out'.[36] In other words, Christopher received ritual acclamations for long life and greetings before Constantine did. It is difficult to believe that the Bulgarians' 'insistence' was wholly spontaneous. It suited their self-regard and self-interest that Peter's father-in-law should be next in line to Romanos, but the timing and the location in full view of the populace (albeit out of ear-shot) seem too finely-tuned to Lekapenan interests to be wholly the product of Bulgarian

[34] Class VII of the gold *nomismata* of Constantine VII (*sic*), showing only Romanos and Christopher, has been described as 'exceedingly common': P. Grierson, *Catalogue of the Byzantine Coins in the Dumbarton Oaks Collection* , III.2, *Leo III to Nicephorus III* (Washington, DC, 1973), p. 534; cf. pp. 529–30, 532; pl. XXXVI: 7.3, 7.4, 7.13 (photos). The class of silver coins mentioned above in the text – class II – may have been issued at the same time as class III, whose inscription names Constantine *before* Christopher: *ibid.*, p. 536; pl. XXXVII: 17.2, 17.3, 18.3, 18.6.

[35] S. Reinach, 'La Reconstruction des murs de Cavalla', *Bulletin de Correspondance Hellénique*, 6 (1882), 267–75, at pp. 268–9. Christopher is named after his brother Stephen as well as after Constantine here, on account of 'the necessities of the metre' (p. 273).

[36] *Theophanes Continuatus* (see n. 8), p. 414.

caprice. Here too, I suggest, is the deft hand of Lekapenan 'public relations', seeking to further Christopher's claim to succeed his father as senior emperor.[37]

If this is so, the marriage, and the publicity which seems to have blazoned forth the marriage, can be seen in a new perspective: as the bonding of two families, neither possessing incontrovertible imperial lineage, and each gaining in status from the fact of the marriage. Each had a stake in the status of the other, the Lekapenoi being far more recent arrivals at the top than was the family of Peter, and this may well underlie the 'official' account's emphasis that Maria 'was delighted at being united with an emperor for a husband', as well as its detailed list of the negotiators on the Bulgarian side, including a monk, bearing a (Bulgarian) golden bull.[38] They are treated almost as if they are culturally comparable with the Byzantines, rather than being members of the 'barbarian nations' of Arethas' letter! This seems to be a case of a foreign marriage contrived for domestic or, more exactly, dynastic political advantage as well as for diplomatic gain. This may be why the wedding receives such fulsome attention in the chronicle. In contrast, those few other foreign marriages that were contracted in the tenth century were mostly either covered up deliberately as being shameful, or passed over in silence as part of the unremarkable stock-in-trade of dealings with reputable but remote foreign rulers. Such dynastic calculations could well also have provoked the denunciation of the Bulgarian marriage as an 'unworthy and unseemly innovation' on the part of Constantine VII Porphy-

[37] The same suspicions were harboured – or relayed from earlier sources – by John Zonaras, *Epitome historiarum*, ed. T. Büttner-Wobst, III (Bonn, 1897), p. 474. But Zonaras' claim that the two younger sons of Romanos were also acclaimed before Constantine is inherently implausible, lacking even circumstantial evidence in corroboration. Cf. Niketas Magistros, *Lettres d'un exilé (928–946)*, ed. and trans. L.G. Westerink (Paris, 1973), p. 30. Christopher's seniority to Constantine was still not clear-cut even after 927. But that it was being advocated is shown by a rare class of *nomisma* (class VIII): its legend names Constantine before Christopher, but Constantine is depicted as beardless and slightly smaller than Christopher, who stands to his father's right (the senior position): Grierson, *Catalogue of the Byzantine Coins* (see n. 34), p. 534; pl. XXXVI: 8.1, 8.2. This class, which has been dated to '*c.* 930', seems to have restored Constantine to the *nomisma*'s design the better to display his inferior status. According to hearsay relayed by Liutprand, Christopher walked ahead of Constantine in public processions but 'soon afterwards' (*post modicum*) died. This would be compatible with a change in the order of processing after the Bulgarian marriage in October 927: *Antapodosis* (see n. 18), III, 37, ed. Becker, p. 91; trans. Wright, p. 128; cf. Bakalov, 'Carskata promulgacija' (see n. 27), p. 37.

[38] *Theophanes Continuatus* (see n. 8), pp. 412–13, 414.

rogennetos. It would not be surprising if Constantine reacted adversely to a political manœuvre-cum-theatre, which attached Bulgarian sympathies to Christopher Lekapenos and ultimately to his male offspring. Constantine, who had been born in the purple and bred in the palace, was in 927 well on the way to being 'sidelined', while Christopher's prospects of succession were markedly enhanced.

This goes some way towards explaining Constantine's antipathy towards Bulgarians in general as being 'always in one way or another opinionated and boastful', in the words of the biography of his grandfather for which he took some credit.[39] It also adds pungency to the vitriol in Constantine's formula for explaining away the Bulgarian marriage to foreign suitors of the future: 'the lord Romanos . . . was a common, illiterate fellow and not from among those who have been brought up in the palace and have followed from the start Roman manners; nor was he of imperial and noble stock, and for this reason he was too arrogant and arbitrary in most of his actions'.[40] This was the reason for Romanos' stepping out of line and marrying the relative of a reigning emperor to a foreign ruler; he was acting thus, Constantine repeats, 'out of a temper, arrogant and self-willed and untaught in virtue'.[41] Constantine's venting of personal spleen is accompanied by a categorical, and significant, assertion: that at the time of the wedding Christopher was 'the third and most junior [emperor], who was still subordinate and had no share in matters of government'.[42] The lattermost assertion jars with a contemporary, if partisan, source, the three poems occasioned by Christopher's death which will be discussed below. The insistence on Christopher's tertiary status at the time of his daughter's wedding represents Constantine's denial of the implications of the ceremonies and acclamations of October 927.

Constantine's aspersions about Romanos bring us to the second main question arising from the marriage: what qualities and attainments did Maria bring to her new country? With a grandfather such as Romanos Lekapenos 'untaught in virtue', how could she live up to Arethas' pious hope that she might 'trans-

[39] *Ibid.*, p. 229. 'The God-hated people of the Bulgarians' feature in another work associated with Constantine, the *De thematibus*, ed. A. Pertusi, Studi e testi, 160 (Rome, 1952), p. 84. The tone of these works was probably set by Constantine, even if his claims to direct authorship are debatable.

[40] Constantine VII, *De administrando imperio* (see n. 2), ch. 13, 149–53, pp. 72–3.

[41] *Ibid.*, ch. 13, 155–6, pp. 72–3. [42] *Ibid.*, ch. 13, 163–4, pp. 74–5.

form' her new people 'to the virtuous life of human kind'? How well qualified was she for this *mission civilisatrice*? The answer, unfortunately, is that we have no direct evidence about Maria's life in Byzantium, personality or degree of education. Nor do we know much about her conduct in Bulgaria, although we learn from a Byzantine chronicle that she took with her in 927 'all kinds of wealth and innumerable household goods (*aposkeuen*)'.[43] Theophanes Continuatus also tells us that she 'often' paid visits to her parents and grandfather back in Constantinople in the early years of her marriage, returning one last time after her father's death and bringing her three children to see their great-grandfather, Romanos.[44] Presumably the 'household goods' would have contained precious silks, *de luxe* ornaments, tableware and furnishing, and here we may have a real point of comparison with the goods which Theophano is supposed to have brought in profusion to the West. As with Theophano, so with Maria, some historians have been inclined to credit her with a degree of political influence which she supposedly exercised on behalf of the Byzantine government. Thus the Bulgarian historian V.N. Zlatarski views her as briefing her father and grandfather about Bulgarian current affairs during her frequent visits to Constantinople, acting virtually as a Byzantine 'agent'![45]

The shortcoming of such speculation is that it fails to take into account Maria's age at the time of her wedding. We do not know the date of Maria's birth, but there is enough circumstantial evidence to permit tentative conclusions as to the age at which she was married. One clue arises from the fact that Maria's father, Christopher, died suddenly four years after her marriage, and is lamented in three poems by an unknown author, writing just after his death.[46] The poet clearly regards Christopher's death as untimely although he regards him as a mature man, accomplished in matters of law and war, rather than being a mere youth. Indeed, the verses relay keenly the blow which Christopher's death dealt to the Lekapenan regime, upsetting all the calculations which had underlain the marriage celebrations: 'he revitalized the old age of his father, flourishing in his turn in majesty, and he nourished [it] with hopes of [his] succession to the throne'.[47] More

[43] *Theophanes Continuatus* (see n. 8), p. 415. [44] *Ibid.*, p. 422.
[45] Zlatarski, *Istorija* (see n. 14), pp. 535–6.
[46] L. Sternbach, 'Christophorea', *Eos*, 5 (1899), 7–21, at pp. 15–19.
[47] *Ibid.*, p. 17.5–6.

pertinently for our purposes, the poet makes clear that Christopher had left a young family: in one poem Christopher himself asks his friends to protect 'my dearest children with their mother' while making Theophanes (the chief negotiator in the talks with the Bulgarians) 'guardian of the family'. This suggests strongly that the children were juveniles and it corresponds with a statement in the Byzantine chronicle that 'his sons were still infants (*nepioi*)' at the time of Christopher's death. The name of only one other surviving child besides Maria herself is known, that of Michael, but others may well have gone unrecorded.[48] Christopher seems to have been married by 912 and in 922 his wife, Sofia, was old enough to be made *augusta*, that is, to take on the formal duties of consort to Romanos Lekapenos, after he lost his wife that year. Sofia must by then have been a mature adult and would have been capable of bearing children for some years before that. Even so, there is no positive evidence indicating that Maria was at the time of her marriage much older than the minimum age for betrothals – twelve years.[49] She was then of, or approaching, child-bearing age, judging by the fact that she had three children to show to Romanos Lekapenos around 932: they must have been born in rapid succession after her marriage. An age of, say, fifteen for Maria in 927 would be consonant with this and with the fact that her siblings – presumably all junior to her – were still in need of a guardian in 931. It would also accord with the poignant tone of the chronicle's description of Maria's parting from her parents, who wept over 'their most dear heart'. Likewise with Maria's frequent visits home to her parents: may not these be symptoms of the home-sickness of an adolescent, rather than an 'agent' reporting back to base?

I suggest, then, that Maria arrived in Bulgaria at too tender an age to be able actively to 'domesticate' 'the barbarian nations' (in Arethas' words),[50] or to play a significant political or diplomatic role. But we should not accept at face value Constantine VII's portrait of the marriage, in which the grandfather Romanos is a

[48] *Ibid.*, p. 15.13, 16; *Theophanes Continuatus* (see n. 8), p. 420; Niketas Magistros, *Lettres* (see n. 37), ed. Darrouzès, p. 29.

[49] Betrothals or marriages could, however, be arranged below this age (at eight or ten years), if the emperor was acting 'out of necessity', according to a mid-twelfth-century jurist: scholion to B.2.3,162, *Ecloga Basilicorum*, ed. L. Burgmann, Forschungen zur byzantinischen Rechtsgeschichte, 15 (Frankfurt am Main, 1988), p. 147; cf. Macrides, 'Dynastic Marriages' (see n. 1), p. 275.

[50] Arethas, *Scripta minora* (see n. 31), I, p. 266.

'common, illiterate' outsider, ignorant of 'Roman manners', a thrust, perhaps, at Romanos' Armenian origins. This would tend to imply that his granddaughter, too, was ignoble and ill bred, and in no position to 'civilize' the Bulgarians. But in fact Maria's mother was *augusta* from 922 onwards. So the girl had the opportunity to learn something of court ceremonial and 'Roman manners', while the Byzantine chronicle makes clear that she had, up to the time of her marriage, been living in the palace – 'her palace-home'.[51] Moreover, we have a hint from the anonymous poems lamenting her father's death that she was old enough to have received some education. One of the poems praises him for his love of his children, a role-model (*typos*) for both boys and girls, while another poem speaks of Christopher's 'burning desire for every work of writing; you draw upon them unstintingly for godly instruction of children' – presumably Christopher's own children.[52] The poet does not specify whether the girls received this education as well as the boys, and of course, this could be merely a eulogistic reference to conventional Bible-reading and fundamental Christian beliefs. But, taken together, the three poems paint a believable portrait of a man of calibre who had high expectations of inheriting the throne from his aging father, and who had a reputation for 'wisdom' among 'the lovers of wisdom', particularly in matters of law, both secular and canon law.[53]

A similar interest in law, learning and piety is to be found in another emperor intent on establishing his regime securely and on gaining legitimacy, Alexios Komnenos; and there is evidence that a thorough religious education was given to Alexios' daughter, Anna Komnene. If we can take Anna as any kind of yardstick, a princess might already by the age of thirteen be well read in the Scriptures.[54] In other words, Maria Lekapena may have had a

[51] *Theophanes Continuatus* (see n. 8), p. 415. One of the anonymous poems indicates that Maria's father had himself been raised in Constantinople: Sternbach, 'Christophorea' (see n. 46), p. 16.27.

[52] *Ibid.*, p. 18.26, p. 16.11–12. [53] *Ibid.*, p. 16.29–31.

[54] Anna is one of a number of educated women of the late eleventh- and twelfth-century Komnenan court who stand in contrast to their immediate predecessors: A.P. Kazhdan and A. Wharton Epstein, *Change in Byzantine Culture in the Eleventh and Twelfth Centuries* (Berkeley, 1985), p. 101. According to the funeral oration for Anna, her parents encouraged their children to study the Scriptures, but strongly disapproved of the exposure of maidens to classical literature: J. Darrouzès, *Georges et Dèmètrios Tornikès: lettres et discours* (Paris, 1970), pp. 242–7, 263, n. 47. On the possibility that Theophano received some elemen-

thorough religious, if not secular, education by the time she married Peter of Bulgaria.

It is likely, then, that Maria arrived in Bulgaria at too early an age actively to play the 'civilizing' role assigned to her by Arethas. Anyway, much of her time in the first years of marriage seems to have been spent on child-bearing, or trips home to Constantinople. Yet she seems to have received a godly, perhaps bookish, upbringing. Admittedly, we are here in the realm of speculation, and to attempt a full answer to our third main question – her impact on Byzantino-Bulgarian relations and on Bulgaria itself – would involve even more speculation. The evidence is sparse and ambivalent and the question itself is misleading, if it encourages us to follow the line of thought of Arethas and most other Byzantines' references to the Bulgarians as a barbarous, upstart people, in need of being 'transformed to the virtuous life of human kind'. They were 'a Scythian people, poor and unclean', ruled by 'a prince clad in leather skins' in words put into the mouth of Nikephoros Phokas by Leo the Deacon. Nikephoros is represented as addressing the envoys of Peter of Bulgaria thus.[55] Nikephoros' words, if taken at face value, would suggest that Maria's *mission civilisatrice* had been a total failure, whether in 'transforming' Byzantine court attitudes towards the Bulgarians, or her husband's sartorial habits.

But the very circumstances in which these words are supposed to have been uttered should make us hesitate to accept them unreservedly. Nikephoros is depicted as railing at the request of Peter's envoys for tribute – tribute which had been paid regularly, apparently, ever since the marriage treaty of 927.[56] And the rituals staged at the Byzantines' eventual victory celebrations over the

tary, if not secondary, education at Byzantium, see Tinnefeld, 'Braut aus Byzanz' (see n. 16), p. 256.

[55] Leo the Deacon, *Historia*, ed. C.B. Hase (Bonn, 1828), pp. 61–2.

[56] S. Ivanov ('Vizantijsko-bolgarskie otnošenija v 966–969 gg.', *Vizantijskij Vremennik*, 42 (1981), 88–100) has argued strongly for a reconstruction of events which relies more heavily on the accounts of John Skylitzes (*Synopsis Historion*, ed. I. Thurn (New York and Berlin, 1973), pp. 276–7) and John Zonaras (*Epitomae Historiarum* (see n. 37), p. 513) than on Leo the Deacon. Nikephoros' speech could well represent the artifice of Leo the Deacon or contemporary propaganda on behalf of Nikephoros, portraying him as responding to outrageous demands for tribute: Ivanov, 'Vizantijsko-bolgarskie otnošenija', p. 99. But Ivanov does not deny that tribute payments continued well into the 960s, and if the speech was propaganda, it played on existing Byzantine preconceptions of the Bulgarians as insolent yokels.

Bulgarians in 971 suggest that the Bulgarian state was regarded with a degree of respect, albeit without enthusiasm. It therefore needed to be dissolved in as solemn and conclusive manner as possible. According to Skylitzes, the son and heir of Peter and Maria, Boris, was ordered 'before the eyes of the citizens' of Constantinople to disrobe, setting aside his crowns and red boots; then 'the Bulgarian crown' of gold was deposited in Hagia Sophia in thanksgiving. Earlier, the emperor, John Tzimiskes, had forborne from riding in a triumphal wagon through the city streets. Instead the wagon's seat was occupied by an icon of the Mother and Child 'which he had taken from Moesia' (Leo the Deacon's classicizing name for Bulgaria); and beneath this prominently positioned icon were laid Bulgarian purple vestments and imperial crowns (*stemmata*).[57] These measures suggest an elaborate attempt to deny the legitimacy of the Bulgarian state, and to demonstrate that the Mother of God had consented that her icon should be transferred from Bulgaria to Constantinople. This seems to be more than just a show of exultation over winning the war, or ridicule at the Bulgarians' pretensions. In other words, Byzantium took the political culture of mid-tenth century Bulgaria more seriously than the reported jibes about a 'prince clad in leather skins' might lead one to suppose. Besides, Boris could claim to be the great-grandson of a senior *basileus* of the Romans, whereas Tzimiskes had mounted the throne just two years earlier.

Ideally, one should pause at this point to explore the level of general culture, literacy, Christianity and order in tenth-century Bulgaria, and also to gauge how far it had developed its own, Slavic, corpus of writings and how far it was still dependent on fresh infusions of Byzantine manuscripts, churchmen and craftsmen. Against this background, we might begin to delineate the

[57] Skylitzes, *Synopsis Historion* (see n. 56), p. 310; Leo the Deacon, *Historia* (see n. 55), p. 158. The proceedings were influenced by the triumph over Abul Asa'ir, celebrated in 956: M. McCormick, *Eternal Victory* (Cambridge, 1990), pp. 171, 173–4. The latter function did not, however, involve a ritual disrobing. The divergences between Skylitzes' and Leo the Deacon's accounts as to the sequence and location of the disrobing are discussed by G. Prinzing, who emphasizes that two different crowns were publicly displayed during the triumph. He connects these with the two crowns which the Bamberg *Gunthertuch* depicts as being presented to a victorious emperor: this large silk may well commemorate Tzimiskes' triumph of 971 rather than that of Basil II over the Bulgarians in 1018 (as is generally supposed): 'Das Bamberger Gunthertuch in neuer Sicht', in *Byzantium and its Neighbours from the mid-Ninth till the Twelfth Centuries*, ed. V. Vavřínek (*Byzantinoslavica*, 54 (1993)), pp. 218–31, at pp. 225–31.

figure of Maria Lekapena, noting, for example, that Greek seems to have been spoken and understood among the Bulgarian ruling elite. This is suggested by finds of graffiti in Greek and perhaps also by some bilingual inscriptions in Slavic and Greek.[58] Therefore Maria would not necessarily have been a wholly isolated figure, even if Greek remained the sole language which she spoke. The question of Maria's role is, in fact, many-layered. On the one hand, one might argue, the tenth-century Bulgarian elite had nothing to learn from the court at Constantinople. It possessed its own 'insignia of empire', credible enough to be paraded in the Byzantine victory celebration in 971, and there is no need to suppose that these were introduced to Bulgaria by Maria or as a result of her presence in Bulgaria. Already in the 920s, Peter's father Symeon was depicted on his seals in the costume of a Byzantine emperor, wearing a *loros* wrapped over his *divitision* and holding an orb and sceptre.[59] In 924 Symeon had received acclamations from his warriors 'in the language of the Romans' (i.e Greek), and this was not a ceremony concocted specially for the watching citizens of Constantinople. Snatches of Byzantine court acclamations are to be found not only on Symeon's seals but also in the Greek-language inscriptions of pagan, ninth-century rulers.[60] And their significance was presumably not lost on the Bulgarians who 'insisted that Christopher should be acclaimed first' at Maria's wedding feast on the Golden Horn.

But in such a situation, one could object, members of the Bulgarian ruling elite, based in their capital of Preslav all the year round, might well still think they had something to learn from Byzantine ceremonial. Maria, who had lived in the imperial palace for some years before her marriage, could have been prized as an authority on the etiquette and other 'Roman manners'

[58] I. Gošev, *Starobălgarski glagoličeski i kirilski nadpisi* (Sofia, 1961), pp. 68–9; T. Totev, 'Les monastères de Pliska et de Preslav aux IX–X siècles', *Byzantinoslavica*, 48 (1987), 185–200, at pp. 189–90; Totev, 'Epigrafski svidetelstva za starobălgarskata pismenost', *Palaeobulgarica*, 12 (1988), no. 2, pp. 83–92, at pp. 91–2; P. Schreiner, 'Die Byzantinisierung der bulgarischen Kultur', in *Kulturelle Traditionen in Bulgarien*, Abhandlungen der Akademie der Wissenschaften in Göttingen, phil.-hist. Klasse, 3. Folge, 177 (Göttingen, 1989), pp. 47–60, at pp. 57–8.

[59] Beševliev, *Inschriften* (see n. 8), pp. 330–1, Abb. 151.

[60] *Theophanes Continuatus* (see n. 8), p. 407; Beševliev, *Inschriften* (see n. 8), pp. 80–1, 247, 261, 277, 330–2; Beševliev, 'Das byzantinische in den protobulgarischen Inschriften', *Byzantiaka*, 7 (1987), 55–63, at pp. 58–61; Schreiner, 'Byzantinisierung' (see n. 59), pp. 57–8.

3. Lead seal of Peter of Bulgaria and Maria Lekapena. Both are named in the legend; hands grasp cross at equal level.

which were the hallmark of those raised in the palace (according to Constantine Porphyrogennetos). And the 'wealth and innumerable household goods' which she brought with her to Bulgaria may well have been admired by, and were perhaps partially distributed to, ladies-in-waiting. Although Maria's own visits to Constantinople apparently ceased after *c.* 932, she presumably remained in contact with relatives at court. Her aunt Helena, the wife of Constantine VII Porphyrogennetos, lived until 961. In other words, Maria, even if not politically active or any kind of 'agent' for the Byzantine government, could have had a role as a kind of 'jewel in the crown' of the palace culture at Preslav, where new residences of senior office-holders and nobles were being built, as well as new churches and monasteries.[61]

Even if we had fuller evidence about Maria's role in her new country, it would probably still be ambivalent. Much would depend on whether one was talking about her role in the 'political culture' of the elite or about the effect or lack of effect of her

[61] N. Mavrodinov, *Starobălgarskoto izkustvo* (Sofia, 1959), pp. 184–97; D. Ovcharov, 'Emergence et développement de la ville de Preslav IX–X siècles', *Bulgarian Historical Review* (1979), no. 2, pp. 51–61, at pp. 59–60. As Totev ('Monastères de Pliska' (see n. 58), pp. 191–2) acknowledges, differentiation between the buildings of Symeon's and of Peter's eras is not always feasible. Even so, the evidence of rebuilding and extension work at some monastic sites and in the palace complex together with finds of seals of Constantine VII suggests that, at the very least, cultural and spiritual vitality persisted through the mid-tenth century; cf. Totev, 'Monastères de Pliska', pp. 193–9.

4. Lead seal of Peter of Bulgaria and Maria Lekapena. Only 'Peter, pious emperor' is named in the legend; his hand is below Maria's.

residence in Preslav on the peasant masses, further afield. What is clear is that Maria's presence in Bulgaria was advertised to the recipients of Peter's messages, on his lead seals. On all but two of the known examples of them, Maria is shown side by side with Peter, *en buste*. On one type of the seals, the legend on the reverse has been read by Bulgarian sigillographers as 'Πέτρος [καὶ] Μαρ[ία] ἐν Χ[ριστ]ῷ αὔ[τοκράτορες] Β[ουλγάρων]'[62] (Fig. 3). This reading is possible, but on the evidence of the transcript made of the legend on two examples of the seals, there is reason to prefer the reading 'Πέτρος [καὶ] Μαρ[ία] ἐν Χ[ριστ]ῷ αὔ[γουστοι] β[ασιλεῖς]'.[63] In either case, the legend is clearly indicating that Maria possessed the same title as Peter and that they jointly exercised authority over the Bulgarians. So the epithet 'mistress of the Bulgarians' may not be an empty title dreamed up by a chronicler

[62] T. Gerasimov, 'Bălgarski i vizantijski pečati ot Preslav', in *Preslav*, II (Sofia, 1976), pp. 129–41, at pp. 129–30 and tablica I: 3–6, p. 127; K. Totev, 'Novopostăpil pečat na car Petăr ot Preslav', *Numizmatika* (1984), no. 3, 28–31, at p. 30, obr. 1, p. 29 (photo).

[63] T. Gerasimov reads the final letters of the legend on one example as 'AYG' and on another as 'AYb' ('Bălgarski i vizantijski pečati' (see n. 62), p. 129). 'AYG' for *Augustus* or Αὔγουστος occurs 'in some form or another. . .on much of the gold coinage. . .from the reign of Basil I to that of Nicephorus', Grierson, *Catalogue of the Byzantine Coins* (see n. 34), III.1, p. 177. A reading of αὔγουστοι βασιλεῖς on this type of Peter's seals would not in itself invalidate the view of Gerasimov and other Bulgarian scholars that the type was issued after 945, in imitation of seals and coins of Constantine VII. The chronology of Peter's seals cannot be discussed in detail here, but it is noteworthy that αὔγουστοι appears on a common class of *nomismata* of Constantine VII and Romanos II: Grierson, *Catalogue of the Byzantine Coins* (see n. 34), III.2, pp. 552–3.

or propagandist sympathetic to Romanos Lekapenos. It may have been a term actually used, in 927 and subsequently, to denote Maria's position. Admittedly, the Greek legend's pronouncement of the parity, or near parity, of status of Maria with Peter would not have been comprehensible to the vast majority of Bulgarians. But the depiction of Maria besides, and on the same level as, Peter, flanking a cross, would have been a clear declaration of their comparable status. On earlier Bulgarian seals, the ruler is always shown alone.

A second type of Peter's seals bears a different legend, 'Πέτρος βασι[λεὺς] εὐσ[εβ]ής'[64] (Fig. 4). The iconography is, however, very similar to that of the type already mentioned. On the face is a bust of Christ, while the reverse is occupied by busts of Peter and Maria flanking a two-barred 'patriarchal' cross, as on the other type. The legend on this type obviously makes no mention of Maria, focusing instead on the piety of Peter. Εὐσεβής was a not uncommon epithet on Byzantine imperial coins, but it probably also reflected the personal predilections of Peter, who was a persistent devotee of holy men and vigilant against heresy. But while the legend singled out this trait of Peter alone, the image on the reverse conveyed the same visual message as that on the first-mentioned type of seal: that Maria and Peter were exercising authority jointly. This would have been evident to the untutored eye from the fact that their two figures are of the same size, and each clasps the staff of the cross with one hand. No less obvious would have been the splendour of their vestments and regalia. Maria's robes are particularly ornate, her main garment being studded with jewels.

The discerning Bulgarian or Byzantine viewer would have found the finer points of the symbolism comprehensible, although he (or she) would have noted certain ambiguities, and also minor variations, in the design. First, and most important of all, the iconography and palaeography – a mixture of Greek and occasional Latin letters – would have been entirely familiar. So, too, with the design, a bust of Christ with a cross behind his head on the face, and the busts of the two co-rulers clasping a patriarchal cross on the reverse. The latter design was to be found on several classes of Constantine VII's gold coins, and also on his lead

[64] T. Gerasimov, 'Olovni pečati na bălgarskite care Simeon i Petăr', *Izvestija na Bălgarskija Archeologičeski Institut*, 12 (1938), 354–64, at Abb. 160, p. 362.

seals.[65] Thus the depiction of Peter and Maria conformed to the contemporary Byzantine method of representing joint rulership. Secondly, Peter occupied the position to the left of the cross (from the beholder's viewpoint): this was the position taken by the senior co-emperor on Byzantine coins and seals and presumably Peter's seals were intended to convey the same message. Thirdly, Peter and Maria are usually shown wearing Byzantine-style clothing and crowns of the same sort as Byzantine emperors and empresses wore. Maria's crown is similar to that of Peter, being a *stemma* (or diadem), with a cross projecting up from the section over her forehead, and *pendilia* hanging down from the *stemma* on either side of her face. Her crown differs from Peter's in being topped by two triangular projections at either end. Similar 'pinnacles' were shown on the crowns of the empresses on Byzantine coins and they merely denoted membership of the imperial house. No great significance need be attached to the fact that the woman's vestments look more sumptuous than the man's; and the *chlamys* which Peter wears over his *divitision* was not inherently less 'imperial' in status than the *loros* which his wife is wearing over her *divitision*.[66] It is, however, noteworthy that on one variant of the first-mentioned type of seal Peter is shown wearing a helmet-like hemispherical crown without any *pendilia*. Maria's crown, in contrast, is a *stemma*, replete with *pendilia*.[67] This variant is, apparently, known on only one example of Peter's seals published hitherto, and this suggests that the marked discrepancy between the crowns was regarded as significant and (at least to the Bulgarians) unpalatable. It would seem that sooner or later remedial action was taken.

[65] Grierson, *Catalogue of the Byzantine Coins* (see n. 34), III.2, pp. 533–6, plates XXXVI, XXXVII; G. Zacos and A. Veglery, *Byzantine Lead Seals*, I.1 (Basel, 1972), nos. 62, 64, 67, pp. 54–5, 56–7, 60; *ibid.*, *Plates* (Basel, 1972), pl. 19.

[66] On these insignia and vestments, see Grierson, *Catalogue of the Byzantine Coins* (see n. 34), I.II.1, pp. 117, 119–23, 127, 129–30; for line-drawings of the 'pinnacles' on the crowns of empresses, see table 13, p. 128; cf. *ibid.*, I.II.2, p. 541; pl. XXXVI: 1 (Constantine VII and Zoe). Peter's vestments seem to be the same on each of the above-mentioned types of seals, but the condition of some of the extant examples and the poor quality of the more recent photographs leaves room for doubt. *Pendilia* are not clearly visible on Peter's crown on the first type of seal, as illustrated in Gerasimov, 'Bălgarski i vizantijski pečati' (see n. 62), tablica I, p. 127: 3, 4, 5. However, they are mentioned in Totev's description of an example of this type: 'Novopostăpil pečat' (see n. 62), at p. 29.

[67] Gerasimov, 'Olovni pečati' (see n. 64), Abb. 158, p. 360; Gerasimov, 'Bălgarski i vizantijski pečati' (see n. 62), p. 129, tablica I, p. 127: 6. *Pendilia* were a common,

5. Lead seal of Basil I and Constantine (drawing published by G. Schlumberger).

6. Lead seal of Peter of Bulgaria and Maria Lekapena. Peter's hand is slightly above Maria's.

Fourthly, on Byzantine seals and coins the senior emperor normally, though not invariably, holds the cross with his hand clearly above that of his co-ruler (Fig. 5). It does not appear from existing reproductions of Peter's seals that this was always the case between him and Maria. On one example, her hand is above that of Peter, on the staff of the cross (Fig. 4).[68] This was, however,

though not indispensable, attribute of tenth-century emperors' crowns: Grierson, *Catalogue of the Byzantine Coins* (see n. 34), III.1, pp. 127, 129.

[68] Gerasimov, 'Olovni pečati' (see n. 64), Abb. 160, p. 362. The exceptions to the norm that the senior emperor's hand was uppermost are discussed in detail in Grierson, *Catalogue of the Byzantine Coins* (see n. 34), III.1, pp. 113–14, 142.

highly exceptional and on the remainder of the illustrated examples of their seals Peter's hand is shown slightly above Maria's hand, or at the same level.[69] The latter position (characteristic of the first type of seals mentioned above) seems to be roughly as common as the former. The two hands, when level, seem to be touching one another, as if symbolizing the 'union' proclaimed by the oration of 927. Such equality of positioning of the hands is not common in Byzantine portrayals of co-rulers.

While these observations would have been made by a Byzantine beholder of the seals, he – and we – might incline to doubt whether these features were deliberate. The isolated variants or unusual aspects of the design could fairly be dismissed as marks of Bulgarian ignorance or technical ineptitude. However, there are grounds for supposing that the Bulgarian government was interested in, and capable of regulating to a fair degree, the design of its seals. The very rarity of the variant showing Maria as having the upper hand on the cross suggests that its symbolism of seniority was understood and that before long steps were taken to rectify this. The find of discards at Preslav – in the vicinity of the seal-striker's workshop – is also an indication of some quality control.[70] That Peter's strikers were no less in command of their technique than their Constantinopolitan counterparts is suggested by their manufacture of a seal made not of lead but of silver. It is said to be the only Bulgarian or, indeed, Byzantine silver seal for the period from the ninth to the twelfth centuries, and it was manufactured by an unusual technique. Two thin circular platelets were each stamped on one side and then were carefully soldered together.[71] The publisher of the seal, J. Jurukova, suggested that the craftsman responsible for this unusual technique might have been Byzantine-born, or at least Byzantine-trained, and this is perfectly possible.[72] The silver seal suggests both Peter's access to high levels of technical competence and a persistent tendency to heed Byzantine conventions, not only in the design

[69] For an example of the former, see Gerasimov, 'Olovni pečati' (see n. 64), Abb. 159, p. 361 (Fig. 6 above). Maria's hand seems to be gripping the staff at the same level as Peter's in, e.g. Gerasimov, 'Bălgarski i vizantijski pečati' (see n. 62), tablica I, p. 127: 3–6. (Fig. 3).

[70] Totev, 'Novopostăpil pečat' (see n. 62), p. 29.

[71] J. Jurukova, 'Srebăren pečat na car Petăr (927–968)', *Numizmatika* (1980), no. 3, pp. 3–12, at pp. 6–7; Jurukova, 'La titulature des souverains du premier royaume bulgare d'après les monuments de la sphragistique', in *Sbornik v pamet na Prof. Stančo Vaklinov* (Sofia, 1984), pp. 224–30, at p. 230; fig. 8(a) and (b), p. 227.

[72] Jurukova, 'Srebăren pečat', p. 7.

7. Lead seal of Peter of Bulgaria of the 960s. The legend reads 'Peter, emperor'.

but also in the correlation of seal weight with coin weight. The seal weighs 2.62 grams, approximately the average weight of the Byzantine *miliaresion*.[73] It most probably reflects the Byzantines' practice of issuing golden bulls of the same weight as their *nomismata* or multiples thereof. The Bulgarian golden bull delivered to Byzantium in the course of the 927 negotiations could well have conformed to the same conventions. (See above, p. 133.) This incidentally serves to remind us that *de luxe* seals were not an invention of Peter's reign.

We may note, as a final indication of Peter's concern with seal design and ability to control it, that seals with intelligible legends and clear designs continued to be struck to the end of his reign. Two examples are known of a type issued in the last years of his reign, between the death of Maria in, probably, the early 960s and Peter's own death in 969. They depict him alone, and represent an up-date on the earlier types. One of the examples is blundered and, most probably, a discard: the letters of the inscription are unreversed and half the seal has broken off along the hollow 'channel' through which a cord attached to the seal was intended to run. But the other example is well preserved and of a high standard of execution. In fact its publisher not unreasonably

[73] *Ibid.*, p. 12. The average weight of ninety-five coins in good condition from Basil I's to Basil II's reign was found to work out at 2.72 grams; the theoretical weight of the *miliaresion* was, however, considerably higher: Grierson, *Catalogue of the Byzantine Coins* (see n. 34), III.1, p. 65.

maintained that the portrayal of Peter, wearing a broad *loros* and with long, grave face and pointed beard, is superior to the representations of Peter and Maria on the earlier seals, being less schematic (Fig. 7).[74] The legend on the reverse reads 'Πέτ[ρο]ς βασιλεύ[ς]'.

It would therefore be rash to dismiss the traits of the main types of Peter's seals as insignificant, while at the same time one should not attach undue weight to rare, and perhaps accidental, minor variants in the design. The positioning of the hands on the cross on the main types of seal could well represent policy, and not a seal-striker's caprice or incompetence. Equally, one should reject the notion that the seals were struck solely for purposes of display, and had little or no practical purpose. This cannot be true of the lead seals, at least. Approximately twenty-two finds have been reported, mainly but not exclusively in and around Preslav, the place of production.[75] This tallies with the impression of Peter's administration gained by Ibrahim ibn Yakub, who visited central Europe in the 960s and observed Bulgarian envoys on their way to the court of Otto I. He states that 'their king enjoys great authority, wears a diadem on his head, has secretaries, heads [of offices] and senior functionaries, and issues orders and prohibitions in a well-advised and regular manner, as is the custom with the greatest monarchs'.[76] Ibn Yakub's assessment offers a backdrop to the triumph which Tzimiskes celebrated after his victory in 971. The Bulgarian symbols of imperial authority and divine protection seem to have rested on a far from derisory administrative base.

This brings us back to the question of Maria's impact on Byzantino-Bulgarian relations. The last word belongs to Liutprand who surely knew what he was talking about in referring to the 'most solid peace' which the marriage had 'established'. One

[74] K. Popkonstantinov, 'Nov pečat na car Petăr', *Numizmatika* (1979), no. 3, pp. 19–21; photo of reverse, showing Peter: obr. 1, p. 19. A second, blundered, example of this type was published by T. Totev, 'Oloven pečat na car Petăr (927–968)', *Numizmatika* (1989), no. 2, pp. 40–1.

[75] Jurukova, 'Titulature des souverains' (see n. 71), p. 230; Totev, 'Novopostăpil pečat' (see n. 62), pp. 28–9; S. Vitlianov, 'Novootkrit carski pečat ot Veliki Preslav', *Numizmatika* (1988), no. 4, pp. 38–40; Totev, 'Oloven pečat' (see n. 74), pp. 40–1.

[76] Ibrahim ibn Yakub, *De itinere slavico quae traditur apud al-Bekri*, ed. and Latin and Polish trans. T. Kowalski, Monumenta Poloniae Historica, n.s. I (Cracow, 1946), pp. 51, 148.

can, indeed, take a negative view, pointing out the evidence of tensions between Bulgaria and Byzantium during the reign of Constantine Porphyrogennetos (who so clearly resented the marriage), and emphasizing that within a few years of Maria's death the two peoples were at war with one another again.[77] But given that the sense of rivalry and mutual suspicion existed and were perhaps indelible, one may argue that the marriage, a partnership expressed in the design of the seals of Peter and Maria, did buy time and forge personal bonds for over a generation: one of Maria's sons was called Romanos after her grandfather. Perhaps no dynastic marriage could reasonably be expected to do more than that.

[77] Constantine VII, *De administrando imperio* (see n. 2), ch. 5, 1–9, pp. 52–3; ch. 8, 20, pp. 56–7; Shepard, 'Bulgaria' (see n. 7).

8

The image of women of the nobility in the German chronicles of the tenth and eleventh centuries

P. BANGE

Introduction

In a chapter (entitled 'The women of the Saxon aristocracy') of his *Rule and Conflict in an Early Medieval Society*, Karl Leyser observes that high-ranking women played a major role in the tenth century, especially in the church.[1] The author mentions, among others, Matilda, the wife of the first king of the Saxon dynasty in Germany, Henry I (876–936; king from 919 onwards); Adelheid, the wife of Henry's son, Otto I the Great; and Theophano, the daughter-in-law of Otto I, whose daughters, Adelheid and Sophia, became the abbesses of large convents. According to Leyser, the authority of these 'grand ladies' achieved the level of that of prelates and lay lords. This was not a new phenomenon. We can observe the same female influence in church matters long before this period, namely in the Anglo-Saxon world of the seventh and eighth centuries.

The question why women played such an important role in Ottonian society is not easily answered. Sources on this issue are in short supply; they will be reviewed later. It is worth remarking, however, that women often outlived their husbands by many years. The empress Adelheid (*c.* 931–99), for instance, outlived her husband by twenty-six years, her son by another sixteen years (and her daughter-in-law by eight years). So she was able to be the regent for her grandson Otto III for three years (991–4), until he

[1] K.J. Leyser, *Rule and Conflict in an Early Medieval Society: Ottonian Saxony* (London, 1979), pp. 49–51.

attained majority. This may be an important reason why women frequently appeared on the stage when decisions had to be taken.

The high death-rate among men, due to the frequent wars and the diseases and epidemics connected with the campaigns, might be a stereotyped explanation for the relatively high life-expectancy of women. When there were no more male heirs available, women – the mother or sisters of the land-owning men – could come into possession of the properties. On the other hand, we have to be aware of the fact that women often died in childbirth.

The sources

Within the limited space of this chapter, it is not possible to sketch a complete picture of the social position of women, especially of high-ranking women, in the tenth and the eleventh centuries. Moreover, the source material that has come down to us from this period does not permit us to draw convincing conclusions. The kind of information provided is mostly biased, and expressed in formulaic and cliché-ridden language. Nevertheless, we have to make the most of what we have, and try to find some traces of the reality that is hidden behind the pictures of women, as they are presented in the historical sources.

We will do so on the basis of two kinds of historical narrative, namely the German chronicles and the annals of the period (the qualification 'German' should be taken in the unrestricted sense of the word). The anecdotes recounted in these narratives developed some common characteristics, typical of the genre, which enable us to consider the narratives as one coherent corpus. Although the annals as well as the chronicles have different origins, in the course of history the two genres merged.[2] Eventually annals superseded the original intention of presenting tables with the series of pre-calculated Easter dates, with some marginal notes concerning historical events. They finally related full-scale history. Chronicles, in their turn, more and more followed the annual sequence in relating the special stories of a king, an abbot or a convent. While Dennis Hay, therefore, uses the term 'annalistic chronicles',[3] he

[2] See for example R.C. van Caenegem and F.L. Ganshof, *Guide to the Sources of Medieval History* (Amsterdam, New York, etc., 1978).

[3] D. Hay, *Annalists and Historians: Western Historiography from the Eighth to the Eighteenth Centuries* (London, 1977), p. 38; see also H. Grundmann, *Geschichts-*

also recognizes, on the other hand, that annals could serve as a basis for stories that were not annalistic in nature.

In order to appreciate these chronicles and annals, we have to read them with a critical eye, and avoid applying modern standards to these texts.[4] Generally, the authors have edifying intentions; their readers have to draw a lesson for the present from the past. Bad as well as good behaviour can be held up as an example and is actually presented as such. Of course, this didactic intention influences both the composition of the text and its reliability as a historical source. The social and cultural outlook of the author is also an influential factor; the writer will select his sources according to his personal preferences.

These texts are further characterized by the lack of causal connections in the stories. The events are presented in a sequential order, and if we do find some causal connections, e.g. between the appearance of a comet and the origin of a famine or inundation, they do not help us to understand the story that is being told. On the other hand, these chronicles and annals contain a wealth of information with regard to the time in which the author lives. The interpretation he gives of certain historical events itself gives insight into contemporary culture. If we can verify his data and compare them with what is related by other sources, we can also compare the different interpretations that were given of the same phenomena. Cross-cultural comparison provides a fine method of gathering historical evidence, when sources are scarce.

The German chronicles

From a cultural point of view the tenth century is an important period. On the analogy of the so-called Carolingian Renaissance, historians also use the term Ottonian Renaissance, in order to characterize the cultural revival of the century. Not without reason the names of the rulers, Charlemagne and Otto the Great, are connected with this cultural revival, because they personally initiated the cultural activities which are the distinguishing marks of the periods.

schreibung im Mittelalter, second edn (Göttingen, 1965), pp. 24–5; K.H. Krüger, *Die Universalchroniken*, Typologie des Sources du Moyen Age Occidental, 16 (Turnhout, 1976), pp. 35.

4 See B. Guenée, 'Y-a-t-il une historiographie médiévale?', *Revue Historique*, 258 (1977), pp. 261–75.

This revival can also be observed in historiography. A great variety of texts were produced by high-ranking monks or clerics, who were mostly in close contact with royal circles, or with the aristocracy in a broader sense; their lines of approach, as shown in these texts, are very similar. They also provide ample evidence for the image of women in these circles, on which this study will focus.

My intention is to show the way in which women are spoken of in these texts, what role they played, and what qualifications are used to indicate their personalities. The data will be organized according to three themes: 1. the appreciation of women in general, both positive and negative; 2. the role women played in politics, with special attention to marriage as a political institution; 3. (expressions of) female devotion. Finally I will try to sketch a general picture of the woman of the nobility, and discuss whether this image, gathered as it is from the German chronicles and annals of the tenth and eleventh centuries, reveals in a reliable way what life was like for a woman of nobility in those days.

Four of the texts used were written in the tenth century: Thietmar of Merseburg's *Chronicon* (975–1018); Widukind of Corvey's *Res gesta Saxoniae* (second half of the tenth century); Adalbert's *Continuatio Reginonis* (same period); Liutprand's *Liber Antapodoseos* (*c.* 920–72). Five texts were selected from the eleventh century: Alpert of Metz's *De diversitate temporum* (first half of the eleventh century); Lampert of Hersfeld's *Annales* (*c.* 1020–after 1077); Wipo's *Gesta Chuonradi II* (eleventh century); Herman of Reichenau's *Chronicon* (second half of the eleventh century) and Frutolf's *Chronicon* (died 1103).[5]

What sort of women do the texts reveal?

All of the women mentioned in the various chronicles and annals were women of a certain prestige and standing. The majority were high-ranking figures: wives of kings and emperors, of counts and dukes and other worldly rulers; also women who played important roles in the religious world as abbesses.

[5] The following abbreviations will be used: Th = Thietmar of Merseburg, W = Widukind, A = Adalbert, Li = Liutprand of Cremona, Alp = Alpertus of Metz, La = Lampert of Hersfeld, Wi = Wipo, H = Herman of Reichenau , F = Frutolf. For the editions used see list of the Primary sources at the end of this chapter.

The ways in which these women are described vary to a large extent, ranging in tone from the positive, via the neutral, to the clearly negative. Because of the clichéd character of the language used by the authors, it is difficult to discover the actual judgement of the writer with regard to a specific woman. In sketching the picture of a queen, a countess or an abbess, the author gives them the features he thinks plausible for a woman in such a position.[6] If she misbehaved, according to his judgement, he expresses his opinion in the appropriate stereotyped terms. As a result, we do not so much discover the real personalities of these ladies, but rather learn about their functions and those qualities of character which were deemed correct for ladies of such rank. We only discover the opinions of the author in this respect, and see the ladies in question through his eyes, thus gaining a reflection of the view of the circles for which he was writing.[7]

From these texts we may infer in general that high-ranking women normally did not play the same role in society as men did. However, they were in fact able to take over the duties and responsibilities of their husbands or sons, if necessary. Women officiating in responsible positions were not seen by the chroniclers of those days as behaving inordinately, even if they assign qualifications to the ladies which make clear that they are regarded as being different from men. Sometimes a chronicler even expresses his approval when a woman behaves like a man, or is said to possess male qualities (Th 76, 124–6; W 178–80). Of course, stereotype female qualities are also accentuated, and not always in a negative way (Th 12, 38, 86).

The general impressions as formulated above will be elaborated on in this chapter.

Appreciation of women in general

When reading the chronicles and annals, one comes to the conclusion that the clearly positive and the explicitly negative descrip-

[6] See R. Strating, 'Adela, heerszuchtige vrouw of vrouwelijke heerser?: de lotgevallen van een gravin en haar verhaal door Alpertus van Metz', in *Vrouw, familie en macht: bronnen over vrouwen in de Middeleeuwen*, ed. M. Mostert *et al.* (Hilversum, 1990), pp. 167–80.

[7] See C.J.C. Broer, 'Echtgenote, deelgenote, lotgenote: over oorkonden als bron voor de vrouwengeschiedenis' (Charters as a source for the history of women), in *ibid.*, pp. 147–65, at pp. 148–9: 'In narrative sources such as chronicles, annals and saints' lives women do not figure very often. Moreover we should consider, that, when they are mentioned, the authors had a very prejudiced image of woman.'

tions of women in these texts are well balanced. We cannot observe any dominance of a negative judgement. Let us consider both aspects.

For obvious reasons, a positive appreciation is formulated on the basis of the piety of women, their prudence and their virtues. For Widukind a combination of beauty and intelligence is commendable (W 118). He dedicated his text to Matilda, daughter of the emperor Otto I. He holds her in such high esteem, that he feels himself unable to describe her virtues adequately: 'cum eius claritas precellat omne quod dicere aut scribere valemus' (W 136). Further on, he mentions the elderly Matilda, the mother of the emperor, and wife of Henry I. He calls her a woman of remarkable sanctity ('mirae sanctitatis feminam' (W 178)), and qualifies himself as too deficient to do justice to her virtue. Also Liutprand of Cremona seems to appreciate the combination of honest beauty and approved manners, when he qualifies a woman as gracious because she excels in both aspects: 'cum forma honestissima tum morum probitate gratiosam' (Li 416). Wipo accentuates the beauty of queen Gisela, who, notwithstanding her high nobility and beautiful appearance, was not haughty at all: 'cum tantae nobilitatis est et formae decentissimae, minimae extollentiae fuit' (Wi 552). In formulating this judgement, he pays the queen a notable compliment, because pride was considered to be the first and the most important of the seven deadly sins.[8]

Thietmar, in describing the empress Theophano, is more reserved in his wordings. There is a certain ambivalence in his appreciation. Although Theophano belongs to the weaker sex ('quamvis sexu fragilis', Th 124), she is very modest and her conduct excellent, which, according to Thietmar, 'is very rare in Greece'. But he obviously praises her highly when he says that she preserved the reign of her son with 'male vigilance' ('regnumque filii eius custodia servabat virili', Th 126). In Liutgard, daughter of the emperor Otto I and his Anglo-Saxon wife Edith, he appreciates her 'male patience' ('virili patientia', Th 76). We observe the same reservedness with Alpert of Metz, when he describes the pious abbess Liutgard: 'amazing that a woman, notwithstanding the frailty of her female sex ('fragilitas feminei

[8] These are: pride, avarice, luxury, wrath, gluttony, jealousy, sloth; see e.g. M. Bloomfield, *The Seven Deadly Sins* (East Lansing, Michigan, 1952); pride was Lucifer's sin, and also Adam's and Eve's, because they wanted to be equal to God; that is why original sin came into the world.

sexus'), could do all this' (Alp 12). We should realize, however, that such a caution could mean an added appreciation: the woman has obviously conquered the frailty of her sex.

Implicitly, the virtuousness of women is appreciated in two anecdotes, related by Thietmar. The first one concerns king Henry I. On Maundy Thursday, Henry, being drunk, compels his wife Matilda, who is resisting furiously, to have sexual intercourse with him. The devil, who, of course, is the 'moving spirit' of the affair, betrays to one of her ladies-in-waiting, that Henry has made his wife pregnant. The lady, however, sees to it that bishops and priests are present at the moment of birth, in order to prevent the devil from arrogating the child (Th 26–8). A little bit further on, he relates a similar story, this time about Uffo, a citizen of Magdeburg, who, drunk as Henry was, on Innocents' Day, forced his wife to meet his wishes. She also became pregnant, and she gave birth to a child with deformed toes. 'Lo,' she said to her husband, 'that is God's revenge.' After baptism, however, the child was accepted among the Innocents, Thietmar knows (Th 28).

Lampert of Hersfeld uses a somewhat curious argumentation in order to prove the pudicity of Matilda of Tuscany. Although her husband, duke Gozelo of Lotharingia, was still alive, she used to live as a widow, because she did not want to leave her native country, Lampert relates. One might at least conclude that theirs was not a happy marriage. Matilda, he relates, was even under the suspicion of an incestuous love-affair with the pope ('nec evadere potuit incesti amoris suspicionem', La 400). Lampert rejects the accusation. If she had committed something immoral, it would not have remained undiscovered in that crowded city, said Lampert (*ibid.*).

Though beauty may be allied to virtue, the opposite is often the case. According to Liutprand of Cremona, Bertha, the widow of the margrave of Tuscany, was a charming and attractive lady, equalled in these respects by her daughter Irmgard ('dulcedine coequalem', Li 338). But Bertha was also a vicious woman. After her husband had died, she managed to remain in possession of power by slyness, gifts and a series of lovers (Li 336). Adela, the notorious countess of Hamaland, had fine looks, but, according to Alpert of Metz, this mask covered a dissolute inner self. The only civilized trait he could discover in her was her gift for weaving ('hec sola humanitas in ea nota est', Alp 10).

Next to impudence, authors impute to some women the instigation of evil. They stir up their husbands to fulfil their evil projects, but try to escape safely when things turn out badly. Adela, the countess just mentioned, was such a woman. She had count Wichman killed, without her husband, Balderich, knowing. Unanimously, however, he was declared to be the culprit, although everybody knew he was not guilty. But he was held responsible because of the malignity of his wife ('propter maliciam uxoris', Alp 66).

The role of women in politics can also be appreciated in a positive or in a negative way. Lampert of Hersfeld and Frutolf disagree in this respect, when judging Beatrice, the margravine of Tuscany. Frutolf says that, on his way back from Italy in 1055, the emperor Henry (III) took along his cousin Beatrice. He treated her in a merciless way because of her insolences ('quasdam insolencias suas', F 70)[9] after the death of her husband. Frutolf, obviously, agrees in his heart with the emperor. Lampert, however, is of a different opinion, even if he does not appreciate the margravine's conduct in all respects. He relates that Beatrice was received in audience by the emperor. She defended her marriage to Geoffrey of Upper Lotharingia, after the death of her husband. In doing so she gave her house, bereaved of a husband, a new protector, as was allowed by the law of nations ('iure gentium'). The emperor accepted the situation, fearing that, otherwise, Geoffrey would link up with his enemies. However, he took Beatrice with him, because she had arranged a marriage without his consent (La 56). The wording of this story shows that Lampert agrees with Beatrice's action, but also with Henry's punishment for the transgression of his rights.

Marriages as part of politics; the role of women in politics

In all the texts under consideration we regularly see that marriages form a part of politics. Women – and also men, there is not much of a difference in this respect – were given in marriage, when this was considered to be favourable for the expansion of territory or, as the case might be, of influence. Widukind, for instance, relates that king Henry gave a woman in marriage to his son Liudolf; she excelled in riches and in noble birth, an important combination

[9] Schmale (see Primary sources: Frutolf and Ekkehard) translates: 'Lebensgewohnheiten die der Sitte widersprechen' (71).

(W 132). The Byzantine emperor Romanos slowed down the aggression of king Symeon of the Bulgarians by giving his granddaughter in marriage to Romanos' son Peter (Li 382); the opinion of the girl was not asked, of course. King Otto even offered duke Berthold of Bavaria the choice between two women: namely the widow of duke Giselbert of Lotharingia or his daughter. Berthold, however, so Liutprand says, preferred to wait for the not yet nubile daughter instead of marrying the mother (Li 442).

A little further on, Liutprand mentions another interesting event. The emperor of Byzantium was looking for a girl for his grandson, and he called upon king Hugh of Italy. Hugh sent back some messengers to explain the situation: Hugh only had daughters by concubines. The emperor saw no objection to that, because, as Liutprand says, in matters of descent, the Greeks take only the father into consideration, not the mother (Li 460).

Thietmar of Merseburg relates that Otto I sent a courier to the court of Byzantium, because he wanted a woman from the imperial house of Constantinople for his son. With magnificent gifts and a select retinue, the niece of emperor John Tzimiskes was sent to Otto, not the girl requested (Th 48f). Otto put up with John's niece, because the emperor whose daughter Otto wanted for his son had been dethroned by John.

From the chronicles we get the impression that, although it was forbidden by the church, it was fairly easy for the nobility to divorce their wives. Thietmar, laconically enough, relates that Boleslav, son of duke Mieszko of Poland, divorced twice before marrying a woman who believed in Christ and who, says Thietmar, was able to guide her husband's unstable heart towards good things (Th 174). Perhaps we may conclude from this story that Boleslav did not leave this wife.

It was, however, complicated for a king to divorce his wife, as we may conclude from the report of Lampert of Hersfeld from the year 1069. King Henry IV wanted to divorce his wife. According to Lampert, there was nothing that Henry could reproach her with in order to justify the separation, but that he himself was not able to consummate the marriage. He wanted a separation, so that both of them might contract a happier marriage. He therefore called to his assistance the archbishop of Mainz. During the diet he took an oath that the queen was still a virgin. Everybody thought the situation dreadful, and, according to Lampert, unworthy of the king's majesty, but yet it was thought advisable not to disapprove of the plans. This did not solve the problem, because, during a synod at Mainz, which was held somewhat later, the papal envoy, Peter Damian, made his appearance – while the queen had been sent away to Lorsch pending the settlement of the affair – and declared that the Holy Father did not approve of the divorce. Now the imperial princes also had the courage to voice their objections. The king decided to abandon the project, but from then on he only shared the name of the empire with his wife. Lampert says: 'He had her, as if he did not have her' ('communicato cum ea solum regni nomine, sic eam habere, quasi non haberet', La 120). This remark, however, is contradicted by the fact, also related by the same Lampert at the year 1071, that the queen, being with the king in Mainz, gave birth to a son, who died shortly after having been baptized.

From another passage in Lampert's *Annales* we gather that marriages were arranged for political reasons. The margrave Azzo of Italy was invested with the duchy of Bavaria, because he had married a daughter of duke Otto. As long as there was peace, he showed his wife marital love and honour ('maritalem affectum et honorem'), and he promoted the interests of his father-in-law. When it occurred to him, however, that he was no longer in the king's favour, he broke off all bonds of affinity: he refused to help his father-in-law, excluded his wife from his embraces and from all intercourse, and sent her back to her father ('filiam eius a complexibus suis et thori consortio segregavit patrique remisit', La 132). There is no evidence whatsoever that he took into consideration the feelings of his wife.

Frutolf relates an event which is reminiscent of Bede's stories of various marriages in England during his lifetime, in the seventh and eighth centuries.[10] King Henry II's sister, Gisela, was proposed to by king Stephen of Hungary. But he was not worthy to receive her, unless he promised that he and his entire people would accept the Christian faith and receive the sacrament of

[10] See P. Bange, 'Angelsaksische (religieuze) vrouwen en hun rol bij het kersteningsproces', in *Willibrord: zijn wereld en zijn werk: voordrachten gehouden tijdens het Willibrordcongres 28–30 september 1989*, ed. P. Bange and A.G. Weiler, Middeleeuwse Studies, 6 (Nijmegen, 1990), pp. 115–27, at pp. 116–17: King Edwin of Northumbria has been told by the brother of his future wife that she, being a Christian, may not marry a pagan. He therefore promises not to impede her Christian faith. Shortly afterwards he also is converted to Christianity (whether or not through his wife's urgings is not clear).

baptism. The king was, indeed, converted to Christianity (F 50). Frutolf adds to the story that the king, as soon as he had made his promise, was devout and pious in good works; divine mercy gave evidence of this by the miracles that happened at his grave after his death. Regrettably, Frutolf does not relate how the Hungarian people were converted. Perhaps we might refer here to a similar situation related by Bede; the king consulted the aristocrats of the realm, and when they agreed and were prepared to follow the king in his transition to Christianity, he took courage to do so. Herman of Reichenau also tells this story, but much more briefly and concentrated more specifically on the queen. According to him, she was given in marriage to the Hungarian king Stephen, when he converted to the Christian faith ('cum se ad fidem Christi converteret'). Giving alms and doing other good deeds, she reached a considerable age (H 652). From this passage it is not clear, however, that the conversion of the king was a condition for his marrying a Christian woman.

Highly placed women could also play an important role in politics, as is clear from several passages in the chronicles and annals. Wipo, for instance, relates the events in 1024. After the death of emperor Henry II, 'the state felt insecure'. There was much trouble and unease in the realm, because the emperor had died without leaving a son.[11] Fortunately, there were wise priests and men of state who were able to put the ship of the fatherland safely into port. The empress Cunegunda, in her turn, devoted all her energy to the interest of the realm, although she was deprived of the support of her husband. She consulted her brothers, bishop Thierry of Metz and duke Henry of Bavaria. With a clear vision, and purposefully, she tried to restore strength to the empire (Wi 530–2). As soon as the princes had chosen a new king,[12] empress Cunegunda handed the royal insignia over to him, and strengthened him in reigning, as much as her sex was allowed to do ('regalia insignia . . . obtulit et ad regnandum, quantum huius sexus auctoritatis est, illum corroboravit', Wi 544).

Lampert of Hersfeld relates a story about queen Agnes, widow of Henry III, who in 1056 took on the regency for her five-year-old son, later to become Henry IV. The supreme power,

[11] Frutolf also tells us this story: the emperor knew that he would not beget any sons, because he only loved his wife as his sister ('consortem regni Cunigundam nunquam cognovit, sed ut sororem dilexit', F 48).

[12] Conrad, a great-great-grandson of Otto I, through his daughter Liutgard.

however, and administration of all necessary matters remained totally with the empress ('summa tamen rerum et omnium quibus facto opus erat administratio penes imperatricem remansit', La 58). For instance, she invested Otto of Northeim with the duchy of Bavaria, of which she herself, after the death of her son Conrad, had been the governor (La 72).[13] The empress, however, was happy to receive advice. Bishop Henry of Augsburg was her most important counsellor. Hereby she could not escape the suspicion of an incestuous love ('unde nec suspicionem incesti amoris effugere potuit'), because there was a widely spread rumour, according to Lampert, that without a shameful relationship the two of them would never have been so close ('quod non sine turpi commercio in tantam coaluissent familiaritatem', La 72). The princes of the realm took grave offence at the affair, because, as Lampert says, in that way their influence was nearly eliminated. They stirred up public opinion against the empress – whether such an incitement had any effect is doubtful – and tried to remove the son from his mother's influence. In the end, the archbishop of Cologne kidnapped the child. The empress resigned, and did not prosecute the inflicted injustice on the basis of the law of nations ('imperatrix nec filium sequi nec iniurias suas iure gentium expostulare voluit', La 74). She decided to withdraw to her private demesnes, and to abandon politics. She would even have withdrawn from the world completely, had it not been for her friends preventing her from doing so. The power of the empress, therefore, was built on a weak foundation. It only subsisted by the grace of the princes. We can imagine, however, that she did not comply so easily with the situation as Lampert tries to make us believe.

Frutolf also tells about the empress Agnes. He is even more clear about the motives of the people in her entourage. She governed in a wise and prudential way, Frutolf says, until some princes, out of envy, removed the boy from his mother, and deprived her of the mastery in the realm (F 72). He is, however, cautious in his judgement of archbishop Anno of Cologne, who kidnapped the king. We cannot say, says Frutolf, whether God's judgement approved of the deed, but it is certain, in his eyes, that it caused much inconvenience (F 72). As soon as Henry had become king (Henry IV), his mother resumed the ducal power in

[13] Conrad, a younger brother of Henry (IV) died in 1055, still very young; Lampert is obviously somewhat confused here about facts.

Bavaria (diet of Regensburg, 1056; F 74). In 1069, however, she abdicated, and went to Rome in order to do penance (F 78). According to Frutolf's story, Agnes remained involved in politics for a longer period than is related by Lampert.

Princesses often accompanied their husbands on their journeys. Several times they also made their own trips. Thietmar relates, that king Henry met his wife Cunegunda in Corvey and that they travelled along together to Paderborn, not far from Corvey (Th 212). Somewhat further down, concerning an event some years later, he mentions that the emperor, on his journey eastward, summoned the queen to come to Paderborn. Subsequently, they travelled together to Magdeburg. Then the queen returned, and the king marched on with his army (Th 418); women were not wanted there. Lampert of Hersfeld shows that such trips were not always pleasant enterprises. In his description of Henry IV's journey across the Alps in 1077, to make peace with the pope, Lampert relates that the queen and her suite were dragged down from the snow-clad mountains on cowhides (La 398).[14] Although we do not read in these chronicles and annals many exact details concerning the *itineraria* of the various kings and emperors, yet we get an impression of their rather restless life, travelling from palace (*palatium/Pfalz*) to palace, and their frequent campaigns. Small wonder that their wives sometimes preferred the quiet of a convent to restless travelling. More reliable data about the routes of emperors and kings are presented by the charters, which they gave on the way. Since empresses and queens often signed those charters with their husbands, we know that they travelled along with them.

Piety

Chroniclers express themselves in a very positive way when appreciating female piety. We may observe this appreciation in various stories about women who prayed for the welfare of their late husbands' souls. Liutprand relates that Matilda, widow of Henry I, was most diligent in having masses said for his soul's salvation. According to Thietmar, she distributed food to the

[14] Liutprand also mentions the impassability of the Alps (456): when king Berengar of Lombardy fled over the Alps, he sent for his wife Willa, who was far advanced in pregnancy. I cannot stop wondering, says Liutprand, that she came afoot over such a desolate mountain ('montes tam asperos atque invios').

poor and even to the birds in order to secure his spiritual welfare (Th 24). Just as Liutprand praises Matilda, so he extols Adelheid, the widow of Otto I. The anxiety she showed to relieve her husband's soul was equalled by nobody (Th 80). Even more is achieved by Adela, the widow of count Gero of northern Thuringia. Together with his sister, Tetta, she founded a monastery in his memory (Th 94–6). Thietmar also tells a story concerning his cousin Matilda, daughter of duke Bernhard of Saxony. At the death of her husband – whom she, at the age of twenty, had been married to for seven years – she took the veil for the love of God and the salvation of her poor consort. She was so steadfast in the service of Christ, so mild, chaste and ascetic, that her approaching death was heralded by all kinds of portents (Th 356).

Duke Ernest of Swabia is depicted as apparently not being at ease that everything would end well. On his death-bed, he asked his faithful retainers to exhort his wife to keep up his honour and not forget him. Thietmar does not specify whether, in the intention of the duke, this also included the celebration of masses for his soul (Th 368).

In many different ways female piety and devotion appear in the texts under consideration. For example, women are mentioned whose husbands were converted to Christianity through their mediation. I have already pointed to the role of the third wife of king Boleslav of Poland. But also his father, Mieszko, was still involved in all kinds of pagan errors ('vario gentilitatis errore implicitum', Th 170). On marrying him, his wife, a Christian Bohemian woman, contrived to bind him to her also in faith. Thietmar then comes up with a rather remarkable passage. Wittingly she practised evil for some time, he says, in order to do good afterwards. For example, after her marriage she tried to please God by not eating meat during Lent and by chastising her body. But on her husband's request, she desisted from it, and finally her husband was persuaded to accept the Christian faith and was converted. In that way, an evil deed gave her a beautiful fruit, says Thietmar (172).

Several passages relate that queens and empresses gave donations to monasteries and even founded convents. Daughters of noble birth were obliged by their parents to enter (imperial) monasteries, and often they became abbesses. This was the case with Adelheid and Sophia, the two eldest daughters of emperor Otto II and his wife Theophano. Adelheid was made a canoness in the convent of Quedlinburg; afterwards she became abbess in the same place. Sophia entered the convent at Gandersheim; she also became abbess there. On the occasion of the birth of Adelheid and of Sophia, gifts and privileges were presented by the empress to the nunneries of Metz and Nivelles.

Sometimes worldly and spiritual interests went together in a rather peculiar way, as is shown by a fine example related by Lampert of Hersfeld. Agnes, the widow of king Henry III, mentioned above, had forsworn all worldly matters out of religious motives. Nevertheless, for once she interfered with politics. On the request of her son-in-law, duke Rudolf of Swabia, she travelled to Worms, in order to assist him against some people who had come to the king with accusations against him. As her motive for complying with his request, Lampert states that she was of the opinion that giving assistance to a man who deserved well of her easily fitted in with her ecclesiastical duties (i.e. that she had forsworn the world). So she came to Worms with a great number of abbots and monks, and freed the duke from all kinds of suspicion (La 160–2).

It is with approval that Thietmar gives a story concerning a recluse, called Sisu. He relates nothing about her descent. For sixty-four years she gave herself to her heavenly spouse as a pure virgin. She lived in complete solitude, never had a fire to comfort her, and wept and prayed continually. He adds a detail, which to us is rather disgusting. She did not chase away the vermin that fed on her; on the contrary, when one fell from her body, she picked it up and put it back in its place (Th 448; Thietmar refers to the example given by Symeon the Stylite – fifth century). She refrained from everything that was not allowed, not in order to conquer perishable glory, but for the chaplet of flowers of heavenly reward (Th 450).

There is another remarkable story told by Thietmar concerning a person in whom piety and unlawful behaviour are united. After the death of his wife, duke Mieszko – already mentioned – married Oda, the daughter of margrave Thierry of the Saxon 'Nordmark', who was a nun in the convent of Calbe. Her misdemeanour was great, in despising her heavenly spouse, and Mieszko did not ask for ecclesiastical permission. But, in Thietmar's opinion, what they did was not bad for the country, because in all respects she furthered the service of Christ. He expresses the hope that God would forgive her offence, because she did so many pious works. To Thietmar it seems that the good effects made the unlawful deed acceptable, perhaps even to God (Th 172).

Image and reality

Although our authors are not very explicit in stating their objectives, we may assume that, at least implicitly, theirs was a double purpose: their readers, both contemporary and future, had to be informed about the events the authors estimated to be of importance; subsequently, they should be enabled to learn lessons from these stories for their own lives. Thietmar makes an exception in this respect. He says he expects from his work profit for himself, now and in the future: 'in presenti et futuri sibi proficere' (Th 4).

The authors reflect reality as they saw it, or, more so, as they thought their readers should know and recognize it. For them, historiography had to serve as a positive or negative example, and preferably also as entertainment, when an anecdote was told. We may think of the bravery of a king or emperor, or the unreliability of a duke or a count, which could not pass unpunished, but also of the example given by astute, wicked, virtuous or pious women. The image of women given by these authors must therefore be considered in this perspective. It also accounts for the stereotypes and the postulated exigencies with regard to women which we encounter in the texts.

The misogyny of which ecclesiastical writers so often give testimony in treatises, sermons or adhortations is not that clearly found in the chronicles and annals under consideration. This is due to the fact that there is always some 'reality', however coloured the wording of it may be, as the point of reference of the story. The presentation of reality mostly has an exemplary function, but not so much as any normative or idealizing text would have. The women mentioned in the texts really existed. They had their very recognizable good or bad qualities, their strong and their weak points.

Reconsidering the stories related in the previous pages, we get the impression that the final judgement of these authors concerning the women they described might be rendered in one single sentence: a woman has to know her place, and what this place is is clear from the beginning. We can elaborate this impression in five statements:

1. The best women are pious women, nuns being the best of all.
2. Female beauty is only to be appreciated when coupled with virtuousness, modesty and piety. Next to these, riches and noble birth are reckoned to be the most important qualities of a suitable candidate for marriage. Beauty, therefore, is not necessarily appreciated as devilish or alluring; when combined with bad qualities of character, however, beauty may lead to undesirable situations.
3. Women should not interfere with the affairs of their husbands.
4. Divorce is esteemed possible, whenever the political situation might demand it, but is not approved of.
5. When governing on her own, a woman needs manly qualities. In fact, she can only be a lady governor when assisted by men. She has to be on her guard, however, against envious aristocrats.

Along these lines, the noble women described fitted into the models and patterns the authors designed for them. In this way, they might serve as examples for good and for evil behaviour. In spite of the model-like features recorded in these texts, the intelligent reader is given a clear impression of the real society of those days, and in particular of the place women occupied in it. Liutprand of Cremona, for instance, did not characterize the margravine of Tuscany in a very positive way, mentioning her cunning and the 'host of lovers' she kept. But from reading in between the lines, we might conclude that the lady in question was utterly capable of maintaining authority in the margraviate, although the means employed, at least in Liutprand's eyes, were socially not quite acceptable (Li 336–8).

Conclusion

The image evoked by the authors of chronicles and annals is necessarily a coloured one. The objective with which they composed their works called for such colouring. They presented reality to their readers as an example, to edify and to instruct. This applies to all events related, whether women were involved or not.

As for women in particular, the authors gave them a fixed position in society, a position that women should know and the limits of which they should not overstep. If the situation, however, required such a transgression, women were allowed to transgress the limits; the author will not immediately pass a crushing judgement on their behaviour. For that reason Thietmar of Merseburg approved, as we have stated, of the empress Theophano, when she took care of the realm of her son Otto with masculine vigilance, while he was under age. In doing so, she avoided troubles and problems concerning the succession to the throne, according to Thietmar.

Our authors, however, were not totally unbiased with regard to the women in their chronicles. They could not be otherwise, being too much influenced by the society they were part of, by the social setting they stemmed from, and by the conventions of their class. As men of their time, they were not able to attribute to women a position that would be equal to that of men in all respects. As clerics, they had a clear-cut opinion about the ideal relationship between man and woman. But being also aristocrats, most of the time closely connected with royal circles or even with the court, they were not able to contest the high position of a lady governor or of an abbess of an imperial monastery. Finally, there is their didactic preoccupation, as mentioned above. All these considerations adduce arguments for the biases found in their stories.

The image of women of the nobility in the German chronicles and annals of the tenth and eleventh centuries is first of all that of an example. Real women, however, were the 'referents' after which the example was modelled. Therefore it is inevitable that when telling stories the authors also hinted at the reality of those days. And that was what we were looking for in studying these texts closely.

Select bibliography

PRIMARY SOURCES

Widukind, *Sachsengeschichte*, Adalbert, *Fortsetzung der Chronik Reginos*, Liutprand, *Werke*, in *Quellen zur Geschichte der sächsischen Kaiserzeit*, ed. A. Bauer, R. Rau, AQDG 8 (Darmstadt, 1971).

Alpert of Metz, *Gebeurtenissen van deze tijd en Een fragment over bisschop Diederik I van Metz*, ed. and trans. H. van Rij (Amsterdam, 1980).

Frutolf and Ekkehard, *Chroniken und die anonyme Kaiserchronik*, ed. F.-J. Schmale and I. Schmale-Ott, AQDG 15 (Darmstadt, 1972).

Lampert of Hersfeld, *Annalen*, ed. and trans. A. Schmidt and W.D. Fritz, AQDG 13 (Darmstadt, 1975).
Thietmar of Merseburg, *Chronik*, ed. and trans. W. Trillmich, AQDG 9 (Darmstadt, 1966).
Rimbert, *Leben Ansgars*, Adam of Bremen, *Bischofsgeschichte der Hamburger Kirche*, Wipo, *Taten Kaiser Konrads II*, Hermann of Reichenau, *Chronik*, in *Quellen des 9. und 11. Jahrhunderts zur Geschichte der Hamburgischen Kirche und des Reiches*, ed. and trans. W. Trillmich, AQDG 11 (Darmstadt, 1968).
For the abbreviations used see n.5

SECONDARY SOURCES

P. Corbet, *Les saints ottoniens* (Sigmaringen, 1986).
Frauen im Frühmittelalter: eine ausgewählte kommentierte Bibliographie, W. Affeldt *et al.* (Frankfurt am Main, 1990).
H.W. Goetz, *Weibliche Lebensgestaltung im frühen Mittelalter* (Cologne, 1991).

9

Ottonian intellectual culture in the tenth century and the role of Theophano*

ROSAMOND McKITTERICK

The association of intellectual culture in Ottonian Germany and the empress Theophano in the title of this chapter raises a number of obvious questions.[1] First of all, Theophano, rightly or wrongly, has been regarded as a representative of Greek culture, and thus as the main source for the introduction of the indisputably Byzantine cultural influences at work in tenth-century Germany.[2] Byzantine artefacts and sumptuous textiles of tenth-century German provenance have been associated with a posited but undocumented and untraceable dowry,[3] or else have been suggested as being part of the baggage of the entourage which may have accompanied Theophano from Byzantium.[4]

I am not qualified to consider the wealth of material art historians such as Hans Wentzel have surveyed, with the ivory plaques and boxes, cameos, silks, gold and silver crosses, enamels,

* This text appeared also in *Early Medieval Europe*, 2 (1993), 53–74.

1 I should first like to record my thanks to Yitzhak Hen for his assistance in checking references when a leg injury had reduced my mobility. I am grateful to Jonathan Shepard for vigorous discussion of many aspects of the topic, and to my audience at Kasteel Hernen in May 1991, in particular to Karl Leyser, for many helpful comments. As it turned out, this was the last time I saw Karl before his death almost exactly a year later; I make this small offering, therefore, to his memory.

2 On these influences see O. Mazal, *Byzanz und das Abendland* (Graz, 1981).

3 H. Wentzel, 'Das byzantinische Erbe der ottonischen Kaiser: Hypothesen über den Brautschatz der Theophano', *Festschrift für Wolfgang Krönig*, *Aachener Kunstblätter*, 40 (1971), 15–39 and 43 (1972), 11–96.

4 See the critical discussion of the various possibilities by H. Wentzel, 'Alte und altertümliche Kunstwerke der Kaiserin Theophano', *Pantheon*, 30 (1972), 3–18. For more recent discussion, however, see the excellent collection of essays in von Euw and Schreiner, *Kaiserin Theophanu*, especially H. Westermann-Angerhausen, 'Spuren der Theophanu in der ottonischen Schatzkunst?', II, pp. 193–218.

and crystal chessmen, flasks and reliquaries now reposing in various ecclesiastical treasuries and museums. I would only wish to observe that there were many ways in which such objects could have reached Germany. Quite apart from other gift-laden Byzantine embassies before 899 and after 945 to and from the Carolingian and Ottonian courts,[5] there are the many contacts between the East and West Franks and Constantinople, with Venice and Ravenna, and with central and southern Italy, especially the Greeks in Apulia and Calabria, which also could have served as a route for objects from Byzantium.[6] Further, the remarkable duplication in the type of object documented by Wentzel, such as the little ivory plaques depicting the Virgin and Child, may represent the development of a particular taste or fashion for this type of artefact on a large scale among the Frankish and Saxon aristocracy, a taste catered to by enterprising merchants and craftsmen.[7] Enhanced knowledge of Byzantium and increased possibility of contact with Byzantium, even if these cannot be documented precisely, may well have been a consequence of Theophano's marriage and have made such objects fashionable. Yet it is arguable that the interest in things Greek apparent here and there in our ninth- and tenth-century sources, now fully documented by Berschin,[8] quite apart from the long-hoped-for marriage with a Greek princess so clearly mirrored in such sources as Liutprand of Cremona,[9] provides the background for an aesthetic appreciation of Greek works of art in the West to which the surviving artefacts bear witness. Otto II's marriage to Theophano might therefore be interpreted as a culmination of the attraction Byzantium had in some western eyes at so many levels, even if the

[5] *Byzantium and the West, c. 850–c. 1200: proceedings of the XVII Spring Symposium of Byzantine Studies*, ed. J.D. Howard-Johnston (Amsterdam, 1988), especially the essays by T.S. Brown, J. Shepard and K.J. Leyser.

[6] See K.J. Leyser, 'The tenth century in Byzantine–Western relationships', in *Relations between East and West in the Middle Ages*, ed. D. Baker (Edinburgh, 1973), pp. 29–63, reprinted in K.J. Leyser, *Medieval Germany and its Neighbours, 900–1250* (London, 1982), pp. 103–37.

[7] Wentzel, 'Byzantinische Erbe' (see n. 3), especially pp. 12–17.

[8] W. Berschin, *Greek Letters and the Latin Middle Ages from Jerome to Nicholas of Cusa*, trans. J.C. Frakes (revised and expanded from the German edition of 1980) (Washington, DC, 1988). See also B.M. Kaczynski, *Greek in the Carolingian Age: The St Gall Manuscripts* (Cambridge, Mass., 1988).

[9] Liutprand of Cremona, *Antapodosis* and *Relatio de legatione Constantinopolitana*, ed. J. Becker, MGH SS XLI (Hanover, 1915), English trans. F.A. Wright, *The Works of Liudprand of Cremona* (London, 1930).

Ottonians' immediate political goals of a firm foothold in Italy are the most obvious context in which to understand the negotiations with Byzantium and their nuptial conclusion.

To what degree can Theophano herself be shown to have been in a position to have exerted any influence on Ottonian culture at all, either indirectly or directly? In consequence, we have to consider the exercise of royal patronage in relation to culture, whether and why the Ottonian rulers might have been in a position to appreciate or patronize intellectual culture, and thus the degree of literacy and learning they display. It is true that to some degree Otto I attempted to emulate Charlemagne in the hospitality he offered to scholars from other countries, such as the *grammatici* Gunzo and Stephen from Novara or Liutprand of Cremona who wrote his notorious *Antapodosis* while at Otto's court. Stephen of Novara, at least, appears to have been brought to Germany in order to teach at Würzburg.[10]

Unfortunately there is no comparable evidence, as far as the Ottonian rulers are concerned, for the exercise of royal patronage such as we have for the Carolingian rulers.[11] With the Carolingians, as is now well known, 'the web of royal favour and patronage extended far and wide in the kingdom, reaching across any regional divisions in order to create the tenuous but potentially intimate and productive relationship between scholar and patron . . . the king's patronage held the promise of material rewards as well as scholarly recognition and many sought it'.[12] Scribes, artists and scholars found their greatest admirers and patrons in the Carolingian rulers, and in the decorated codices presented to the rulers, or produced in ateliers closely associated with the court, such as the Ada group and Coronation Gospels group under Charlemagne, the Lothar court school at Aachen and

[10] M. Manitius, *Geschichte der lateinischen Literatur des Mittelalters*, I, *Von Justinian bis zur Mitte des 10. Jahrhunderts* (Munich, 1911), pp. 531–6; Berschin, *Greek Letters* (see n. 8), pp. 174–82 and see B. Bischoff and J. Hofmann, *Libri Sancti Kyliani: die würzburger Schreibschule und die Dombibliothek im VIII. und IX. Jahrhundert* (Würzburg, 1952), p. 25.

[11] I summarize here my arguments from 'Royal patronage of culture in the Frankish kingdoms under the Carolingians: motives and consequences', in *Committenti e produzione artistico-letteraria nell'alto medioevo occidentale*, Settimane di Studio del Centro Italiano di studi sull'alto medioevo, 39 (Spoleto, 1992), pp. 93–129.

[12] R. McKitterick, 'Charles the Bald (823–877) and his library: the patronage of learning', *English Historical Review*, 95 (1980), 28–47.

the Hofschule manuscripts produced for Charles the Bald, we can observe some of the finest pieces of Carolingian book production extant. Analyses of Frankish royal patronage have tended hitherto to concentrate on the personal pleasure and edification on the part of the Carolingian kings, with books and objects made in ateliers apparently organized to serve the king's wishes, or emanating from the court and stimulating activity in order to serve essentially selfish concerns. The evidence relating to Charlemagne, Louis the Pious, Louis the German, Charles the Bald and Lothar has been assessed in order to determine the personal interests of the king, the difference patronage of culture made to his personal possessions, especially his library, his interaction with the scholars at court and the degree to which his exercise of patronage reflects his personal piety. The activities of artists and scribes working for such Carolingian rulers as Lothar and Charles the Bald indicate the gathering together of craftsmen from different centres and with different training behind them to work for the royal court and to provide books for the chapel, for the personal use of the king and his family, and for presentation to selected recipients. These court ateliers were complemented by work produced on commission in other centres throughout the kingdom. Queens, too, were active patrons, and a number of fine books, donated to particular ecclesiastical centres, such as the handsome Sacramentary (New York, Pierpont Morgan Library G 57) commissioned from St Amand and presented by Queen Ermintrude to the convent of Chelles, can be associated with them.

In contemporary Carolingian sources, emphasis is placed upon the king's personal intervention and involvement in the promotion of scholarship and closely interwoven with the Christian piety of the kings, though Notker Balbulus gives us some idea that the favouring of scholars also had the wider purpose of promoting scholarship throughout the kingdom.[13] We have, too, Carolingian legislation insisting on correctness in speech and writing and on the encouragement of learning.[14] The gathering together of artists and scribes or the commissions to artists and scribes elsewhere to produce work both for the king's personal use

[13] Notker Balbulus, *Gesta Karoli*, I, c. 1, *Quellen zur karolingischen Reichsgeschichte*, III, ed. R. Rau, AQDG 7 (Darmstadt, 1975), p. 322.

[14] For example, the *Admonitio generalis*, MGH Cap[itularia] I, no. 22, c. 72, p. 60 and the *De litteris colendis*, MGH Cap. I, no. 29, p. 79 and P. Lehmann, 'Fuldaer Studien', *Sitzungsberichte der bayerischen Akademie der Wissenschaften, phil. hist. Klasse* (1927), pp. 4–13.

and enjoyment and for donation to other centres as part of a strategy of royal piety and largesse can thus be fully documented.[15]

With the Carolingian evidence, moreover, we are able to go still further to explore the motives and consequences of patronage. It is clear from the manuscript evidence in particular that royal patronage is not just random aesthetic pleasure or arcane intellectual curiosity, but an organized and determined assembly and deployment of resources to carry out what appear to be specific aims and objectives. If one looks beyond the sheer number of Gospel Books produced in the royal ateliers of Charlemagne, for example, one can see that what was being disseminated was a particular text, namely, a Carolingian edition of the Gospels. Patronage for the Carolingian rulers was inextricably bound up with the themes of *correctio* and *emendatio*. Not only Gospel Books and Psalters, but also corrected texts or texts copied from exemplars regarded as authoritative, were prepared, under the auspices of Pippin III, Charlemagne and Louis the Pious, of Sacramentaries and canon law, the Homiliary, the Bible, the Rule of Benedict and the secular laws of the people under Frankish rule. In the patronage of music, too, can be discerned, according to the accounts presented by both Einhard and Notker Balbulus,[16] the desire to sing and perform the music correctly and to disseminate the same chants and melodies to different centres.[17] A very similar liturgy was sung in churches all over the Carolingian Empire, thereby reinforcing the political control exerted by the Carolingians in the cultural and religious spheres.

For the Carolingians therefore, the patronage of book production and intellectual culture was primarily for the promotion of their royal power as Christian kings and for the consolidation of the Christian faith by disseminating the key texts on which that faith was based. By contrast, no such motives are as yet discernible in relation to the Ottonian rulers, despite the political inspiration provided for the Ottonian rulers by their Carolingian predecessors. I stress 'as yet', for work on tenth-century manuscripts has

[15] See, for example, T.A. Heslop. 'The production of de luxe manuscripts and the patronage of King Cnut and Queen Emma', *Anglo-Saxon England*, 19 (1990), 151–95.

[16] Einhard, *Vita Karoli*, c. 26, in *Quellen zur karolingischen Reichsgeschichte*, I, ed. Rau, p. 198; Notker, *Gesta Karoli*, I, cc. 7 and 10 (see n. 13), pp. 330–2, 336.

[17] See S. Rankin, 'Carolingian Music', in *Carolingian Culture: Emulation and Innovation*, ed. R. McKitterick (Cambridge, 1993), pp. 274–316.

not so far been conducted with the intensity and precision that has been apparent in the study of ninth-century books, notably in the work of Bernhard Bischoff. Much still remains to be charted for the book production of the tenth century.[18]

For the moment I wish to focus on what the manuscript evidence may have to tell us concerning the exercise of royal patronage under the Ottonian rulers and whether we have anything comparable to the Carolingian royal libraries and promotion of scholarly activity emanating from the court. As far as Henry the Fowler, Otto I and Otto II are concerned, we do not. One Gospel Book (Coburg, Kunstsammlung der Veste, Nr. I) produced at Metz in *c.* 860 is thought to have been a gift from King Aethelstan to Otto I and his mother Queen Matilda; it was at the royal convent of Gandersheim, where Otto II's daughter Sophia was abbess, by the beginning of the eleventh century.[19] A further Gospel Book, now London, British Library Cotton Tiberius A.II, written at Lobbes at the end of the ninth century, was probably given by Otto to Aethelstan.[20] Both therefore were arguably diplomatic gifts but, unlike such gifts made by the ninth-century Carolingian rulers, neither appears to have been specially commissioned for the occasion. One or two ivories have also been linked with Otto, as has the marvellous crown now in the Schatzkammer in Vienna.[21] Only the Gospels from Quedlinburg, now in New York, Pierpont Morgan Library, M 755 (Corvey, s.x) and a couple of associated manuscripts in Baltimore (Walters Art Gallery, W751, Corvey, s.x) and Rheims (Bibliothèque Municipale 10, Corvey, s.x) were once claimed to be from a scriptorium writing for members of the court. These are now attributed to Corvey, which raises a different set of problems I have discussed elsewhere.[22] For the moment it seems to be the case

18 A magnificent contribution has been made, however, by H. Hoffmann, *Buchkunst und Königtum im ottonischen und frühsalischen Reich*, MGH Schriften, 30,1 (Stuttgart, 1986); see also H. Mayr-Harting, *Ottonian Book Illumination: An Historical Study* (London, 1991).

19 Hoffmann, *Buchkunst* (see n.18), p. 9 and see S. Keynes, 'King Athelstan's books', in *Learning and Literature in Anglo-Saxon England: Studies Presented to Peter Clemoes on the occasion of his Sixty-Fifth Birthday*, ed. M. Lapidge and H. Gneuss (Cambridge, 1985), pp. 143–201 at pp. 189–93.

20 Hoffmann, *Buchkunst* (see n. 18), p. 9 and Keynes, 'King Athelstan's books' (see n. 19), pp. 147–53.

21 P.E. Schramm and F. Mütherich, *Denkmale der deutschen Könige und Kaiser* (Münich, 1981), nos. 67, 68 and possibly, 77, 141 and 145.

22 Hoffmann, *Buchkunst* (see n. 18), pp. 128, 129 and R. McKitterick, 'Continuity and innovation in tenth-century Ottonian culture', in *Intellectual Life in the Middle*

that the early Ottonian rulers had no one atelier, or even a group of ateliers, on which they could call for books either for their personal use or as gifts.

Otto II is known to have given a book to Magdeburg and was recorded in the eighteenth century as having given one containing a representation of him and his wife, Theophano, to Gandersheim.[23] Ekkehard IV in his *Casus sancti Galli*, moreover, records Otto's interest in the books at St Gallen and how he took a number of them away with him, including a quadripartite Psalter with its text set out in four columns with the three Latin versions of the Psalms and one in transliterated Greek, perhaps to aid him in the learning of Greek (Bamberg, Staatsbibliothek, Bibl. 44, St Gall, s.x^{in} (909)). [24] Its origin is thought to lie in Italy and it is one of a number of western Greek texts from St Gallen which were copied and used in western ways with no obvious sign that Byzantium had any role in their original production.[25] It is of interest, however, that a copy was later made of this Psalter and is linked to Essen where Otto's daughter, Sophia, was abbess (Essen Münsterschatz, Essen, s.x/xi and a further copy was made at Cologne, now Cologne, Dombibliothek 8, s.x/xi).[26] It appears to have been Otto II rather than his son who initially inspired the Master of the Registrum Gregorii, that is, the artist of the single leaf now in Chantilly, Musée Condé 14bis (Trier, s.x^{ex}), to portray the enthroned emperor receiving homage from the four provinces. The Gospel Book now in Paris (Bibliothèque Nationale lat. 8851, Trier, s.x^{ex}), with its four imperial medallions, is another instance, though the real efflorescence of ruler portraits is in celebration of Otto III and, in particular, Henry II and Henry III.[27]

Not until the very end of the tenth and beginning of the eleventh century therefore can a group of manuscripts be associated with the ruler with any certainty. From the very last years of

Ages: Essays Presented to Margaret Gibson, ed. L. Smith and B. Ward (London and Rio Grande, Ohio, 1992), pp. 15–24.

[23] Thietmar, *Chronicon*, III, 1, ed. R. Holtzmann with German trans. by W. Trillmich, AQDG 9 (Darmstadt, 1974), p. 84; Hoffmann, *Buchkunst* (see n. 18), p. 38.

[24] Ekkehard IV, *Casus sancti Galli*, c. 16, MGH SS II, p. 147; Hoffmann, *Buchkunst* (see n. 18), p. 368.

[25] Kaczynski, *Greek in the Carolingian Age* (see n. 8).

[26] Berschin, *Greek Letters* (see n. 8), pp. 149, 198.

[27] Hoffmann, *Buchkunst* (see n. 18), pp. 468, 483.

Otto III's reign we have the famous quartet of codices, Munich, Bayerische Staatsbibliothek, Clm 4453 (Gospels), Bamberg Staatsbibliothek Bibl. 22 (Song of Songs, Proverbs of Solomon, glossed Book of Daniel) and 76 (glossed Book of Isaiah) and Lit. 5 (Troper), all produced by scribes and artists trained at Reichenau.[28] These are thought to have been made for Otto's personal use. The same atelier went on, as Henry II's Gospels, the *Pericopes* and the Bamberg Apocalypse (perhaps originally ordered for Otto III: Munich, Bayerische Staatsbibliothek, Clm 4452 and Clm 4454, Bamberg Staatsbibliothek, Bibl. 240, Reichenau, s.xi^{in}) indicate, to serve Otto's successor Henry II.[29] Whether Reichenau presented these manuscripts to the ruler in order to win favour or whether they were commissioned by the ruler from Reichenau can no longer be ascertained. Reichenau's position in the Ottonian kingdom has still to be clarified, or it may have been producing books for export to wealthy patrons, both lay and ecclesiastical, in a way analogous to that of Tours in the mid-ninth century.[30] What is clear, however, is that there was no larger purpose to such commissions or gifts, as far as the rulers were concerned, than to provide sumptuous royal books.

A further potential source of information concerning Otto III's patronage of book production and intellectual culture might be thought to be the large number of books of different origin which Florentine Mütherich has suggested were once part of Otto III's personal library.[31] The forty-four books she discusses reflect Otto's education and intellectual tastes as well as the high office and its requirements of their owner. The books include volumes presented to him early in his reign, such as the diminutive prayer Book from Mainz now in Pommersfelden (Schlossbibliothek MS 347, Mainz, c. 990) written by the female scribe, Duriswint, in

[28] *Ibid.*, pp. 333, 308, 309, 311, 309 respectively. For further discussion see F. Mütherich, 'Peinture', in L. Grodecki *et al.*, *Le siècle de l'an mil* (Paris, 1973), 87–93; Mayr-Harting, *Ottonian Book Illumination* (see n. 18), especially I, pp. 203–8 and II, pp. 214–28.

[29] Hoffmann, *Buchkunst* (see n. 18), pp. 332, 333, 309.

[30] R. McKitterick, 'Carolingian book production: some problems', *The Library*, 6th series 12 (1990), 1–33 and McKitterick, 'Carolingian Bible production: the Tours anomaly', in *The Early Medieval Bible: Its Production, Decoration and Use*, ed. R. Gameson, Cambridge Studies in Palaeography and Codicology, 1 (Cambridge, 1994), pp. 63–79.

[31] F. Mütherich, 'The library of Otto III', in *The Role of the Book in Medieval Culture*, ed. P. Ganz, Bibliologia: elementa ad librorum studia pertinentia, 4 (Turnhout, 1986), pp. 11–26.

gold on purple dyed parchment,[32] and some remarkable Gospel Books, such as Manchester, John Rylands Library 98 (Trier, s.x/xi), possibly made for Otto's coronation in 996,[33] the Morgan Golden Gospels (New York, Pierpont Morgan Library, Morgan 23, Trier, s.x$^{4/4}$),[34] and the Liuthar Gospels in Aachen (Domschatz, Ottonenevangeliar, Reichenau, s.x/xi).[35]

The largest group of books identified by Mütherich is from Italy, some of them apparently given to Otto by his Greek tutor Johannes Philagathos. A list of these books was entered *c.* 1000 in an early ninth-century medical text from Lorsch (Bamberg Staatsbibliothek, med.1) and included texts of Orosius, Persius, two copies of Livy, Fulgentius, capitularies, Isidore of Seville, *In Isagogas Porphirii minus commentum Boethii* and two glossaries. Some of these are still extant among the manuscripts in Bamberg, not least a fifth-century uncial Livy and another Livy from the ninth century written in central Italy (Bamberg, Staatsbibliothek class. 35a and 34).[36] Other Italian manuscripts in Bamberg from the tenth or early eleventh century contain texts on subjects such as science, music and philosophy, and include such authors as Jerome-Gennadius *De viris illustribus*, Augustine *De haeresibus* (Bamberg, Staatsbibliothek, patr. 87), Priscian (Bamberg, Staatsbibliothek, class. 4), Quintilian (Bamberg, Staatsbibliothek, class. 44), Calcidius (Bamberg, Staatsbibliothek, class. 18), the Epitome of Livy by Florus (Bamberg, Staatsbibliothek, class. 51) and a late eighth-century copy of Cassiodorus' *Institutiones* from Monte Cassino (Bamberg, Staatsbibliothek, Bibl. patr. 61). These accord with the scholarly interests of the king indicated by other manuscripts with clear implications of royal ownership. To these can be added books associated with the royal library of the Carolingian ruler Louis the Pious, such as Pliny's *Naturalis historia* and the *Epistolae morales* of Seneca (Bamberg, Staatsbibliothek, class. 42 and 46, court scriptorium of

32 Hoffmann, *Buchkunst* (see n. 18), p. 255 and *Vor dem Jahr 1000: abendländische Buchkunst zur Zeit der Kaiserin Theophanu: Ausstellung des Schnütgen-Museums, Köln 1991* (Cologne, 1991), pp. 92–6.

33 Hoffmann, *Buchkunst* (see n. 18), p. 479.

34 *Ibid.*, p. 482 and E.A. Lowe, 'The Morgan Golden Gospels: the date and origin of the manuscript', in *Studies in Art and Literature for Belle da Costa Greene*, ed. D. Miner (Princeton, 1954), pp. 266–79, reprinted in *E.A. Lowe, Palaeographical Papers 1907–1965*, ed. L. Bieler (Oxford, 1972), pp. 399–416.

35 Hoffmann, *Buchkunst* (see n. 18), p. 307.

36 Schramm and Mütherich, *Denkmale* (see n. 21), nos. 89 and 90, p. 150.

Louis the Pious, s.ix^1)[37] as well as such late Antique manuscripts as the Quedlinburg Itala (Berlin, Deutsche Staatsbibliothek, lat. fol. 485, Rome, s.v^1) perhaps given by Otto to his sister Sophia[38] and the *Notitia dignitatum*, known only through later copies, such as the fragments now in Augsburg (Fürstlich-Oettingen-Wallerstein'sche Bibliothek, 1.2.2°37, s.x^1? Rheinland) and the copy now in Munich (Bayerische Staatsbibliothek, Clm 10291, Speyer, s. xvi).[39] Some ninth-century West Frankish manuscripts of theology, philosophy and history, mostly by Carolingian authors such as John Scotus Eriugena (Bamberg, Staatsbibliothek, philos. 2, Soissons, s.ix^1), Paschasius Radbertus (Bamberg, Staatsbibliothek, patr. 88, N. France, s.x^1), Hucbald of St Amand (*De musica*, Bamberg, Staatsbibliothek, Var. I, Rheims, s.x), Hincmar of Rheims (*Vita Sancti Remigii*, Bamberg, Staatsbibliothek, Hist. 162, Rheims, s.x), Heiric of Auxerre (Bamberg, Staatsbibliothek, patr. 46, Rheims, s.ix^2) and Richer, appear to have been given to Otto by Gerbert of Rheims, along with West Frankish copies of such texts as Isidore's *De natura rerum* (Bamberg, Staatsbibliothek, Bibl. patr. 61, E. France, s.ix$^{1/3}$), Martianus Capella (Bamberg, Staatsbibliothek, Bibl. patr. 39, Fleury with glosses in Rheims hand, s.ix^2), Quintilian (Bamberg, Staatsbibliothek, Bibl. class. 45, France, s.x), Boethius, *De arithmetica* (Bamberg, Staatsbibliothek, class 5, produced at Tours *c.* 845 and presented to Charles the Bald, and Bamberg, Staatsbibliothek, class. 14 perhaps actually copied in Germany early in Otto's reign) and Augustine (Bamberg, Staatsbibliothek, patr. 21, NE. France, ix^2). Indeed, it was Richer's autograph copy (Bamberg, Staatsbibliothek, Hist. 5, Rheims, 995–8) of the *Historiae* that came into royal possession. One can only speculate as to how such manuscripts as the Pliny, Seneca and Boethius from the Carolingian royal library came to be in the Ottonian royal library a century and a half later. A possible route may have been through King Odo of West Francia's gifts to Arnulf of Carinthia.[40]

[37] B. Bischoff, 'Die Hofbibliothek unter Ludwig dem Frommen', in Bischoff, *Mittelalterliche Studien*, III (Stuttgart, 1981), pp. 171–86.

[38] I. Levin, *The Quedlinburg Itala*, Litterae textuales (Leiden, 1985).

[39] J.J.G. Alexander, 'The illustrated manuscripts of the *Notitia Dignitatum*', in *Aspects of the Notitia Dignitatum*, ed. R. Goodburn and P. Bartholomew, British Archaeological Reports, Supplementary series 15 (Oxford, 1976), pp. 11–50 and *Texts and Transmission: A Survey of the Latin Classics*, ed. L.D. Reynolds (Oxford, 1983), pp. 253–7.

[40] R. McKitterick, *The Frankish Kingdoms under the Carolingians, 751–987* (London, 1983), p. 272.

Otto III's library is a wonderfully diverse and scholarly collection, but in relation to Ottonian intellectual culture and book production it has some odd features. For one thing, as Florentine Mütherich has pointed out, there is no contemporary work extant dedicated to Otto himself by a German scholar of his day.[41] Only in a small group of manuscripts, moreover, do we have any that were arguably acquired for use by Otto or his court advisers. These manuscripts, dated to the ninth and tenth centuries, include the Institutes of Justinian (Bamberg, Staatsbibliothek, iur. I, Italy. s.x), to which had been added the capitulary of Otto I issued from Pavia in 971 and a tract on the ranking of papal and Byzantine officials, a volume of canon law and polemics against pope Formosus (Bamberg, Staatsbibliothek, can. 1, Italy, s.ix/x) with added verses by Otto's chancellor Leo of Vercelli and the poem *Roma caput mundi*, and what Fuhrmann has described as a dossier of documents relating to the coronation of 962 (Bamberg, Staatsbibliothek, can. 4, Italy s.x^{2}).[42] These include the pseudo-Isidorean decretals and the text of the *Constitutum Constantini* from which a certain amount of political theory concerning the imperial position *vis-à-vis* the pope and the church might be derived. Yet all are of Italian origin and all predate Otto's reign by some decades. The total corpus of books associated with Otto produces only the small group of liturgical books from Reichenau with any discernible link with the ruling house and actually of German origin. Only one other, a copy of Boethius perhaps given to Otto by his first tutor Bernward of Hildesheim, was copied by a German scribe.[43] All the others were supplied from West Francia and Italy, mostly by means of gifts from Otto's teachers rather than as a result of his own initiative. Whether or not this can be taken as a reflection on the poverty of Ottonian intellectual culture, though I doubt it, what it does seem to indicate is Otto's absorption in Italian affairs and lack of contact with what was going on in his German realm. In such a context the sumptuous gifts from Reichenau look like an appeal for attention and recognition and an affirmation of what his contemporary scribes and artists could achieve. Certainly the Italian orientation of Otto III's cultural

[41] Mütherich, 'The library of Otto III' (see n. 31), p. 22.

[42] H. Fuhrmann, 'Konstantinische Schenkung und abendländisches Kaisertum', *DA*, 22 (1966), 143–51.

[43] Bamberg Staatsbibliothek, Class 14 (Germany, s.x), see H. Fischer, 'Die königliche Bibliothek in Bamberg und ihre Handschriften', *Zentralblatt für Bibliothekswesen*, 24 (1907), 364–93.

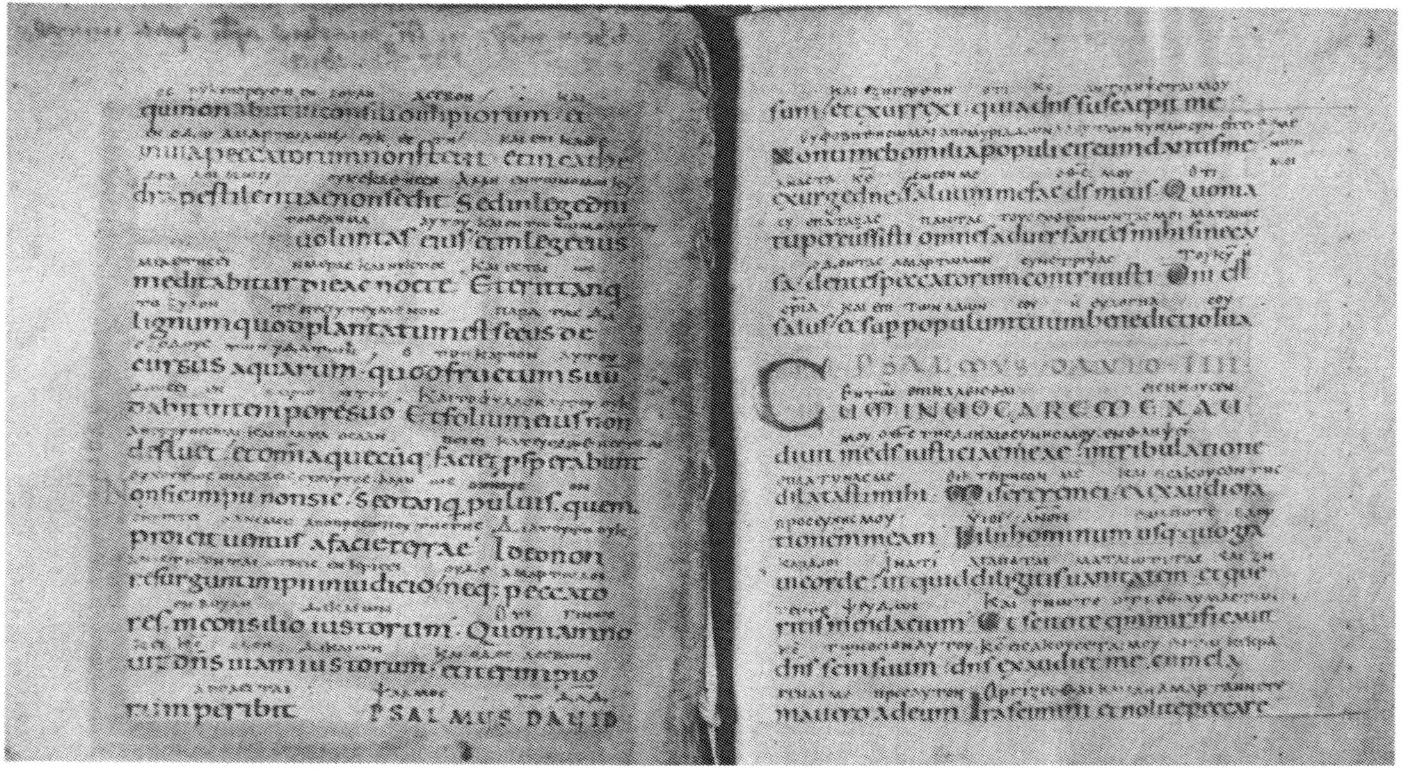

8. Trier Stadtbibliothek MS 7/9 8°, fols. 2v and 3r. (I am grateful to the Stadtbibliothek/Stadtarchiv, Trier, and to Dr Reiner Nolden for permission to reproduce these pages.)

interests contrasts sharply with the cultivation of German centres of book production under Henry II.

The almost total absence of any manuscripts that can be associated directly with Byzantium, or which contain Greek, moreover, is striking. Only in the St Gallen Quadripartite Psalter, borrowed by Otto II from St Gallen, and presumably inherited by Otto III (Bamberg, Staatsbibliothek, Bibl. 44. St Gallen AD 909), and in the Greek alphabets in majuscule and indifferent minuscule added in the tenth century to Bamberg, Bibl. patr. 61, fol. 131v, a copy of Gregory of Tours' *De cursu stellarum* and Isidore of Seville's *De natura rerum*, is any Greek to be found at all. The overwhelming impression, moreover, is of Italy as the primary source of supply of older books acquired from a variety of different sources and by various means. There is no systematic patronage of particular centres, no group of scholars associated with the court, no royal role in the dissemination of particular texts, no cultivation of contemporary scholarship, no court atelier, no sign even of occasional sponsorship of individual scholars or craftsmen.

It would perhaps seem unfair to set the Ottonian rulers against the Carolingian yardstick were it not for the facts, first of all that Charlemagne himself was regarded, at least by Otto III, as a model for the exercise of kingship[44] and, secondly, that comparable resources to those enjoyed by the Carolingian rulers were available to the Ottonians, as we shall see. Nevertheless it is clear that, apart from the personal intellectual interests of Otto III, we must look elsewhere for developments in Ottonian culture, even if no further than the women of the Ottonian dynasty.

What, for example, of Theophano herself? In Trier Stadtbibliothek there is a magnificent Latin and Greek Psalter (MS 7/9 8° Trier, s.x^{ex}) (see Fig. 8). Five scribes were responsible for its copying, the first of whom, writing in gold on purple-dyed parchment, was none other than the scribe and artist known as the Master of the *Registrum Gregorii* who was also responsible for the resplendent marriage charter of Theophano drawn up in April 972 (Staatsarchiv Wolfenbüttel 6 Urkunde 11), and the Gospel Books containing portraits of Otto II mentioned earlier.[45] The main text of the Psalter is the Latin *Psalterium Romanum*, written

[44] See, for example, Thietmar, *Chronicon*, IV, 47 (see n. 23), pp. 162–4.

[45] Hoffman, *Buchkunst* (see n. 18), pp. 488 and 103–16, 176. The manuscript is small, 164 mm x 128 mm, 203 folios long with only fifteen lines to a page.

in a heavy formal caroline minuscule, with all the letters clearly separated and with virtually no abbreviations. A Greek interlinear translation is provided in Greek uncials. The lay-out is appropriate for a reader who had training in Greek and wished to learn or to understand Latin. One could in fact learn Latin from it. By contrast, it is worth noting that the two other bilingual Psalters extant from Ottonian Germany in the tenth century are designed for Latin readers wishing to learn Greek: Bernkastel-Kues Cusanusstift 10 (Fulda, s.x) represents a tenth-century descendant of the bilingual Psalters recorded at Fulda in the mid-ninth century but with tenth-century corrections in a Greek hand.[46] Manuscripts such as this offer a precious glimpse of occasional Greek visitors to, or resident in, the monasteries of the Ottonian kingdom. Bernkastel-Kues Cusanusstift 9, written north of the Alps in the late ninth or early tenth century, contains, in three columns to a page, the Greek text transliterated into Roman letters in caroline minuscule, the Latin Vulgate text and the Greek text in Greek uncial. Allgeier has proposed that this manuscript was designed to serve as an introduction to the Greek language for a Latin reader and, because some Greek articles were excluded in order to achieve verbal symmetry, that the Psalter in fact provided an elementary textbook of Greek vocabulary.[47]

Although it is not possible to associate Bernkastel-Kues Cusanusstift 9 with anyone in particular, it is likely that the Trier Psalter, in Latin for a Greek reader, on the other hand, represented a commission, perhaps from the Ottonian court. If we accept that the use of gold usually indicates a royal recipient, and appreciate the significance of the same scribe being associated with the Psalter and with Theophano's marriage charter, it seems likely that the most obvious recipient of a book to assist a reader of Greek to learn Latin was Theophano herself.[48] The necessity to learn the

[46] *Ibid.*, p. 144. Compare B. Bischoff, 'Das griechische Element in der abendländischen Bildung des Mittelalters', in his *Mittelalterliche Studien*, II (Stuttgart, 1967), pp. 246–75, at p. 253 and n. 35.

[47] A. Allgeier, 'Exegetische Beiträge zur Geschichte des Griechischen vor dem Humanismus', *Biblica*, 24 (1943), 261–88 at 269, and see also Berschin, *Greek Letters* (see n. 8), pp. 192–3.

[48] Compare G. Franz's entry in *Vor dem Jahr 1000* (see n. 32), no. 38, p. 142, where he states his preference for the Psalter (dated 985–93) being made for Archbishop Egbert (977–93), without, however, any supporting evidence. Berschin, *Greek Letters* (see n. 8), p. 192, stops short of accepting the traditional designation of the book as the 'Psalter of Theophanu' and describes Archbishop Egbert as the '*spiritus rector* of this manuscript'.

language of the country to which one moved on marriage is well documented. In the case of Rotrud, a daughter of Charlemagne betrothed to Constantine VI, it is the clerics who accompanied her for whom we have some indication that they were to learn Greek, whereas tutors were sent beforehand to teach Greek to Hedwig of Swabia in readiness for her marriage.[49] In the case of Theophano, however, no such preparation is recorded. It is likely, indeed, that there had been no time for such advance preparation and Theophano was set to the task of learning Latin on her marriage.[50] The bilingual Psalter, presenting a no doubt familiar text to her, would have been one way of assisting her and was commissioned for her use by someone connected with the court, the most likely person being, in my view, Queen Adelheid. The bilingual Psalter serves as a symbol for Theophano's place in the Ottonian world. She had to learn the language and the ways of the people whose queen she had become.[51]

That Theophano became an Ottonian queen in all respects and not just in name has to be appreciated if we are to assess whether or not she was able to play a part in Ottonian intellectual culture. Theophano, whose parentage is uncertain, is generally accepted as being the niece of the emperor of Byzantium, John Tzimiskes.[52] We know nothing and hear nothing about her before her marriage to Otto II in Rome in April 972. Her marriage charter and contemporary accounts of the wedding at the time give the impression that she was very young.[53] That she was indeed very

[49] Einhard, *Vita Karoli*, c. 19 (see n. 16), p. 190; Berschin, *Greek Letters* (see n. 8), pp. 108–10 and K. Neff, *Die Gedichte des Paulus Diaconus* (Munich, 1980), pp. 67–8; Ekkehard IV, *Casus sancti Galli*, 90, ed. H. Haefele, AQDG 10 (Darmstadt, 1980), p. 184.

[50] On the chronology of the marriage see G. Wolf, 'Wer war Theophanu?', in von Euw and Schreiner, *Kaiserin Theophanu*, II, pp. 385–96 and his references.

[51] Similar examples of Byzantine princesses marrying into foreign royal houses can be cited, such as Maria Lekapena of Bulgaria. S. Runciman, *The Emperor Romanus Lecapenus and his Reign: A Study of Tenth-Century Byzantium* (Cambridge, 1929, reprinted 1988), pp. 97–8; J. Shepard, 'A marriage too far?: Maria Lekapena and Peter of Bulgaria' (this volume).

[52] W.H.R. von Collenburg, 'Wer war Theophanu?', *Genealogisches Jahrbuch*, 64 (1964), 49–71. Wolf, 'Wer war Theophanu?' (see n. 50), pp. 387–8, rehearses the arguments and argues that she was the niece of John Tzimiskes' first wife, a member of the Skleros family. G. Wolf, 'Nochmals zur Frage: Wer war Theophanu?', *BZ*, 81 (1988), 272–83, provides details of earlier literature.

[53] See, for example, Widukind, *Res gestae Saxonicae*, III, c. 71, *Quellen zur Geschichte der sächsischen Kaiserzeit*, ed. H.E. Lohmann, in A. Bauer and R. Rau, new edn, AQDG 8 (Darmstadt, 1977), p. 176, who refers to her as *puella*; and see M.

young is supported by the fact that the birth of her first child was not until 975 and that in the next five years she proved her fertility by giving birth to four further children. She would, however, presumably have been required to be capable of conceiving and to have reached the customary minimum age for marriage before she was married to Otto II. We may envisage therefore, a young girl of twelve or thirteen years old; of a not-deprived background and surely relatively elevated social status in the Byzantine aristocracy, who may have spent some time at the royal Byzantine court, and who may have received the standard education for a girl with good connections in Byzantium, whatever that was.[54] She was married into a family, and, indeed, a people, with a long tradition of strong-minded and forceful queens.[55] Surely she would have needed to be educated in the Saxon way, just as her counterpart, Bertha, illegitimate daughter of Hugh of Arles, had her name changed to Eudokia and was educated in Byzantine imperial ways on her marriage to the soon-to-be emperor Romanos II.[56]

The obvious person to instruct Theophano in Ottonian ways was Adelheid, with help perhaps from Matilda, abbess of Qued-

Uhlirz, 'Studien über Theophanu, I und II', *DA*, 6 (1943), 442–74, and W. Ohnsorge, 'Die Heirat Ottos II. mit der Byzantinerin Theophanu (972)', reprinted in his *Ost-Rom und der Westen: gesammelte Aufsätze zur Geschichte der byzantinisch-abendländischen Beziehungen und des Kaisertums* (Darmstadt, 1983), pp. 128–72. Compare also M. Stratmann, 'Die Kaiserin Theophanu in den erzählenden Quellen des 11. und 12. Jahrhunderts', in von Euw and Schreiner, *Kaiserin Theophanu*, II, pp. 413–23.

54 A.E. Laiou, 'The role of women in Byzantine society', *JÖB*, 31/1, *XVI Internationaler Byzantinischer Kongress, Wien 4–9 Oktober* (Vienna, 1981), 233–60, and Robert Browning, 'Literacy in the Byzantine world', *Byzantine and Modern Greek Studies*, 4 (1978), pp. 39–54. This view is shared by F. Tinnefeld, 'Die Braut aus Byzanz – Fragen zum Theophanus Umfeld und gesellschaftlicher Stellung vor ihrer abendländischen Heirat', in *Kaiserin Theophanu Prinzessin aus der Fremde – des Westreichs Grosse Kaiserin*, ed. G. Wolf (Cologne, Weimar and Vienna, 1991), pp. 247–61, who also adds a useful *caveat* as far as Theophano's likely childhood environment is concerned. The possibility that Theophano was married before she reached puberty, however, cannot be excluded. Byzantium would permit child-marriages for reasons of state: see R. Macrides, 'Dynastic marriages', in *Byzantine Diplomacy*, ed. J.E.B. Shepard and S. Franklin (Belfast, 1992), p. 275. I am grateful to Jonathan Shepard for these references.

55 See K.J. Leyser, *Rule and Conflict in an Early Medieval Society: Ottonian Saxony* (London, 1979), pp. 49–74. P. Corbet, *Les Saints ottoniens: sainteté dynastique, sainteté royale et sainteté féminine autour de l'an mil* (Sigmaringen, 1986) and F.-R. Erkens, 'Die Frau als Herrscherin in ottonisch-frühsalischer Zeit', in von Euw and Schreiner, *Kaiserin Theophanu*, II, pp. 245–60.

56 Liutprand, *Antapodosis*, V, 20 (see n. 9), p. 466; see Runciman, *The Emperor Romanus Lecapenus* (see n. 51), p. 196.

linburg (954/5–99), Otto II's sister. What relations were like between these women in the early years is unknown. Formal acknowledgement was made by Theophano and Otto in calling their first-born child Adelheid, after her grandmother, and one suspects that Adelheid would have been a somewhat domineering mother-in-law who had taken the young bride firmly in hand.[57] Charters between the years 976 and 981 in which Theophano intervenes, fully in accordance with long-established Frankish custom for the making of gifts by queens, appear to reflect the debt Theophano owed to the kindness of the nuns of Herzebrock, Nivelles, Gandersheim (where Otto I's niece Gerberga was abbess), Herford and S. Maria in Cosmedin in Ravenna, that is, some of the convents on the royal *iter* where Theophano stayed to give birth to her babies or was cared for in the difficult five years of almost non-stop pregnancy and a growing clutch of small children.[58] The close family connections of many of these convents with the royal house, many of them actually presided over by royal abbesses, is one indication of how Theophano herself was absorbed into the family and came under the influence of mother- and sister-in-law and aunts by marriage. It is also in a number of these family convents that the most innovative of Ottonian literary and historiographical writing was done, not least the Terentian plays of Hrotsvit.[59] It was to female members of the royal house that some of these works were dedicated or by whom they were commissioned. Works celebrating the queens of the Liudolfing dynasty, moreover, were also produced. We need only to recall the two Lives of Queen Matilda written by a nun at Nordhausen in about 975, possibly on commission from Otto II or Adelheid, which constitute the most eloquent proclamations of a distinctive ideal of sanctity, of a peculiarly royal and feminine sanctity that was of far-reaching importance for the sense of identity and religious ideals of the Ottonian royal house.[60] It fell

[57] M. Uhlirz, 'Studien ber Theophanu III', *DA*, 9 (1951–2), 122–35, discusses the significance of these names. See also O. Perst, 'Zur Reihenfolge der Kinder Ottos II. und der Theophano', *DA*, 14 (1958), 230–6; Wolf, 'Wer war Theophanu?'(see n. 50), p. 389, suggests that Sophia was named after Theophano's mother.

[58] Uhlirz, 'Studien über Theophanu III' (see n. 57). On the *iter* and the royal monasteries see John W. Bernhardt, *Itinerant Kingship and Royal Monasteries in Early Medieval Germany, 936–1075* (Cambridge, 1993).

[59] P. Dronke, *Women Writers of the Middle Ages* (Cambridge, 1984), pp. 5–83 and his references. See also C. Villa, *La 'Lectura Terentii'* (Padua, 1984), pp. 99–132.

[60] Corbet, *Les Saints ottoniens* (see n. 55), pp. 120–234.

to the royal women, too, to uphold the status of the dynasty.[61] To this possibly self-appointed task can be linked Widukind of Corvey's *Res gestae Saxonicae* dedicated to Matilda, abbess of Quedlinburg and Otto I's daughter.[62] It was also Matilda who commissioned the *Annales Quedlinburgenses*.[63] Hrotsvit of Gandersheim's *Gesta Ottonis* commissioned by Gerberga, Otto I's niece, and her *Primordia coenobii Gandersheimensis* on the origins of Gandersheim composed in 973 or so, are further contributions on the part of the female members of the royal family to the recording of their dynasty's history.[64] This writing of history by and for women of the Liudolfing house has rightly been stressed by Elisabeth van Houts as indicating their function as transmitters of information about their families and as preservers of tradition and a historical past.[65] Yet the levels of culture implied by such a role must also be stressed, for it is quite clear from the extant sources relating to such royal female religious houses as Quedlinburg, Gandersheim, Essen, Nordhausen or Susteren and the aristocratic foundations of Niedermünster, Fischbeck, Herford and Meschede, Gernrode, Hilwartshausen and Lamspringe, that education was available in some of them, and that they possessed, even if they themselves did not produce, their own books.[66] If the male members of the royal house showed only an occasional interest in learning, the queens and royal daughters and nieces were far more active, and it is a subject that needs far fuller investigation than is

[61] See K. Sonnleitner, 'Selbstbewusstsein und Selbstverständnis der ottonischen Frauen im Spiegel der Historiographie des 10. Jahrhunderts', in *Geschichte und ihre Quellen: Festschrift für Friedrich Hausmann zum 70. Geburtstag*, ed. R. Härtel (Graz, 1987), pp. 111–19.

[62] Widukind, *Res gestae Saxonicae*, preface, ed. Lohmann (see n. 53), p. 16.

[63] *Annales Quedlinburgenses*, MGH SS III, pp. 18–90 and the discussion by K. Sonnleitner, 'Die Annalistik der Ottonenzeit als Quelle für die Frauengeschichte', *Schriftenreihe des Instituts für Geschichte: Darstellungen*, 2 (Graz, 1988), 233–49.

[64] *Carmen de Gestis Odonis I Imperatoris* and *Primordia Coenobii Gandesheimensis* of Hrotsvit, in *Hrotsvithae Opera*, ed. H. Homeyer (Paderborn, 1970). See also the discussion by G. Althoff, 'Causa scribendi und Darstellungsabsicht: die Lebensbeschreibungen der Königin Mathilde und andere Beispiele', in *Litterae Medii Aevi: Festschrift für Johanne Autenreith zu ihrem 65. Geburtstag*, ed. M. Borgolte and H. Spilling (Sigmaringen, 1988), pp. 117–33.

[65] E. van Houts, 'Women and the writing of history in the early Middle Ages: the case of abbess Matilda of Essen and Aethelweard', *Early Medieval Europe*, 1 (1992), 53–68.

[66] B. Bischoff, *Mittelalterliche Schatzverzeichnisse*, I (Stuttgart, 1967) and R. McKitterick, 'Frauen und Schriftlichkeit im Frühmittelalter', in *Weibliche Lebensgestaltung im frühen Mittelalter*, ed. H.-W. Goetz (Cologne, 1991), pp. 65–118 at p. 115.

possible here. Theophano herself, however, does not appear in this intellectual context, and apart from the part she may have played in the appointment of her son's tutors, there is little evidence for any role played by her in the intellectual culture of her time, either in promoting the existing Latin culture of the German realm or in introducing Greek texts or authors to her adopted country.

It is arguable that even her political position as regent and the much discussed title *coimperatrix* owe more to the Frankish and Saxon context than to any whisper of Byzantine influence. From at least 29 April 974 Theophano is referred to as *consors regni* and *coimperatrix*. *Consors regni* at least had been a title used before by such Frankish queens as Richardis, wife of Charles the Fat, and by Adelheid when still married to King Lothar of Italy.[67] *Coimperatrix* appears to be a new title. It has been argued that this is a consequence of contemporary or fairly recent Byzantine examples.[68] It is certainly possible. A vivid visual image of a Byzantine empress portrayed as a female counterpart to an emperor was of course available to Otto II in San Vitale at Ravenna and the magnificent portraits there in mosaic of Justinian and Theodora, where interpretation of their relative status and of the significance of the differences between the two portraits is left entirely to the beholder. Nevertheless, an acceptable hypothesis of a Byzantine model would have to be matched by the assumption of the plausibility of Ottonian acceptance of a Byzantine and therefore, presumably by definition, alien, idea in the tenth century. The concepts need not have been as polarized as this implies, however, for Ottonians in the 970s could well have latched on to Byzantine titles, modes of expression or iconography to express graphically or, possibly, more grandiosely, notions of the status of the royal spouse which already existed among them, but for which adequate vocabulary or visual images had been lacking hitherto.

Given the use already in Ottonian documents of words such as *consors regni* and *augusta*, the activities of Adelheid as empress, and

[67] Uhlirz, 'Studien über Theophanu III' (see n. 57) and K. Uhlirz, 'Die Interventionen in den Urkunden des Königs Otto III. bis zum Tode der Kaiserin Theophanu', *Neues Archiv*, 21 (1896), 115–37.

[68] Uhlirz, 'Studien ber Theophanu III' (see n. 57). See also W. Ohnsorge, 'Das Mitkaisertum in der abendländischen Geschichte des früheren Mittelalters', *Zeitschrift der Savigny-Stiftung für Rechtsgeschichte*, Germ. Abt. 67 (1950), 307–35 and M. Uhlirz, 'Zu dem Mitkaisertum der Ottonen: "Theophanu coimperatrix"', *BZ*, 50 (1957), 383–9.

the prominent role women played in Ottonian political and ecclesiastical life, however, Theophano's position could also be interpreted as a logical consequence of the development of female royal influence as queen dowager or queen in the absence of a royal wife for her son the emperor. This is in contrast to recent Byzantine experience where there is no instance in the tenth century of a Byzantine *augusta* taking the helm for long. The tendency there, if we think of Theophano, widow of Romanos II and mother of Basil II and Constantine III, who wed Nikephoros II Phokas, was of the need of a widowed empress to gain a strong new emperor-husband. In the west, however, it was not only Theophano who grasped the reins of government on occasion. Otto II's sister Matilda played a key role, alongside Adelheid and Theophano, in 984, and was left in charge when her nephew Otto III went to Rome in 997.[69] Adelheid, moreover, is as prominent in the political intrigues of the Ottonian realm revealed in Gerbert of Rheims' letters as Theophano, and so, for that matter, is Adelheid's daughter by her first marriage, Emma, queen of the Franks.[70] The lives of Henry I's queen Matilda, referred to earlier, make her strong influence within the kingdom very clear.[71] There are also earlier examples of Frankish royal women playing a prominent role as regents for their sons and as *de facto* rulers of the kingdom, to mention only the Merovingian examples of Balthild, Nantichild and Brunhild,[72] the Carolingian Plectrude in the eighth century attempting to safeguard the inheritance of her grandsons,[73] and the empress Engelberga in the ninth century and her activities as regent in Italy,[74] to say nothing of contemporaries

[69] Thietmar, *Chronicon* (see n. 23), IV, 40–2, pp. 176–80 and *Annales Quedlinburgenses*, 984–985 (see n. 63), pp. 65–7; Leyser, *Rule and Conflict* (see n. 55), p. 44.

[70] *Die Briefsammlung Gerberts von Rheims*, ed. F. Weigle, nos. 6, 20, 52, 74, 97, 103, 117, 119, 120, 128, 138, 204, 208, 215, MGH Die Briefe der deutschen Kaiserzeit (Berlin, Zurich, etc., 1966), 28, 42, 81, 104, 127, 133, 144, 146–8, 155, 165, 246, 248, 256.

[71] *Vita Mahthildis reginae antiquior*, ed. R. Köpke, MGH SS X, pp. 573–82, and *Vita Mahthildis reginae (posterior)*, ed. G.H. Pertz, MGH SS IV, pp. 282–302. Corbet, *Les Saints ottoniens* (see n. 55), pp. 120–234.

[72] J.L. Nelson, 'Queens as Jezebels: the careers of Brunhild and Balthild in Merovingian history', in *Medieval Women*, ed. D. Baker, Studies in Church History, Subsidia I (Oxford, 1978), pp. 31–78.

[73] Fredegar, *Continuationes*, 7–9, *The Fourth Book of the Chronicle of Fredegar with its Continuations*, ed. J.M. Wallace-Hadrill (London, 1960), pp. 86–8.

[74] See, for example, the letters exchanged between Engelberga and Pope John VIII, MGH Epistolae Vll, nos. 44, 82, 91, 94, 212, 293, pp. 42–3, 77–8, 86–7, 88–9, 190–1, 255–6 and C.E. Odegaard, 'The Empress Engleberga', *Speculum*, 26 (1951), 77–103 and G. Pochettino, 'L'imperatrice Angleberga, 850–890', *Archivio Storico Lombardo*, 5th series 48 (1921), 39–149.

such as Aelfthryth, wife of the Anglo-Saxon king Edgar[75] and Adelheid herself as Lothar of Italy's widow.[76] Exertion of a forceful influence in politics, if not actual power, was not apparently something necessarily bestowed by any constitutional right. Much depended on the personality, and the family, of the women concerned and the degree to which they had committed support from the male officials and advisers, especially leading churchmen, who supported the ruler.[77] The queen's position is always defined in relation to a son, grandson or husband. Theophano was acting as an Ottonian queen in the political turbulence that ensued on her husband's death and in the gifts she made in gratitude for services rendered to her.

However, a lack of total familiarity with Ottonian culture may have militated against Theophano playing anything other than a passive role as far as the royal patronage of intellectual culture was concerned. It was her mother- and sister-in-law and aunt by marriage, together with her daughters, Adelheid and Sophia (and perhaps Matilda too), who were the active royal participants in, and occasionally promoters of, Ottonian intellectual and cultural life.[78]

In Ottonian Germany as a whole, however, it appears to have been episcopal patronage, rather than royal patronage, which was the deciding factor in the degree of literacy and educational achievement. The cathedral schools of Trier under bishop Ruotbert (931–56), Augsburg under Udalrich, Eichstätt under Starchand and Utrecht under Balderich were notable, and many boys

[75] P. Stafford, 'The king's wife in Wessex', *Past and Present*, 91 (1981), 3–27 and P. Stafford, *Queens, Concubines and Dowagers* (London, 1983), especially pp. 124–7, 164–5.

[76] See *Die Lebensbeschreibung der Kaiserin Adelheid von Abt Odilo*, ed. H. Paulart, *Mitteilungen des Instituts für österreichische Geschichtsforschung*, Ergänzungsband 20/2 (1962), 'Das Epitaphium', cc. 3, 9 and 15, pp. 32, 36 and 40; 'Das Wunderbericht', c. 2, pp. 46–8. F.P. Wimmer, *Kaiserin Adelheid, Gemahlin Ottos I. des Grossen in ihrem Leben und Wirken von 931–73* (Regensburg, 1897) and Corbet, *Les saints ottoniens* (see n. 55), pp. 81–110.

[77] E. Ward, 'Caesar's wife: the career of the Empress Judith, 819–829', in *Charlemagne's Heir: New Perspectives on the Reign of Louis the Pious*, ed. P. Godman and R. Collins (Oxford, 1990), pp. 205–31 and see the comments by Stafford, *Queens, Concubines and Dowagers* (see n. 75).

[78] See, for example, V. Elbern, *Das erste Jahrtausend* (Düsseldorf, 1962), nos. 376, 378, 382, 383, 384, 385; *Kunst und Kultur im Weserraum 800–1600* (Corvey, 1966), no. 162; P. Perst, 'Die Kaisertochter Sophie Äbtissin von Gandersheim in Essen, 975–1039', *Braunschweigisches Jahrbuch*, 38 (1957), 5–46, and the patronage of history writing above, p. 186.

were sent there for training.[79] Other bishops employed one of the visiting scholars called to Germany by Otto. Bishop Poppo of Würzburg, for example, had Stephen of Novara as head of his cathedral school for many years.[80] Wolfgang, later bishop of Regensburg, had taught in the cathedral school at Trier when Henry, Poppo's brother, was archbishop there between 956 and 964.[81] Bruno himself restored the school of Cologne and was active in Lotharingia and Liège, already celebrated for its learning under bishop Ebrachar.[82] Bruno's school friends Adalbero and Gauzlin were active promoters of their cathedral schools at Metz and Toul respectively once they became bishops.[83] Hilward of Halberstadt and Balderich of Speyer were both educated at St Gallen.[84] Archbishop Frederick of Salzburg was helped in his cathedral school by Liudfrid the schoolmaster and Otto's own son William stimulated renewed interest in learning at Mainz.[85]

[79] Othloh, *Vita sancti Wolfgangi episcopi Ratisbonensis*, c. 7, MGH SS IV, pp. 528–9; Gerhard, *Vita sancti Oudalrici episcopi augustani*, c. 1, ed. G. Waitz, in H. Kallfelz (trans.), *Lebensbeschreibungen einiger Bischöfe des 10.-12. Jahrhunderts*, AQDG 22 (Darmstadt, 1973), p. 54; S. Weinfurter, *Die Geschichte der Eichstätter Bischöfe des Anonymus Haserensis*, c. 11, Eichstätter Studien, NF 24 (Regensburg, 1987), pp. 47 and 125–8 (and *Anonymus Haserensis*, c. 11, MGH SS VII, p. 257); Ruotger, *Vita sancti Brunonis archiepiscopi Coloniensis*, c. 4, ed. I. Ott, in Kallfelz, *Lebensbeschreibungen*, p. 184.

[80] Othloh, *Vita sancti Wolfgangi episcopi Ratisbonensis*, c. 4, MGH SS IV, p. 528.

[81] *Ibid.*, c. 7, p. 529.

[82] Liège continued to flourish under bishop Notker (972–1008): see Anselm, *Gesta episcoporum Tungrensium, Traiectensium et Leodiensium*, c. 24, MGH SS VII, p. 201; Gozechin of Mainz, *Epistola ad Vacherum itidem scholasticum olim discipulum*, cc. 7–8, PL 143, cols. 885–908 at col. 889; and Aegidius Aureaevallensis, *Gesta episcoporum Leodiensium*, MGH SS XXV, p. 60. See also G. Kurth, *Notger de Liège et la civilisation au Xe siècle* (Brussels, 1905). On the school at Cologne see Sigebert, *Vita Deoderici episcopi Mettensis*, MGH SS IV, 1.2, pp. 464–5; R. Kottje, 'Schreibstätten und Bibliotheken in Köln Ende des 10. Jahrhunderts', in von Euw and Schreiner, *Kaiserin Theophanu*, pp. 153–64; I. Jeffré 'Handschriftliche Zeugnisse zur Geschichte der Kölner Domschule im 10. und 11. Jahrhundert', in *ibid.*, I, pp. 165–71; and P.C. Jacobsen, 'Lateinische Dichtung in Köln im 10. und 11. Jahrhundert', in *ibid.*, I, pp. 173–89.

[83] See W. Wattenbach and R. Holtzmann, *Deutschlands Geschichtsquellen im Mittelalter: die Zeit der Sachsen und Salier*, I, *Das Zeitalter des ottonischen Staates*, revised edn ed. F.J. Schmale (Darmstadt, 1978), pp. 179, 182, 186–7. On Gauzlin of Toul see also MGH SS IV, pp. 487–9.

[84] *Vita Meinwerci*, c. 3, MGH SS XI, p. 108, Compare Wattenbach-Holtzmann, *Deutschlands Geschichtsquellen* (see n. 83), p. 213.

[85] Wulfhere, *Vita Godehardi anterior*, c. 6, MGH SS XI, p. 172, and compare Wattenbach-Holtzmann, *Deutschlands Geschichtsquellen* (see n. 83), pp. 200 and 284; Manitius, *Geschichte der lateinischen Literatur* (see n. 10), pp. 701, 714. Several Ottonian scholars, such as Widukind of Corvey and Adalbert of St Maximin,

Archbishop Adalbert of Magdeburg founded the cathedral school at Magdeburg led by Ohtrich, one of the most famous philosophers of his day, and Bernward of Hildesheim was educated there.[86] Bishop Otwin, formerly a monk of Reichenau, and abbot of St Moritz at Magdeburg, promoted learning at Hildesheim.[87] Corvey and Gandersheim in Saxony, Hersfeld in Hesse, St Gallen in Swabia, St Pantaleon in Cologne and Laubach in lower Lotharingia were the most celebrated for their learning. Other foundations sought at least to establish good schools, such as Herford and Werden in Saxony, Fulda in Hesse, Reichenau in Swabia, Einsiedeln in Bavaria and St Maximin of Trier in Lotharingia. Valuable information concerning the schools and curricula can be obtained from the accounts of the early education of Bruno of Cologne, Bernward of Hildesheim and Ulrich of Augsburg.[88] Bruno was entrusted to bishop Balderich of Utrecht to be instructed in the liberal arts.

> He made great progress in his understanding of his lessons in school . . . after he had learnt the rudiments of grammar . . . he began with his teacher to read the poetry of Prudentius. . . Thereafter there was no branch of Latin and Greek learning that his lively mind did not investigate. . . Whatever new and important developments were taking place in history, rhetoric, poetry and philosophy, Bruno knew about it and would investigate it with the learned men at the court.[89]

This text, if not a hagiographer's hyperbole, is one of our few indications that there may have been some scholars at Otto I's court. If we knew a little more it might serve to ameliorate the rather bleak picture I have painted concerning the intellectual interests of at least one of the Ottonian rulers.

Ulrich of Augsburg was entrusted by his parents to St Gallen,

later archbishop of Magdeburg, appear to have spent some time at Mainz. On the Mainz *scriptorium* in the later tenth and early eleventh centuries see Hoffmann, *Buchkunst* (see n. 18), pp. 226–73.

86 Thangmar, *Vita sancti Bernwardi episcopi Hildesheimensis*, c. I, ed. G. Pertz, *Lebensbeschreibungen* (see n. 79), p. 274.

87 *Translatio sancti Epiphanii*, c. 4, MGH SS IV, p. 249.

88 An informative, if uncritical and insufficiently documented introductory survey is C.E. Lutz, *Schoolmasters of the Tenth Century* (Hamden, Conn., 1977).

89 Ruotger, *Vita Brunonis* (see n. 79), c. 5. Note also the reference to the *scola* at the *palatium* where Bruno could indulge to the full his intellectual interests at his brother's court. Compare c. 8 where Bruno is able to take the books he needs with him when the court travels.

where he would be able to learn about the religious life and acquire some learning. Ulrich was taught grammar by a monk called Waninc, and he was also instructed daily in matters of religion and all the other school subjects.[90] Bernward's parents saw that he was taught by his uncle Folcmar, a pious deacon, and bishop Osdag of Hildesheim, where he learnt to write poetry, rhetoric, dialectic, the arts of script, illumination and metalwork and of building in wood and stone. He subsequently went for further training at Mainz.[91] A succession of bishops trained in the various schools are recorded in connection with these schools as well as from Liège. All reveal how much a learned bishop or abbot was respected. This is spelt out also in the case of Rather of Verona by Liutprand, who 'because of his piety and his knowledge of the seven liberal arts was made bishop'.[92] Anselm's *Gesta episcoporum Leodiensium*, moreover, notes that 'many churches rejoiced to have as their pastors men trained by [Ebrachar, bishop of Liège (959–71)], among them Gunther, archbishop of Salzburg, Rothard and Erluin, who succeeded one another in the see of Cambrai, Haimo, bishop of Verdun and Adalbold, bishop of Utrecht'.[93]

Learning in the liberal arts of the tenth-century schools, therefore, was one essential qualification for office in both the secular and ecclesiastical administration. Almost without exception, moreover, these bishops, active in their sees in the promotion of the cathedral schools and of learning generally, were monks from the 'reformed' monastic centres. That they were made bishops rather than abbots meant that in the course of the tenth century the monastic schools appear to have been eclipsed by the cathedral schools in the East Frankish kingdom as far as education was concerned. These cathedral schools preserved the traditional forms of education – Bible study, Church Fathers, Latin classics

[90] *Vita sancti Oudalrici*, c. 1, *Lebensbeschreibungen* (see n. 79), p. 54.

[91] *Vita sancti Bernwardi*, cc. 1 and 2, *Lebensbeschreibungen* (see n. 79), p. 274 and 276.

[92] Liutprand, *Antapodosis*, III, 42; ed. and trans. Wright, *Works of Liudprand* (see n. 9), p. 132.

[93] Anselm, *Gesta episcoporum Leodiensium* (see n. 82), c. 25, p. 205. On all the episcopal schools and possible, if tenuous, links with the court (largely in a practical context) see J. Fleckenstein, 'Königshof und Bischofschule unter Otto dem Grossen', *Archiv für Kulturgeschichte*, 38 (1956), 38–62, reprinted in J. Fleckenstein, *Ordnungen und formende Kraft des Mittelalters: ausgewählte Beiträge* (Göttingen, 1989), pp. 168–92. Anselm's comments, however, are not necessarily to be read as tributes to the scholarship of these men.

and a few contemporary authors. It is only occasionally, in the form of chronicles, verses and minor works, that there is any literary creativity. In the monasteries, however, no longer the principal educational centres, there was rather more in the way of literary and above all creative musical and liturgical production.

Some interest in Greek is evident in the so-called Greek grammar included in a general collection of grammars made by Froumund of Tegernsee at the end of the tenth century.[94] Apart from the Gospel Book of the second half of the tenth century now in Vienna, but possibly written in Constantinople itself, there is hardly any sign of an interest in, or knowledge of, Greek culture to any greater extent than was evident in the Carolingian world, though there are now indications in new work on Ottonian culture that the tenth century may, in some respects, have surpassed the ninth.[95] Ottonian intellectual culture was thriving in the tenth century: much teaching, learning, and a continuation of traditions is apparent, and very occasionally some original literary and scholarly endeavour, especially in history and hagiography, can be documented. All this, however, seems to have taken place with very little involvement from any member of the royal family, let alone Theophano herself.

94 See C.E. Eder, *Die Schule des Klosters Tegernsee im frühen Mittelalter im Spiegel der Tegernseer Handschriften*, Münchener Beiträge zur Mediävistik und Renaissance-Forschung, Beiheft (Munich, 1972), pp. 39–41; W.J. Aerts, 'The knowledge of Greek in western Europe at the time of Theophano and the Greek grammar fragment in MS Vindob. 114', in *Byzantium and the Low Countries in the Tenth Century: Aspects of Art and History in the Ottonian Era*, ed. V.D. van Aalst and K.N. Ciggaar (Hernen, 1985), pp. 78–103; G. Sporbeck, 'Froumund von Tegernsee (um 960–1006/12) als Literat und Lehrer', in von Euw and Schreiner, *Kaiserin Theophanu*, pp. 369–78.

95 See, for example, Berschin, *Greek Letters* (see n. 8), and the important comments made by W. Berschin, A. Bayer, N. Staubach, G. Sporbeck and A. von Euw in their contributions to the section 'Das griechisch-lateinische Mittelalter' in von Euw and Schreiner, *Kaiserin Theophanu*, I, pp. 327–400. The Vienna manuscript is Österreichische Nationalbibliothek cod. gr. 240: see Mazal, *Byzanz und das Abendland* (see n. 2), no. 377.

10

Froumund's Greek: an analysis of fol. 12v of the Codex Vindobonensis Graecus 114, followed by a comparison with a Latin–Greek wordlist in MS 179 Auxerre fol. 137v ff

W.J. AERTS

On an earlier occasion I published an article on the Greek grammatical fragment which can be found on fols. 13r–15v of the MS Vindobonensis Graecus 114 (hereafter Vind. 114).[1] The question was whether this fragment could be considered a sign of renewed or increased knowledge of the Greek language, due to the arrival of the Byzantine princess Theophano in Western Europe to be the wife of Otto II and empress of the Ottonian Empire. My conclusions were:

1. Since the fall of the western part of the Roman Empire the knowledge of Greek was at a very poor level. Even scholars such as Isidore of Seville (sixth/seventh century), Bede (seventh/eighth century), and John Scotus Eriugena (ninth century) had only a superficial and defective knowledge of Greek.
2. In Italy the situation was more favourable as a consequence of the presence of the Byzantines in southern Italy and of Greek monasteries in Rome and elsewhere.
3. What was known of Greek was chiefly based on bilingual (Greek–Latin) texts of the Bible and on transmitted Greek–Latin wordlists.
4. The Greek grammar in Vind. 114 has in fact nothing to do with Greek, but is a rather clumsy 'hellenization' of the (Latin) grammar of Donatus.

MS Vind. 114 has on fols. 3–24 extensive glosses in the margins, written by Froumund of Tegernsee (*c.* 965–1008), who is also

[1] W.J. Aerts, 'The knowledge of Greek in Western Europe at the time of Theophano and the Greek grammar fragment in MS Vindob. 114', in *Byzantium and the Low Countries in the Tenth Century: Aspects of Art and History in the Ottonian Era*, ed. V.D. van Aalst and K.N. Ciggaar (Hernen, 1985), pp. 78–103.

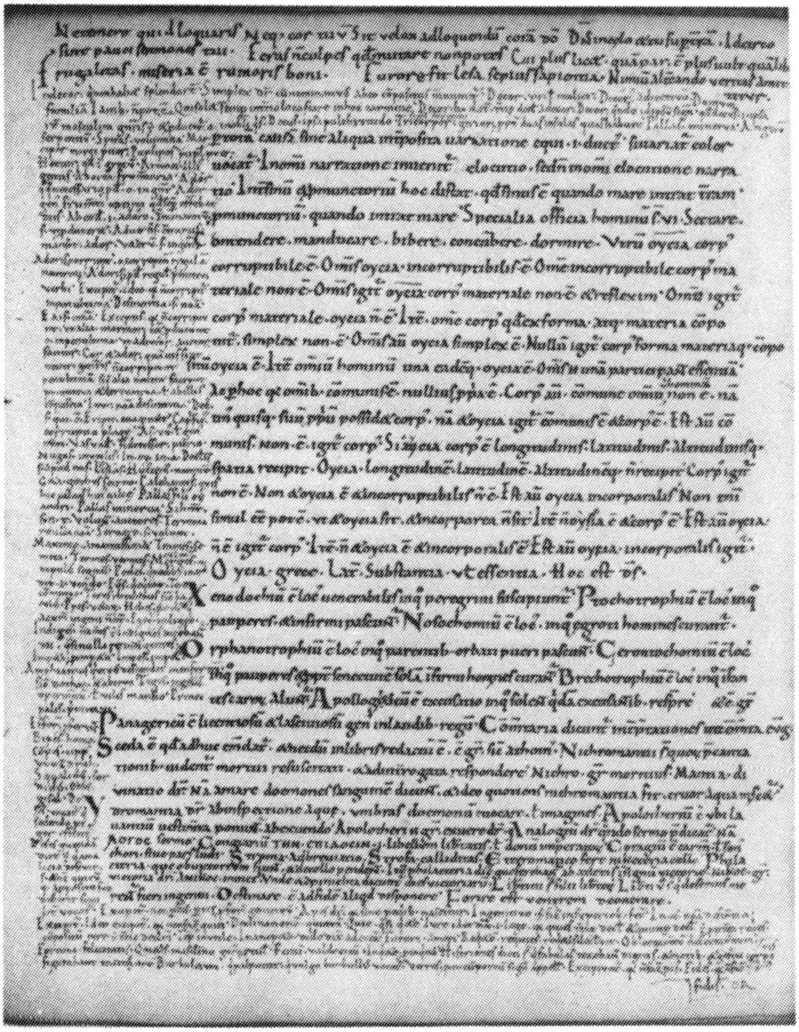

9. Codex Vindobonensis Graecus 114, fol. 12v.

responsible for the major part of the main texts. The subjects mostly bear a grammatical character and are often extracts from and/or comments on the *Institutiones* of Priscian. On the fol. (12v) (Fig. 9) which precedes the Greek grammatical fragment is another series of *graeca* which will be analysed in this paper as a confirmation of the thesis that, if the arrival of Theophano may have stimulated some interest in the Greek language, the knowledge of Greek was not essentially furthered and remained based on material which was already available in the West. There are, of course, some exceptions to this rule, but besides their being exceptional, they have no connection with the coming of Theophano. One may mention the Latin/Italian/Modern Greek wordlist of Monza,[2] a Latin/Greek list from Avranches and another from Auxerre.[3]

As to Froumund, he was ordained a priest at a rather advanced age and he himself considered teaching and the composition of occasional poetry his main tasks. He loved to use Greek, but more *pour épater le bourgeois* than to demonstrate a basis in real knowledge. His activities are recorded in Cologne, Feuchtwangen and Tegernsee.

On fol. 12v starts, rather unexpectedly, the discussion of a number of Greek words: to begin with, the notion *ousia*, followed by a consideration of fourteen lines. Then comes the series *xenodochium*, *ptochotrophium*, *nosochomium*, *orphanotrophium*, *gerontochomium*, *brechotrophium*, *apollogiticum*,[4] *panagericum*, *commentaria* (*sic!*), *sceda*, *nichromantii*, *ydromantia*, *apolotherium*, *analogium*, *congiarium/epidosin*, *coragium*, *stroma* and *strofa*. The words that follow (*philacteria*, *nikos*, *anikos*, etc.) have been taken from quotations from the third Satire of Juvenal.

The endings in *-ium/-um* instead of *–ion/-on* show already that we have to do with a Latin source. The six first-mentioned (*xenodochium* to *brechotrophium* (the latter is, of course, a mistake for *brephotrophium*)) are qualified by analogous definitions:

2 See e.g. *Monza*.

3 Krijnie Ciggaar, 'Byzantine marginalia to the Norman conquest', with an appendix by W.J. Aerts 'The Latin–Greek wordlist in MS 236 of the Municipal Library of Avranches, fol. 97v.', in *Anglo-Norman Studies*, 9 (1987) (= Proceedings of the Battle Conference 1986, ed. R. Allen Brown), 43–64, 65–9. For Auxerre, see L. Delisle: 'Manuscrits de la Bibliothèque d'Auxerre', *Le Cabinet Historique*, 23 (1877), 10–5. The transcription of this vocabulary is worked out in the second part of this article.

4 The *i* in the syllable *-gi-* has been written above a deleted *e*.

xenodochium	e[st]	loc[us] venerabilis	in	quo	peregrini suscipiuntur
ptochotrophium	,,	,,	,,	,,	pauperes et infirmi pascuntur
nosochomium	,,	,,	,,	,,	[a]egroti homines curantur
orphanotrophium	,,	,,	,,	,,	parentibus orbati pueri pascuntur
gerontochomium	,,	,,	,,	,,	pauperes et propter senectutem solam infirmi homines curantur
brechotrophium	,,	,,	,,	,,	infantes carorum aluntur[5]

In the last sentence a word before or after *carorum* is missing: *egentes* or perhaps *carentes*. Similar qualifications can, with some variation, be found in the Codex Sangallensis 912 from St Gallen, see e.g. *CGL* IV, 211, 25: 'brephotrophium locus venerabilis in quo infantes aluntur'.

The line along which these 'definitions' found their way is probably the following: in the chapter *De sacrosanctis ecclesiis* (I, 2, 22, cf. also 23) of the *Institutiones* of the emperor Justinian I it was decreed that legacies made to churches and other non-profit institutions were free of taxes. The text runs as follows: 'sancimus res ad venerabiles ecclesias vel xenones vel monasteria vel ptochotrophia vel brephotrophia vel orphanotophia vel gerontocomia vel si quid. . .etc. . .liberas immunes esse.' Elsewhere (in I, 2, 19) the word *xenodochium* is also used. Further propagation of these terminologies seems to have taken place through the *Capitula Caroli Magni* II, § 29. Peculiar is Froumund's spelling *-chomium* instead of *-comium*. The same peculiarity is to be found in *CGL* V, 522, 31 (= Excerpta ex codice vaticano 1469): 'gnosochomium locus venerabilis in quo aegroti homines curantur'.

The following group of words, *apollogiticum* to *analogium*, goes back to Isidore of Seville, on the understanding that the process of transmission did not fail to leave behind the traces of wear. Froumund notes: 'apollogiticu[m] e[st] excusatio in q[u]o solent q[u]ida[m] excusantib[us] resp[onde]re. et est graecum.' The text in Isidore (VI, 8, 6) runs as follows: 'apologeticum est excusatio, in quo solent quidam accusantibus respondere. in defensione enim

5 The letters between brackets have been indicated *per ligaturam* or *per abbreviationem*.

aut negatione sola positum est; et est nomen graecum.' Striking is the fact that Froumund has changed the (common and factually correct) spelling with *-ge-* into *-gi-*. In this case it is possible that Froumund's attention was drawn to the fact that the pronunciation of Greek η was altered from [æ:] into [i:]. On the other hand he seems to associate the word with the name Apollo. Another mistake which escaped Froumund's notice is the pointless form *excusantibus* instead of the correct *accusantibus*. The sentence 'In defensione . . . ' is omitted, as well as the word *nomen*.

The following definition: 'panagericu[m] e[st] licentiosu[m] et lasciviosu[m] gen[us] in laudib[us] regu[m]' has also been borrowed from Isidore (VI, 8, 7). But Isidore has the correct *panegyricum* and the necessary addition *dicendi* after *genus*. For the rest, Isidore uses the same definition with, however, a longer explanation.

As to the word that follows, *commentaria*, one may wonder why Froumund ranges this among the Greek words. The explanation is probably that in the definition 'com[men]taria dicunt[ur] int[er]p[re]tationes ut com[men]ta ev[an]g[elii]' the last word is of Greek origin. Also in this case we have to do with an abridgement of a text of Isidore (VI, 8, 5): 'commentaria dicta, quasi cum mente. sunt enim interpretationes, ut commenta iuris, commenta evangelii.'

For *sceda* we find this definition: 'sceda e[st] q[uo]d adhuc em[en]dat[ur]. et necdu[m] in libris redactu[m] e[st]. e[st] gr[aecum] sic[ut] athom[us].' Whereas Froumund is rather immoderate in the use of a superfluous *h*, here we miss one. Isidore VI, 14, 8 gives the correct *scheda* (=σχέδη) with the same definition except for the last four words. There Isidore adds: 'et est nomen graecum sicut et tomus'. In that way the odd *athomus* of Froumund becomes clear: it concerns the Greek word τόμος and of course not the word ἄτομος. The *a* has its origin in a carelessly written or understood ligature &, whereas *tomus* has been provided again with a superfluous *h*.

Interesting is the term that follows, *nichromantii*. Again, Isidore is more explicit and clear (VIII, 9, 11): 'necromantii sunt, quorum praecantationibus videntur resuscitati mortui divinare et ad interrogata respondere. νεκρός enim graece mortuus, μαντεία divinatio nuncupatur: ad quos sciscitandos cadaveri sanguis adicitur. nam amare daemones sanguinem dicitur. ideoque quotiens necromantia fit, cruor aqua miscitur, ut cruore sanguinis facilius provocentur.' I have underlined the words which are lacking in Froumund. In addition, there are a number of variations: *nichromantii*; *nichro* instead of νεκρός; *mantia* instead of μαντεία, *dicitur* instead of *adicitur* as a consequence of the adaptation of the sentence; *dicunt* instead of *dicitur*; *et ideo* instead of *ideoque*; *miscetur* instead of *miscitur*. Here it should be noticed that some of these variations already occur in the so-called Italian group (group 2) of manuscripts of Isidore, especially in Karolinus Wolfenbuettelanus (hereafter K) (=Weissenburg 64, beginning of the eighth century). In K *enim* is missing; K reads *dicunt*, together with Bernensis 101 (B), group 1; K also has *et ideo*.

This lemma has another problem. It is not clear why in *nichromantii* and *nichro* an *i* has taken the place of the correct *e*. Did it emerge from the idea that the *e* represented a Greek η? Or did the inventor of this spelling have an association with the word *niger*? As has been stated before, Froumund likes to give his Greek words a Greek 'flavour' by means of the *h*. The spelling *nichro-* for *nekro-*, however, occurs very seldom. No list in *CGL* offers this kind of spelling, only *Du Cange Latinus* quotes two instances from documents dating from 996 and 1181. The first has *nichromanticus*, the second *nychromanticus*. The confusion with *niger* is less strange than it seems to be. A peculiar poem, named *Graecismus*, written by Eberhard Bethuniensis (twelfth century), has the following distich in ch. 8, where words of Greek origin are discussed:

> Mors nigros est, nigromantiam dic inde venire,
> estque nicos victus, anicos inde venit.

Here *nigros* is clearly meant to function as a contamination of νεκρός and *niger*. This idea can be strengthened by a passage in *De casibus sancti Galli*, ch. 2 of Ekkehard (IV, 980–1060), where black magic and necromancy are connected: *libri nigri – necromantici*. From there the *Glossarium Latino–Germanicum* of Diefenbach offers the following explanation s.v. *nigromantia*: 'nederduits de zwarte kunst: schwarz kunst die do ist mit uffsehung der dotten mit den der nigromanticus zaubert oder mit den drijen ersten schollen die der pfaff würfft ynsz grab oder mit den wydhopffen die do lauffen by den greberen'.[6]

[6] Taken from the *Variloquus* ('Vocabularius predicatorum', end fifteenth century). The text says as much as: black magic which exists in calling up the dead with whom the nigromanticus practises sorcery, or with the first three clods of earth which the priest throws into the grave, or with the hoopoes that walk about the grooves (or graves).

The series continues with *ydromantii*. Here, too, the source must be Isidore (VIII, 9, 12), who writes: 'hydromantii ab aqua dicti. est enim hydromantia in aquae inspectione umbras daemonum evocare, et imagines vel ludificationes eorum videre ... '. This phrase has been shortened to: 'ydromantia d[icitu]r ab inspectione aqu[a]e. umbras doemonu[m] evocare. [ve]l imagines.' The changes are clear enough; the only remarkable thing is the spelling *ydro-*, which occurs again in MS K.

The next term, *apolotherium*, is a corruption of the original *apodyterium*, which Isidore defines (XV, 2, 41) as: 'apodyterium, ubi lavantium vestimenta ponuntur, ab exuendo scilicet dictum; ἀποδύειν enim graece exuere dicitur.' It seems that somewhere in the transmission the letters *-od-* have been 'simplified' > *-ol-* (a kind of haplography), whereas the change *y* > *o* probably arose from a confusion with the idea *lotus* < *lautus* from *lavare*. In other wordlists one can more than once find the interchange of *d* and *l*: *apolyterium* (from λύω or possibly λούω). The spelling *-th-* probably points again to Froumund's preference for the *h*. This lemma makes clear in any case that Froumund's knowledge of Greek was very poor, in fact non-existent. His explanation of *exuere* even more clearly demonstrates his ignorance: his transcription *apolotheri* (*H*)[7] is apparently meant to be a Greek infinitive on *-in* = -ειν, built on a non-existent stem.

Froumund continues with 'analogiu[m] d[icitu]r q[ua]ndo sermo p[rae]dicat[ur], nam ΛΟΓΟΣ sermo', a rather careless reflection of Isidore XV, 4, 17: 'analogium dictum quod sermo inde praedicatur; nam λόγος Graece sermo dicitur' (*dictum* is lacking in MS K). Moreover, from the words that follow in Isidore's text, 'quod et ipsud altius situm est', it becomes clear that the intended signification is 'pulpit'. Because *quod inde* has been replaced by *quando*, the original meaning has disappeared and has almost taken the signification of 'sermon', 'preaching'. One should notice that Froumund writes λόγος with Greek letters (small capitals) just like Isidore.

Greek spelling appears also in the next lemma: 'congiarium ΤΗΝ ΕΠΙΔΟΣΙΝ i[d est] libellum lib[er]tatis [ve]l donu[m] imperator[um]'. Instead of *libertatis* one has to understand *liberalitatis* ('liberality'). Though this word has been mentioned twice in

7 The H represents the word *enim*, as in Isidore's text. In Froumund's text the *-n* of the infinitive has been omitted.

Isidore (XVI, 26, 7 and 8), in this case Froumund must have had another source, because the idea ἐπίδοσις ('free giving', 'largesse' (given to soldiers) = Lat. *donativum*) is lacking in Isidore's work. In the lists of *CGL*, however, the translation ἐπίδοσις for *congiarium* occurs at least sixteen times. Another definition is δωρεὰ Καίσαρος (*CGL* II, 503, 13 and II, 282, 45, in this latter case with the addition that *congiarium* also means a measure of capacity: six pints).

It is unclear from what source Froumund borrowed his definition of *coragium*: 'coragiu[m] e[st] carm[en] [ve]l son[us] chori, sive pars ludi'. The word does not occur in Isidore. The Glossaria are somewhat more helpful without offering an obvious solution. In *CGL* IV, 45, 6 = 500, 28 we read: 'coragio pars est in ludis quando proverbia dicuntur', and in V, 593, 49 'puer[orum] est ludus quando proverbia dicunt'. In other terms, it concerns a part of a theatrical performance or manifestation in which (young) players (slaves?) say special sayings (to the public?; entr'acte?). Here Isidore (XVIII, 16, 2) gives some useful information. Speaking on *ludus* he first derives the word from *Lydus* ('Lydian'), because the Lydians immigrating into Etruria were supposed to have taken with them their rites from their homeland. Then he mentions Varro, who derives the word from *lusus*: 'quod iuvenes per dies festos solebant ludi exultatione populum delectare'. Elsewhere in *CGL* (IV, 397, 9) *choragium* is described as *ornatus mimicus* (*vel mimici*), i.e. the outfit of mimics, which fits rather well in the terminology *summum choragium*, which refers to the central storehouse of theatrical requisites in the Roman Empire.[8] With these data one may conclude that in Froumund's definition the words *pars ludi* comprise a reminiscence of the traditional description, whereas the formula *carmen vel sonus chori* indicates that Froumund saw a connection with Greek χορός/*chorus*. It is then striking that *coragium* has been spelled without the 'indispensable' *h*.

The two following lemmata: *stroma.adbreviatio* and *strofa. calliditas* are based on a misunderstanding and/or on a distorted transmission.The wordlists in *CGL* give for *stroma* either the meaning *varietas* (cf. V, 585, 21: 'stromaton liber ex variis rebus

[8] Cf. e.g. *Corpus inscriptionum Latinarum*, ed. Th. Mommsen, III (Berlin, 1873), no. 348; VI (Berlin, 1876), no. 297; see also *Der Kleine Pauly*, I (Stuttgart, 1964), c. 1159 *s.v. choragium*.

aut diversis auctoribus compositum')[9] or *lectulus* (V, 389, 17). The signification *adbreviatio* has no reference to *stroma*. The mistake could have originated from the partial omission out of a lemma, e.g. *stroma* < *variatio* [or *lectulus*], *syntomia* > *adbreviatio*.[10] As to *strofa* . *calliditas* there is some support in *CGL* V, 389,7, where *strofa* has been interpreted as *callida versutia* (cf. IV, 287, 36 *praeversio* (= *perversio*) *fraus impostura*). The 'normal' signification is, however, 'turn', 'twist', 'suppleness', besides, of course, 'strophe' of a poem.

As mentioned above, the first Greek word noted by Froumund is the noun οὐσία, in 'pseudo-Greek' spelling: *oycia*. Isidore does mention the word (= *substantia*) in II, 26, 10 ff. In this case, however, Froumund borrowed the definition literally from the writing *Periphyseon* of John Scotus Eriugena. From 'utrum ousia corpus corruptibile est' as far as 'non est igitur corpus' inclusive, the passage is the same as in *Periphyseon* I, p. 146, 19–30, edited by I.P. Sheldon-Williams with the collaboration of L. Bieler (Dublin, 1968). The rest is in conformity with p. 148, 7–9 and 13–17. The differences are few in number:

146,	27	proprie	Froumund	propria
	28/29	proprium	"	propium
	29	non	"	nam
148,	8	autem	"	[missing]
	14	igitur	"	"
	15	et[3]	"	"
	16	non[2 or 3]	"	"

The most striking deviation is 148, 13, *incorporalis*, where Froumund has *incorruptibilis*.

As far as can be distilled from the *apparatus criticus* and the Introduction in the edition of Sheldon-Williams and Bieler, this fragment was unknown to the editors of the *Periphyseon*. Froumund apparently made use of a manuscript which had a number of differences which do not occur in the MSS collocated by Sheldon-Williams and Bieler.

Fol. 12v of MS Vindob. 114 is an interesting page to show the level of the knowledge of Greek in Western Europe in the time of the empress Theophano. As to Froumund, though he certainly

[9] Clearly a circumscription taken from the indication of the *Miscellanea* = Στρωματεῖς of Clement of Alexandria.

[10] This kind of mistake is not uncommon in these wordlists, e.g. *Monza*, 16 and *CGL*, III, 175, 18–21.

had a great interest in Greek, he apparently had no other material at his disposal than that which traditionally circulated in the libraries of 'cultural' monasteries. And even if it had come to his knowledge that contemporary Greek was completely different in character from that which could be learnt from the traditional wordlists, it is clear that he did not make any effort to 'update' his command of the language of his interest. One should not reproach him with this: opportunities to meet Greek-speaking 'colleagues' were very scarce in the German countries, perhaps even more scarce than in France or in Italy. The wordlist of Monza has already been mentioned. As a contrast with Froumund's series of Greek words I quote a number of lines from a MS from Auxerre (MS 179, fol. 133v).[11] The writing dates, according to Delisle, from the twelfth century. It is a bilingual (Latin–Greek) text, with the Greek text written in Latin characters. Delisle does not offer a Greek transcription, which I add here in a third line. He only calls attention to two copies (A and B) of this text, which sometimes give an alternative reading.

Bonus	dies	tibi.	Bonus	vesper	tibi.	Multis	annis	faciat
Calos	ymera	si.	Calos	yspera	si.	Poli	coron	pissem
Καλῶς[12]	ἡ μέρα	σοι.	Καλῶς	ἡ σπέρα	σοι.	Πολὺ <ν>	χρονὸν [?]	ποίσῃ
							καιρὸν [?]	

vivere	te	Deus	Audi	tu,	domne	mi.
na	se	o theos.	Aquis	te,	afendim	men.
νὰ <ζήσῃ>	σ[ε]	ὁ θεός.[13]	'Ακούῃς	το,	ἀφέντη	μου.[14]

Quid	tu	vis,	frater	mi?	Quid	audisti		de
ti	te	celis,	adelfe	men?	ti	aquis	to	apeto
τί	[(π)τε]	θέλεις,	ἀδελφέ	μου;[15]	Τί	ἀκούεις	το	ἀπὲ τὸ <ν>
						ἀκούσ <α> τε		ἀπὸ

[11] This list was published by Léopold Delisle in *Le Cabinet Historique*, 23 (1877), 10–5. I thank Dr K.N. Ciggaar for drawing my attention to this interesting vocabulary.

[12] This text has many difficulties. Here one would expect καλή, not καλῶς, unless the person who wrote this text was confused by the masculine form of the Latin adjective *bonus*, and one should read καλός. Instead of ἡ μέρα one can read ἡμέρα, but one should observe the parallel. *Coron* is puzzling. One could understand *coron* either as *ceron* = καιρόν or as a mistake for χρονόν. In both cases a masculine πολύν is necessary.

[13] *Pissem na se* does not bring in a reasonable Greek text. I suppose that *pissem na* stands for ποίσῃ νά. Possible, but improbable, is a 'classic' optative ποιήσαι νά. The author of the text apparently identified *na* with *vivere* and *se* with *te*, unaware of the fact that νά is a particle, which should be followed by a verb.

[14] I have written το and μου on the ground that copy A has *to* instead of *te* and *mon* instead of *men*.

[15] Copy A reads *tu* instead of *te*. I see three possibilities for the interpretation: either *te* (or *tu*) should be *to*, or one should understand τίπτε, or the author incorrectly construed a *te* from Latin *te*.

imperatore	greco?	Quid	facit	imperator?
vasilio	romeco?	ti	pissem	vasilios?
βασιλιᾶ<ν>	ῥωμαιϊκό<ν>?[16]	Τί	ποιήσει	<ὁ> βασιλιᾶς;

?	?	Quid	boni	dat?	Satis	nummos
Francis	calom	ti	kalo	docem?	Pola	lacotina
Φράγκοις	καλόν [?].[17]	τί	καλὸ	<ἔ>δωκεν;[18]	Πολλὰ	<ὁ>λοκότινα

et	arma.	Gloria	tibi	domne.	Donne [*sic*],	ubi	vis	ire?
que	armata.	Doxa	si	kirrie.	Afendan,	pia	celis	ypa
καὶ	ἅρματα.[19]	Δόξα	σοι,	κύριε.	Ἀφέντα μ',	ποίᾳ	θέλεις	ὑπᾶ<ν>?[20]

Ad		castellum.	Habitas	tu	castel?	Etiam.	Tibi	placet,	ubi	est
oto		castro.	Menis	to	castro?	Ne.	Si	levis,	po	ne
ὡ<ς>	τό	κάστρο.[21]	Μένεις	<σ>τὸ	κάστρο;	Ναί.	Σὺ	λέγοις [?],	ποῦ	'νε
στὸ		κάστρο.						λέγῃς [?]		

castellum?	Ubi	est		via	ad	castellum?	Vide	viam!
castro?	Po	ne		strata	oto	castro?	Thoris	stratam!
<τὸ?> κάστρο?[22]	Ποῦ	'νε	<ἡ>	στράτα	στὸ	κάστρο;	Θωρεῖς	στράταν![23]

16 Instead of *audisti* copy A reads *audistis*. If *aquis* = ἀκούεις is correct, the following τό is superfluous. But probably *aquis to* should be read as ἀκούστε or ἀκούσατε, which agrees better with *audistis*. For ἀπὲ instead of ἀπὸ see Hatzidakis, 152; Jannaris, § 1519.

17 Since the Latin counterpart is lacking, it is difficult to understand what was meant: 'Hail to the Francs' (?).

18 I suppose that ἔδωκεν is a better option than ἔδωσεν. Perhaps one should read: καλό 'δωκεν.

19 The ὁλοκότινον, ὁλοκοτίνιν, λοκοτίνιν is a Byzantine (golden) denarius. Instead of *ypa* the copy A reads *ipa*.

20 The significance of the sentence is clear, but the Greek comprises a number of problems. *Afendan* probably stands here for Ἀφέντα μου, though as a vocative Ἀφέντη μου is the normal form. The etymological ground form αὐθέντης had a vocative αὐθέντα (see LSJ s.v.). The 'translation' *pia* for *ubi* is strange. Why not *pu* just as in the next line *po* ? There are three possibilities: 1. *pia* stands for ποίᾳ (sc. ὁδῷ) = 'by which way?', 2. ποῖ = 'whither?' + adverbial -α, 3. πῇ = 'which way?' + adv. -α. For the first mentioned use one may compare the *Chronicle of Morea*, 6594 '(βουλὴν ἀπῆρεν...) τὸ ποίαν ὁδὸν νὰ πιάσουσιν κ' εἰς ποῖον μέρος νὰ ἀπέλθουν. For stem + adverbial -a formation, see e.g. ἐκειά = ἐκεῖ (see Hatzidakis *MNE*, I, 55), for ταχιά 'early' (*Erotokritos*, II, 71), for συχνιά (*ibid*., II, 343, 353). Finally *ypa* (copy A: *ipa*) must be an infinitive, though a construction with νά + subj. would be 'normal'. For θέλω + inf., see e.g. *Ptochoprodromos*, Eideneier, IV, 581 and *Ptochoprodromos*, Hesseling, III, 405: θέλουσιν ὑπάγειν. In Medieval Cypriotic θέλω + inf. expresses the future tense, see Menardos, 76; W.J. Aerts, 'Periphrastic constructions of the future tense, especially with ΜΕΛΛΕΙΝ, in Medieval Cypriotic', in Ἐπετηρίς τοῦ Κέντρου Ἐπιστημονικῶν Ἐρευνῶν Κύπρου, XII (1983), 152. For the contracted forms of ὑπάγειν see Hatzidakis *MNE*, I, 241; Jannaris, § 996, 3.

21 If *oto* is correct, one has to understand ὡς τό, but the first *o* may be a mistake for *s*, read στό.

22 *Si levis* seems to be incorrect. *Si* perhaps stands for σοι, but then *levis* is incomprehensible to me: the *-s* ending does not harmonize with σοι. The only solution which I see for the moment is a derivation of λέγειν to be taken as an optative: 'you may say, please...'. The insertion of το is not necessary, but seems to be the logical consequence of the reasoning.

Prope	est	castellum.	Qualis	homo	est	prefectus?	Per	Deum,
Sima	ene	castro.	Pios	atropos	ene	estraiget ?	Maten	cetu,
Σιμὰ	ἔνε	<τὸ> κάστρο.[24]	Ποῖος	ἄνθρωπος	ἔνε	ὁ στρατηγός;[25]	Μὰ τὸν	θεόν,

bonus.	Habet	conjugem	et	infantes?	Etiam.	Si	ieris,	faciet
calos.	Equit	innecam	que	pedia ?	Ne.	Na	ipas,	pissem
καλός.[26]	Ἔχει[τ]	γυναῖκαν	καὶ	παιδία;[27]	Ναί.	Νὰ	ὑπᾶς,	ποιήσει
	Ἔχει	τὴν 'ναῖκαν				Ἄν,		ποίσῃ

tibi	bonum.		Habes	aliquid	et	ut	vendas?	Non habeo,
si	calon.	Franc	equis	tipote	que	amna	pulissem?	Uqu esquo,
σοι	καλόν.[28]	Φράγκε,	ἔχεις	τίποτε	καὶ	ἐννὰ	πουλήσῃς;[29]	Οὐκ ἔ[σ]χω,

domine,	non	decem.	Habes	aurum,	nummos,	vestem	et	aliquid?
lurie [*sic*],	uqu	deca.	Equis	crisa,	quesia,	pannum	que	tipote?
κύριε,	οὐκ	δέκα.[30]	Ἔχεις	χρυσᾶ,	κ<αρτ>έσια [?],	πάννον	καὶ	τίποτε;[31]

23 I have changed the phrase in comparison to Delisle, who reads 'Ubi est via? Ad Castellum, inde viam?' *Ne* = εἶναι, respectively εἶνε, respectively ἔνε. The next lines clearly write ἔνε =. Instead of *vide* the Latin text has *inde*, which I have altered, because of the Greek translation. Θωρῶ = νεωρέω ('to see') and στράτα ('road') frequently occur in medieval texts, especially from Cyprus and Crete. As to υωρεῖς as a translation of *vide*, the Greek text has an indicative instead of an imperative, but one could interpret <νὰ> θωρῇς.

24 For σιμά 'nearby' = κοντά see e.g. *The Chronicle of Morea*, 1279P, 1352, 1661H, 2481, etc. (14 times). Also in Cypriotic, but seldom in Machairas (340, 12 ed. Dawkins).

25 The rendering of the word ὁ στρατηγός is less than adequate, but the intention seems clear.

26 I suppose that the rendering θεόν for *cetu* is correct, but Χριστόν is a possibility.

27 One can waver between the supposition that the *t* is superfluous and has originated from the *t* in Latin *habet* or that the *in-* of *innecam* should be linked with the *t*, as a consequence of which 'ναῖκαν = γυναῖκαν, unless *t in–* is a haplography for *tin in-*. The first solution seems to be the more obvious one, because παιδία has no article either.

28 Νά as introduction of a hypothetical clause is possible (see Tzartzanos, § 245.II, p. 63), but more logical would be ἄν. Perhaps the composer of the list heard no difference. Nor did he apparently notice any difference in the forms of the verb ποιεῖν. Καλόν = καλό (neuter).

29 The vocative is missing in Latin. *Et*, respectively καὶ, is in fact superfluous. If my identification *amna* = ἐννά is correct, we have to do with the common form of this particle in Cypriotic. As usual, the author neglects the ending: *-sem* instead of *-sis*.

30 Perhaps one has to transcribe οὐκί or οὐχί, which also fits in better before δέκα. Instead of ἔχω, which implies a superfluous *s* in the transcription, one can read ἴσχω, a possible but less common alternative. I must accept the transcription of Delisle but palaeographically speaking *lurie* is very close to *kirie*.

31 The term *quesia* must indicate the plural of a piece of money, but of which one? If some letters dropped out, the interpretation καρτέσια (Venetian coins in use on Cyprus) corresponds with the beginning and the end of the term mentioned. Alternatives are γροσία, καρτσά or κερατσία for which see Kriaras ΛΜΕΔΓ and Machairas, ed. Dawkins II, 88 and Wordlist. Πάννος was a Greek loan-word borrowed from Latin, see Sophocles, *Lexicon*.

Habeo.	Vis	mercari?	Non	vel [*sic*]	volo.	Habes	panem?
Esquo.	Celis	nagorassem?	Uqi	dem	celo.	Esquis	sumin?
Ἔ[σ]χω.	Θέλεις	ν' ἀγοράσῃς;[32]	Οὔκ,	δὲν	θέλω.	Ἔ[σ]χεις	ψωμίν;

Habeo,	et	vinum,	et	carnem,	et	caseum,	et	uva	ovium
Equo,	que	crassim,	que	crias,	que	turim,	que	alga	anesget
Ἔχω,	καὶ	κρασίν,	καὶ	κρέας,	καὶ	τυρὶν	καὶ	αὐγά,	ἂν ἔχετε

allia	et		et	uva	et	castaneas	et	pira;
scorda	que	cromedia	que	taphilia,	que	castaneas	que	apidia;
σκόρδα	καὶ	κρομμύδια	καὶ	<σ>ταφίλια	καὶ	καστανέας	καὶ	ἀπίδια.[33]

et	cultellum	et	spatam	et	lanceam,	et	equum	et	loricam,
que	macherium	que	spatim	que	condarium,	que	talogum	que	bromum,
καὶ	μαχαίριον	καὶ	σπάθην	καὶ	κοντάριον,	καὶ	τἄλογον	καὶ	? ,

et	ollam	et	parapsidem	et	?	et	? ,	et	solutares
que	topin	que	pignata	que	scifum	que	calatum,	que	calias
καὶ	τουπὶν	καὶ	πήγματα [?]	καὶ	σκύφον	καὶ	κάλαθον,	καὶ	καλίγια[ς][34]

et	pergammenum,	et	piscem,	et aquam	flumen,	aquam,	
que	cartim,	que	obsarium,	que	potamium,	nerro,	tubias,
καὶ	χαρτίν,	καὶ	ὀψάριον,	καὶ	ποτάμιον,	νερό(ν),	τουβία[?],

32 *Nagorassem* shows again the non-differentiated ending. One may also read ν'ἀγοράσω, but this fits less well in the conversation. For ἔ[σ]χω see n. 30.

33 The passage as a whole is clear enough, except for the words *uva ovium* on the Latin side. *Uva* should be *ova* ('eggs'), and the Greek rendering, though inadequate, gives with *alga* = αὐγά the right intention. *Ovium* has no function at all (unless it originally resided under the Greek term ᾠόν = 'egg'), the Greek side seems to mean ἂν ἔχετε ('if you have' = 'perhaps you have (also) ...'). The onions disappeared on the Latin side, and on the Greek side some misunderstanding rose about *castaneas*, which in Latin indicates both the fruits and the tree ('chestnuts' and 'chestnut trees'). The Greek translation should have been κάστανα = 'chestnuts', not καστανέας = 'chestnut trees'.

34 The copy B has *cutellum* instead of *cultellem*. *Bromum* may be what it is, it does not correspond with *loricam*. An adequate translation would give θώρακα – θωράκιον, whereas *bromum* scarcely can be connected with other than either βρῶμα = 'food' or βρόμον acc. of βρόμος = 'oats' (see LSJ and Kriaras ΛΜΕΔΓ s.v. βρόμος (1) and Koukoules ΒΒΠ, V, 259). Perhaps there was some gap or the author made a mistake, forgetting the Greek equivalent of *lorica* and the corresponding Latin equivalent of *bromum* (*hordeum*?). The Greek word τουπίν or τυπίον is in use for τυροφόρον δοχεῖον = 'a barrel for cheese-making', see Koukoules ΒΒΠ, V, 329. For the same purpose also κάλαθοι were in use (Koukoules, *ibid.*). Striking is the presence of the Greek-looking *parapsidem* on the Latin side, but this loan-word had already found its way into classical Latin, often in the correct form *paropsis* (< Gr. πάροψις, cf. Juven., III, 142: 'quam multa magnaque paropside cenat?'), but usually with the spelling *parapsis*. We find the word in this form also in Isidore 20, 4, 10: 'parapsis quadriangulum et quadrilaterum vas, id est paribus absidis'! Here, too, the Greek equivalent does not correspond with the Latin word. Πήγματα has perhaps also to do with the process of cheese-making, cf. Aristotle, *Historia animalium*, 516a4 ('that which makes to curdle') (LSJ). Under *calias* we probably have to understand καλίγια = shoes, though the Latin equivalent is somewhat obscure (= **sutulares*? = *subtelares* > Fr. *souliers*).

		ferrum,	mensam,	lapidem,	librum,
brachias,	clocleitrium,	siderum,	trapesium,	petram,	biblum,
βρακία[?]	? ,[35]	σίδηρον,	τραπέζιον,	πέτραν,	βίβλον,

litteras,	gallina,	vaccas,	vitulum,	sues,	oves,	naves.
garamata,	urnitia,	geladia,	muscum,	surridia,	probata,	carabia.
γ[α]ράμματα,	ὀρνίθια,	γελάδια,	μόσχον,	χοιρίδια,	πρόβατα,	καράβια.[36]

Dies Lune,	dies Martis,	dies Mercurii,	Jovis,	Veneris,	Saturni,
Dextera,	triti,	tetrardi,	pesta,	parascenem,	sabbato,
Δευτέρα,	τρίτη,	τετάρτη,	πέμπτη,	παρασκευή[ν],	σάββατο,

Dominica.	Corona,	pili,	caput,	oculi,	aures,	nasus,	os,
kirriechim.	Galgala,	malia,	cephalis,	obmatia,	ptia,	miti,	stoma,
κυριακή[ν].[37]	? ,[38]	μαλλιά,	κεφαλή,	ὀμμάτια,	ἀφτία,	μύτη,	στόμα,

lingua,	dentes.	Barba,	gene,	manus,	digiti,	pedes,	viscera.
glosa,	dentia.	Genia,	maxilla,	cheria,	dactilia,	podaria,	cardia.
γλῶσσα,	δόντια.	Γένεια,	μαξίλλα,	χέρια,	δακτύλια,	ποδάρια,	καρδία,[39]

[35] This part of the list has a number of incomprehensible items. It is not clear why the lemma *aquam* has been mentioned twice. Should one read *aquam fluminis* – <νερὸ(ν)> ποτάμιον? For τουβίον = 'legging' (or τουβίον = 'tassel') see Sophocles, *Lexicon*. With *brachias* is probably meant βρακία plural of βρακί(ον) = 'trousers'. As to *clocleitrium* my imagination falls short. One may think of κοχλιάριον = 'spoon' (Isidore mentions the word under the household ware: 20, 4, 13: 'coclear ab usu prius coclearum dictum'. In the form *coglari* it occurs also in *Monza*, 29 with the Greek translation *cotali* = κουτάλι) or κ<α>λὸ κλι<ν>τ<ή>ριον = 'a good couch'.

[36] For ὀρνίθον = 'hen' see Sophocles, *Lexicon*, for ἀγελάδι and γελάδι, Kriaras ΛΜΕΔΓ. In the spelling *surridia* one may suppose a dialectal pronunciation such as χιουρίδια, cf. Hatzidakis *MNE*, II, 230 (Leuktra). On Cyprian χ followed by *i*-sound > *s*, see Menardos, 6. *Monza*, 43 has a similar notation: *porco* - *surilo*, which I transcribed as χιουρίλο(ν) (respectively χοιρίλο(ν)).

[37] In *Monza*, 59–65, there is also a list of names of the weekdays, beginning with Sunday. The spelling *dextera* looks more like an association with Latin *dexter* than that *x* should be pronounced as *s* or *ss*, which would bring us to a pronunciation *destera* as in southern Italian Greek (Bova), see *Monza*, 60. *Tetrardi* recalls the form τετράς as used in *Monza*, 62. The peculiar notation *pesta* for 'Thursday' reminds us of southern Italian *pefti* (cf. Caracausi). *Monza*, 63, is of no help since the text there is practically illegible.

[38] One can only guess what was meant with *galgala*. In the sphere of the games one can try ἔπαθλα = 'prizes' as confused with στέφανος = 'wreath', 'crown'. If *corona* was understood as a 'head-gear' one may guess κάλυμμα. Possible, but too far-fetched, seems a mental leap like *corona* (in the circus) > σφενδόνη > κάγκελλα (= *carceres*, which were to be found under the σφενδόνη, see Koukoules ΒΒΠ, III, 17).

[39] Copy B ends after *dentes* / *dentia*. This list of parts of the body corresponds in a number of aspects with the list in *Monza*, though there are also differences. *Cephalis* has a superfluous *s*, though also the word κεφαλίς = 'little head' exists. It is, however, too unusual a word to make it the probable term in this context. Striking is *obmatia* for ὀμμάτια, where *Monza*, 3, has *ubtarmia* = ὀφτάλμια, *CGL*, III, 394, 43 *obtalmi*. *Ptia* shows the same spelling as *Monza*, 6, *apti* = αὐτί. *Glosa* (with one *s*), the same as in *Monza*, 14. *Monza*, 50, had a 'better' *odonta* for 'tooth'.

Benedic	me,	pater,	mater!	Bone	adjuvet	te	Deus!
Eblois	em,	despota,	roda!	Calo	sosis	e	o theos!
Εὐλόγησέ	μ<ε>,	δέσποτα,	? !	Καλῶ<ς>	σώσῃ	σε	ὁ θεός![40]

Palmites,	vinea.	Camisia	mea.
Climata,	ampelia.	Ilmati	mon.
Κλήματα,	ἀμπέλια.	Ἱμάτι	μου [?].[41]

It will be clear that this wordlist of Auxerre is of a totally different character from fol. 12v of the MS Vind. 114, written by Froumund. In this case we have to do with a list such as the Vocabulary of Monza, that is to say that on the Greek side someone tried to record 'modern' i.e. contemporary Greek, someone who saw himself confronted with the difficulty of rendering the Greek words in the Latin alphabet. Moreover, it is clear that this person, whatever the reason for his interest may have been, had no real command of the language either: he noted what he thought he heard, and he made a lot of mistakes. In a number of cases, in rendering the Greek words he was guided by the endings of the Latin ones. Another problem of the list is that it gives the impression of being copied from an earlier one. In the course of the transmission a number of lemmata have been dropped out and some of the mistakes could be the result of this transmission. But at the same time it is clear that this list originates from a contact between someone from the West and a Greek person, or someone who had a reasonably good knowledge of contemporary Greek.

For *barba Monza*, 15, has the less correct ἡ γενειάς. Μαξίλλα as a Greek translation for *gene* (= *genae*) is a very strange mistake, *maxilla* being no less Latin. One should expect παρειαί or γνάθοι. Ποδάρια is correct = πόδια. Also somewhat strange is the interpretation of *viscera* = 'entrails' as the specific καρδία = 'heart'.

40 Here we happen to find two cases of wrong division of the words: the *e* of *em* belongs to the imperative εὐλόγησε = εὐλόγησον. In the second case the (final) *s* of *sosis* must be connected with the following *e*. The simplest things are sometimes unsolvable: after *pater* – δέσποτα a lemma *mater* – δέσποινα (or μήτηρ, μητέρα, μάνα, etc) might be expected: a circumscription like ῥόδα = 'roses', however much mothers deserve such a poetical indication, is very unlikely.

41 *Camisia* already occurs in Hieronymus, *Epistula*, 64, 11 (St Jérôme, *Lettres*, ed. J. Labourt, III (Paris, 1953), p. 127, 12). Isidore gives the following definitions in 19, 21, 1: 'Poderis est sacerdotalis linea, corpori adstricta et usque ad pedes descendens; unde et nuncupata; quam vulgo camisiam vocant'; 19, 22, 29: 'Camisias vocari quod in his dormimus in camis, id est in stratis nostris.' The Greek transcription has two mistakes: the *l* in *ilmati* is superfluous and *mon* should be *mou*. The pronoun *mea* makes it probable that one should understand Ἱμάτι μου. Theoretically one could imagine *ilmati mon* = *i[l]mati[m]on* = ἱμάτιον.

Whether the list was made for crusaders or was the result of an incidental conversation is not easy to decide. Neither does the question whether the list reflects a distinct (modern) Greek dialect permit an easy answer. Some traces point to Cyprus (ἕνε, ἐννά, 'ναῖκα, etc.) or Crete, but these are, in my opinion, not clear enough to justify a definite conclusion. In any case, it is a very interesting example of real contact between the western and Byzantine worlds.

Abbreviations and select bibliography

Caracausi = Girolamo Caracausi, *Testi neogreci di Calabria: indice lessicale* (Palermo, 1979).

CGL = G. Loewe and G. Goetz: *Corpus Glossariorum Latinorum*, I–VII (Leipzig, 1888–1901 and reprinted 1923).

The Chronicle of Morea = *The Chronicle of Morea*, ed. J. Schmitt (London, 1904 and reprinted Groningen, 1967); Τὸ Χρονικὸ τοῦ Μορέως, ed. P.P. Kalonaros (Athens, 1940).

Erotokritos = V. Kornaros, *Erotokritos*, ed. S.A. Xanthoudides (Athens, 1952) (small edn).

Hatzidakis = G.N. Hatzidakis, *Einleitung in die neugriechische Grammatik* (Leipzig, 1892 and reprinted Hildesheim, 1977).

Hatzidakis *MNE* = G.N. Hatzidakis, Μεσαιωνικὰ καὶ Νεοελληνικά, I-II (Athens, 1905–7 and reprinted 1992).

Isidore = Isidori Hispalensis Episcopi, *Etymologiarum* ... *Libri XX*, ed. W.M. Lindsay, Oxford Classical Texts (Oxford, 1911).

Jannaris = A.N. Jannaris, *An Historical Greek Grammar* (London, 1897 and reprinted Hildesheim, 1987).

Juven. = Juvenalis, *Satirae*, ed. L. Canali and E. Barelli (Milan, 1960).

Koukoules ΒΒΠ = F. Koukoules, Βυζαντινῶν Βίος καὶ Πολιτισμός, I–VI (Athens, 1948–55).

Koumanoudes = S.A. Koumanoudes, Λεξικὸν Λατινοελληνικόν (Athens, 1854).

Kriaras ΛΜΕΔΓ = E. Kriaras, Λεξικὸ τῆς Μεσαιωνικῆς 'Ελληνικῆς Δημώδους Γραμματείας (Thessalonike, 1966–).

Lampe = G.W.H. Lampe, *A Patristic Greek Lexicon* (Oxford, 1961).

LSJ = H.G. Liddell, R. Scott and H. Stuart Jones, *A Greek–English Lexicon* (Oxford, 9th edn, 1940).

Phalieros, 'Ερωτικά = Marinos Phalieros, 'Ερωτικὰ "Ονειρα, ed. A. F. van Gemert (Thessalonike, 1980).

Menardos = S. Menardos, Γλωσσικαὶ Μελέται (Nikosia, 1969; revised articles in reprint).

Monza = W.J. Aerts, 'The Monza Vocabulary', in *Studia Byzantina et Neohellenica Neerlandica*, ed. W.F. Bakker, A.F. van Gemert and W.J. Aerts (Leiden, 1972), pp. 36–73.

Papadopoulos = A.A. Papadopoulos: Ἱστορικὸν Λεξικὸν τῆς Ποντικῆς Διαλέκτου (Athens, 1958–).

Ptochoprodromos, Eideneier = *Ptochoprodromos*, ed. H. Eideneier, Neograeca Medii Aevi, V (Cologne, 1991).

Ptochoprodromos, Hesseling = *Ptochoprodromos*, ed. D.C. Hesseling and H. Pernot (Amsterdam, 1910).

Sophocles, *Lexicon* = E.A. Sophocles, *Greek Lexicon of the Roman and Byzantine Periods* (Cambridge, Mass., 1914).

Tzartzanos = A.A. Tzartzanos, Νεοελληνικὴ Σύνταξις (Athens, 1946–53).

11

The art of Byzantium and its relation to Germany in the time of the empress Theophano*

JACQUELINE LAFONTAINE-DOSOGNE

The Byzantine princess Theophano entered history through her marriage to Otto II, emperor of Germany, in 972. Otto I had sought from the emperor of Byzantium a purple-born consort for his son and co-emperor, but two diplomatic missions led by Liutprand of Cremona had failed to achieve this object. Evidently, such a request still appeared presumptuous to the Byzantine court, which was, however, prepared to betroth to him a niece of the reigning emperor, John I Tzimiskes. The young princess arrived at Rome, where the marriage was celebrated on Easter Day, 14 April; afterwards she was crowned as empress by the pope.[1]

The wedding is registered in a document deposited in the archives of Wolfenbüttel (Niedersächsisches Staatsarchiv, 6, Urk. 11). This 'diploma' was drawn up by the Imperial Chancery at Rome; it contains a list of the gifts and estates with which Theophano was presented. Inscribed on purple parchment in letters of gold, as Carolingian documents had sometimes been

* I wish to thank, most warmly, Andrew Palmer, who has greatly improved my English text. Owing to the drastic limitation of footnotes I have only given general references according to the subdivisions of this article. The location of the works of art I deal with is indicated in the text.

[1] For general information on Theophano and her time see: ***Byzantium and the Low Countries in the Tenth Century: Aspects of Art and History in the Ottonian Era***, ed. V.D. van Aalst and K.N. Ciggaar (Hernen, 1985), and, most important, von Euw and Schreiner, *Kaiserin Theophanu*. See also L. Grodecki, F. Mütherich, *et al.*, *Le Siècle de l'An Mil*, L'Univers des formes (Paris, 1973); P. Lasko, *Ars sacra 800–1200*, The Pelican History of Art (Harmondsworth, 1972); *Ornamenta ecclesiae: Kunst und Künstler der Romanik*, Schnütgen-Museum, 3 vols. (Cologne, 1985). Many works of art mentioned in this article are reproduced in those books as well as in the other studies referred to in the following notes. I could not use the important catalogue ***Bernward von Hildesheim und das Zeitalter der Ottonen***, Dom- und Diözesanmuseum Hildesheim, Römer- und Pelizeus-Museum (Hildesheim, 1993).

prepared, it contains also busts and medallions of Christ, the Virgin Mary and the Apostles which betray the influence of Byzantium. The background has a pattern strongly reminiscent of Byzantine silks, with a number of large contiguous medallions containing representations of animals, the spaces between being decorated with stylized vegetation. Such features recur in ornate Ottonian manuscripts of the following decades.

Among the estates listed there were some in the northern and southern Low Countries which had belonged to Matilda (d. 968), the grandmother of Otto II; for example, the abbey of Nivelles, of which Theophano was the last lay abbess. The court was frequently on the move and several times resident in Nijmegen, where Theophano died on 15 June 991, although she was buried, according to her wish, in the monastery of St Pantaleon at Cologne, of which she had been the benefactress. Pantaleon, a saint with a great following in Byzantium, was already venerated in Italy during the ninth century.

At the death of Otto I in 973, Otto II became sole emperor with Theophano as his *co-imperatrix*. Leaden medallions, sculpted ivories and manuscripts all represent the imperial couple as equals; this is not typical of western art, which suggests once more that Byzantium had furnished the model. Two leaden medallions (at St Petersburg and Helsinki) show, on the obverse, Christ blessing Otto and Theophano and, on the reverse, the Cross with double cross-bar and Greek inscriptions. All these things are typical of Byzantium, rather than the West.

The Ottonians championed the renovation of the *imperium romanum*, claiming equality with the Christian emperors of the East. These ideas inform the famous ivory plaque in the Musée de Cluny, which was probably carved in 982. A tall Christ stands on a pedestal and blesses Otto and Theophano, who are wearing the robes and the crowns of Byzantine emperors. The inscriptions combine Latin letters with Greek: 'OTTO IMP[erator] P[o]MAN[orum] A[ugustu]C et ΘΕΟΦΑΝΩ IMP[peratrix] A[ugustu]C'. Note that the gender of the word 'emperor' is unchanged. For Byzantine officialdom Otto was no more than *Imperator Francorum*: the title of *Imperator Romanorum* is inspired by Byzantine imperial titulature. The plaque also shows a figure prostrate at Christ's feet below the emperor. This is presumably the donor, who has been identified as John Philagathos, the Calabrian monk who became bishop of Plaisance and orchestrated the *rappro-*

chement of the empires of East and West. The Greek inscription in the field calls upon the Lord to help His servant John, a well-known Byzantine formula. Both the style and the presumptuous title suggest that the artist, perhaps a Greek, executed this work in Italy or in Germany, not in Constantinople. Yet the iconography is purely Byzantine. Compare the plaque in the Cabinet des Médailles at Paris which represents the coronation of Romanos II and Eudokia (945–9) by Christ. The recent re-identification of the emperor as Romanos IV has been contested, notably because it does not conform to the type of the beardless emperor. If the earlier date be accepted, this Byzantine plaque, more refined and better balanced than that of Otto II and Theophano, might well be seen as its antecedent.

By contrast, the Castello Sforzesco possesses an ivory of a purely western – most probably Milanese – style, representing, as it would seem, Otto II, Theophano and the young Otto III, all at the feet of Christ, who is surrounded by the Virgin Mary, St Maurice and two angels. The divine personages are named in inscriptions, but OTTO IMPERATOR is the only designation referring to the imperial family. This plaque was presumably created while the court was resident in Italy, perhaps in 982. Otto II died in Rome in 983, whereupon Theophano assumed the regency. She was a good empress. According to Otto Demus she was not a *porphyrogennetos* but an empress born.

No doubt Theophano brought with her to the West some Byzantine *objets d'art* and commissioned, with her court, several others. Sumptuous and refined, Byzantine art had a fascination all of its own.[2] Already in an earlier age Byzantine objects had

[2] For Byzantine art, cf. for example J. Beckwith, *Early Christian and Byzantine Art*, The Pelican History of Art (Harmondsworth, 1970); J. Lafontaine-Dosogne, *Histoire de l'art byzantin et chrétien d'Orient*, Institut d'études médiévales (Louvain-la-Neuve, 1987). For its connection with the West, O. Demus, *Byzantine Art and the West* (New York, 1970); K. Weitzmann, 'Various aspects of Byzantine influence on the Latin countries from the sixth to the twelfth century', *DOP*, 20 (1966), 1–14; K. Wentzel, 'Das byzantinische Erbe der Ottonischer Kaiser: Hypothesen über den Brautschatz der Theophano', *Aachener Kunstblätter*, 43 (1972), 11–96; Wentzel, 'Byzantinische Kleinkunstwerke aus dem Umkreis der Kaiserin Theophano', *Aachener Kunstblätter*, 44 (1973), 43–86; J. Lafontaine-Dosogne, 'L'art byzantin en Belgique en relation avec les croisades', *Revue Belge d'Archéologie et d'Histoire de l'Art*, 61 (1987), 13–47; Lafontaine-Dosogne, 'Die byzantinische Kunst nach dem Ikonoklasmus bis zur Mitte des 11. Jahrhunderts', in von Euw and Schreiner, *Kaiserin Theophanu*, II, pp. 63–85; Lafontaine-Dosogne, 'L'influence artistique byzantine dans la région Meuse-Rhin du VIIIe au début du XIIIe siècle',

arrived on the banks of the Rhine and the Meuse, especially from Ravenna, a Byzantine 'exarchy', and from Rome, which remained a Byzantine city until the mid-eighth century. Imported silk and other goods are attested from Merovingian times and the city of Pisa played a central role in this commerce. In addition, Byzantine emperors were unstinting in the gifts with which their diplomats presented the rulers of the West; many valuable objects came to Germany in this way. Certain Byzantine rituals had been adopted already, by Clovis, Charlemagne, Charles the Bald. The Greek language was not unknown: Bruno, brother of Otto I and archbishop of Cologne, had studied Greek with Balderich, bishop of Utrecht (d. 976). But the influence of Byzantium in Germany after the marriage of Otto II and Theophano was more direct.

Florentine Mütherich regards the style displayed by the court, in its fashions of dressing and otherwise, in the figured representations of Cologne, for example, as a reflection of the splendour brought to it by the Byzantine princess. We may compare the superb representation of the Virgin Mary as an imperial personage in a Reichenau manuscript which may have been inspired by Theophano herself (Universitätsbibliothek Heidelberg, cod. sal. IXb, fol. 40v). Of Theophano herself few portraits survive. That on the Cluny ivory is hardly realistic; but there is a little bust in a medallion at the *Incipit* of St Matthew in the Saint-Gereon Gospels (Historisches Archiv Köln, cod. W 312, fol. 22r) which may represent Theophano. Thietmar of Merseburg created a manuscript in Magdeburg containing such a portrait; but this is now lost. He describes it as follows: 'imperatricisque Theophanu imago auro splendet formata' ('and the image of the empress Theophano adorns it, created with gold').

As for works of art, Hans Wentzel has made an interesting attempt to attach a number of pieces now in German collections to the person of Theophano; but he has too little justification for dating some of the pieces to the tenth century. Some are dated exactly, others can only be dated approximately, and so cannot be used to prove this theory. Correct method should also take account of the possibility that some pieces which are indeed of the tenth century were brought from Byzantium to the West in the time of the Crusades. Portable objects, such as manuscripts, ivories, gold and silver items, jewelry, and textiles, were capable

in *Byzantine East, Latin West: Art Historical Studies in Honor of Kurt Weitzmann* (Princeton, forthcoming).

of exerting a stylistic influence and of providing iconographic models at the same time. There may have been model-books through which Byzantine monumental painting was studied in the West, but none have been preserved; apart, perhaps, from the frescoes of St George in Oberzell, which date from the end of the tenth century, there are no examples of Byzantine influence in this province of art before the romanesque period. As for portable painted icons, not many are preserved from this period; they probably were not disseminated in the West for reasons of theology. Nor did Byzantine sculpture, most of which was architectonic, have much impact beyond the Italian peninsula.

I propose to consider here a selection of works in these different categories dating from the splendid period of the Macedonian Renaissance and to establish links with works of art preserved in Germany with the aim of defining certain influences.

Manuscripts[3]

The Middle Byzantine period (843–1204) produced the best illuminated manuscripts, many of them sumptuously bound in precious metals, enamels, precious stones and plaques of ivory. As works of literature they attest to the breadth of Byzantine intellectual interests: the Old Testament, especially the Psalms; the New Testament, represented by Gospel Books, Lectionaries and Acts of the Apostles; Menologia, saints' lives and homilies; also works of profane literature, science and history. These manuscripts were created in *scriptoria*, such as those attested for the Great Palace of Constantinople, the patriarchate and certain monasteries, such as that of Stoudios. The imperial *scriptorium* was developed by literary emperors of the tenth century, such as Leo VI the Wise and, above all, Constantine VII Porphyrogennetos, who was writer, scholar and artist all at once, and who commissioned copies of the ancients. In terms of art, the tenth and eleventh centuries manifest, broadly speaking, two tendencies or orientations: the humanistic orientation towards Antiquity and the medieval orientation towards the Christian faith, tendencies

[3] Cf. K. Weitzmann, *Die byzantinische Buchmalerei des IX. und X. Jahrhunderts* (Berlin, 1935); V.N. Lazarev, *Storia della pittura Bizantina* (Turin, 1967); I. Spatharakis, *The Portrait in Byzantine Illuminated Manuscripts*, Byzantina Neerlandica, 6 (Leiden, 1976); *Vor dem Jahr 1000: abendländische Buchkunst zur Zeit der Kaiserin Theophanu*, Schnütgen-Museum (Cologne, 1991); H. Mayr-Harting, *Ottonian Book Illumination: An Historical Study*, I, *Themes*, II, *Books* (London, 1991).

capable of coexistence. As in manuscripts of the early Byzantine period, there is a contrast between the transcendental treatment of Christian themes from the New Testament and the antique style adumbrated by Old Testament illustrations and profane images.

It will be instructive to examine a few examples. The first manuscript dated after Iconoclasm is the gorgeous collection of homilies by Gregory of Nazianze and other texts (Paris, Bibliothèque Nationale, gr. 510), executed for Basil I between 880 and 883; this is followed by a series of *de luxe* imperial codices of the Macedonian dynasty. The iconography is very rich in imperial portraits and christological scenes. The clarity of the compositions, the tranquil weightiness of the figures, the subtlety of the colouring announce the neo-classical phase which will be manifested in the tenth century, certainly in Constantinople, if not elsewhere. The Joshua scroll in the Vatican Library (gr. 431) and the great Paris Psalter (BN gr. 139) are good representatives (not without some academicism) of the classically inspired style and the technical perfection of books produced in the capital in the tenth century. They also display a repertory of motifs, especially personifications, deriving from the art of Antiquity. Antique illusionism is also practised, with more freedom, in some religious manuscripts, such as the Bible of Leo the Patrician (Vat. Reg. 1) or the Gospels gr. 21 in the Saltykov-Ščedrin Library at St Petersburg. In the Bible, borders are adorned with a simple uncial inscription, for the Byzantines liked to exploit their writing for aesthetic effect.

The Evangelists are represented as ancient philosophers, in a classical architectural setting, in the Stauronitika 43 on Mount Athos; in a Gospel Book in London (British Library, Add. 28815) (mid-eleventh century), they sit in a less specific architectural frame but their instruments are minutely detailed. Those portraits became classics of Byzantine art and strongly influenced the West. 'The Evangelist Luke' in the Trier Gospels in Prague (Museum of Czech Literature, MS D.F.III,3, fol. 104 v°) and 'Gregory the Great' by the Master of the Registrum Gregorii at Trier (Stadtbibliothek, Hs. 171/1626), respectively from *c.* 980 and 984, are good examples; note that the instruments for writing are less realistic than in the Byzantine miniatures. Ottonian christological cycles match those created for the Byzantine illustrated lectionaries. The miniatures of the *Codex Egberti* made in Reichenau *c.* 985 (Trier, Stadtbibliothek, cod. 24) are clearly the product of such influence. Such cycles were also produced at Cologne, for instance in the Saint-Gereon Sacramentary (BN lat. 817, 996–1002). Individual tableaux such as the Dormition of the Virgin could have been influenced by carved ivories or other models. In the Lives of SS Kilian and Margaret, especially the latter, in a manuscript from Fulda dating from the last quarter of the tenth century (Hanover, Niedersächsische Landesbibliothek, MS I.189), these early cycles betray a strong Byzantine influence.

About the end of that century, a style better suited to the religious and more severe ideal of transcendency spread through Byzantium, as we find in the Menologion of Basil II (Vat. gr. 1613). This hagiographic compilation (of which only one half has been preserved) contains 436 miniatures attributable to eight different painters; it represents an important step in the constitution of the iconography of the saints and of christological commemorations in the liturgy. The busts of Christ and of the Virgin in two miniatures of the *Codex aureus* from Speyer conserved at the Escorial (Real Biblioteca, cod. Vit. 17, 1043–6) have been compared with some representations in this Menologion and are probably likewise the work of a Greek artist. The more sumptuous Psalter of Basil II in the Biblioteca Marciana at Venice (Marc. gr. 17), which was probably made after his victory over the Bulgarians in 1017, opens with an impressive image of the Bulgaroktonos, the new Joshua, protected by God and by military saints, and dominating the peoples he has defeated. Such an image, which has its roots in early Byzantine art, seems to have had no echo in the West. By contrast less unusual Byzantine imperial protocols were adopted for certain magnificent representations of Otto II and Otto III: an isolated miniature of the Master of the Registrum Gregorii at Chantilly (Musée Condé), where Otto II is surrounded by Germania, Francia, Italia and Alamania; and a double composition showing Otto III surrounded by his court and attended by personifications of the provinces of his empire. The latter is in the late tenth-century Gospels from Reichenau (Munich, Bayerische Staatsbibliothek, Clm. 4453, fols. 23v°–24r°).

Otto III also appears in *proskynesis* before Christ in his Book of Hours at Pommersfelden (Gräflich-Schönbornische Schlossbibliothek, cod. 347), produced at Mainz in 983–91. The same attitude is seen in the Lectionary of Everger, bishop of Cologne (Erzbischöfliche Diözesan- und Dombibliothek, Dom Hs. 143, fol. 3v–4r): he is prostrated before the apostles Peter and Paul, who are designated by faulty Greek inscriptions. Everger was a friend of Theophano and such gestures certainly reveal a certain atmosphere at the court of the Byzantine empress. Indeed in their iconographic interpretation of the divine right of emperors, the Ottonians went still further than the Byzantines. The Byzantine concept of *Christomimesis*, the emperor being like Christ on earth, is carried to extremes in the apotheosis of Otto III which adorns the Gospels offered by Liuthar to the emperor (Reichenau, 996–1000, at Aachen, Domschatzkammer, pp. 30–1). Otto, crowned by the Hand of God, sits in majesty in a mandorla surrounded by the symbols of the Evangelists; the roll before him probably alludes to the Gospel; his throne is sustained by the Earth; on the opposite page, Liuthar stands, presenting the book.

Other representations are more familiar, such as the coronation by the enthroned Christ of Henry II and Cunegunda, presented to him by SS Peter and Paul, in this emperor's Book of Pericopes (Reichenau, 1002–14, at Munich, Bayerische Staatsbibliothek, Clm. 4452). This rather resembles Christ crowning Peter and Irene in the Egbert Psalter in the Museo Archeologico at Cividale. In the Hitda Codex (Cologne, about 1000, at Darmstadt, Hessische Landes- und Hochschulbibliothek, Hs. 1640, fol. 6r°), the abbess offers the book to St Walburgis, much in the same way as Leo the Patrician offers his Bible to the Virgin.

The Byzantine manuscripts which produce the scientific works of Antiquity have greatly contributed to our knowledge of ancient sciences and arts. In the *Theriaka* by Nikander (Paris, Bibliothèque Nationale, suppl. gr. 247) the scientific illustrations are accompanied by charming mythological and idyllic scenes; the *Hippiatrika* in the Biblioteca Laurenziana at Florence (Plut. LXXIX, 7, eleventh century) combines antique compositions with borders similar to those of the Gospel *canons*; the Pseudo-Oppian *Kynegetika* at Venice (Marc. gr. Z. 479) perpetuates ancient representations of animals which may have provided models for the decorative arts. Poetry was not so fortunate. Homer was considered essential reading for schoolboys, but no illustrated manuscripts of his epics have been preserved. As for the historical manuscripts, we do not have any illustrated examples from the period but one can form an idea of what they were like from later chronicle-manuscripts, the Skylitzes at Madrid (Biblioteca Nacional, Ms Vitr. 26.2, twelfth century) and the Bulgarian

Manasses in the Vatican (slav. II, fourteenth century). The sources affirm that historical themes were illustrated at that time in monumental painting, so there is no reason to doubt that there were illustrated books of history as well.

The typological variety of Byzantine manuscripts is not reflected in Ottonian manuscripts, which essentially deal with imperial and religious matters. Otto III, as we know, had in his possession an illuminated copy of Boethius' *Arithmetica*, but this was a Carolingian work. Secular iconography is rare; one might mention the calendar with an allegorical cycle of the year and a personification of *Annus* himself from a manuscript made in Fulda at the end of the tenth century (Berlin, Staatsbibl. Preussischer Kulturbesitz, MS theol. lat., fol. 192). As a matter of fact, Ottonian illumination was linked to various centres of production and continued to be impregnated from the Carolingian tradition. Nevertheless, it adopted new trends in iconography, compositional structures, and style from Byzantine art. Some illuminated Byzantine manuscripts certainly did exist in Germany at the time of Theophano, but it seems that none has been preserved, either in Germany, or in Belgium, or in the Netherlands.

The ivories[4]

Byzantine ivories display a variety of types: diptychs and triptychs, plaques, caskets, pyxides and so on, which were used in both religious and secular contexts. The industry of ivory was very old in the Greco-Roman world; it made use of elephant tusks imported from India or Africa. The technique of ivory-carving is difficult; it is something between sculpture, as to the relief, and painting, as to the frame, the iconography and, on occasion, the polychromy. A great number of ivories were made up to the eleventh and twelfth centuries, but after that they became rarer.

Some ivories represent the coronation of an emperor. The plaque in the Pushkin Museum in Moscow, on which Christ is crowning Constantine Porphyrogennetos, seems to be linked to his re-installation as sole sovereign in 945. It is a noble work, with a new sense of depth and drapery and an elegant elongation of the

[4] Cf. A. Goldschmidt and K. Weitzmann, *Die byzantinischen Elfenbeinskulpturen des X.-XIII. Jahrhunderts*, 2 vols. (Berlin, 1930, 1934); D. Gaborit-Chopin, *Ivoires du moyen âge* (Fribourg, 1978); J. Fleming, *Byzantinische Schatzkunst* (Berlin, 1979); *Splendeur de Byzance*, Europalia-Grèce, 82 (Brussels, 1982).

figures. The coronation by Christ of Romanos II and Eudokia, which has already been cited, breathes an air of classicism and serenity. The plaque of Otto II and Theophano must have been inspired by some such model. Let us also recall the Milan plaque, which represents the imperial Ottonian family at the feet of Christ in an entirely western style; from an iconographic point of view, one may consider that it outdoes all Byzantine models, which never represented the entire imperial family in *proskynesis*. Liturgical objects may sometimes assume a political meaning, as is the case with the precious *situla* at Aachen (in the Cathedral Treasury), on which Otto III sits enthroned. The occasion of its creation was either his anointing or the opening of Charlemagne's shrine, which was ordered by him.

Among Byzantine caskets, that in the Cathedral Treasury at Troyes (tenth/eleventh century), tinted with purple, is interesting for its imperial iconography; it depicts the entrance into a subdued city, scenes of hunting and a phoenix. Numerous caskets adorned with rosette-borders display secular motifs. The most famous of them is the Veroli casket, at the Victoria and Albert Museum in London, which boasts compositions inspired by classical mythology and drama, such as the Rape of Europa, the Sacrifice of Iphigeneia, scenes from the cycle of Hercules, Dionysus and the Maenads, Bellerophon and so on. It is also a technically dazzling work of art, demonstrating a deep understanding of the classical style which can only have existed in the imperial workshop; it is datable to about the end of the tenth century.

Christian motifs are the most numerous, though. Caskets were preferably adorned with biblical subjects: one example is the Genesis casket at Darmstadt (Hessisches Landesmuseum, eleventh/twelfth century). More frequently plaques, diptychs and triptychs bear christological motifs. These were intended to be placed on a public or a private altar; like the diptychs, they might be folded to be taken on a journey. Individual plates might be used for book-covers or as icons. They are carved with solemn representations of Christ, his Mother and his saints, alone or arranged in groups. For example, on the Harbaville triptych in the Louvre, the principal place is occupied by the Deesis, flanked by the various categories of saints, standing or in bust. On a triptych in the British Museum, the Crucifixion appears in the central part and some saints are depicted on the wings. The Virgin usually takes the attitude of the Hodegetria – the 'shower of the way' –

bearing the Infant, sitting, standing or in demi-figure. Two beautiful central parts of a triptych preserved separately at Utrecht (Rijksmuseum Het Catharijneconvent) and at Liège (Saint-Paul Cathedral Treasury) display the type of the standing Hodegetria. Except for John the Baptist and the Apostles, individual saints are rarely represented. Standing Apostles are found carved on three plates at Vienna (Kunsthistorisches Museum), Venice (Museo Archeologico) and Dresden (Grünes Gewölbe): they are admirable works, made, according to the inscriptions, for the use of Constantine Porphyrogennetos, and closely related in style to the coronation plaque of that emperor at Moscow. Compositions from the Dodekaorton, illustrating one or more of the twelve great liturgical feasts, are numerous.

It seems that such portable objects, especially overtly Christian ones, were readily conveyed to the West, where they exerted both an iconographic and a stylistic influence, and where some were reused for other purposes. Many triptychs lost their wings; the central parts were reused as plaques, which often served to adorn bindings, more often, indeed, than in Byzantium itself. Some imperial Ottonian manuscripts provide revealing examples. The splendid Evangeliary of Otto III at Munich (Staatsbibl., Clm. 4453) was adorned with a beautiful ivory of the Dormition of the Virgin and also, in the upper part, with a stone bust of Christ, which seems not to have been noted. Another Gospel Book of Otto III, made in Reichenau (Aachen, Domschatzkammer) shows an Hodegetria in bust surrounded by a precious goldsmith's border with christological scenes and symbols of the Evangelists, which is of western workmanship. Another Hodegetria constitutes the central part of the binding of a Sacramentary from Fulda about 1000 (Bamberg, Staatsbibl., Lit. 1), surrounded by a silver border carved with secular motifs, including the Seasons and 'inhabited' vine-scrolls. Four plaques representing Christ, the Virgin, St Peter and St Paul, all standing, were used as a binding for the Prayer Book of Henry II, now kept at Bamberg (Staatsbibl., Lit. 8, beginning of the eleventh century). A plaque with four scenes, the Nativity, the Baptism, the Crucifixion and the Descent from the Cross, was inserted in the cover of the Gospels of Adelheid, Otto III's sister, the abbess of Quedlinburg. A part of a triptych with the Virgin Hodegetria in demi-figure adorns a Latin Gospel Book of the late tenth century at the University of Jena; its great elegance bespeaks a Constantinopolitan workshop and it may even have belonged to Theophano herself.

It was, at least in part, through such objects that the iconographical types of Christ and especially of the Virgin spread throughout Germany. The same applies to some scenes in manuscripts, like the Dormition of the Virgin or the Deesis (for example, the Deesis in Otto III's Prayer Book, with the emperor below between Peter and Paul, fol. 2r°). As for the ivory caskets, some were also imported into the West as containers for relics. They may have provided models for the casket-reliquary at Munich (Bayerisches Nationalmuseum) adorned with Apostles and zodiacal signs, which is dated to the end of the tenth century.

The goldsmith's craft and enamel-work[5]

In Byzantium, gold and silver were used in secular art to display status by wearing jewelry or using a dinner-service; in the religious sphere, liturgical vessels, reliquaries, crosses and icons were often made with precious metals. They were also used for manuscript-bindings, for lamps and, as some sources say, for plaques set in pieces of furniture. Traditional techniques like working in relief and chasing were used, as was that of filigree. Precious stones and pearls are often set in gold and the way this was done recalled an earlier period and revealed the Byzantine taste for polychromy. However, in this period enamels were largely used in addition. Byzantine craftsmen had mastered the refined technique of cloisonné enamel, by smelting the smalts between thin golden threads welded on a ground of gold, electron or silver-gilt which gleams through the translucent enamel. In the eighth and ninth centuries such enamels were still a little heavy, with a green background. But the artisans soon achieved perfection. This highly skilled workmanship was reserved for the emperor, the court and the church; there existed a workshop in the Great Palace itself.

The insignia and the crowns of emperors are known to a large extent from their representations, whether in the mosaics of Hagia

[5] Cf. K. Wessel, *The Byzantine Enamels from the Fifth to the Thirteenth Century* (Shannon, 1969), English edition; *Ornamenta ecclesiae* (see n. 1); M.-M. Gauthier, *Emaux du moyen âge occidental* (Fribourg, 1972); *Le Trésor de Saint-Marc de Venise*, Grand Palais (Paris, 1984); J. Lafontaine-Dosogne, 'Email et orfèvrerie à Byzance, au Xe–XIe siècle, et leur relation avec la Germanie', in *Kunst im Zeitalter der Kaiserin Theophanu: Akten des Internationalen Colloquiums veranstaltet vom Schnütgen-Museum Köln 13–15. Juni 1991*, ed. A. von Euw and P. Schreiner (Cologne, 1993), pp. 61–78.

Sophia at Constantinople (Leo VI, Alexander, Constantine IX and Zoe), or in miniatures, on ivories and on coins. Crowns with gems are adorned with a cross at the top and *pendilia* of pearls hanging from both sides of the face; those of the empresses are higher and surmounted with pinnacles. The sceptre and the globe are ceremonial attributes; they may be replaced in certain circumstances by a purse, a diploma, a book or a weapon. No imperial crown has been preserved, except for that of Leo VI at San Marco in Venice, which served as an *ex-voto*; this crown carries a bust of the emperor. But, among the crowns that the Byzantines sent to foreign princes as gifts or marks of suzerainty, two still exist at the National Museum in Budapest. The one that Michael VII Dukas sent to Geza I of Hungary (the base of the 'crown of St Stephen') bears the enamelled portraits of the emperor, his son and Geza, in strict order of precedence. The one that Constantine IX Monomachos offered to Andrew of Hungary was made for a woman; it is an extraordinary piece, both as to its structure and as to its iconography. Seven high enamelled golden plaques represent the emperor flanked by Zoe and Theodora, who are flanked in turn by two female dancers and the personifications of Sincerity and Humility, together with cypresses and birds, charming motifs evoking the princely arts of luxury and leisure. The sensational discovery of Preslav, in Bulgaria, has revealed among other things some small curved enamel plates decorated with secular motifs, such as the Ascension of Alexander, which once belonged to a diadem. Similar plates with religious subjects have been reused in the binding of the Book of Pericopes of Henry II at Munich (Bayer. Staatsbibl., Clm. 4452); these probably came from a diadem of Theophano herself.

The crowns worn by Otto II and Otto III in the miniatures which were mentioned above are inspired to some extent by those of the Byzantine emperors. The magnificent crown of the empire preserved in the Kunsthistorisches Museum at Vienna was made in the second half of the tenth century, but redesigned in the eleventh. It is adorned with stones and pearls, has four curved enamel plates representing Christ between two seraphim, Isaiah in front of king Ezechiel and the prophets Daniel and Solomon; the phylacteries that they hold so oddly on their arms recall the roll of Otto III in his apotheosis. The cloisonné enamels have rich colours, but are less masterfully executed than Byzantine enamels, especially as to the outlines.

Byzantine necklaces, diadems, ear-rings, pectoral crosses, pendants, bracelets and rings have not been preserved in great numbers from this period. Fortunately, there have been some recent discoveries, such as the rare pair of enamelled bracelets or gauntlets decorated with birds and flowers from Thessalonike now in the Archaeological Museum there, probably from the end of the ninth century; and the jewels found in Preslav, dated before the middle of the tenth century: a superb twofold golden necklace with enamelled plates and medallions, pearls and stones, elaborate ear-rings and rings, all evidently produced for the Byzantine court. Enamels were also used to embellish ecclesiastical vestments and even the harnesses of horses. As for the jewels executed in Germany, those attributed to the empress Gisela, about 1000 (or, according to a recent hypothesis, to Agnes, in the middle of the eleventh century), are very beautiful indeed and betray the influence of Byzantium.

Religious objects have survived in greater numbers. These are of various types, made of all kinds of materials and worked by every known technique. The most splendid is the great Reliquary of the Wood of the Cross (or *staurotheke*) in the Cathedral Treasury at Limburg an der Lahn; it was made for Basil the Proedros, a bastard of Romanos I and a patron of the arts. It was brought to Germany by the crusader Ulrich von Uelmen, after the capture of Constantinople by the Latins in 1204. It is a silver-gilt flat casket, enamelled and set with precious stones; the sliding cover is decorated with the Deesis and the Apostles; on the inside plate is the *loculus*, a hollow recess made for the Holy Wood, and this is surrounded by different kinds of angels; the fine chased plate at the back is sealed with a foliated cross. Other reliquaries of the Holy Cross take the form of triptychs or of crosses. They are numerous in the West, where most of them were brought in the time of the Crusades. In 1156, Wibald, abbot of the Stavelot Monastery, brought back from Constantinople two little triptychs which were then set in the great Mosan triptych presently in the Pierpont Morgan Library at New York. Such triptychs were imitated in the West, as we can see from the *staurotheke* of Martin Le Roy in the Louvre. The Cathedral Treasury of Halberstadt is exceptional in holding two small reliquaries of St Demetrios, one with an enamelled image of the saint on the cover, which is of the tenth century, the other one in silver, which is of the eleventh. Some objects were reused as reliquaries in the West; a rich *artophorion* (casket for liturgical bread) in the form of a church, in silver-gilt and niello, probably made in Antioch in the second half of the tenth century, was made into a reliquary for Anastasius the Persian (in the Cathedral Treasury at Aachen).

We come now to liturgical vessels, that is, to patens and chalices. A beautiful series came into the possession of the Treasury of San Marco at Venice as a result of the pillage of the Constantinopolitan churches after the conquest in 1204. The translucent stones in a gold or silver setting, embellished with enamels, precious stones and pearls, make an impression of great richness. There is an alabaster paten framed with a gemmed border and adorned in the centre with an enamelled medallion of Christ, an almost abstract design which represents a great aesthetic achievement. The two chalices in sardonyx bearing the name of the emperor Romanos II are beautiful and distinguished pieces, adorned with enamels on small round or rectangular plates. The fact that there are so few golden or silver vessels in the treasury is probably due to the fire of 1231 or to the melting-down of a number of pieces after the conquest by Napoleon. A silver-gilt paten, of the mid-eleventh century, has fortunately been preserved in the Cathedral Treasury at Halberstadt; it is decorated with a Crucifixion surrounded with very elaborate ornamental motifs and an inscription. It was brought by bishop Konrad after the fall of Constantinople.

Crosses are well represented, ranging from the most simple to the richest type, to be placed on an altar, worn in procession or suspended from the neck. Superb examples of processional crosses are found in the Great Lavra on Mount Athos and in the Benaki Museum at Athens, the latter being from Adrianople. The iconography of these processional crosses is very interesting. As for the pectoral crosses, we should mention the cross-reliquary in the Cathedral Treasury at Tournai, worked in gold and set with stones and pearls, which is dated between the eighth and the eleventh centuries, though it was brought to Tournai by a crusader in 1205. The pretty enamelled cross in the Rijksmuseum at Amsterdam is also worthy of note. Some superb crosses were made in Germany in our period. Two of them were produced for the abbess Matilda, the older of the two between 973 and 982; they are richly decorated with enamels and stones. The Lothair cross, doubtless a gift of Otto III to Aachen Cathedral (where it is still kept), and the later imperial cross in the Kunsthistorisches Museum at Vienna are of an extraordinary sumptuousness. All these crosses have only one cross-bar.

Byzantine book-covers are sometimes beautiful products of the goldsmith's craft, in plain chased gold or silver, or set with enamels, stones and pearls. The Treasury and the Library of San Marco in Venice own some precious examples, framing icons of Christ or the Virgin. We have already seen how Byzantine ivories were reused in some manuscript bindings in Germany. The plaque of St Demetrios in Berlin (Staatl. Museum Preussischer Kulturbesitz, Kunstgewerbemuseum) is one example of an enamel icon reused in a binding. Western ivories were used too; the Carolingian Crucifixion on the Book of Pericopes of Henry II, for example. On the golden cover of the *Codex aureus* from Echternach, made in Trier between 983 and 991 (Nuremberg, Germanisches Nationalmuseum), Theophano and Otto II are represented among other personages, with enamelled borders, around a contemporary western ivory-carving of the Crucifixion.

Still more precious are those Byzantine icons which are enamelled on chased silver-gilt, such as the two plaques with an effigy of St Michael (full figure on the one; bust on the other), in the Treasury of San Marco. They were probably placed in a sanctuary dedicated to this archangel. They are surely the product of an imperial workshop: the empress Zoe owned an icon of Christ of a similar type. Nothing of this sort was produced in the West. The casket of the Codex of Uta, abbess of Niedermünster (Munich, Bayer. Staatsbibliothek), which was made in Reichenau in the first quarter of the eleventh century is perhaps not unrelated in type to these Byzantine works with its enamelled ornamentation of an icon of Christ enthroned, which is executed in high relief. Finally, plaques of precious metal are sometimes found on church furniture, such as the enamels of the famous Pala d'Oro in San Marco at Venice. Germany preserves some sumptuous examples of this technique: the *antependium* in the Cathedral of Aachen, that in the Musée de Cluny, and also the pulpit of Henry II in the Cathedral of Aachen, which is crafted like a precious object with gold, filigree, reused ivories and stones, and brown varnish.

Glass and crystal[6]

Byzantine *de luxe* glassblowers seem to have developed a very skilful technique in the Macedonian period; some beautiful examples in the Treasury of San Marco bear witness to this. One extraordinary enamelled glass bowl, a very refined product of, most probably, the eleventh century, is adorned with mythological figures – the style may be inspired by the ancient glyptic- and pseudo-Kufic inscriptions. This object has all the characteristics of the Renaissance and must be a product of the imperial glassworks. Cut glassware is represented by cups with knots, by lamps and by patens in colourless or greenish glass set with precious stones. Certain cups which might originally have been lamps and vases have been reused as reliquaries in the West. Some examples are preserved in the treasuries of Halberstadt and Quedlinburg (where there is a reliquary made for Otto III). However, it should be noted that the series of so-called Hedwig glasses, dated by Hans Wentzel in the tenth century, are actually no older than the twelfth.

Rock crystal, as it seems, was less favoured by the Byzantines, for very few pieces from our period are known, nor indeed from earlier periods either. The experts do not agree about the attribution of some objects, whether they belong to Antiquity, to Byzantium or to Islam. This applies particularly to certain crystal objects in the Treasury of San Marco, such as the lamp in the form of a fish or the 'grotto of the Virgin'. Nevertheless, the sources record that Basil I gave Louis the German a big crystal object in 872. In the same collection, a bucket and a vase, both very simple, are considered to be Byzantine. The head of a lion reused in a reliquary in the Cathedral Treasury at Halberstadt is a Byzantine creation of the tenth century. The collections in Quedlinburg, Borghorst, Cologne and Essen preserve some pretty flasks, made perhaps for perfumes, which are thought by some to be Byzantine. Certain of the vases now attributed to Egypt or Iraq could be Byzantine, too; in that field, as in those of ceramics and sculpture, some iconographic themes, mostly involving animals, are held in

[6] Cf. A. Grabar, 'La verrerie d'art byzantin au moyen âge', *Monuments Piot*, 57 (1971), 89–127; Wentzel, 'Das byzantinische Erbe', and 'Byzantinische Kleinkunstwerke' (see n. 2); Lafontaine-Dosogne, 'Die byzantinische Kunst' (see n. 2); *Le Trésor de Saint-Marc* (see n. 5).

common. But, on the whole, this material was not appreciated by the Byzantines. Rock crystals were reused in some Ottonian works of art, for instance the pulpit of Henry II at Aachen or the reliquary-cross of Bertha of Borghorst in the church of St Nikodem; but it is difficult to detect their origin. The manufacture of crystal objects in the West would not develop until the twelfth century.

Textiles[7]

In Theophano's time textiles were an artistic and commercial activity of first significance for Byzantium. Constantinople remained the greatest producer, although some provincial workshops were active, too. Textiles of linen and wool were certainly produced; but silk, a traditional symbol of luxury and prestige, was the object of artistic researches and was placed under the severe protection of the state. Silk was manufactured not only for clothes but also for curtains in front of windows and doors, which explains why many silks are of heavy quality. Merchants, most of them Italian, travelled to Constantinople to obtain such textiles at source, in order to export them to the West and sell them there. Silk textiles were also appreciated as 'diplomatic gifts' from the emperors to their western visitors. Sometimes they were illegally exported: Liutprand of Cremona was arrested by the Byzantine customs officers when leaving Constantinople in 968 for smuggling silk! Most of the Byzantine silks known today are in cathedral treasuries in Western Europe, or have been taken from such treasuries. They have often been used for wrapping relics and venerated corpses, which explains their preservation. Such silks are always samites (a kind of serge), but there were different methods of weaving.

The dating of many Byzantine silks is problematical, especially because of the persistence of traditional secular motifs. Some silks of the tenth and eleventh centuries bear the names of emperors; these indicate both the date and the place of production, namely in the textile factories attached to the Great Palace. The oldest (a sheet of silk decorated with lions, which was formerly at Auxerre) was made for Leo VI the Wise; another, formerly at Sieburg, but

[7] Cf. O. Falke, *Kunstgeschichte der Seidenweberei*, 2 vols. (Berlin, 1913); Beckwith, *Early Christian and Byzantine Art* (see n. 2); Lafontaine-Dosogne, 'Die byzantinische Kunst' (see n. 2), and 'L'influence artistique byzantine' (see n. 2).

now in the museum at Berlin-Köpenick, was made for Romanos I and his son Christopher in 921–3. Lions are the most frequent motifs used in this period; they may be seen as heraldic animals or symbols of sovereignty. The most beautiful example is a big fragment of curtain from the shrine of St Heribert (*c.* 1002) in the Erzbischöfliches Diözesanmuseum at Cologne. The decoration is composed of superb yellow lions with blue eyes tiered in registers on a purple background; the inscriptions between the faces of each pair of lions mention Basil II and Constantine VIII (976–1025). Eagles, another imperial symbol, spread their wings on some superb textiles, such as the chasuble of St Albuin in the Cathedral Treasury at Brixen-Bressanone, or that in the church of St Eusebius at Auxerre. Other animal motifs are less frequent: tigers on an early silk in the Musées Royaux d'Art et d'Histoire at Brussels, elephants on a tenth-century silk in the Cathedral at Aachen, which, according to the inscription, was made in the Zeuxippos workshop of the Great Palace. This famous silk was regrettably replaced in the shrine of Charlemagne in 1988. The griffins on the shroud of St Siviard in the Cathedral of Sens are enhanced with golden threads, a sign of slightly later craftsmanship. All these motifs have a remarkable decorative efficiency; they sometimes exhibit Islamic influences, perfectly assimilated to Byzantine style.

Some of these motifs exerted an influence in the West. The tiered registers of lions on a decorative page of the Gospel Book from Echternach at Bremen (*c.* 1039, Staatsbibliothek, Hs. b.21) were certainly inspired by the Cologne silk or one like it. Another manuscript from Echternach, the *Codex aureus* at Nuremberg (before 1039, Germanisches Nationalmuseum, Hs. 2°156142), contains an ornamental page with bands displaying geometrical and zoological elements: lions, griffins, birds with ribbons around their necks, all of which belong to the Byzantine repertory. The models were surely sumptuous silks offered as gifts by the Byzantine emperors to western potentates.

According to some sources, human representations, both imperial and religious, also existed on Byzantine textiles. The silk of bishop Gunther in the Cathedral Treasury at Bamberg, although very much damaged, offers a splendid and unique testimony to this. A scene of imperial triumph is woven in it, most probably that of Basil II, who is represented on horseback, crowned by the personifications of Constantinople and Athens. Such pieces could not possibly have been the objects of commerce.

Gunther no doubt obtained it on his visit to the Byzantine capital in 1064–5; when he died, it was used as his shroud. In other cases, Byzantine textiles were used as clothing by the dignitaries of the court and of the church. Rich imperial cloaks were made of silk imported from Byzantium, but embroidered in Germany, such as the mantle of Henry II, probably executed in Bavaria about 1020 (in the Diözesanmuseum at Bamberg). Indeed, Germany could not produce silk because it was not possible to cultivate the silk-worm in such a climate, although silk could be produced in Italy or in Spain.

Conclusion

Although the documentation is fragmentary, the impression which emerges from an examination of these objects is that Byzantine influence on German art was considerably reinforced at the time of Theophano. Iconographic and stylistic trends in the various artistic techniques all testify as much. In the eleventh century, this influence is perhaps less direct; but by that time it had been well assimilated. Nevertheless, the German objects exhibit neither an archaizing nor a secular trend, though both of these were strong in Byzantium during the Macedonian Renaissance. The Ottonians were most interested in certain imperial and religious themes; but in both cases their interest was limited. The use they made of imperial themes sometimes oversteps the bounds of Byzantine decorum, as we have seen in some representations of Otto II and particularly of Otto III. In a number of cases Byzantine objects have been given a new setting or put to a new use. In the history of artistic interaction between Byzantium and the West, the period of Theophano left its mark; not until the Crusades flooded Europe with Byzantine objects, especially after the taking of Constantinople by the Latins in 1204, would the West receive such generous exposure to the rich influence of the material culture of Byzantium.

12

Imperial art in Byzantium from Basil I to Basil II (867–1025)

E. VOORDECKERS

The marriage of Otto II to the Byzantine princess Theophano in 972 was a peaceful encounter between two imperial ideas and ambitions. On the one hand there was the Greek imperium, which originated in the New Rome and was considered to be unique and universal because of its uninterrupted continuation of the tradition of the old *Imperium Romanum*. On the other hand there was the Western European imperium, 'renovated' in 962, which, as the Carolingians had done before, claimed new power and a special relationship with Italy as the heir of Old Rome.

The marriage was at the same time a meeting of two cultures, especially of two artistic movements, which were to receive the name of *Renaissance*; the 'Macedonian Renaissance', named after the ruling dynasty in Constantinople, and the 'Ottonian Renaissance', named after three successive emperors of the Saxon dynasty, who ruled from 936 until 1002. It is generally assumed that the impact of the Macedonian upon the Ottonian Renaissance was considerable, because the former flourished in an earlier period and was artistically superior to the latter. The role of Theophano herself in this encounter is by no means clear; let it be noted in passing that she was hardly thirteen or fourteen years old when she married Otto II.

In all probability Theophano did not arrive empty handed at the German court. It seems, however, impossible to identify one single object of art that belonged to her personally. Liutprand of Cremona and other negotiators of the Ottonians may have brought artefacts to the West before 972 and other objects may have arrived as diplomatic gifts during the reign of Otto II, the regency of Theophano (983–91), the reign of her son Otto III (until 1002) and that of his successor, Henry II (1002–24), the last emperor of the Saxon dynasty. It makes no sense, though, to use *objets d'art* manufactured in Byzantium but never exported, or exported to the German Empire only after the first quarter of the eleventh century, in order to demonstrate the role of Byzantine art in the Macedonian–Ottonian artistic encounter. Neither, when evaluating the impact of the Macedonian upon the Ottonian Renaissance, should we take into account indirect Byzantine influence (via central and northern Italy or through the Carolingian Renaissance).

For the investigation of the impact and the effects of the Macedonian Renaissance on Ottonian art, our starting-point should be a thorough understanding of the specific characteristics of Macedonian art, in particular its historical and ideological context, its forms, its contents and its definable stylistic features.

The empire that betrothed Theophano as a pseudo-*porphyrogennetos* to the Ottonians in 972 was at the height of its power and prestige. It was a state governed according to a legal system with an exceptionally advanced economic and social legislation. Its cultural and religious *Commonwealth* stretched out as far as Syria and the Caucasus, Venice and southern Italy, and from 988 onwards even as far as the Baltic Sea. The imperial dynasty, enjoying the devotion of the populace, ruled in Constantinople in a *sacrum palatium*, following the rhythm of liturgy prescribed by a luxurious and refined ceremonial, imperial as well as ecclesiastical in character.

In the Byzantine Empire under the Macedonian dynasty, the imperial court was the centre of cultural and more specifically artistic life. The emperor and the court had almost unlimited financial resources at their disposal. The imperial workshops held the monopoly of the manufacture of precious metals, ivory, silk and other sumptuous materials. One emperor of the dynasty, Constantine VII Porphyrogennetos, was a skilled painter and goldsmith himself. The imperial ideology was based on religion and for that reason artefacts often served as a tribute to God, especially when made under imperial patronage for the Byzantine church, the patriarchate or the monastic establishment. The art of the Macedonian Renaissance should therefore be considered imperial art.

It seems that two important provinces of artistic activity, architecture and monumental painting, did not play a part in the exchange of influences between Macedonian and Ottonian art: the objects simply could not be transported. In the context of this article it is therefore sufficient to mention that Basil I and Constantine VII in particular concerned themselves very closely with the conservation of the old architectural patrimony, which was threatened more than once by earthquakes, for example in 869. As a result of this concern for and consequently interest in architecture the palaces were continuously rebuilt and redecorated, new church-types were developed (domed inscribed cross plan, dome on corner squinches, triconch) and new monastical complexes were built (the imperial foundation of the Lavra Monastery on Mount Athos in 963 and of the monastery of Hosios Loukas in the first half of the eleventh century).

On the other hand it is well known that, after the iconoclast controversy had been settled, in these newly created architectural types as well as in the renovated older types (the Church of the Holy Apostles in Constantinople, for example) a severely hierarchical monumental decoration programme[1] was developed, perfectly well adapted to the pyramidical edifices. The revelation of the Christ Pantokrator, depicted in the dome and authenticated by the image of His Incarnation in the apse (Theotokos mosaic of 867 in Hagia Sophia in Constantinople) descended to the believers through depictions on the vaults of His manifestation in scenes from the Gospels that had been attributed the status of great festivals on account of their theophanic significance. This monumental decoration was executed in mosaics, as it had been during Justinian's reign. Its palette of warm colours and its glittering golden light in the background rivalled the marbles on the walls and the floors in splendour.

As a matter of fact only portable artefacts played a part in the Macedonian–Ottonian artistic encounter: illuminated manuscripts, textiles, icons on wood, ivory and precious metal, religious objects such as liturgical vessels and reliquaries.

A very limited number of manuscripts, dealing with secular as well as religious matters, with a continuous narrative illustration, deriving from late antique and early Byzantine rolls,[2] or with

[1] O. Demus, *Byzantine Mosaic Decoration: Aspects of Monumental Art in Byzantium* (London, 1948).

[2] Vat. Pal. gr. 431 (Joshua Roll, the tenth century); Paris, BN, gr. 74 and Florence Laurent. Plut. VI 23 (Gospel Books dating from the eleventh and twelfth centuries).

antique illustrations in a rediscovered Hellenistic style, displaying allegorical personifications and mythological themes,[3] and a series of ivory caskets[4] decorated in the same way, are peculiar objects which have survived from the Macedonian Renaissance. It is striking that these objects were always expressly made for someone in particular, for instance the emperor, exalted court-officials, etc. All the other works of art, that is the greater part, served for the ecclesiastical cult and imperial ceremonial and show a remarkable homogeneity as to style and content. They pre-eminently represent the new art, meant for all classes of Byzantine society. Monumental art derived its iconographical themes and style from the same source. What is true of the Ottonian Renaissance is therefore also true of the Macedonian Renaissance: its vigorous and innovating artistic activities are of greater importance than its sparing use of elements of style, executed in an academic way, deriving from the Hellenistic or early Christian past.

Characteristic of the art of illumination is the autonomous and monumental nature of its compositions and the sober clarity of its style. The order of the miniatures in a manuscript is no longer determined by the narrative but by the liturgy. The miniatures were adapted to the new manuscripts developed for use at the Divine Liturgy and the offices of the canonical Hours:[5] Gospel-Lectionaries such as the famous Gospel-Lectionary of Trebizond (Petropolitanus, gr. 21)[6] and its rival in the sacristy of the Lavra Monastery on Mount Athos,[7] which both date from the end of the tenth century and were imperial gifts (the extremely rich Athos Gospel-Lectionary, Dionysiou 587m,[8] made in the Stoudios Monastery in Constantinople in the middle of the fifteenth century, contains both the text and the illustrations of

[3] Paris, BN, gr. 510 (Homilies of St Gregory of Nazianzos, the Theologian, 880–2), Vat. Reg., gr. 1 (Bible of Leo the Patrician, first half of the tenth century), BN, gr. 139 (Psalter, middle of the tenth century), Paris. Supplem. gr. 247 (*Theriaka* of Nikander, tenth century).

[4] A. Goldschmidt and K. Weitzmann, *Die byzantinischen Elfenbeinskulpturen des X.–XIII. Jahrhunderts*, I, *Kästen* (Berlin, 1930).

[5] K. Weitzmann, 'Byzantine Liturgical Psalters and Gospels', in Weitzmann, *Collected Studies* (London, 1980).

[6] V.D. Lichačeva, *Vizantijskaja miniatjura* (Moscow, 1977), pls. 5–10; V.N. Lazarev, *Istorija vizantijskoj živopisi* (Moscow, 1986), pls. 105–6.

[7] S.M. Pelekanidis *et al.*, *The Treasures of Mount Athos: Illuminated Manuscripts*, III (only in Greek) (Athens, 1979), pls. 6–8.

[8] *Ibid.*, I (Athens, 1974), pls. 189–277.

the new cycle of the eleven Resurrection Gospels for Sunday matins and the related *Exaposteilaria* and *Eothina*, composed by the emperors Leo VI and Constantine VII);[9] Psalters showing new techniques of illustration, such as marginal miniatures and a close and often exciting link, based on both biblical and historical analogies, between the illustrations and the literal as well as the deeper meaning of the text (the so-called *Khludov Psalter*, Mosquensis, Hist. Mus., 129, of the third quarter of the ninth century and its imitations);[10] Synaxaries (for example, the so-called *Menologion* of Basil II, Vat. gr. 1613, of the end of the tenth century)[11] and collections of the sixteen selected liturgical homilies by St Gregory of Nazianzos, the Theologian.[12] Synaxaries as well as collections of homilies were used for lecture during the morning office, on normal days and on great festivals respectively.

Icons painted on wood are rare in this period; the material was considered inappropriate to the elevated themes represented, especially when they were intended for public worship. On the other hand, the quantity of enamelled icons and of icons made of precious metal and ivory is impressive. At that time, no doubt, icons were also sometimes expressly made for individuals and were used for personal devotions. Such icons can usually be recognized by size, form (for example triptychs) and iconography (enamelled medallions depicting patron-saints or saints protectors, in the margins of larger icons, wooden panels depicting similar saints, etc.). The magnificent golden icon of the archangel Michael dressed in the vestment of an emperor (first half of the tenth century) in the Treasury of San Marco at Venice[13] should, however, be regarded as a work of art made for public worship. Iconographic mistakes do not normally occur in Byzantine icons. The most striking example of the opposite is to be seen – so it seems – on the three well-known triptychs depicting the Deesis (from the second quarter to the end of the

[9] *Dimanche: office selon les huit tons 'Οκτώηχος*, La Prière des églises de rite byzantin, 3 (Chevetogne, 1972), pp. 53, 139–48, 151–8.

[10] M.V. Ščepkina, *Miniatjury Chludovskoj Psaltyri* (Moscow, 1977).

[11] *Biblioteca Apostolica Vaticana: Liturgie und Andacht im Mittelalter*, exhibition Cologne, Erzbischöfliches Diözesan-Museum (Cologne, 1992), no. 19, pp. 114–19.

[12] G. Galavaris, *The Illustration of the Liturgical Homilies of Gregory Nazianzenus*, Studies in Manuscript Illumination, 6 (Princeton, 1969).

[13] H.R. Hahnloser *et al.*, *Il Tesoro di San Marco*, II, *Il Tesoro e il Museo* (Florence, 1971), no. 17, pp. 25–7, pls. XIX–XXI; *Le Trésor de Saint-Marc de Venise*, exhibition Paris, Grand Palais (Paris, 1984), no. 12, pp. 141–7.

tenth century) in Rome (Palazzo Venezia, with an inscription of Constantine VII Porphyrogennetos), the Vatican and Paris (the Louvre Museum),[14] and on the cover decorated with a depiction of the Deesis of the equally well-known great reliquary of the Wood of the Cross (964–965) in the Cathedral of Limburg an der Lahn,[15] where the *Theotokos* is placed on the left-hand side and St John *Prodromos* on the right-hand side of Christ. The only explanation for this anomaly is that here the view of the individual beholder was given more prominence than the expected theophanic view, which as a rule determines liturgical art.

A close examination of the material shows that a very large number of icons, whether painted on wood, made of ivory or precious metal, or enamelled, had a function in public worship; more particularly they were used for the decoration of the architrave (*epistylion*) of the chancel-barrier (*templon*).[16] From the middle of the tenth century onwards they showed depictions that were also developing in monumental painting and book-illumination: those of the enlarged Deesis and the cycle of the great festivals. Evidence of this phenomenon is to be found not only in the literary sources of that period, but also in what is left of particular works of art: an enlarged Deesis of the tenth century carved in ivory plaques, now in the Staatsbibliothek at Bamberg and in the Dumbarton Oaks collection in Washington[17] (we will come back to this later), the second half of an enamelled cycle of the great festivals, originally consisting of twelve parts, inserted into the upper range of the famous Pala d'Oro in San Marco at Venice,[18] and more fragments of similar cycles carved in ivory, preserved in various museums. In addition, the three very refined ivory plaques, each depicting two apostles and bearing the same inscription, which refers to the patronage of the emperor Constantine VII (now in the Museo Archeologico at Venice, in the Kunsthistorisches Museum at Vienna, and in the Grünes Gewölbe

[14] A. Goldschmidt and K. Weitzmann, *Die byzantinischen Elfenbeinskulpturen des X.–XIII. Jahrhunderts*, II, *Reliefs* (Berlin, 1934), nos. 31–3, pp. 33–5, pls. X–XIII; D.T. Rice and M. Hirmer, *The Art of Byzantium* (London, 1959), pls. 98–102; *Byzance: l'art byzantin dans les collections publiques françaises*, exhibition Paris, Louvre (Paris, 1992), no. 149, pp. 233–6.

[15] Rice and Hirmer, *The Art of Byzantium*, pl. 124 and X.

[16] Studies of M. Chatzidakis, V.N. Lazarev and K. Weitzmann.

[17] Goldschmidt and Weitzmann, *Elfenbeinskulpturen*, II (see n. 14), nos. 65–7, pp. 44–5, pls. XXV–XXVI.

[18] H.R. Hahnloser *et al.*, *Il Tesoro di San Marco*, I, *La Pala d'Oro* (Florence, 1965), pls. XLII–XLVIII.

at Dresden),[19] probably also used to adorn the architrave of a chancel-barrier.

Pairs of icons, enamelled or made of precious metal (in all probability not carved in ivory), representing the, preferably, standing figures of Christ and the Mother of God, or the Crucifixion and the Anastasis, also embellished the covers of Gospel Books (for example in the Treasury of San Marco, and in the Marciana Library at Venice, and in the sacristy of the Lavra Monastery on Mount Athos)[20] to show them in the so-called Little Entrance during the celebration of the Divine Liturgy. Liturgical vessels carved in precious stone (onyx, sardonyx, alabaster) and reliquaries were adorned with luxurious icons in the same way.

During the Macedonian dynasty, imperial art was, of course, at the disposal not only of the church and the liturgical cult, but also of the emperor himself for the embellishment of the imperial palaces and life at court in general. Purple and silk were monopolies of the imperial workshops which manufactured the rich and embroidered (mostly with pearls and precious stones) vestments worn by the emperor, the imperial family and the court dignitaries, as can be concluded from iconographical documentation. These workshops also produced the silk hangings to curtain off the door and window openings in the imperial palace. The most beautiful examples of these date from the reign of Basil II (976–1025) and have been preserved mainly in treasuries of Western European churches: the silk with eagles from the shroud of St Germain in the church of Saint-Eusèbe at Auxerre,[21] the silk with elephants in the Cathedral of Aachen, in which Otto III wrapped Charlemagne's relics in the year 1000,[22] and especially the silk with stylized lions from the St Heribert shroud in the Erzbischöfliches Diözesanmuseum at Cologne, which bears the names of Basil II and his brother and co-emperor Constantine VIII (see p. 229).[23] It is not impossible and is perhaps even prob-

[19] Goldschmidt and Weitzmann, *Elfenbeinskulpturen*, II (see n. 14), nos. 43–5, pp. 38–9, pl. XIX.

[20] Pelekanidis and Christou, *Treasures of Mount Athos*, III (see n. 7), p. 24; Hahnloser, *Il Tesoro di San Marco*, II (see n. 13), nos. 35–8; *Le Trésor de Saint-Marc de Venise* (see n. 13), nos. 9, 14, 19.

[21] Rice and Hirmer, *The Art of Byzantium* (see n. 14), pl. 132; *Byzance: l'art byzantin* (see n. 14), no. 285, p. 377.

[22] Rice and Hirmer, *The Art of Byzantium*, pl. 130; an inscription refers to the imperial manufactory of the baths of Zeuxippos in Constantinople.

[23] *Ornamenta ecclesiae: Kunst und Künstler der Romanik in Köln*, exhibition Cologne, Schnütgen-Museum (Cologne, 1985), II, no. E.94, pp. 326 and 329.

able that these two emperors are depicted on a purple-coloured ivory casket in the Cathedral Treasury at Troyes as two horsemen leaving a (the) city to go lion-hunting.[24]

With the exception of representations on coinage, the emperors of the Macedonian dynasty are relatively seldom portrayed. Between 880 and 882 Basil I and his family were depicted in the first illuminations (fol. A–C) of the Parisinus gr. 510,[25] the complete collection of the forty-five homilies by Gregory of Nazianzos, the Theologian, with an abundance of illuminations. A highly interesting mosaic portrait of the emperor Alexander (912–13), the most insignificant emperor of the dynasty, is not easily found in the most hidden place on the vaults of the north gallery in Hagia Sophia at Constantinople,[26] and one wonders whether this place was chosen by Alexander himself, or before, by his elder brother and predecessor Leo VI, who held him in contempt and kept him away from official life in the empire. A third example is the unusual depiction of Basil II dressed as an Old Roman *imperator* in one of the first illuminations of his private Psalter (Marcianus gr. 17).[27] The depiction alludes to his victory over the Bulgarians in 1017 and should be associated with the silk tapestry, unique to its genre, now preserved in the Cathedral Treasury at Bamberg, depicting Basil II on horseback celebrating his victory of 1017 by a triumphant entry into Athens and Constantinople,[28] where he was offered diadems crested with peacock's feathers.

The depictions of this period in which the religious aspects of the imperial ideology are emphasized are of greater importance. In the Treasury of San Marco at Venice, for example, a small votive crown of Leo VI[29] is preserved embellished with a series of enamelled medallions depicting the emperor as *isapostolos* ('one equal to the Apostles'), surrounded by Apostles and Church Fathers. The same concept helped to shape the ivory handle of the

[24] Goldschmidt and Weitzmann, *Elfenbeinskulpturen*, I (see n. 4), no. 122, p. 63, pls. LXIX–LXX; Rice and Hirmer, *The Art of Byzantium* (see n. 14), pls. 152–3; *Byzance: l'art byzantin* (see n. 14), no. 168, pp. 258–9.

[25] *Byzance et la France médiévale*, exhibition Paris, Bibliothèque nationale (Paris, 1958), no. 9, pp. 5–7; *Byzance: l'art byzantin* (see n. 14), no. 258, pp. 346–8.

[26] Lazarev, *Istorija vizantijskoj živopisi* (see n. 6), pl. 133.

[27] Rice and Hirmer, *The Art of Byzantium* (see n. 14), p. 25, pl. XI.

[28] S. Müller-Christensen, *Das Bamberger Gunthertuch* (Bamberg, 1966).

[29] Hahnloser, *Il Tesoro di San Marco*, II (see n. 13), no. 92, pp. 81–2, pls. LXXII–LXXV; *Le Trésor de Saint-Marc de Venise* (see n. 13), no. 8, pp. 117–24.

sceptre of the same emperor (Staatliche Museen, Berlin),[30] which shows Christ flanked by Peter and Paul on the obverse, and the emperor receiving the imperial crown out of the hands of the *Theotokos* ('Mother of God') on the reverse. The personal relationship of the emperor to Christ is shown on a wooden icon from 944 preserved in the monastery of Mount Sinai,[31] depicting Constantine VII as the Syrian king Abgar of Edessa receiving the *Mandylion* (a cloth bearing the direct imprint of Christ's features), and especially on the famous coronation ivory of the same emperor in the Museum of Fine Arts in Moscow,[32] and the one of his brother, Romanos II (with his wife Eudokia), in the Cabinet des Médailles, Paris,[33] both dating from the years between 944 and 949. But the clearest illustration of the imperial ideology is the large mosaic on the tympanum in the narthex of Hagia Sophia at Constantinople, depicting the emperor Leo VI in the prostrated position of *proskynesis* (reverence performed in the presence of the king, which is common in Byzantine court-ceremonial), extending his hands to the enthroned Christ in prayer as the Theotokos does in a medallion above his head.[34] It can be concluded from all these examples of Macedonian imperial iconography that an emperor is never depicted enthroned or standing on a *suppedaneum*, but that these symbols of power are reserved for Christ alone.

The art of the Macedonian Renaissance is characterized by a remarkable unity of purpose, namely the splendour of the liturgy, ecclesiastical as well as imperial, by its unity of iconographical elaboration, and by its unity of style in all genres and materials. This unity in art was the result of the powerful influence of the great artistic metropolis and of the imperial patronage. There is, for example, no difference in destination, iconography or style

[30] Goldschmidt and Weitzmann, *Elfenbeinskulpturen*, II (see n. 14), no. 88, pp. 52–3, pl. XXXV; A. Effenberger, *Staatliche Museen zu Berlin: das Museum für spätantike und byzantinische Kunst* (Mainz, 1992), no. 122, pp. 210–12.

[31] K. Weitzmann, *The Monastery of Saint Catherine at Mount Sinai: The Icons*, I (Princeton, 1976), no. B.58, pp. 94–8, pls. XXXVI–XXXVII.

[32] Goldschmidt and Weitzmann, *Elfenbeinskulpturen*, II (see n. 14), no. 35, p. 35, pl. XIV; Rice and Hirmer, *The Art of Byzantium* (see n. 14), pl. 96; A. Bank, *Byzantine Art in the Collections of the Soviet Museums* (Leningrad, 1977), pl. 122.

[33] Goldschmidt and Weitzmann, *Elfenbeinskulpturen*, II (see n. 14), no. 34, p. 35, pl. XIV; *Byzance: l'art byzantin* (see n. 14), no. 148, pp. 232–3 and 204.

[34] A. Grabar, *La peinture byzantine* (Geneva, 1953), p. 91; Rice and Hirmer, *The Art of Byzantium* (see n. 14), pl. 93; Lazarev, *Istorija vizantijskoj živopisi* (see n. 6), pl. 130.

between the representations of 'the Washing of the Feet' in the narthex of the church of the Hosios Loukas Monastery (early eleventh century),[35] in the Gospel-Lectionary of Trebizond (Petropolitanus gr. 21, tenth century),[36] on an ivory in the Staatliche Museen at Berlin,[37] and on a small square icon on wood in the collection of the Sinai Monastery[38] (both the ivory and the icon originally part of an architrave decoration and both dating from the tenth century).

Furthermore this art is characterized by its erudition, classical as well as religious, and by its use of the formulae of rhetoric, which were also popular in Byzantine secular and ecclesiastical literature. One should have an eye for the emphasis of a gesture which stresses the essence of an image, and for the connections expressed by significant juxtapositioning of figures, whether internal to the composition or in relation to its borders. In the upper zone of the two side-panels of an ivory triptych from the middle of the tenth century depicting the Crucifixion, which is now in the Cabinet des Médailles at Paris,[39] the ivory carver picked out the prophets Elijah and John the Baptist (or *Prodromos*, the 'Forerunner'), whereas the other medallions in these side-panels are reserved for the Apostles, the Church Fathers and the martyrs. On the obverse of a book-cover of gold embellished with pearls and precious stones, preserved in the Marciana Library at Venice (MS lat. cl. 1, 100),[40] which dates from the same period as the Paris triptych, the central enamelled representation of Christ stands in a similar relation to the enamelled medallion of Elijah, which is placed directly beneath the figure of Christ on the lower border; here, too, the other medallions on the borders are reserved for portraits of the Apostles.

35 *Ibid.*, pl. 156.

36 Lichačeva, *Vizantijskaja miniatjura* (see n. 6), pl. 10; Lazarev, *Istorija vizantijskoj živopisi* (see n. 6), pl. 106.

37 Goldschmidt and Weitzmann, *Elfenbeinskulpturen*, II (see n. 14), no. 13, p. 28, pl. IV; Effenberger, *Staatliche Museen* (see n. 30), no. 125, pp. 216–17.

38 Weitzmann, *Mount Sinai: Icons*, I (see n. 31), no. B.56, pp. 91–3, pl. XXXV; Lazarev, *Istorija vizantijskoj živopisi* (see n. 6), pl. 182.

39 Goldschmidt and Weitzmann, *Elfenbeinskulpturen*, II (see n. 14), no. 39, p. 37, pl. XVI; *Byzance: l'art byzantin* (see n. 14), no. 150, pp. 236–7.

40 Hahnloser *et al.*, *Il Tesoro di San Marco*, II (see n. 13), no. 36, pp. 48–9, pl. XXXIV; *Le Trésor de Saint-Marc de Venise* (see n. 13), no. 14, pp. 152–5. Cf. E. Voordeckers, 'Elie dans l'art byzantin', in *Elie le Prophète: bible, tradition, iconographie*, ed. G.F. Willems, Publications de l'Institutum Judaicum (Leuven, 1988), pp. 155–95, at pp. 182–3.

In spite of the marriage of Theophano and Otto II, the differences between the Byzantine and the Ottonian Empires and between the two Renaissances remained considerable. The Ottonians had a different imperial ideology; the coronation ivory of Otto II and Theophano (Musée de Cluny, Paris)[41] is a clumsy imitation of the ivory of Romanos II and Eudokia mentioned above (Cabinet des Médailles, Paris), and is – iconographically speaking – an exception and not at all a representative model for Ottonian conceptions of emperorship. The Ottonian emperors like to be depicted enthroned; a depiction such as the one showing Otto III not only seated on a throne but also surrounded by a mandorla, which, as if that were not enough, is surrounded by the symbols of the four Evangelists, must have seemed nothing short of theological ignorance and presumptuous insolence to his Byzantine contemporaries (Gospel Book from Reichenau (996–1000), preserved in the Cathedral Treasury at Aachen).[42] Architecture in the Ottonian Empire was of a different nature, the religious edifices were differently arranged and there was no monumental decoration programme at all. The liturgy and the organization of the liturgical year were also different: both were intended for the commemoration of episodes from the Gospel, rather than for their actual soteriological realization. The Ottonians made use of other liturgical books than the Byzantines, even though it is possible that the Ottonian Sacramentaries were influenced by the Byzantine liturgical books as to the order and the style of their illustrations. Finally, the Ottonian Renaissance was not aware of the theological authenticity that legitimated and determined – in a hierarchy of differentiated theophanic values – every representation in Byzantine art after Iconoclasm.

Nevertheless the impact of Macedonian art on Ottonian art is sometimes clearly perceptible. The miniatures in some manuscripts show traces of Byzantine influence in their composition and iconographical elaboration. The clearest examples are the Evergerius Lectionary from the end of the tenth century in the

[41] Goldschmidt and Weitzmann, *Elfenbeinskulpturen*, II (see n. 14), no. 85, pp. 50–1, pl. XXXIV; *Byzance: l'art byzantin* (see n. 14), no. 160, pp. 247–9.

[42] Page 31, from Reichenau, *c.* 1000. Cf. E.G. Grimme, *Das Evangeliar Kaiser Ottos III. im Domschatz zu Aachen* (Freiburg, Basel and Vienna, 1984); *Vor dem Jahr 1000: abendländische Buchkunst zur Zeit der Kaiserin Theophanu*, exhibition Cologne, Schnütgen-Museum (Cologne, 1991), no. 36, pp. 134–8.

Cathedral Treasury at Cologne[43] (copying, though not without mistakes, the Greek inscriptions of its Byzantine model) and the Book of Prayers,[44] made in Mainz between 983 and 991, for the young Otto III, which is now preserved in Pommersfelden. One of the illuminations of the latter manuscript shows the young Otto surveyed by a *spatharios* and praying to an enthroned Christ in the typical Byzantine *proskynesis*,[45] just like the emperor Leo VI on the above-mentioned famous mosaic of the central tympanum in the narthex of Hagia Sophia at Constantinople. In the Cologne Lectionary Evergerius is represented in the same position, though praying not to Christ but to the apostles Peter and Paul.[46] Another illustration of the Book of Prayers at Pommersfelden[47] shows Otto in the orant posture, flanked by Peter and Paul who implore him in a Deesis composition. In the upper zone of this composition the Mother of God is placed at the left-hand side of Christ, imitating the same anomaly as occurs in the famous Byzantine Deesis triptychs at Rome and Paris and on the cover of the above-mentioned, equally famous cross-reliquary in Limburg an der Lahn (taken from Constantinople to Germany not before 1204).

A last observation concerns the Byzantine ivories that have been re-used in the decoration of Ottonian book-covers. Some of them, four representations of the Theotokos Hodigitria, were possibly part of the dowry of the empress Theophano; they were applied to the covers of a Sacramentary from Corvey (last quarter of the tenth century, now in the Staatsbibliothek at Leipzig),[48] of a Sacramentary from Fulda (*c.* 1000, now in the Staatsbibliothek at Bamberg),[49] of the above-mentioned Gospel Book of Otto III from Reichenau (the same date, now in the Cathedral Treasury at Aachen),[50] and of a Gospel-Lectionary from Reichenau (end of the tenth century, now in the Bibliothèque Nationale,

[43] Erzbischöfliche Diözesan- und Dombibliothek, Dom MS 143. Cf. *Ornamenta ecclesiae* (see n. 23), I, no. B.3, pp. 151–2.

[44] Pommersfelden, Gräflich Schönborn'sche Schlossbibliothek, MS 347. Cf. *Vor dem Jahr 1000* (see n. 42), no. 21, pp. 92–6.

[45] Fols. 20v–21. Cf. *Vor dem Jahr 1000* (see n. 42), pp. 94–5, pls. 73–4.

[46] Fols. 3v–4. Cf. *Ornamenta ecclesiae* (see n. 23), I, p. 151.

[47] Fol. 2. Cf. *Vor dem Jahr 1000* (see n. 42), Abb. 6, p. 17.

[48] Rep I 4° 57. Goldschmidt and Weitzmann, *Elfenbeinskulpturen*, II (see n. 14), no. 133, pp. 62–3, pl. XLVIII.

[49] Lit. 1. Goldschmidt and Weitzmann, *Elfenbeinskulpturen* (see n. 14), II, no. 139, p. 64, pl. L.

[50] *Ibid.*, II, no. 129, p. 62, pl. XLVII; *Vor dem Jahr 1000* (see n. 42), no. 36, pp. 134–8, pl. 106.

Paris).[51] A fifth plaque, showing Christ Pantokrator, adorns the cover of an Epistolarium from Reichenau (between 960 and 980, now in the Fitzwilliam Museum at Cambridge);[52] and a carving, representing the Dormition of the Theotokos, is applied to the cover of a second Gospel Book of Otto III from Bamberg (*c.* 1000, now at the Staatsbibliothek at Munich).[53] Finally four ivories, showing, frontally, Christ and the Theotokos, and, in profile, Peter and Paul, were applied to the covers of the Books of Prayer of the last Saxon emperor (successor of Otto III) Henry II and his wife Cunegunda between 1002 and 1012 (now in the Staatsbibliothek at Bamberg);[54] together with a fragment of an ivory depicting an archangel in the Dumbarton Oaks Collection at Washington,[55] they were identified by K. Weitzmann[56] as fragments of the enlarged Deesis zone of an architrave decoration. The Dormition plaque in Munich is probably of a similar origin. It should be noticed that it is improbable that these carvings (with the possible exception of the ivory depicting the Pantokrator at Cambridge) were considered suitable and adequate for the binding of a liturgical manuscript by a Byzantine artist. Of greater significance is the conclusion that ivory plaques, such as those on the cover of the Bamberg Prayer Books and the Munich Gospel Book that had come to Germany before the end of the millennium, are no more than *spolia*, like the spoliated enamels lost during the sack of Constantinople in 1204, now decorating the Pala d'Oro in San Marco at Venice. Is it possible that these objects were no longer in use for their original purpose at the time they were taken to the West? If so, this would only indicate that they had been replaced by better objects.

51 MS latin 10514 (*Evangiles de Poussay*); Goldschmidt and Weitzmann, *Elfenbeinskulpturen*, II, no. 134, p. 63, pl. XLIX; *Byzance: l'art byzantin* (see n. 14), no. 161, pp. 249–52.

52 McClean Collection in the Fitzwilliam Museum at Cambridge, 30; Goldschmidt and Weitzmann, *Elfenbeinskulpturen*, II, no. 148, p. 65, pl. LII.

53 Munich, Staatsbibliothek, Clm 4453; Goldschmidt and Weitzmann, *Elfenbeinskulpturen*, II, no. 1, p. 25, pl. I; Rice and Hirmer, *The Art of Byzantium* (see n. 14), pl. 119.

54 MSS A.II.54 and 55, from the Bamberg Cathedral Library. Goldschmidt and Weitzmann, *Elfenbeinskulpturen*, II, nos. 65 and 66, pp. 44–5, pls. XXV–XXVI; Rice and Hirmer, *The Art of Byzantium*, pl. 154.

55 Goldschmidt and Weitzmann, *Elfenbeinskulpturen*, II, no. 67, p. 45, pl. XXVI; Rice and Hirmer, *The Art of Byzantium*, pl. 83; K. Weitzmann, *Catalogue of the Byzantine and Early Mediaeval Antiquities in the Dumbarton Oaks Collection*, III, *Ivories and Steatites* (Washington, DC, 1972), no. 40, pp. 101–5, pl. LXXI.

56 K. Weitzmann, 'Die byzantinischen Elfenbeine eines Bamberger Graduale und ihre ursprüngliche Verwendung', in *Festschrift H. Usener* (Marburg/Lahn, 1967), pp. 11–20.

13

Did Theophano leave her mark on the Ottonian sumptuary arts?*

H. WESTERMANN-ANGERHAUSEN

The influence of eastern cultural values on the West has always been sustained at various levels of society. This is as true of the tenth century, when a Byzantine princess was crowned empress of the Ottonian Empire, as of any other. Although they travelled with different aims, merchants and bishops, diplomats of the nobility, monks and scholars, pilgrims and artisans alike were part of this cultural traffic.[1] The impulses gained by Ottonian art from Byzantium were not always intentionally given, being rather the by-products of scholarly and diplomatic missions. Ottonian architects, illuminators, textile-workers, sculptors or goldsmiths thus achieved stylistic innovations which in some cases had a very limited effect, though in others they spread rapidly and initiated a broad preoccupation with new models.

Contacts between East and West and the tendency of the West to imitate eastern models have roots reaching far back into Merovingian times.[2] Although there was nothing new about the western preoccupation with Byzantine art at the turn of the millennium, the Ottonian Renaissance was very different in character from the Carolingian one. Conditions for a revival of the arts under the Saxon rulers had become more complex: Ottonian artists no longer harked back exclusively to Antiquity or to

* This text also appeared in German in *Kaiserin Theophanu: Prinzessin aus der Fremde – des Westreichs Grosse Kaiserin*, ed. G. Wolf (Cologne, 1991), pp. 263–78.

1 W. Berschin, *Griechisch–lateinisches Mittelalter: von Hieronymus bis zu Nikolaus von Kues* (Berne and Munich, 1980); for Ottonian times see pp. 211 ff, for Theophano see pp. 222 ff.

2 Principally, H. Vierck, 'La chemise de Sainte-Bathilde à Chelles et l'influence byzantine sur l'art de cour mérovingien au VIIe siècle', in *Centenaire de l'abbé Clochet, 1975: actes du Colloque international d'archéologie* (Rouen, 1978), pp. 521 ff.

Byzantine models, but also to their Carolingian transformations, using and emulating them all.

What then was the influence of Theophano on, say, Ottonian goldsmiths' craft? The patronage and influence of a single person is not to be confused with the general influence of Byzantine painting and sumptuary arts on the renaissance of art under the Saxon emperors.[3]

In many centres of Ottonian art Byzantine models were used, as we said, together with the older Carolingian sources; both were at the disposal of the great patrons of the age and their craftsmen. The paths by which a broad stream of models became known in the Ottonian Empire are hard to trace individually. And it is difficult to define how exactly a Byzantine ivory, a product of the goldsmith's craft or an actual model or sketch might have helped to shape a specific Ottonian object. In spite of the broad range of possibilities, art historians have been inclined to connect the Byzantine influence on Ottonian works of art with a single name, that of the princess from Byzantium who became part of the family, politics and history of the Saxon dynasty.

The arrival of Theophano in Italy in 972, as the bride of Otto II, suggests the image of an impressive retinue consisting of artists and craftsmen, a fairy-tale dowry of everyday objects[4] as well as objects representative of the treasury, which were not only admired and given away, but also imitated. Not until the end of Otto the Great's reign does Ottonian patronage really become apparent; it only reaches its peak in the time of his son and grandson, as is evidenced by the donations, far into Salian times, of sumptuous books and liturgical vessels. Indeed, stylistically speaking, there is only a very small number of Ottonian works of art before the year 972. Therefore it seemed logical to connect Theophano not only with the ever-growing influence of Byzan-

[3] The essays of H. Wentzel, 'Das byzantinische Erbe der ottonischen Kaiser: Hypothesen über den Brautschatz der Theophanu', *Aachener Kunstblätter*, 40 (1971), 11–84; *Aachener Kunstblätter*, 43 (1972), 15–39; 'Byzantinische Kleinkunstwerke aus dem Umkreis der Kaiserin Theophanu', *Aachener Kunstblätter*, 44 (1973), 43 ff; a review of new aspects: *Byzantium and the West: XVIIIth Spring Symposium of Byzantine Studies* (Oxford, 1987).

[4] The basis for this in the written sources is more laconic than the conclusions drawn from them, especially by Wentzel (see n. 3): Widukind, *Res gestae Saxonicae*, III, ed. H.E. Lohmann and P. Hirsch, MGH SRG in us. schol. (Hanover, 5th edn, 1935), pp. 148–9: 'cum magno exercitu et claris muneribus'; Thietmar, *Chronicon*, II, 15, ed. R. Holzmann, MGH SRG (1935), pp. 56–7: 'mox magnificis muneribus comitatuque egregeio'.

10. Marriage charter of Theophano, 972, detail (Niedersächsisches Staatsarchiv, Wolfenbüttel, 6 Urk 11).

tine art on the West after 972, but also with the significantly greater number of the works of art produced after this date.

One of the earliest, most beautiful and especially 'Byzantine' highlights of Ottonian book-illumination is the magnificent ceremonial document[5] which records the donations made to Theophano at her wedding to Otto II in Rome at Whitsun, 972 (Fig. 10). Ornamental borders at the top and the sides of the document, as well as the golden ink on purple parchment, can also

[5] D. Matthes, 'Die Heiratsurkunde der Kaiserin Theophanu', *Veröffentlichungen der niedersächsischen Archivverwaltung*, Beiheft 16 (Wolfenbüttel, 1972); Matthes, 'Die Heiratsurkunde der Kaiserin Theophanu', *Sonderveröffentlichung der niedersächsischen Archivverwaltung anlässlich des X. internationalen Archivkongresses in Bonn* (Braunschweig, 1984); cf. also my essay in von Euw and Schreiner, *Kaiserin Theophanu*, II, pp. 193–218.

be found in other imperial documents, which demonstrate their importance by their extraordinary form. The best example is the *Ottonianum* drawn up at the coronation of Otto I in Rome, 962, which grants the pope all the privileges he had effectively held since the time of Charlemagne.[6] Both the *Ottonianum* and the marriage charter of Theophano presuppose richly decorated Byzantine imperial charters. But the rich ornament of Theophano's charter goes far beyond the regular decorative apparatus of eastern and western charters typical of imperial chancelleries. The extraordinary patterning of the background, the double row of great medallions with their animal ornamentation, and the dark blue spandrels in between with their pattern of red tendrils, transform the parchment with its text into a tableau reminiscent of a luxurious silk from the imperial workshops on the Bosporos. We can, indeed, trace most decorative elements of the charter's adornment, so atypical of chancellery usage,[7] back to Byzantine textiles. Given the scope of this chapter, a critical reference to the possible textile models would lead too far. The same is true of the extensive and profound discussions about the charter in recent historical, diplomatic and art-historical literature.[8] For our purposes it is sufficient to point out that the animal medallions and their patterned background go far beyond the formal appearance of a regular document and suggest some abnormality not only in the form but also in the function of the charter. This has led to historical and art-historical speculation as to the date of the charter (whether it was made immediately in 972 or later) and as to the real purpose of the object and its significance as a political or legal instrument. These speculations will not be dwelt upon here. Nor do the lack of a seal, the spelling-mistakes, the disproportion between the physical length of the parchment and the length of the text bear on our investigation, which concerns the traces left by Theophano herself in Ottonian art. This is not the place to decide whether the empress carried the charter with her on her

[6] W. Georgi, 'Ottonianum und Heiratsurkunde 962/972', in von Euw and Schreiner, *Kaiserin Theophanu*, II, pp. 135 ff; also A. von Euw, 'Ikonologie der Heiratsurkunde der Kaiserin Theophanu', in von Euw and Schreiner, *Kaiserin Theophanu*, II, pp. 175 ff.

[7] Although H. Hoffmann, *Buchkunst und Königtum im ottonisch-frühsalischen Reich* (Stuttgart, 1986), pp. 113 and 116, mentions Byzantine charters with medallion-patterns and figured top borders as something that could be 'gut möglich gewesen aber nicht strikt zu beweisen', nothing comparable to the Theophano charter has survived.

[8] Summarized by Hoffmann, *Buchkunst* (see n. 7), pp. 103–16.

travels and hung it like a luxurious tapestry[9] or whether it was put on show to demonstrate the status and privileges[10] of Theophano as a co-empress. Such extraordinary explanations could only have been elicited by an object with an extraordinary appearance. The transformation of an imperial charter into a sumptuous object is effected by extravagant decoration,[11] borrowed from other artistic disciplines. The ornamented top border is a veritable imitation of goldsmith's work with *émail cloisonné*. The medallions recall imperial silks with motifs of animals fighting. But within the medallions, the contours and the composition of the animals themselves seem much more fluid, clear and detailed than would be possible in a woven or embroidered representation. This has suggested metal-work as a possible source for the animal scenes.[12] The red tendril ornament in the dark blue spandrels between the medallions is of great elegance and precision. The painting itself is of the highest quality, not only in the small busts and animals imitating enamel-work, but also in the animal groups in the great medallions, which, by comparison, have a monumental aspect, and, indeed, in every detail of the decorative system. Everything is subject to the same standard of high artistic discipline. This 'charter' is a masterly conception that did not leave anything to chance; it proves its quality in every detail by its most imaginative integration of different decorative elements into one homogeneous whole. The sumptuous metamorphosis of Theophano's marriage-charter is effected through quotations from different artistic disciplines and different stylistic periods. This is obviously what the artist intended; it was only possible in a special situation.

In the older literature, the charter, taken to come from an itinerant imperial chancellery that could not be directly localized, was tentatively compared with Saxon book-illumination.[13] Konrad Hoffmann recently placed the charter of Theophano in a stylistic context that had not been considered before by his claim that the Master of the *Registrum Gregorii* was its creator.[14] Its

[9] Wentzel, 'Das byzantinische Erbe' (1971) (see n. 3), p. 76.

[10] W. Ohnsorge, 'Die Heirat Kaiser Ottos II. mit der Byzantinerin Theophanu (972)', *Braunschweigisches Jahrbuch*, 54 (1973), 53.

[11] Hoffmann, *Buchkunst* (see n. 7), p. 113: 'Wie dem auch sei, wiederum ist nur die allgemeine Konzeption aus derartigen byzantinischen Vorbildern zu erklären, die Ausführung im Einzelnen ist westlichen Mustern verpflichtet.'

[12] Matthes, 'Die Heiratsurkunde' (1972) (see n. 5), p. 49, no. 41, fig. 41.

[13] Hoffmann, *Buchkunst* (see n. 7), criticizing the Corvey localization.

[14] *Ibid.*, pp. 116 ff; because of lacking competence, the present author cannot contribute to the discussion about the script and the consequent localization to Fulda of

stylistic character is the same as that apparent in the work of this extraordinary Ottonian artist. Important decorative elements, especially the red spandrel-fillings on a blue background which are obviously constructed of compass-drawn curves and the paired animals of the top border, go back to the same stratum of models from which the Gregory Master developed his decorative vocabulary, namely the Carolingian illuminations of Tours, available in several manuscripts in the Ottonian libraries of Trier.[15] Touronian book-illuminations can be shown to have stimulated book painters in Trier since the 970s. The step-by-step development of the Ottonian Renaissance out of Carolingian models as a process of copying, paraphrase, transformation and recreation can be followed in an exemplary fashion from one initial to the next in the two volumes of Gregory the Great's *Moralia in Hiob*,[16] originating from St Maximin in Trier. Here, as well as in later manuscripts of the Gregory Master, Hoffmann shows convincing parallels for the heart-shaped and cruciform flower-patterns in the spandrels between the animal medallions of the charter.[17] The paired animals of the top border can be paralleled in a similarly convincing way with Touronian inventions as they appear for instance on fol. 8r of the Vivian Bible, here and there imitating goldsmith's work (Fig. 11). In the jewelled borders on the long sides of the Egbert shrine we find the same animals enamelled. The tendril ornaments of the charter are compared by Hoffmann with very similar heart-shaped flowers and characteristic links at branching-off points in the slightly larger enamels on the small

the Gregory master. Hoffmann's comparisons of motif and style of the ornamental patterns in the charter with ornamental and figural enamels of the Egbert workshop are convincing, however. As I have shown earlier, the connections between the goldsmiths and the book painters working for Egbert of Trier can be well defined. H. Westermann-Angerhausen, 'Die Goldschmiedearbeiten der Trierer Egbertwerkstatt', Beiheft der Trierer Zeitschrift, 36 (1973), for the ornamental enamels and their Touronian and Ottonian parallels pp. 53 ff, for the Evangelist symbols on the Egbert shrine and their parallels in the miniatures of the Gregory master pp. 66 ff.

[15] C. Nordenfalk, 'Beiträge zur Geschichte der touronischen Buchmalerei', *Acta Archeologica*, 7 (1936), 281 ff; H. Schnitzler, 'Südwestdeutsche Kunst um das Jahr 1000 und die Schule von Tours', *Trierer Zeitschrift*, 14 (1939), 154 ff; J.M. Plotzek, 'Die Anfänge der ottonischen Trierer Buchmalerei', *Wallraf–Richartz Jahrbuch*, 32 (1970), 7 ff.

[16] J.M. Plotzek, 'Zur Initialmalerei des 10. Jahrhunderts in Trier und Köln', *Aachener Kunstblätter*, 44 (1973), 101 ff, especially p. 102.

[17] Hoffmann, *Buchkunst* (see n. 7), pp. 103 ff, especially pp. 107–16, e.g. fol. 1v of the Trier Moralia, Trier Stadtbibliothek Hs. 2209/2328, or Manchester, John Rylands Library, lit. lat. 98, fol. 14v.

11. Vivian Bible (Paris, Bibliothèque Nationale, MS lat. 1, fol. 84).

sides of the Egbert shrine and in the borders of the *Codex aureus* from Echternach, both donations of archbishop Egbert and of the empress Theophano, and made in a workshop with close connections to the Ottonian *scriptorium* of Trier.[18] Consequently, we can localize the stylistic origin of several important decorative elements of the charter in Trier, and it seems a logical conclusion that some of the strange motifs that turn up in the document can

[18] Westermann–Angerhausen, 'Die Goldschmiedearbeiten' (see n. 14), pp. 55 f and 79 ff.

also be localized in the artistic context of Trier. The Gregory Master is the very person we can most readily credit with the ability to combine the small decorative elements common to both the *scriptorium* and the goldsmith's workshop with the monumental animal pairs that only he himself could have transformed from a model in textile- or possibly in metal-work[19] to drawings of such classical character.

We do not intend to credit the Gregory Master with yet another 'work' to augment his 'œuvre', although it is tempting to connect the name of this well-defined artistic personality, who stands for a particular style and, indeed, a school of book-illumination, with one of the earliest and most impressive products of Ottonian imperial art. Instead, we will try to define more precisely the artistic intention behind this magnificently homogeneous conception. Given the convincing stylistic localization of the ornamental elements of the charter, it becomes evident that the stylistic instruments used to evoke the impression of truly oriental splendour were not imported from abroad. They were not, in fact, 'Byzantine'. We do not see a participant in the 'invasion of Greek artists in the retinue of the empress Theophano'[20] at work here, but rather an Ottonian painter, probably schooled in Trier under the impression of Carolingian, Touronian models. With wit and intuition he used stimuli from other artistic media,[21] the arts of weaving and metal-work, in order to create an almost fairy-tale paraphrase of a 'normal' sumptuous imperial document. The historical and diplomatic[22] evidence for the merely ceremonial function of this document, which may have been useless as a legal instrument, are corroborated by stylistic evidence. Thus we can conclude that the document was primarily intended to impress upon contemporaries the importance of the imperial wedding between the eastern and western empires. This document was made to look more Byzantine than anything ever seen or imagined. A Byzantine craftsman in the retinue of Theo-

[19] See n. 12. [20] W. Burger, *Abendländische Schmelzarbeiten* (Berlin, 1932), p. 45.

[21] 'Copies' from other media occur elsewhere in Trier book painting as well: in the Gospels of the Sainte Chapelle we find inventions of the Gregory master, head-capitals that can be explained as a direct reflex of roman spoliate capitals still visible in Egbert's time in the Cathedral of Trier, see H. Westermann-Angerhausen, 'Blattmasken, Maskenkapitelle, Säulenhäupter: Variationen über ein vorgegebenes Thema', *Boreas: Münsterische Beiträge zur Archäologie*, 6 (1983), 202 ff.

[22] See n. 10.

phano would most probably have adhered much more strictly to the regular chancellery patterns for a document like this. The very fact that such rules are being played with, albeit at an extremely high level of craftsmanship, affords a surprising insight into the process set in motion in Ottonian art by 'Byzantium'. We are not witnesses to the passive absorption of foreign models. Instead, the local stylistic language proves to be so supple and expansive that it can simulate a foreign idiom by its own means. According to this interpretation, Theophano's presence caused the invention of this extraordinary form, although neither she herself nor her retinue influenced its stylistic appearance directly.

Since the series of essays by Hans Wentzel,[23] the name of Theophano has been linked with the concept of the 'Byzantine heritage of the Ottonian emperors', consisting of objects that are often connected, at least hypothetically, with imperial donations of Ottonian and Salian times. They are luxury objects, such as chess pieces and perfume bottles and other sumptuous vessels of semiprecious stone, precious textiles and ivories admired as strange and valuable, preserved and given new functions in church treasuries and princely collections. It is not easy to prove that they all came from the dowry of Theophano; and even if they did, this would not actually answer the question about Theophano's direct influence on Ottonian art. Apart from ivories[24] and textiles,[25] the direct impact of these luxury objects on the changing character of Ottonian styles up to and shortly after the turn of the millennium is not easy to prove, whereas the influence of Byzantine books on the style and iconography of Ottonian book-illumination is more directly evident.[26] The trend towards increasing preciousness, as instanced by the 'carpet-pages'[27] of Echternach book-illumination, seems to have been a delayed

[23] See n. 3.

[24] E.g. the copy of a Byzantine ivory for the precious Gospels of Bernward of Hildesheim, see L. Stamm-Saurma, 'Die auctoritas des Zitates in der bernwardinischen Kunst', *Schriftenreihe der Kommission für niedersächsische Bau- und Kunstgeschichte bei der Braunschweigischen wissenschaftlichen Gesellschaft* (Göttingen, 1988), III, pp. 105 ff.

[25] F. Mütherich, 'Malerei', in L. Grodecki, F. Mütherich *et al.*, *Die Zeit der Ottonen und Salier* (Munich, 1973), p. 88.

[26] A. von Euw, 'Die Kölner ottonische Malerschule: Synthese der künstlerischen Strömungen aus Ost und West', in von Euw and Schreiner, *Kaiserin Theophanu*, I, pp. 251 ff.

[27] For the history of carpet-pages see K. Nordenfalk, *Codex Caesareus Upsaliensis: An Echternach Gospel-Book of the Eleventh Century* (Stockholm, 1971), pp. 97 ff.

reaction if one supposes that it was in the year 972 (and only then) that the textiles which inspired it were brought to Germany.

The great number of luxury objects of Byzantine provenance that are linked with Ottonian times, whether contemporary or classical treasures, did not in themselves change a stylistic tradition. Spolia such as the cameo of Augustus in the Lothair cross[28] at Aachen, the agate and rock crystal vessels set in the ambo[29] at Aachen, the crystal bottles set in the reliquary cross of Borghorst[30] or the Byzantine enamels set in the cover of the pericopes of Henry II[31] do not have the effect of changing a style. Instead, these precious alien elements integrated into Ottonian or Salian goldsmiths' works display the same phenomenon as in the charter of Theophano: the spolia, 'quotations' of motif and style, far from bringing about an assimilation to the admired model. The foreign elements achieve a new contextual meaning in the stylistic and iconographical 'syntax' of Ottonian and Salian work.

So much is lost in the field of metal-work from around the turn of the first millennium that we shall never be able to gain as clear – though fragmentary – a picture of it as of book-illumination. Most of what has survived can be classified as monumental goldsmith's craft, works of ecclesiastical or imperial representation, usually of important dimensions: antependia, book-covers, large processional or altar crosses and reliquaries. Apart from these objects for ecclesiastical use, Ottonian goldsmiths, as in any other time, were most probably occupied very largely with the production of chains, bracelets, ear- and finger-rings, fibulae, belt buckles, and precious table-vessels.[32] The comparatively large

28 H. Wentzel, 'Alte und altertümliche Kunstwerke der Kaiserin Theophanu', *Pantheon*, 30 (1972), 3 ff, ill. 1 and Wentzel, 'Byzantinische Kleinkunstwerke' (see n. 3), p. 76, ill. 29.

29 E. Doberer, 'Studien zum Ambo Kaiser Heinrichs II. im Dom zu Aachen', in *Karolingische und ottonische Kunst: Werden, Wesen, Wirkung*, Forschungen zur Kunstgeschichte und Christlichen Archäologie unter dem Patronat von Georg von Opel, 3 (Wiesbaden, 1957), pp. 308 ff; H. Appuhn, 'Das Mittelstück vom Ambo Heinrichs II.', *Aachener Kunstblätter*, 32 (1966), 70 ff.

30 H. Westermann–Angerhausen, 'Westfälische Goldkreuze und ihre Voraussetzungen in Rheinland und Niedersachsen', in *Rhein und Maas*, II, *Kunst und Kultur 800–1400* (Cologne, 1973), pp. 187 ff.

31 F. Steenbock, *Der kirchliche Prachteinband im frühen Mittelalter* (Berlin, 1965), p. 131, no. 50, ill. 71.

32 See generally, H. Roth, *Kunst und Handwerk im frühen Mittelalter* (Stuttgart, 1986), pp. 40 ff and 131 ff. A predominance of ecclesiastical goldsmithing is, however, maintained by V.H. Elbern, *Goldschmiedekunst im frühen Mittelalter* (Darmstadt, 1988), pp. 12, 13.

number of liturgical vessels preserved need not indicate a decline in secular metal-work. The picture is simply out of proportion because the tradition of grave gifts no longer existed. In the central regions of Ottonian rule archaeological sources for liturgical goldsmithing begin to dwindle long before the year 1000. Conditions and motivations for ecclesiastical goldsmith's craft at this time probably differed from those for secular jewelry. As in book-illumination, Carolingian models played a major role for treasury objects, but in contrast to book-illumination it is seldom possible to show 'the role of copies' by directly juxtaposing Carolingian and Ottonian treasure objects, because they have survived even more sparsely than books. The recently proposed redating of the nail reliquary kept in the Ottonian Egbert shrine has shown the problems of distinction between Carolingian and Ottonian metal-work.[33] The role of models in the development of Ottonian and Salian goldsmith's work should not be underrated, but recurrences of motif and style characterize the Ottonian Renaissance in book-illumination in a different way than in the treasure arts. The exemplary function of an important reliquary or gemmed cross, for instance, lay in its venerability, and this again meant that it had to be identifiable through its characteristic decoration and form. An ecclesiastical goldsmith was bound by the formal and material identity of an 'old-fashioned' but venerated model, as can be shown by comparing the *Codex aureus* of St Emmeram with the *Codex aureus* of Echternach.[34] Whether or not the secular goldsmiths stuck to tradition in the same way as can be supposed for ecclesiastical art is hard to determine; they might have been able to adapt their stylistic vocabulary more easily to changing fashion. We know that jewelry was produced in all the great centres of ecclesiastical goldsmith's craft, but of this hardly anything has survived. The liturgical objects that we know of from the different centres can be grouped regionally and chronologically. The amount of jewelry preserved from the

[33] For the Carolingian character of the verroterie cloisonnée on the Egbert shrine, see Schulze-Dörrlamm, *Die Kaiserkrone* (see n. 39), no. 78; H. Westermann-Angerhausen, 'Das Nagelreliquiar im Trierer Egbertschrein: das "künstlerisch edelste Werk der Egbertwerkstätte"?', in *Festschrift für Peter Bloch zum 11. Juli 1990*, ed. H. Krohm and C. Theuerkauff (Mainz, 1990), pp. 9 ff.

[34] O.-K. Werckmeister, *Der Deckel des Codex Aureus von St. Emmeram: ein Goldschmiedewerk des 9. Jahrhunderts* (Baden-Baden and Strasbourg, 1963); R. Kahsnitz, Kommentarband zur Faksimile-Ausgabe (Frankfurt and Stuttgart, 1982), pp. 115 ff; Westermann-Angerhausen, 'Die Goldschmiedearbeiten' (see n. 14), p. 99.

central parts of the Ottonian realm is so small that stylistic differences do not really tell us much.[35] In contrast to the jewelry of earlier periods, preserved in larger quantities, it is not easy to construct hypothetical contexts or to find workshop affinities between jewelry and ecclesiastical goldsmith's work. This means that it is almost impossible to construct a detailed chronology or define regional characteristics for secular jewelry from the probable Ottonian and Salian centres of production.

Therefore, it is very difficult to judge the only coherent group of women's jewelry from the turn of the millennium. After its discovery in Mainz, Otto von Falke[36] attributed it to the empress Gisela, the wife of Conrad II (1027–39), because he recognized similar or identical decorative elements in the stone settings and filigree of the imperial crown. Von Falke was convinced that it dated back to the time of this ruler because of the inscription on the pearled bow. Since then, the majority of scholars have accepted two phases of production for the imperial crown. The body proper with its eight plates is now generally thought to have been made either for the coronation of Otto I in 962 or for that of his son Otto II in 967, whereas the bow and the cross are taken to have been added by Conrad II.[37] The hoard of Mainz, still usually associated with the imperial crown, consists of stylistically very different objects, which therefore might have been made at different times. It contains fibulae, ear-rings, rings, needles and two pieces of ceremonial jewelry, *maniakon* and *lorum*, modelled on elements of Byzantine imperial dress. Like the imperial crown, at least part of this hoard has been dated before the turn of the millennium.[38] The hoard has been understood to be a collection accumulated by several female rulers, consisting of ceremonial jewelry and insignia handed down together with 'modern' pieces for daily use; the latest of these were made in the time of Conrad

[35] J. Taralon, 'Die Kleinkünste in ihrer geographischen Verteilung', in *Die Zeit der Ottonen und Salier* (see n. 25), pp. 289 ff.

[36] O. von Falke, *Der Mainzer Goldschmuck der Kaiserin Gisela* (Berlin, 1913).

[37] For the imperial crown and discussion of the literature see most recently H. Fillitz, *Die Schatzkammer in Wien: Symbole des abendländischen Kaisertums* (Vienna, 1986), pp. 165–6; G.J. Kugler, *Die Reichskrone: die Kronen des Hauses Österreich*, V (Vienna, 1987), pp. 148–55; R. Staats, *Theologie der Reichskrone: ottonische 'renovatio imperii' im Spiegel einer Insignie*, Monographien zur Geschichte des Mittelalters, 13 (Stuttgart, 1976).

[38] P.E. Schramm and F. Mütherich, *Denkmale der deutschen Kaiser und Könige* (Munich, 1962), p. 168, no. 144; H. Westermann-Angerhausen, 'Ottonischer Fibelschmuck: neue Funde und Überlegungen', in *Jewellery Studies*, 1 (1983–84), 20 ff.

II, when the treasure was evidently hidden in the vault in Mainz, only to be rediscovered in 1880.

While this chapter was being completed, Mechthild Schulze-Dörrlamm[39] presented two studies on the imperial crown and jewelry, showing on the basis of archaeological methods that the crown as a whole was made in the time of Conrad II and that the imperial women's jewelry did not, as was assumed before, take several decades to accumulate, but was made during a fairly short period even later than the crown for Agnes of Poitou (1043–77), wife of Henry II. She established these new datings of the imperial jewelry and crown on a statistical basis, using a system of co-ordinates associating twenty defined decorative elements with identical or similar details from fifty-eight goldsmiths' works from the early ninth century to the end of eleventh century. The principal result of this examination is that the crown and the hoard, dated to the times of Conrad II and of Henry III, show very strong Italo–Byzantine influence and may even have been made for the imperial Salian court by Byzantine craftsmen in Germany or northern Italy.

This would eliminate the possibility of dating at least some of the pieces from the hoard, namely the jewelry belonging to ceremonial dress, to the time of Theophano, because the crown with its comparable decorative apparatus has been removed from the context of the coronations of 962 or 967. The role of Theophano in Ottonian goldsmith's craft would thereby lose most of its material foundation.

As I have earlier tried to show in detail (see n. 5), a comparative analysis of the characteristic double-storeyed stone settings on the imperial crown does not necessarily favour a late dating, because important elements of the minute decorative apparatus constituting the settings can already be paralleled by works from the first half or shortly after the middle of the tenth century. The most important witness is the gemmed cross given to Monza by king Berengar in the first third of the tenth century. Its stones are held by double-storeyed settings similar to those of the crown, the lower storey consisting of short cylindrical golden pillars. Apart from this example from the Mediterranean, of old under Byzan-

[39] M. Schulze-Dörrlamm, *Die Kaiserkrone Konrads II. (1024–1039): eine archäologische Untersuchung zu Alter und Herkunft der Reichskrone* (Sigmaringen, 1991); Schulze-Dörrlamm, *Der Mainzer Schatz der Kaiserin Agnes: neue Untersuchungen zum sogenannten 'Gisela-Schmuck'* (Sigmaringen, 1991).

tine influence, there are also Frankish monuments originating in the area which was later to become part of the Ottonian realm. A group of golden hair- or veil-needles in Bonn shows that Frankish goldsmiths – in their own time also occupied with assimilating Byzantine models – had already invented complicated multi-storeyed settings from which those of the crown could have been developed, although certainly not in a direct line. Although it is hard to trace, there is therefore nevertheless evidence for a strongly rooted tradition of craftsmanship and style in the centre of Frankish–Carolingian–Ottonian territory. This tradition makes objects such as the crown and the jewelry hoard possible without necessarily having to postulate a massive influence of Italo–Byzantine goldsmithing around and after the middle of the eleventh century.

The development of the goldsmith's craft around the year 1000 can certainly not be explained without ever-recurring influence of Byzantium or more generally of the Mediterranean, but it would be even less understandable if we failed to take into account the basic tradition of Frankish and Carolingian craftsmanship which was reacting to these influences from the South and the East. Although lack of archaeological material makes it difficult to prove, this indigenous tradition could explain some decorative elements that Schulze-Dörrlamm cannot find parallels for after the turn of the millennium, thus weakening the strength of her statistical arguments.

The Ottonian Renaissance involved a process of encounter and assimilation in the field of the arts; the artisans worked at various centres of production, close to the court and the great ecclesiastical and secular patrons, enjoying direct access to foreign models in the form of gifts of honour, 'souvenirs' or luxury imports. This means that Byzantine stimuli from book-illumination as well as from the goldsmith's craft could elicit an immediate response. The centres of the Ottonian and Salian treasury arts were emphatically also centres of innovation.

Many late datings in the books of Mechthild Schulze-Dörrlamm are made by comparing works from those centres of Ottonian and Salian goldsmithing with works mostly from archaeological sites that would seem peripheral in relation to Ottonian Germany, from Nordic, Slav, north Italian or Mediterranean contexts; she often dates or redates an Ottonian or Salian work of art on the basis of an archaeologically dated piece in this 'periphery'. In the centre of Ottonian territory, archaeological sources do not allow a reconstruction of the jewelry arts in all their complexity, especially in the early years of Otto I and Otto II, i.e. in the time of Theophano; there are too few precisely dated objects. Looking at the many pieces of jewelry in the hoard, it is easy to establish differences in stylistic character between the fibulae and the ceremonial objects, the *maniakon* and the *loros*. Besides, within the large group of fibulae, the differences in style could well point to production within a longer period of time and in different areas.

Many important decorative elements not yet apparent on the crown or only evident in simple combinations turn up in great numbers and in intricate combinations on the conical pairs of fibulae of the hoard. Here, they seem to have been used in a more experienced manner, accumulating minute elements in *à jour* filigree compositions to achieve the effect of virtuoso craftsmanship. This speaks for a development from simpler to more intricate forms within the context of Ottonian–Salian jewelry. Byzantinizing elements are included in both the 'early' and the 'late' pieces of the jewelry hoard and the crown; there is no need to believe that early Ottonian goldsmiths could not have used this 'vocabulary' as readily as their colleagues in the eleventh century.

Important byzantinizing elements are stringed pearls or small filigree globes soldered almost freely between two storeys of a stone setting. They are used in the same way as comparable elements in book-illumination: in the Ottonian goldsmith's craft, although we cannot fully trace its development, Byzantine models were not slavishly copied. Rather, a varying group of decorative elements was integrated at will into an Ottonian context; the strange vocabulary was used to create a 'Byzantine' effect. This does not mean that Byzantine craftsmen had to be imported in greater numbers. The written sources report on Theophano's passion for jewelry and costly dress in a rather critical fashion.[40] In spite, or rather because of this, her example was probably followed avidly. The fibulae of Minden and Schleswig[41] of the early eleventh century and the New York sapphire

[40] Otloh of St Emmeram, *Liber visionum*, XVII, MGH SS XI, p. 385.

[41] For the fibulae of Minden and Schleswig, Westermann-Angerhausen, 'Ottonischer Fibelschmuck' (see n. 38).

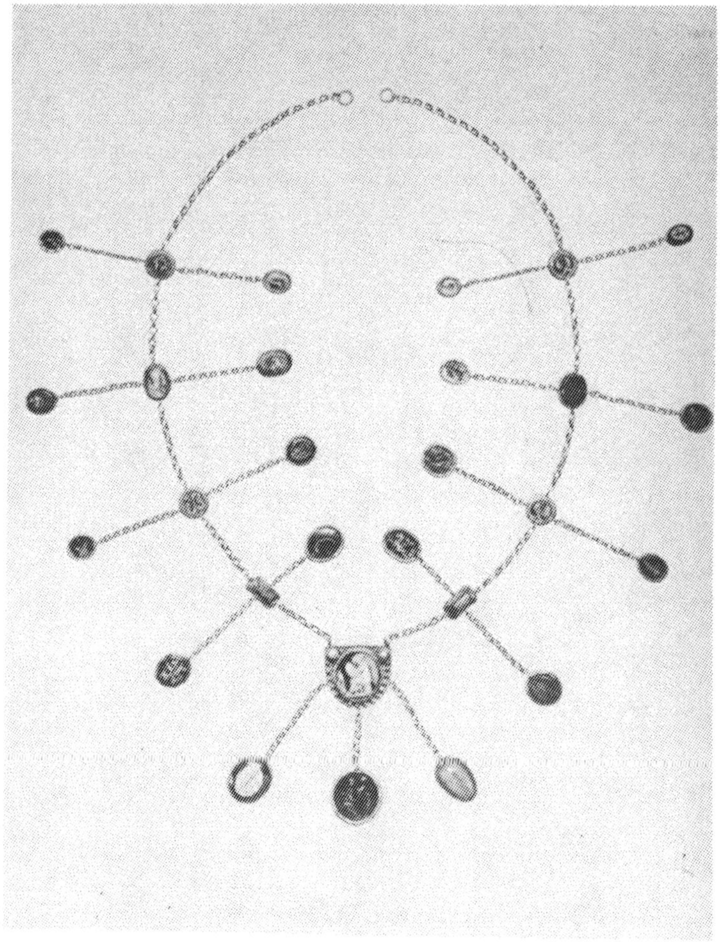

12. Maniakon (Berlin, Staatliche Museen zu Berlin – Preussischer Kulturbesitz, Kunstgewerbemuseum, Inv. Nr. 62, 44).

fibula, from the reign of Otto III,[42] show by their very similarity to those of the imperial hoard that local craftsmen far away from Mainz were able to react to new fashions. As with the search for Greek learning,[43] the adaptation of Byzantine or more generally Mediterranean models in the goldsmith's craft and book-illumi-

[42] For a tentative chronology see *ibid.*, with the dating of the New York fibula to the time of Otto III; H. Westermann-Angerhausen, 'Eine unbekannte Fibel aus dem ottonischen Kaiserinnenschmuck?', *Mainzer Zeitschrift*, 70 (1975), 69 ff.

[43] N. Staubach, 'Graecae Gloriae: die Rezeption des Griechischen als Element spätkarolingisch-frühottonischer Hofkultur', in von Euw and Schreiner, *Kaiserin Theophanu*, I, pp. 343 ff.

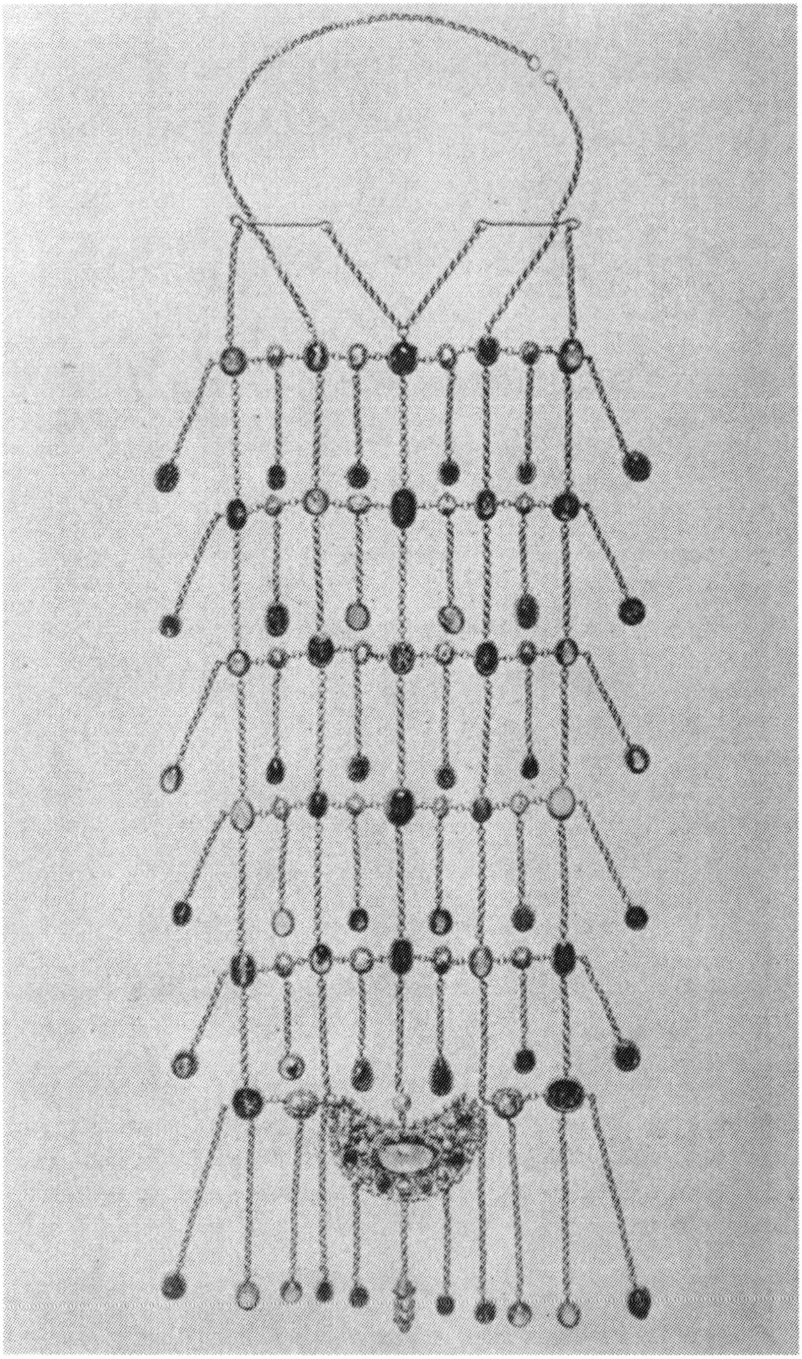

13. Loros (Berlin, Staatliche Museen zu Berlin – Preussischer Kulturbesitz, Kunstgewerbemuseum, Inv. Nr. 62, 45).

nation had already been going on before the marriage of Theophano and this process retained momentum far beyond the middle of the eleventh century. Ottonian goldsmiths – like Carolingian ones before them – had been preoccupied with Byzantium before Theophano was ever in a position to influence patronage. The old, early dating of the imperial crown can be taken as evidence for this opinion.

The cross on the crown, together with the pearled bow, used to be considered as a later addition (from the time of Conrad II) to the early Ottonian crown proper. One decorative element is common to both parts, the small filigree globes that divide two storeys of a setting. This element can be traced back to earlier and later Mediterranean and Byzantine works, though there it is used in a different stylistic context. It also turns up in the 'late' fibulae of the jewelry hoard as well as in the related fibulae of Minden and Schleswig. Since it is common to so many objects, its use on the bow and cross of the crown could be interpreted as an intentional imitation of a decorative element typical of the crown proper.

All authors, including Mechthild Schulze-Dörrlamm, speak of the 'archaic' character of the plates of the crown itself, as opposed to the cross, bow and monumental *Reichskreuz* definitely connected with the name of the emperor Conrad II. One reason for this could be that the plates were not made in the time of Conrad II, but earlier. They are not archaic because the later eleventh century used decorative elements 'which had been in use for a long time in Byzantine craftsmanship, but which were only adopted by German goldsmiths in the course of the eleventh century';[44] rather, the imperial crown was modern, because it was already experimenting with these decorative elements in the 1060s. Therefore the imperial crown can be said to be on the same stylistic level of development as the charter of Theophano. This marks the beginning of Ottonian Renaissance just as clearly as do the products of the *scriptorium* of archbishop Egbert at Trier. In contrast to artefacts of the eleventh century using the same typical decorative elements in much more complex combinations, the crown is evidence for a phase of stylistic innovation. The comparable decorative elements which are used in the same 'simple' manner on the ceremonial pieces of jewelry in the hoard should therefore also be classed as early Ottonian inventions in Byzantine

[44] Schulze-Dörrlamm, *Die Kaiserkrone* (see n. 39), p. 102.

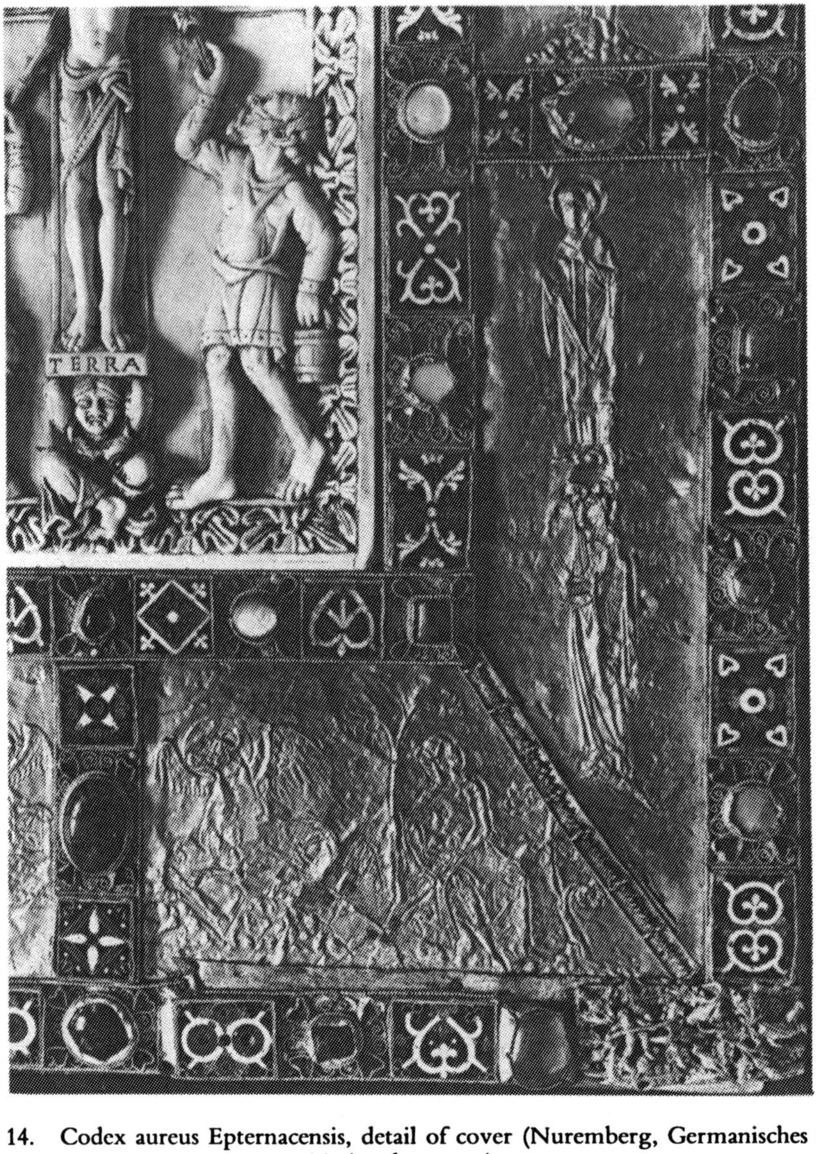

14. Codex aureus Epternacensis, detail of cover (Nuremberg, Germanisches Nationalmuseum).

style, rather than Italo–Byzantine artefacts of the later eleventh century (Figs. 12 and 13).[45] They are significantly different from all representations of *loros* or *maniakon* in painting and sculpture; and this is due chiefly to their greater sophistication and spaciousness. Stones, enamels or pearls are positioned between lengths of gold chain in a wide-meshed net, making the individual elements look rather small. Theophano's jewelry on the Cluny ivory[46] is heavier and more densely set by comparison. Jewelled collars, depicted or actually preserved, such as the one of Preslav[47] or the collar of Maria-Ecclesia in the Petershausen Sacramentary,[48] are very different from the *maniakon* of the imperial hoard, because they are built up radially from a solid necklace. The Mainz *maniakon* with its chain elements branching off inwards and outwards, thus necessitating a supporting fabric, owes nothing to Byzantine designs. It cannot be proven that the Mainz *maniakon* was actually made for Theophano. But the style of its decorative detail relates it to the crown, and a comparison with 'normal' jewelled collars of this type shows that the Mainz *maniakon* is an original invention. Like the marriage-charter, we can therefore call it an early Ottonian paraphrase of a Byzantine model; a paraphrase, moreover, that would not have come into existence without the appearance of Theophano in Germany.

The most distinct trace of Theophano in Ottonian sumptuary

[45] Schulze-Dörrlamm, *Der Mainzer Schatz* (see n. 39), pp. 91 ff and 96 ff.

[46] For the Cluny ivory see A. Goldschmidt and K. Weitzmann, *Die byzantinischen Elfenbeinarbeiten des X.–XIII. Jahrhunderts* (Berlin, 1934), II, no. 85, ill. XXIV; Schramm and Mütherich, *Denkmale* (see n. 38), no. 73; P.E. Schramm, *Die deutschen Kaiser und Könige in Bildern ihrer Zeit 751–1190*, new edn ed. P. Berghaus, N. Gussone, *et al.* (Munich, 1983), no. 91.

[47] M. Schulze-Dörrlamm, 'Juwelen der Kaiserin Theophanu: Ottonischer Schmuck im Spiegel zeitgenössischer Buchmalerei', *Archäologisches Korrespondenzblatt*, 19 (1989), 415, ill. I,2. The components of the Byzantine jewelled collar which has been reconstructed from the curved enamel plaques from the Theophano cross and the nail-reliquary at Essen are, by the way, western Ottonian, and cannot be reasonably compared with the icon of St Michael in the Treasury of San Marco; they can easily be distinguished from the real Byzantine plaques at the end of the Theophano cross, see L. Cüppers and P. Mikat, *Der Essener Münsterschatz* (Essen, 1966), pp. 57 ff, distinguishing the different enamels.

[48] Schulze-Dörrlamm, 'Juwelen' (see n. 47), ill. II. For the Petershausen Maria Ecclesia as a reflex of the appearance of Theophano see A. von Euw, 'Der Darmstädter Gero-Codex und die künstlerisch verwandten Reichenauer Prachthandschriften', in von Euw and Schreiner, *Kaiserin Theophanu*, I, pp. 191–225, especially p. 210; A. von Euw, 'Das Sakramentar von Petershausen', in *Vor dem Jahr 1000: abendländische Buchkunst zur Zeit der Kaiserin Theophanu, Katalog Schnütgen-Museum* (Cologne, 1991), pp. 122 ff.

arts is, no doubt, her own image as *donatrix* on the golden book-cover of Echternach from the Trier workshop of archbishop Egbert (Fig. 14). Unfortunately, the donation of a precious book for Magdeburg, mentioning a golden cover with the images both of Otto II and Theophano, is lost. According to Gunther Wolf the Echternach book-cover was given on the occasion of the 250th anniversary of the death of the monastery's founder, Willibrord (658–739).[49] A historical consciousness manifests itself, not only in the date of the donation, but also in the whole figural and ornamental programme of the cover, which is composed around the death of Christ, interpreted as the fountain of the church's missionary efforts. Around the great central Crucifixion ivory, we see a procession, led by Mary and Peter, the patrons of the church of Echternach, with Willibrord, founder of Echternach, and Benedict, father of the monastic order, followed by the apostles to the Germans, Ludger and Boniface. Below them stand Theophano and her son, Otto III, not in the traditional pose of donors but rather as equal partners with the saints in the ceremony of the *adoratio crucis* (Adoration of the Cross), and at the same time as participants and bearers of the 'apostolic' missionary task. This is a most impressive way of showing how Theophano accepted and blended with a tradition she encountered because she understood it and knew how to put it to use.

The picture of the princess from Byzantium as a revolutionizing exponent of foreign influence vanishes behind this fragile[50] golden image. What remains in its place is the impression of a ruler and patron who did not impose her foreign descent either on politics or on art. She neither presided over nor engineered a climate of openness to the creative preoccupation with things Byzantine in the Ottonian Empire; she was part of it herself.

[49] G. Wolf, 'Zur Datierung des Codex Aureus Epternacensis', *Hemechat*, II, 42 (1990), 147 ff.

[50] W. Messerer, 'Zur byzantinischen Frage in der ottonischen Kunst', *BZ*, 52 (1959), 46.

14

The palace of Nijmegen in the tenth and early eleventh centuries*

BERT THISSEN

On 14 April 972, Otto II, son of the German emperor Otto I (962–73), who had already been co-king and co-emperor for a few years, married the Byzantine princess Theophano, who was crowned empress on this occasion. It was an event of great importance, not least for the two persons most directly involved. For Theophano it meant, among other things, a change from a sedentary existence to a life characterized by restless and constant travelling.

The Byzantine emperors ruled their empire from their permanent residence in Constantinople. Because Byzantium had inherited the centralism of the ancient Roman Empire, they had a large, hierarchically organized machine of government at their disposal, which was capable of administering the empire from one place. To a certain extent the role of Constantinople as a permanent imperial residence was also a logical consequence of the fact that, in some respects, the unwritten constitution of Byzantium resembled that of an ancient city-state. In this constitution not only the emperor and the army but also the senate, originally an institution of the city, and the urban population of the capital had autonomous political authority. Constantinople, aptly referred to by the German historian Peter Schreiner as 'the Byzantine empire *in nuce*',[1] was therefore the place where the internal political relations of this empire were determined. As a consequence, the emperor had every reason to manifest himself here

* The subject of this article will be dealt with in more detail in my thesis on the palace of Nijmegen (in preparation).

1 Peter Schreiner, *Byzanz*, Oldenbourg Grundriss der Geschichte, 22 (Munich, 1986), p. 6.

and there was no political necessity to travel. The imperial palaces outside Constantinople were actually no more than country seats or residences subsidiary to the Great Palace in the capital. It was in that city that the imperial court with its impressive pomp and ceremony gave shape to an ideology that raised the emperor to a sacral position above ordinary mortals and captivated many leading figures from the senate, the people, the army and civil service.

Though not 'born in the purple', porphyrogennete, Theophano came from the imperial palace (*augusti de palatio*) and was therefore familiar with life at the Byzantine court.[2] Because of her marriage she moved to the court of the Ottonian sovereigns. Neither in their 'Roman' Empire nor in their German kingdom, which was their actual realm, did they have a capital. They were doomed to a never-ending *peregrinatio imperii*. In his famous article 'Ottonian Government', the late Karl Leyser called these continual migrations of the king 'the most essential and carefully administered institution of the Ottonian and Salian *Reich*'.[3] This underlines the great importance of this itinerancy of the German kings in the tenth and eleventh centuries and it implies that their government was otherwise little institutionalized. The kingdom of the Ottonians owed its existence in the first place to a network of personal relations around the king. German historians therefore speak about a *Personenverbandstaat* and some of them even prefer not to use the word 'state' in this respect at all.[4] Government institutions to rule territories hardly existed here, and so governing the kingdom from one permanent place was absolutely inconceivable.

The constitution of the kingdom – if we may call it a constitution – also made travelling necessary. The king himself was with his court the only unifying and centralizing element. There was no senate or hierarchically organized professional army, which is certainly consistent with the low level of organization and functional differentiation in this relatively primitive society. The way in which the kingdom had come into existence was also

2 *Vita Mahthildis reginae antiquior*, MGH SS X, p. 581.

3 Karl Leyser, 'Ottonian government', in Leyser, *Medieval Germany and its Neighbours 900–1250* (London, 1982), pp. 69–102, at p. 94.

4 See Hagen Keller, 'Zum Charakter der "Staatlichkeit" zwischen karolingischem Reichsreform und hochmittelalterlichem Herrschaftsausbau', *Frühmittelalterliche Studien*, 23 (1989), 248–64. Compare Timothy Reuter, *Germany in the Early Middle Ages c. 800–1056* (London and New York, 1991), p. 208.

the reason that a *populus* as a homogeneous constitutional factor was lacking. Instead, the kings had to deal with a number of different peoples (*gentes*) and other regional groups, spread all over the empire, partly in the form of duchies, partly in the form of entities without a recognizable institutional framework. In this situation important decisions, like the acceptance of a new king, had to be taken or at least confirmed by each community separately. Although there was a powerful supraregional nobility that regularly visited the court, particularly during government assemblies and on Christian holy days, it was nevertheless necessary for the king to visit particular regions at regular intervals to assert his rights and enforce certain decisions 'on location'.

The constant travelling of the kings was therefore in the first place politically inspired and it cannot be explained, as older historians have suggested, by an economic necessity to consume the production surpluses of royal domains on the spot. The example of certain big monastic communities that were supplied by transport services from a great distance shows that, strictly speaking, such an economic necessity did not exist. It is clear, though, that economic motives could influence the king's itinerary: particular territories were probably visited more than others by the king because of his many royal estates and rights there. These territories are called *Kern-* or *Königslandschaften* or *Zentralräume* in German historiography. Tenth-century examples were the area of the Harz mountains (eastern Saxony and northern Thüringen), where the Ottonians had many patrimonial possessions of old, and parts of Lower Lotharingia (in the area around Aachen) and the Rhine-Main area (around Frankfurt), where many royal estates still dated from the Carolingian period.

The travels of the kings were never strictly private and the palaces they visited were therefore never private seats either. Exaggerating a little, one might say that in this kingdom without a capital (*Reich ohne Hauptstadt*) each palace was a capital in itself, though only for some time. When a king and his court visited a palace, it became the representative seat of the sovereign and the functional centre of his kingdom; as such it was the counterpart of the Great Palace in Constantinople. However, these temporary residences of a travelling court could never equal the Byzantine palace in splendour; from a functional point of view they always had the character of a regional centre. The *Repertorium der deutschen Königspfalzen* (Repertory of German Royal Palaces), which is currently being compiled, focuses precisely on this relation with the regions. This project is based on the point formulated by W. Berges 'How the king's meeting with regional and local forces takes place in reality'.[5]

It would be a mistake to think that all palaces were more or less similar. The German kingdom was not a modern unitary state, so these palaces cannot be compared with modern regional administrative centres. They were scattered all over the empire and had a high degree of individuality, each being determined by its own specific past and regional context. There were ancient Carolingian palaces and new Ottonian ones, palaces where the king and his large retinue could stay for a long period of time and palaces where they would soon have encountered problems with provisioning. Moreover, the Ottonians did not stay only in royal palaces, but also in royal manors (often barely distinguishable from palaces), in monasteries (with moderation) and in episcopal cities (Otto III did so increasingly after 991).

All in all, the picture of the places where the Ottonians ruled and stayed is very heterogeneous and they can hardly be epitomized in a few 'ideal types'. This also applies to the places where Theophano stayed from her marriage in 972 until her death in 991. Her itinerary, as it was published by Gunther Wolf a few years ago, records 107 different stopping-places, of which twenty-three are in Italy and the others are scattered all over the German kingdom.[6] In every respect it reflects the itinerary of Otto II (973–83) and Otto III (983–1002) in these years. As a matter of fact, it is largely derived from it, as there are hardly any direct records of her own travelling.

Below, one palace will be discussed in more detail: Nijmegen. Here Theophano stayed eight times, near here she gave birth to her son Otto III and presumably a twin sister in 980 and here she died eleven years later. The palace of Nijmegen was certainly a prominent place in the world this Byzantine princess entered because of her marriage and to a certain extent it may perhaps be called typical of this world. It has been claimed that Theophano

[5] See Herman Heimpel, 'Bisherige und künftige Erforschung deutscher Königspfalzen', *Geschichte in Wissenschaft und Unterricht*, 16 (1965), 461–87, at p. 470. Compare Thomas Zotz, 'Vorbemerkungen zum Repertorium der deutschen Königspfalzen', *Blätter für deutsche Landesgeschichte*, 118 (1982), 177–203 and *Die deutschen Königspfalzen*, ed. Zotz (Göttingen, 1983–).

[6] Gunther Wolf, 'Itinerar der Prinzessin Theophano/Kaiserin Theophanu', *Archiv für Diplomatik*, 35 (1989), 237–54.

personally preferred this palace.[7] We shall see whether any proof of such preference can be found.

Nijmegen is situated on the left bank of the river Waal, on the extreme tip of a range of hills stretching far to the south via the present-day German towns of Cleves and Xanten (Fig. 15). In the Middle Ages it was part of the most north-westerly deanery of the archbishopric of Cologne. The town has a great Roman past, both from a civil and a military point of view, and over the past few years archaeological investigations have led to the conclusion that the place was continuously inhabited between Antiquity and the Middle Ages.[8] For the tenth century three topographical elements should be distinguished: 1. The palace, which in all probability was situated at the place where later the Valkhof castle was built. Here, high above the river, an army camp was situated in the late Roman period and here the Staufen palace was built as a castle in the late Middle Ages. 2. A rural settlement with a church directly south of the palace. 3. A settlement in the depression west of the palace along the river. The archaeological remains of this last settlement, which was situated on the site of a Roman civilian settlement and which was enclosed with a Roman wall on the landward side, are of a rural character. However, presumably only the agricultural landward side of this settlement has so far been traced and on the riverside there was probably a more commercial zone, as was the case in the much larger port of trade of Dorestad. In later times that zone was washed away by the river.[9]

The earliest written evidence of the palace of Nijmegen dates from the second half of the eighth century. A visit by Charlemagne (768–814) to the *palacium publicum* of Nijmegen in the spring of 777 is mentioned by his biographer Einhard.[10] This visit

[7] Compare K.N. Ciggaar, 'The Empress Theophano (972–991)', in *Byzantium and the Low Countries in the Tenth Century: Aspects of Art and History in the Ottonian Era* (Hernen, 1985), pp. 33–76, at pp. 33–4, 37–40.

[8] See J.H.F. Bloemers and J.R.A.M. Thijssen, 'Facts and reflections on the continuity of settlement at Nijmegen between AD 400 and 750', in *Medieval Archaeology in the Netherlands*, ed. J.C. Besteman *et al.* (Assen and Maastricht, 1990), pp. 133–51.

[9] See Herbert Sarfatii, 'De vroege topografie van middeleeuws Nijmegen (7e–13e eeuw)', in *Feestbundel aangeboden aan prof. dr. D.P. Blok*, ed. J.B. Berns *et al.* (Hilversum, 1990), pp. 321–31.

[10] *Annales regni Francorum*, s.a. 776, AQDG 5, p. 36, cp. *Diplomata belgica ante annum millesimum centesimum scripta*, ed. M. Gysseling and A.C.F. Koch, Bouwstoffen en

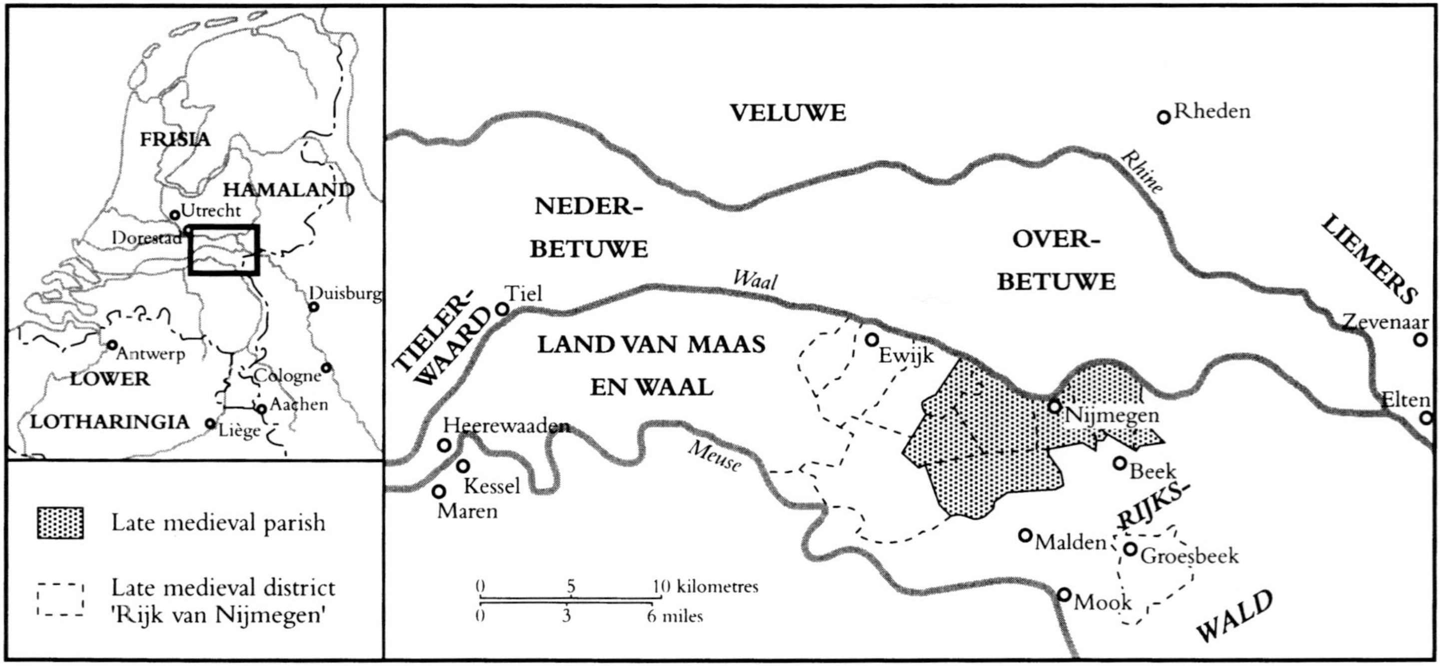

15. Medieval Nijmegen and its surroundings.

is often taken as *terminus ante quem* for the building of a palace at Nijmegen by Charlemagne. Einhard reports that during his reign Charlemagne started to build several palaces and in this connection he mentions Ingelheim and Nijmegen in particular.[11] One should bear in mind, however, that there is no record of a visit to Nijmegen for a period of some thirty years after 777, until 804, and that it is only in the last years of Charlemagne's life that the palace becomes an important place of residence. Einhard also suggests that of the various building projects started by Charlemagne only a few were completed ('opera . . . plurima . . . inchoavit, quaedam etiam consummavit'). The fact that the librarian Gerwardus, who was temporarily responsible for the building of palaces, was present here in 828[12] possibly also shows that Charlemagne did not live to see the completion of the palace which he started at Nijmegen. It is conceivable, therefore, that the palace of 777 was, indeed, a Merovingian palace, situated on a Roman fiscal estate and that it dated back to seventh-century Frankish expansion, which also left other traces. At some time between 777 and 804 Charlemagne embarked on the replacement of this palace by a new Carolingian one. At about the same time he built a palace at Ingelheim, which can be said not to have played a major role until under Charlemagne's successors.[13]

In the winter of 880/1 the palace of Nijmegen was occupied by the Northmen. It is recorded that they enclosed Nijmegen with solid ramparts and walls and established themselves in the royal palace.[14] After a siege by Louis the Younger (876–82) they finally retreated and set fire to the palace and fortification.[15] It is doubtful whether this was a thorough destruction. It would certainly have

studiën voor de geschiedenis en de lexicografie van het Nederlands, 2 vols. (Brussels, 1950), I, p. 178 (*Actum Niumaga palacio publico*). All references to Nijmegen in the written sources up till 1247 have been collected in *Bronnenboek van Nijmegen (eerste eeuw na Chr.–1247)*, ed. P. Leupen and B. Thissen, Nijmeegse studiën, 10 (Nijmegen, 1981), which also mentions all visits by rulers, as do the many volumes of the *Regesta imperii*, ed. J.F. Böhmer *et al.*

11 Einhard, *Vita Karoli*, c. 17, AQDG 5, p. 186.

12 *Translatio et Miracula sancti Marcellini et Petri*, lib. IV, c. 7, MGH SS XV, p. 258.

13 See K. Weidemann, 'Ausgrabungen in der karolingischen Pfalz Ingelheim', in *Ausgrabungen in Deutschland*, 4 vols. (Mainz, 2nd edn, 1975), II, pp. 437–46, at pp. 440–1 and C. Brühl, *Fodrum, gistum, servitium regis*, Kölner Historische Abhandlungen, 14, 2 vols. (Cologne and Graz, 1968), I, p. 20, n. 61.

14 *Annales Fuldenses*, s.a. 880, AQDG 7, p. 114: 'vallo firmissimo et muris circumdantes'.

15 Regino von Prüm, *Chronicon*, s.a. 881, AQDG 7, p. 260: 'palatium una cum munitione'.

taken months to demolish thoroughly a palace that had been built in the course of many years. The Northmen did not have that much time. In any case the palace must have been restored quickly, because in the nineties of that century it was visited regularly. The fact that in the Ottonian and Salian periods Nijmegen is still referred to as *palatium*[16] is also an indication of continuity. In that time this term became a rather exclusive designation for the most important palaces and was used for those dating from the Carolingian period in particular.[17]

In 1047 a new large-scale attack took place. In the autumn of that year duke Godfrey of Upper Lotharingia and other magnates from Lotharingia rebelled against the emperor Henry III (1039–56) and attacked several strongholds which were under his royal authority. Their first target was the palace of Nijmegen, which was set on fire at the end of September or the beginning of October. Among the towns that followed were Verdun, which was taken by siege and set on fire, and Liège, which narrowly escaped the same fate. This attack marks the beginning of a wide gap in the history of Nijmegen: the palace, which had been very important in the preceding years, remained unvisited for a long time. It is questionable, though, whether the rebels managed to destroy the palace irreparably during their raid. In this context it is important that some rulers still visited Nijmegen before Frederick Barbarossa (1152–90) started large-scale building activities in the second half of the twelfth century. Henry V (1106–25) was here in 1125 and Conrad III (1138–52) in 1145 and 1151.[18] The *palatium* is explicitly mentioned on the occasion of the visit of 1151. Rahewin, Frederick Barbarossa's biographer, describes it as 'very massive indeed, yet seriously in disrepair by reason of neglect and age'.[19] In essence it was therefore probably still the Carolingian palace. The fire of 1047 had not completely destroyed it, but in the literal and figurative sense it had probably made it lustreless and therefore unattractive as a residence. The thorough restoration that Barbarossa then started, although he

[16] E.g. MGH DD O III, 235 (18 December 996): 'in palacio nostro, quod dicitur Novimagio'.

[17] A. Gauert, 'Zur Struktur und Topographie der Königspfalzen', in *Deutsche Königspfalzen*, II (Göttingen, 1965), pp. 1–60, at p. 46. Compare Zotz, 'Vorbemerkungen' (see n. 5), p. 179 and especially Brühl, *Fodrum* (see n. 13), I, p. 159.

[18] Bishop Otto and Rahewin, *Gesta Friderici I*, lib. I, cc. 68, 69, AQDG 17, p. 276 and MGH DD Conradi III, 251.

[19] Bishop Otto and Rahewin, *Gesta Friderici I*, lib. IV, c. 86, AQDG 17, pp. 710–12.

failed to complete it himself, was an attempt to change this state of affairs.

In summary, we may conclude that three successive palaces can be distinguished at Nijmegen: a pre-Carolingian (possibly seventh-century), a Carolingian and a Staufen palace. The Ottonians visited a palace that dated back in all essentials to the Carolingian period.

Within the royal palace in a broad sense, i.e. the *Königspfalz* taken as a complex settlement, three main topographical and functional parts are generally distinguished: the palace in the narrow sense (*palatium*), the fortification (*castrum*) and the manor (*curtis*). The church or chapel (*ecclesia* or *cappella*) may be added as a fourth element.[20] This division into palace, chapel, fortification and manor is the basis of the following discussion.

1. For a long time the palace at Ingelheim, as it was reconstructed by Christian Rauch after excavations in *c.* 1910, was considered as the 'ideal type' of the Carolingian palace. Renewed investigations at Ingelheim after 1960 and excavations elsewhere (Aachen, Paderborn, Frankfurt) have shown, however, that there was probably a greater variety than was initially assumed. Nevertheless, from the perspective of Nijmegen, the restored reconstruction of the palace of Ingelheim deserves particular attention, because these two palaces are bracketed together by Einhard and because they are thought to have been built in the same period. The plan is rectangular, with one side built out into an apse. Opposite is the *aula regia*, a representative building with a big hall. Also remarkable are various colonnades on the inside of this complex of buildings.[21]

Archaeologically only a few fragments have so far been found of the Carolingian *palatium* at Nijmegen, fragments that were reused in the Staufen period. They include Carolingian capitals, which are an indication of the presence of columns.[22] In the

[20] See A. Gauert, 'Königspfalzen', in *Handwörterbuch zur deutschen Rechtsgeschichte*, II (Berlin, 1978), cc. 1044–55, at cc. 1049–51, as well as G. Streich, *Burg und Kirche während des deutschen Mittelalters*, Vorträge und Forschungen, Sonderband 29, 2 vols. (Sigmaringen, 1984).

[21] Günther P. Fehring, *Einführung in die Archäologie des Mittelalters* (Darmstadt, 1987), pp. 130–3.

[22] G. Lemmens, 'De burcht van Barbarossa', in *Het Valkhof te Nijmegen*, Catalogi van het kunstbezit van de Gemeente Nijmegen, 3 (Nijmegen, 1980, 2nd edn 1984), pp. 59–72, at pp. 71–2.

written sources the palace is described in laudatory terms, e.g. by Regino of Prüm (*c.* 908) as 'palatium ingentis magnitudinis mirique operis' and by Lampert of Hersfeld (*c.* 1080), when he writes about the events in 1047, as 'domus regia miri et incomparabilis operis'.[23] It is interesting that Einhard's description of the Carolingian palaces at Ingelheim and Nijmegen as 'palatia operis egregii' is repeated in a modified form by Rahewin in the twelfth century: he describes them as 'palatia . . . pulcherrima fabricata et regias clarissimo opere decoratas'. Thomas Zotz suggested as a translation: 'royal houses and richly decorated halls'. In his opinion the two passages show in their interrelationship that the Carolingian concept of *palatium* included both elements, house and *aula regia*.[24] The Staufen palace that was built at Nijmegen during Rahewin's life did indeed have various *domus* and an *aula imperialis*.[25] But Rahewin must also have known the situation before Barbarossa's building activities and consequently he is also a reliable witness for the ancient palace.

The usual retinue of the German king was estimated by Carlrichard Brühl at more than a thousand persons in the eleventh and twelfth centuries. In the tenth century it must have been more modest, but on special occasions, such as the days when the king held court, it might have been much larger.[26] It will therefore not always have been possible to accommodate the complete royal retinue in the palace. A passage in the anonymous *Vita* of Louis the Pious (814–40) concerning a great assembly at Nijmegen in the autumn of 830 shows that accommodation outside the actual palace was used. At a certain moment during that assembly conspirators against the king gathered in the dwelling-place (*habitaculum*) where his son Lothar had found accommodation. The next day this son entered the *regia domus* (the palace) at the invitation of his father.[27] So next to the palace (with the *aula* and dwelling of the king) we find a *habitaculum* as a separate topographical element.

[23] Regino von Prüm, *Chronicon*, s.a. 881, AQDG 7, p. 260, and Lampert of Hersfeld, *Annales*, s.a. 1046, AQDG 13, p. 46.

[24] Bishop Otto and Rahewin, *Gesta Friderici I*, lib. IV, c. 86, AQDG 17, p. 712 and Zotz, 'Vorbemerkungen' (see n. 5), p. 182.

[25] See B. Thissen, 'Die Pfalz Nimwegen zwischen Reichs- und Territorialgewalt (1247–1371)', in *Residenz und Territorium am Niederrhein*, ed. Klaus Flink and Wilhelm Janssen, Klever Archiv, 14 (Cleves, 1993), pp. 33–66, at p. 63.

[26] Brühl, *Fodrum* (see n. 13), p. 170. Compare Wolfgang Metz, *Das Servitium regis* (Darmstadt, 1978), pp. 60–3.

[27] *Vita Hludowici imperatoris*, c. 45, AQDG 5, pp. 336–8.

2. The best-preserved part of the palace of Nijmegen is the octagonal chapel which can still be found in a corner of the ancient castle grounds. The patron-saint of this chapel was St Nicholas, to whom various churches and chapels were dedicated in these regions from *c.* 1000 onwards. In the past this building was considered to be Roman or Carolingian and at present it is mistakenly attributed to Theophano by some people. Art historians, however, are unanimous in dating it to the eleventh century, around 1030, to be more precise.

Professor Aart Mekking has in a study not yet published iodentified the chapel of Saint-Nicolas-aux-Mouches in Liège, which was consecrated in 1030, as a direct model for the chapel at Nijmegen and has pointed out that it has a certain similarity to the so-called 'Bernold churches' in the diocese of Utrecht (*c.* 1040–*c.* 1055). Mekking opts for a date shortly after the attack on the palace in 1047. He interprets it as a symbol of regained imperial authority and as part of a restoration programme.

It should be observed, however, that there is no written evidence whatsoever of a large-scale restoration or a manifestation of royal authority in Nijmegen shortly after 1047. On the contrary, the palace, which in the very last years before 1047 was a very important residence, is completely lacking from the royal itineraries for the next seventy-five years. Although it is not impossible that after the fire some restoration did take place, the written sources seem to indicate that this raid brought the role of the palace as a royal symbol abruptly to an end. The palace did not recover its significance for a long time.

In the late Middle Ages another chapel, dedicated to St Martin, was situated more centrally on the castle grounds. Of this chapel the apse and a small part of the choir have been preserved. It is generally accepted that it dates back to the Staufen period and it must have been part of Barbarossa's palace. But Mekking now believes that this chapel also shows some similarity to the eleventh-century 'Bernold churches'. If so, St Martin's Chapel is an older building redesigned by Barbarossa. Whether it is from the eleventh century, as Mekking assumes, or even older, is a question that must be left aside for the moment.

As it is not known for certain whether there was a chapel dating from the time before the eleventh century, the possibility that the parish church of Nijmegen also served as a palace church for a considerable time should be taken into account. There was an analogous situation at Ingelheim, where a designated palace chapel was only built late in the Ottonian period: before that time the church of St Remigius was used as such.[28] The parish church of Nijmegen, which, according to Piet Leupen, was dedicated to St Stephen (not to St Gertrude, as Willem van Berchen, the fifteenth-century historian, reports), was part of the rural settlement (*villa*) south of the palace and was demolished to allow the extension of the castle's fortifications in the thirteenth century. This church (*ius patronatus* and tithes) belonged to the Chapter of the Holy Apostles in Cologne, reportedly from the foundation of the Chapter in *c.* 1021. Its property was probably donated to the Chapter by its founder, archbishop Pilgrim of Cologne, who might therefore be considered to have been the owner of the church in the tenth century; it is possible that this relationship of Cologne with Nijmegen dates back to the period of Frankish expansion in the seventh century.[29]

3. For a long time the Carolingian palaces were regarded as combinations of a *curtis* (manor) and a *palatium*, without fortification. Only with the new palaces of the Ottonians would this combination be relinquished in favour of the combination *palatium–castrum*.[30] It is not clear whether the palace of Nijmegen was unfortified to begin with. There must, however, have been a fortification as early as the ninth century. In written sources Nijmegen is already called *castrum* in 830, 837 and 846.[31] It is conceivable that in these cases a fortification of the whole settlement, rather than of the palace in the narrow sense, is meant. It was clearly the *palatium* as a building that, according to Regino of Prüm, offered the Northmen a *tutissimum receptaculum* in 880, even though they had themselves further fortified the *munitio* in which they were besieged with ramparts.

From that time no fortification is mentioned in the sources until the thirteenth century. By then the Staufen castle has clearly become the centre of the royal possessions in the region. Although in the intervening period Nijmegen is not described as a *castrum* (it

[28] See H. Schmitz, *Pfalz und Fiskus Ingelheim* (Marburg, 1974), pp. 308–11 and Weidemann, 'Ausgrabungen' (see n. 13), p. 446.

[29] P. Leupen, 'Het oudste patrocinium van Nijmegens parochiekerk', *Archief voor de geschiedenis van de katholieke kerk in Nederland*, 21 (1979), 131–45.

[30] See Gauert, 'Zur Struktur' (see n. 17) and Gauert, 'Königspfalzen' (see n. 20), but (for a different opinion) also Weidemann, 'Ausgrabungen' (see n. 13), pp. 445–6.

[31] Theganus, *Vita Hludowici imperatoris* (addition III), AQDG 5, p. 252; *Annales Bertiniani*, s.a. 837, AQDG 6, p. 32; *Annales Xantenses*, s.a. 846, AQDG 6, p. 348.

is usually referred to without further designation, occasionally as *palatium*, *villa*, *curia*) it may by no means be inferred from this that in the Ottonian and Salian periods it remained unfortified, for in those unsafe times that would have been inconceivable. On the contrary, there is reason to assume that Nijmegen was not only fortified, but that thanks to its fortification it also functioned as a regional centre.

Franz Beyerle has shown that, from the tenth century onwards, a number of places in the Middle Rhine area (such as Speyer, Worms, Mainz, Bingen and Koblenz), as well as, for example, Trier on the Mosel, were centres of so-called *Burgbannbezirke* (castle-ban districts): districts within which the population of sometimes a score of villages or more were obliged to contribute to building, maintaining and guarding the fortifications of the principal place, a *civitas* or other fortified centre, in exchange for protection in times of war and exemption from tolls at the local market. The castle-ban, under which these obligations could be enforced, was a royal prerogative, which was often granted to episcopal churches and monasteries in the second half of the tenth century.[32]

Beyerle assumes that such castle-ban districts also existed on the lower reaches of the Rhine. He refers to Duisburg, where an inscription (now lost) from the twelfth century showed that the inhabitants of Hösel were exempt from tolls, except during the annual fair, because they helped maintain the fortifications.[33] He also refers to Utrecht, in particular to the charter of 2 June 1122, in which the emperor Henry V confirmed the privileges that the inhabitants of Utrecht had been granted by bishop Godebold of Utrecht (1114–27), stating that all those who have to help with the fortification of the *civitas* of Utrecht are exempt from paying tolls when they come there to trade.[34]

Since the publication of Beyerle's article, which went almost

[32] Franz Beyerle, 'Zur Wehrverfassung des Hochmittelalters', in *Festschrift Ernst Mayer* (Weimar, 1932), pp. 31–91.

[33] Wolfgang Müller, *Urkundeninschriften des deutschen Mittelalters* (Kallmünz, 1975), 3 (pp. 49–51 and Tafel 1, with date: [1111–1125?]). Compare Beyerle, 'Zur Wehrverfassung' (see n. 32), pp. 58–9: 'obsequuntur enim ad munimen civitatis in muro et vallo'.

[34] *Oorkondenboek van het sticht Utrecht*, ed. S. Muller Fz. *et al.*, I (Utrecht, 1920), 308 (pp. 282–3): 'Omnes etiam, qui Traiectensem civitatem munire debent vallo, ab omnimodo theloneo liberos esse concedimus, quandocunque eandem civitatem causa mercandi adierint.' Compare Beyerle, 'Zur Wehrverfassung' (see n. 32), p. 65, n. 3.

unnoticed in the Low Countries, these problems have hardly been investigated in this area. Nevertheless, there is reason to assume that more examples could be found. Adriaan Verhulst connected the *libertas castrensis operis* of Antwerp, which is mentioned for the first time in a charter from 1242, with these Ottonian castle-ban districts. It concerns a large area which stretched as far as the Dutch border and beyond, and within which the scores of villages 'que ad opus castri Antwerpiensis pertinent' contributed to building and maintaining the castle of Antwerp and were exempt from paying toll there. This *vrijheid van den borchwerke* (freedom of the castle works) lasted until far into the modern age, including an ever-increasing number of places.[35]

Another possible example is the royal manor of Tiel on the river Waal. Sources from the sixteenth century in particular report that the inhabitants of Culemborg and Buren and the surrounding area and the inhabitants of seventy-two parishes in the districts of Nederbetuwe, Tielerwaard and Maas en Waal were exempt from paying tolls in exchange for a payment every seven years, the so-called *zevenjaarsgeld*, by which they were released from an obligation to dig for the fortification of the town. The written evidence is of a relatively recent date, but the area indicated does not correspond to any known administrative district of a later date; its size indicates an importance that Tiel had in the tenth century, but lacked in later times. Moreover, the *zevenjaarsgeld* (seven-year payment) can be clearly distinguished from the usual *bolwerken* (the obligation to contribute to the fortifications of the town) of the late Middle Ages, with which it co-existed.[36]

For Nijmegen such evidence is not available, but owing to its situation and its characteristic settlement it may no doubt be added to this list.

4. As to the fourth element of the palace, the *curtis* (manor), the sources from the Ottonian period do not give much information. In fact, only a few tenth-century confirmations of the Carolingian donation of the *nonae* of forty-four royal *villae* to the Chapter of Our Lady in Aachen by the Carolingian king Lothar II (855–69)

[35] Adriaan Verhulst, 'Het ontstaan en de vroege topografie van Antwerpen van de Romeinse tijd tot het begin van de 12e eeuw', in *De stad Antwerpen van de Romeinse tijd tot de 17de eeuw*, ed. L. Voet *et al.* (n.p., 1978), pp. 13–40, at pp. 30–1.

[36] See E.D. Rink, *Beschrijving der stad Tiel* (Tiel, 1836), pp. 8, 239–40 and Jan Kuys, *De ambtman in het kwartier van Nijmegen (ca. 1250–1543)* (Nijmegen, 1987), p. 271.

can be cited. These forty-four *villae* were situated in an area that stretched from Nijmegen in the north to Bastogne and neighbouring villages in the southern Ardennes. In fact, this area may be regarded as one large *Königslandschaft*, of which Nijmegen was the northern point. The *nonae* were a second tithe levied from the yield of these *villae*, in addition to the regular tithe to support the church. Of the donation by Lothar no charter has been handed down, only a number of confirmations, starting with that of Arnulf (887–95) in 888, which was followed by that of Henry I (919–36) in 930 and that of Otto I in 966.[37] A great difficulty is, of course, that we do not know to what extent these confirmations still reflected an existing situation. It is unclear if *ministri* of the *villae*, the royal fiscal officials, were still responsible for transferring the *nona pars* of the yield.

The other sources date from earlier or later. In a royal charter of 826 the *villa Bechi* (Beek) is mentioned, which is situated 'iuxta fiscum nostrum qui dicitur Niumaga' (next to our *fiscus* of Nijmegen). Leupen, who was the first to discuss this charter, identifies this *fiscus* with the *villa* of Nijmegen and he assumes that both corresponded with the parish of Nijmegen. In the Carolingian period it not only consisted of Nijmegen, but probably also of the territories of various later villages (Ooij, Persingen, Ubbergen, Wercheren, Hees, Hatert, Neerbosch and Weurt, and possibly also Malden and Groesbeek), an area of approximately 12×6 km.[38] The *fiscus* or *villa* of Nijmegen was probably organized as a bipartite domain with a directly exploited demesne (*terra salica*) and dependent tenancies. An indication of this is the late-medieval toponym *Rikessalike/Selick* as the name of a large leasehold originally possessed by the king.

It is hard to imagine that a *fiscus* or *villa* of this size, being partly virgin territory, formed the complete material basis which the king could fall back on when staying at Nijmegen. In the twelfth century at least, this basis must have been more solid, for in the famous *Indiculus curiarum que pertinent ad mensam regis Romanorum* (better known as *Tafelgüterverzeichnis*), a list of *curiae* that had to contribute to the maintenance of the Roman king, Nijmegen

[37] MGH DD Lotharii II, 43, Arnulfi, 31, Henrici I, 23 and Ottonis I, 323.

[38] *Codex Diplomatico Parmense*, I, *Secolo VIIII*, ed. U. Benassi (Parma, 1910), no. 1. Compare P. Leupen, 'Nijmegen en het Rijk', in *Königtum und Reichsgewalt am Niederrhein*, ed. Klaus Flink and Wilhelm Janssen, Klever Archiv, 4 (Cleves, 1983), pp. 57–78.

appears to be one of the *curiae* charged highest in its own geographical region (the Rhineland), together with, for example, Aachen.[39] There must have been other revenues, therefore, than those from the *villa* alone.

These will probably have been produced in the first place by the other royal estates in the vicinity.[40] The imperial forest Rijkswald (called *Ketelwoud* at the time), where Otto III was born in 980, was attached to the *villa*. As an enclave within this forest, which at the time must have stretched beyond Cleves, was situated Groesbeek, which in 1040 is referred to as a *royal villa*. South of it, on the river Meuse, was situated Mook, which, until the donation to two Chapters in Aachen in *c*. 1079, had been directly in royal hands. Beek and Ewijk, on the other hand, do not seem to have been direct royal possessions in the Ottonian period: in 949 Otto I donated them as confiscated property to St Florin's Church in Koblenz. Within a 50 km range, other royal estates can be found in the Ottonian period, e.g. at Zevenaar, Rheden, Heerewaarden with Maren and Kessel, and Tiel. It is very likely that these estates were involved in maintaining the court when it stayed at Nijmegen. The royal estate at Tiel is of special interest, because it was granted to Theophano as part of her dower on the occasion of her marriage in 972. In the twelfth century the charges imposed on Tiel are half as high as those imposed on Nijmegen, according to the above mentioned *Indiculus curiarum*.

Moreover, the estates of loyal followers of the king or those of ecclesiastical institutions with strong ties to the king may have played a role in the maintenance of the royal table, particularly if these estates came from the king in the first place. The property that count Wichman of Hamaland donated to his monastic foundation of Elten is an example. His donation was confirmed by Otto I in 970, who explicitly stated that part of the property had come from the king.[41] Other examples are the numerous old possessions of the imperial abbey of Lorsch in Betuwe, Liemers and elsewhere in the region and the property of the chapter of St Adalbert of Aachen in Neder-Betuwe and Maas en Waal

[39] *Das Tafelgüterverzeichnis des römischen Königs*, ed. Carlrichard Brühl and Theo Kölzer (Cologne and Vienna, 1979), p. 53.

[40] See for the following survey Guido Rotthoff, *Studien zur Geschichte des Reichsguts in Niederlothringen und Friesland während der sächsisch-salischen Kaiserzeit*, Rheinisches Archiv, 44 (Bonn 1953), *passim*; Leupen, 'Nijmegen' (see n. 38), *passim*.

[41] MGH DD O I, 397.

(*c.* 1000).[42] There is, however, no direct indication in the written sources of any service rendered to the king (*servitium regis*) by these ecclesiastical institutions while he stayed at Nijmegen.

It is possible that revenues from trade and traffic played a role. Wolfgang Metz pointed out that, as early as the tenth and eleventh centuries, many royal residences were of some significance as trading-places.[43] Moreover, many Carolingian royal *fisci* and certainly all centres of Ottonian castle-ban districts had a market. In Nijmegen the market cannot have been of much significance in the Ottonian period, because there is no evidence of coins minted here in this period (mintage in the ninth–thirteenth centuries is a certain indication of a market and the number of coins found is some measure of its significance). The first coin that has been identified as possibly having been minted in Nijmegen dates from the reign of Conrad II (1024–39).[44] Nijmegen does not seem to have had any significant active trade in the Ottonian period. The oldest toll-tariff of Koblenz (eleventh century), containing a comprehensive list of trading-places in this area, does not mention merchants from Nijmegen. The first archaeological traces of urban development date from the tenth/eleventh century, while the earliest written indication (a royal grant of mutual exemption from tolls in Worms and Nijmegen) dates from 1184.[45]

How important the palace of Nijmegen was from a political point of view is to be measured in the first place by its role in the royal itinerary. It is therefore necessary to establish how often the palace was visited, when these were special occasions, how long the visits lasted, etc. In this respect one should bear in mind that the sources provide only limited information on the royal *iter* (progress). In his important study on the kingdom of Otto I, Eckhardt Müller-Mertens calculated that for only 3% of the reign of this king is his place of residence explicitly mentioned in the sources and that for

[42] E.g. *Codex Laureshamensis*, ed. Karl Glöckner, 3 vols. (Darmstadt 1929–36 and reprinted 1975), I, cc. 24, 75, 96–118, 143b, 162, III, cc. 3613, 3797, 3817 (concerning Lorsch) and MGH DD O III, 262 (concerning St Adalbert at Aachen).

[43] Metz, *Servitium* (see n. 26), pp. 50–2.

[44] See Bernd Kluge, *Deutsche Münzgeschichte von der späten Karolingerzeit bis zum Ende der Salier (ca. 900 bis 1125)* (Sigmaringen, 1991), pp. 48 and 158 (no. 105).

[45] *Urkundenbuch der Stadt Duisburg*, I, ed. Werner Bergmann *et al.* (Düsseldorf, 1989), no. 15.

Table 1. *Visits of rulers to Nijmegen*

Ruler	Reign	Years total	Visits	Visit/ *n* years	Feasts	Assemblies (other)
Charlemagne	(768–814)	46	4	11.5	4	–
Louis the Pious	(814–40)	26	9	2.9	–	4
Lothar I	(840–55)	15	1	15	–	–
Lothar II	(855–69)	14	1	14	–	–
[Charles the Bald		1]				
Louis the Younger	(876–82)	6	1*	6	–	–
Arnulf	(887–95)	8	1	8	–	–
Zwentibald	(895–900)	5	1	5	–	–
[Charles the Simple		1]				
Otto I	(936–73)	37	3	12.3	–	1†
Otto II	(973–83)	10	5	2	–	–
Otto III	(983–1002)‡	19	5	3.8	–	1
Henry II	(1002–24)	22	7	3.1	2	1
Conrad II	(1024–39)	15	5	3	4	–
Henry III	(1039–47)	8	3	2.7	1	–

[Charles the Bald and Charles the Simple were western Frankish kings and probably gained their way to Nijmegen by force.]
* Siege only † Whitsuntide

‡ Theophano:	(983–91)	8	3	2.7	–	–

10% of that time there is some reason to doubt whether the place named was actually his place of residence.[46] Fortunately we may assume that the sources give us information on the most significant part of a king's reign, viz. the part that was already considered memorable by his contemporaries.

The first table shows how frequently each individual ruler (until 1047) is said to have visited Nijmegen, both in absolute terms and in relation to the time he reigned. Also, a survey is given of the number of visits on the occasion of certain feasts (Easter, Christmas and from 1002 also Whitsun), because as a rule these visits were connected with a ritual coronation (*coronatio*; *Festkrönung*) or at least a solemn 'going crowned' (*coronatus progrediri*; *unter Krone gehen*) of the king, as well as with a court day. On such days, and at other assemblies, the king presented himself in his full regalia and in a representative ambiance to many people.[47]

[46] Eckhardt Müller-Mertens, *Die Reichsstruktur im Spiegel der Herrschaftspraxis Ottos des Grossen* (Berlin, 1980), p. 91.

[47] See Carlrichard Brühl, 'Krönen- und Krönungsbrauch im frühen und hohen Mittelalter', *HZ*, 234 (1982), 1–31.

How demanding the court was on such occasions appears from the fact that once (953) Otto I even had to cancel an Easter celebration in the great palace in Aachen at the last moment, because the necessary preparations had not been made ('quia nichil sibi dignum ibi paratum esset').[48]

Table 1 shows that the number of visits of each ruler varied. On closer consideration, however, there appears to be some hidden continuity. Three of Charlemagne's four visits took place after 804, when the construction of his new palace was nearing its completion; so in the last few years of his reign there was one visit per 3.3 years. For the rulers from Lothar I to Otto I the great political instability in the region should be taken into account. They were confronted with attacks of Northmen with western Frankish aspirations (two western Frankish kings actually resided at Nijmegen) and with rebellious magnates from Lotharingia. It was only in the tenth century that Otto I managed to achieve a certain stability. He himself went to Nijmegen relatively seldom, but his successors visited the palace with the same frequency as Charlemagne after 804 and Louis the Pious (814–40). Thus, in the years between 777 and 1047, the frequency of the visits of the king to Nijmegen in politically stable times is a constant factor. The rhythm of Theophano's visits in the period of her regency (983–91) conforms to the pattern.

The table further shows that both the early Carolingians and Henry II and his successors regularly used the palace of Nijmegen for the celebration of feasts and for assemblies. Moreover, in 1018 a synod took place there and in 1036 king Henry, son of the emperor Conrad II, and the Danish princess Cunihild were married in this palace.

The importance of Nijmegen as a 'festal palace' (*Festpfalz*) in the eleventh century is all the more remarkable, because of the general shift towards the episcopal cities as places of residence during the festal days from the later years of the reign of Otto III onwards. Müller-Mertens, however, has pointed out that a regional differentiation should be made. In the younger parts of the empire, where there were no traditional political centres to fall back on, the cities were often visited, whereas in the older parts the Carolingian and Ottonian palaces remained relatively

[48] Widukind, *Res gestae Saxonicae*, lib. III, c. 14, AQDG 8, p. 136.

Table 2. *Visits of Ottonian rulers to places of residence in Lower Lotharingia and 'Frisia-Hamaland'*

	Henry I				Otto I				Otto II				Otto III*				Henry II			
	v	d	f	a	v	d	f	a	v	d	f	a	v	d	f	a	v	d	f	a
Aachen	1	1			8	87	3	4	5	25	2		$8^{(1)}$	$230^{(2)}$	$4^{(1)}$	1	10	51	1	2
Cologne					7	35	1	4	2	2	1		$8^{(5)}$	$78^{(75)}$	$4^{(2)}$		8	14		
Nijmegen					3	43		1	5	40			$5^{(3)}$	$60^{(55)}$		1	7	39	2	1
Duisburg	1	1			2	5		1	3	3			4	5	1		4	4		
Utrecht					1	3			3	30	1						3	6		
Tiel									1	20			$1^{(1)}$	$13^{(13)}$			1	39		
Bonn	1	3							1	1							1	1		
Liège													1	1			3	5	1	
Werden																	1	1	1	

* The superscript numbers refer to the period of regency of Theophano (983–91)
v = visits d = days f = feasts a = assemblies (other than feasts)

important.[49] It is this continuity of royal interest of the ancient Carolingian palaces (and it is not for nothing that they are still referred to as *palatia*!), which ultimately provides the explanation of Nijmegen's prominence as a *Festpfalz* in the eleventh century. An ancient, though interrupted, tradition was continued here, where the necessary facilities already existed.

Table 2 gives the profile of the palace of Nijmegen during the Ottonian period in a comparative survey. The comparison includes a number of places within a regional framework, including both Lower Lotharingia and the area to the north of it, named 'Frisia-Hamaland' by Müller-Mertens.[50] It makes sense to combine these two areas, as Nijmegen was situated exactly on the border between them. In the table the most important places of residence in this combined area are listed.

As Table 2 shows, Henry I seldom visited this area, which he could not get properly under control. From Otto I onwards, a constant clustering of the four most important places of residence emerges, of which Nijmegen is one, after Aachen (the regular place of coronation of the kings) and Cologne (seat of the archbishop and archchancellor). Gradually other places also become more important, without this central group losing its prominent position. The occasional long visits of Otto II and Otto III to Tiel were undoubtedly connected with the fact that the *curtis* (manor) of Tiel was part of Theophano's dower.

The first Ottonians preferred to celebrate the feasts in their homeland, Saxony. The table shows, however, that gradually more feasts came to be celebrated in the western area, especially at Aachen and Cologne, but also elsewhere, in particular by Henry II. He celebrated Easter twice at Nijmegen. From that time until 1047 this place was a very important *Festpfalz*.

So far we have only been able to distinguish a few central functions of Nijmegen in the tenth century. Nijmegen was the centre of a large ancient parish and possibly also of the royal domains in the surrounding area, including the imperial forest. The existence of a castle-ban district and a relatively unimportant market in Nijmegen is plausible, but cannot as yet be proven. So

[49] Eckhardt Müller-Mertens, 'Reich und Hauptorte der Salier: Probleme und Fragen', in *Die Salier und das Reich*, ed. Stefan Weinfurter, 3 vols. (Sigmaringen, 1991), I, pp. 139–58, at pp. 154–5.

[50] Müller-Mertens, *Reichsstruktur* (see n. 46), pp. 83–5 and maps.

far as is known, there was no count in residence there. Moreover, Gennep, on the river Meuse, seems to have been the principal place of the only *pagus* in this area mentioned in the contemporary sources, the *pagus Ganipi*.[51] What did the royal palace at Nijmegen add to these central functions?

In the second half of the eighth century Charlemagne built his new palaces at Aachen, Ingelheim and Nijmegen, apparently with the intention of creating a link between the ancient western Frankish and the new eastern Frankish parts of his empire. For Nijmegen this function became particularly prominent in 830, when Charles' son Louis the Pious, who distrusted the western Franks, convened a general assembly in Nijmegen precisely because the eastern Franks were also able to come there.[52] But the division of the empire in the ninth century radically changed the political landscape and soon another function of Nijmegen became more important: that of 'border-palace' between the *Königslandschaft* around Aachen in the south on the one hand and the peripheral zone in the north-west ('Frisia-Hamaland'), which was threatened by many dangers, on the other. This function is clearly perceptible as early as 837. In that year Northmen invaded *Frisia* and caused havoc in Dorestad. Louis the Pious came to Nijmegen with military forces, whereupon the Northmen withdrew.[53] There are later examples also from which it appears that, in times of acute danger, Nijmegen served as an outpost of the authority of the king and in general was a link between centre and periphery in his kingdom.

Only seldom do the sources give an indication of the daily routine of the rulers who visited Nijmegen. Louis the Pious is reported to have gone to Nijmegen twice in order to hunt there ('causa venandi').[54] Thietmar of Merseburg reports that, during a longer stay in Lent of 1003, Henry II first devoted himself to seeking the Empire of God and only after that to satisfying his physical needs.[55] The palace apparently provided facilities for

51 MGH DD O I, 115.

52 *Annales Bertiniani*, s.a. 830, AQDG 6, p. 12: 'Noviomago ... ubi Saxones et orientales Franci convenire potuissent.'

53 *Ibid.*, s.a. 837, AQDG 6, p. 32.

54 *Annales regni Francorum*, s.a. 817 and 825, AQDG 5, pp. 112, 140.

55 Thietmar of Merseburg, *Chronicon*, lib. V, c. 28, AQDG 9, p. 222: 'ibi moratur, primo regnum Dei iusticiamque eius querere, postea humane fragilitati studens necessaria suggerere'. Compare Matthew 6:33: 'Seek ye first the Kingdom of God, and all the rest shall be added unto you.'

both activities. In general, however, the rulers, like Theophano and Otto III according to the *Annales Quedlinburgenses*, will have gone there in order to govern.[56] Unfortunately, there is a limited amount of evidence about the way the Ottonian rulers governed from this palace. Specifically, this is provided by a few narrative sources and some thirty royal charters in which a legal act taking place in Nijmegen was laid down (*actum Noviomago*).[57]

Of these thirty charters fourteen were intended for a person or institution outside Lower Lotharingia and 'Frisia-Hamaland'. There are charters for recipients in Upper Lotharingia (the archbishop of Trier), in Hessen (the monastery of Fulda), in eastern Saxony (the monastery of Gandersheim) and even various charters for recipients in Italy (the diocese of Pavia, the abbot of Bobbio, the church of Parma). Thus it appears that during a visit of the ruler, Nijmegen functioned as the temporary centre of the kingdom and even of the Holy Roman Empire. Unfortunately the charters do not, as a rule, contain any lists of witnesses, but often a few persons are mentioned thanks to whose intervention the legal act took place. These persons are often relatives of the ruler (e.g. Theophano and duke Henry of Bavaria, *nepos* of Otto III) or at least persons who are very close to the king and who follow him on his travels during a longer period of time (e.g. archbishop Willigis of Mainz, archchaplain and archchancellor of the German kingdom, and bishop Hildebald of Worms, chancellor).

The sources report that at various assemblies held at Nijmegen many people were present ('multi adessent') from everywhere ('in conventu totius populi; undique frequentissimi illuc convenirent').[58] The names of persons present are mentioned only a few times. At the *generale placitum* led by Otto I in 949 the following people were present: the archbishops of Trier and Cologne, the bishops of Utrecht, Metz, Paderborn and Liège, the dukes of Lotharingia and Swabia, some four counts and others who remain unnamed.[59]

Of the thirty charters which mention a royal *actum* at Nijmegen

[56] *Annales Quedlinburgenses*, s.a. 991, MGH SS III, p. 68: 'vel imperando vel regendo'.

[57] To this one letter, directed to Theophano (July–September, 986), can be added: *Lettres de Gerbert (983–997)*, ed. Julien Havet (Paris, 1889), ep. 89, pp. 80–1.

[58] Alpertus of Metz, *De diversitate temporum*, ed. Hans van Rij (Amsterdam, 1980), lib. I, c. 3 and lib. II, c. 16, pp. 14, 74; MGH DD O I, 111.

[59] MGH DD O I, 111.

sixteen were intended for a recipient either in Lower Lotharingia (twelve of these distributed among the palace chapel in Aachen, the abbey of Stavelot and the monastery of Nivelles) or in 'Frisia-Hamaland' (two for the monastery of Elten, one for the episcopal church of Utrecht and one for count Theodoric of Holland). Two other charters were intended for recipients elsewhere (the monastery of Prüm, ecclesiastical institutions at St Omer) but concerned possessions in Lower Lotharingia and 'Frisia-Hamaland'. All the cases of royal administration of justice at Nijmegen known from that time concern parties or possessions in these same two areas (the abbey of Susteren; the abbey of Stavelot; the monastery of Nivelles; count Balderich and his wife Adela and their behaviour, for example towards the monastery of Elten).

The impression the charters convey is confirmed by reports about personal visits in the narrative sources. It is reported, for example, how in 1018 a large group of inhabitants of the present province of South Holland came to Nijmegen to lodge a complaint with the emperor about count Theodoric of Holland ('cuncti comprovinciales cesari in Niumagun queruntur'). Henry II thereupon sent troops on a punitive expedition.[60] Another example shows how possessions in the vicinity of Nijmegen were sufficient reason for an abbot from northern France to visit the palace: Reginald, abbot of St Omer, came to king Otto in the royal palace of Nijmegen (probably in July 956) with relics of St Omer in an attempt to regain usurped property on the other side of the Rhine that belonged to the monastery.[61] We owe the only 'court scene' at Nijmegen that has come down to us to a visit that Poppo, the later abbot of Stavelot-Malmédy, paid to Nijmegen probably in 1015. As a prior of the monastery of St Vedast in Arras he had to take care of certain possessions in the Betuwe at the time. On his visit to the court he was confronted with *ludi histrionum* and with an emperor, Henry II, who feasted his eyes on a spectacle in which a naked man whose body had been smeared with honey was exhibited to bears.[62] Finally, an example of traffic in the opposite direction. Alpert of Metz reports that Liutgard, the abbess of Elten, was consulted by people from the palace (of

60 Thietmar of Merseburg, *Chronicon*, lib. VIII, c. 28, AQDG 9, p. 470.

61 Folcwinus the Deacon, *Gesta abbatum s. Bertini Sithiensium*, c. 109, MGH SS XIII, pp. 630–1.

62 *Vita Popponis abbatis Stabulensis*, c. 12, MGH SS XI, p. 301.

Nijmegen) 'ad suarum rerum capiendum consilium' (in order to obtain advice about their own business).[63]

All this provides sufficient reason to conclude that Lower Lotharingia and 'Frisia-Hamaland' together formed the hinterland of the palace at Nijmegen. It was not an administrative district in the modern sense with an administrative centre linked exclusively with that district. After all, during royal visits the importance of Nijmegen as an administrative centre was not limited to that district, but was felt all over the *regnum*, indeed throughout the *imperium*. Besides, the district contained other royal residences, of which two (Aachen and Cologne) were clearly more important than Nijmegen. Lastly, many royal charters intended for recipients in these areas were issued in distant parts of the empire.

The above discussion can be summarized as follows. By her marriage Theophano became a member of an itinerant court. Indeed, from 972 onwards she led an itinerant life herself. Of the 107 places of residence of the empress that are known, Nijmegen stands out as the place that is connected with two important moments in her life: the birth of her son Otto III and her death. However, there is no reason to assume that Theophano had a personal preference for Nijmegen. The palace was part of the Carolingian heritage which had devolved upon the Ottonians and which was the infrastructure on which their kingship in these regions rested. Theophano used the palace of Nijmegen in exactly the same way as her father-in-law, her husband and her son, that is as a regularly visited seat of government, which was particularly important as the political centre on the border between Lower Lotharingia and 'Frisia-Hamaland', but not as a festal palace as Charlemagne did and as did Henry II and his successors. When she went there, it was in all probability for political routine, 'vel imperando vel regendo', rather than because of any strong personal preference for Nijmegen.

[63] Alpertus of Metz, *De diversitate temporum* (see n. 58), lib. I, c. 3 p. 12.

15

The so-called women's gallery in the medieval church: an import from Byzantium*

HILTJE F.H. ZOMER

Introduction

Although galleries[1] are not at all uncommon, they have so far been studied neither fully nor systematically. In the literature that does exist the gallery is discussed only indirectly, for example within the general description of a church or in relation to the liturgy. The question is never put, let alone answered, why galleries should have made their appearance in certain places and at certain times.

In German literature the gallery is often referred to as the *Frauenempore*. This name has its origin in the idea that the gallery was built as a special place for women in order to separate them from men during services.[2] From the third century onwards, liturgical texts recommended the separation of the sexes in churches.[3] Nowhere, however, is it stated that women had to be

* This chapter is part of a general thesis about galleries, which is now in preparation.

[1] A gallery is a partial upper storey with a floor and a roof, found, as a rule, above the side aisle and/or the narthex of a church. It is accessible by means of a stairway and opens onto the nave by means of an arcade.

[2] See for example C. Coüasnon, *The Church of the Holy Sepulchre in Jerusalem* (London, 1974), p. 32; K.G. Holum, *Theodosian Empresses: Women and Imperial Dominion in Late Antiquity* (Berkeley, Los Angeles and London, 1982), p. 140; F. Möbius, 'Basilikale Raumstruktur im Feudalisierungs-Prozess: Anmerkungen zu einer Ikonologie der Seitenschiffe', *Wissenschaftliche Zeitschrift Ernst-Moritz-Arndt-Universität*, gesellsch. und sprachwiss. Reihe (1980), 19–23; H. Möbius, *Die Stiftskirche zu Gernrode* (Berlin, 1972), p. 13; F. van de Paverd, *Zur Geschichte der Messliturgie in Antiocheia und Konstantinopel gegen Ende des vierten Jahrhunderts* (Rome, 1968), p. 26; C. Strube, review of T.F. Mathews, *The Early Churches of Constantinople: Architecture and Liturgy* (see n. 11), *BZ*, 67 (1974), 408–13, at p. 411.

[3] Hippolytus of Rome, *Traditio Apostolica*, *Syriac Didascalia* and *Constitutiones Apostolorum*; see also K. Gamber, *Liturgie und Kirchenbau* (Ratisbon, 1976), 24;

accommodated in galleries. If scholars have assumed that the galleries in the Byzantine Empire and in Western Europe were reserved for women, that is for two reasons: first because separate galleries for women were designed in later synagogues, and second because the sixth-century Greek word for a gallery means 'women's place'. But if galleries were a way of obeying this general liturgical instruction, how is it that churches with galleries are found only in certain areas and then mainly in conventual churches where the separation of the sexes was least necessary? Some of the earliest examples are the churches of John Stoudios and SS Sergios and Bakchos in Constantinople, both monastic churches, where women were not normally admitted.

Equally indefensible is the theory, maintained with a special tenacity in the French literature, that the gallery was built to support the heavy barrel-vault, since churches with a wooden roof sometimes had galleries too.[4] Besides, there were many other solutions to the problem of the heavy vault. It remains unclear why builders should have chosen the gallery as the solution in some churches.

Nor can the gallery be explained as a mere stylistic feature. The theory of the gradual spread of a type of church with a gallery from Constantinople to other specified areas is untenable because the gallery-church also occurs in such isolated and remote places as, for example, St Cyriacus in Gernrode. If galleries are explained by stylistic influence from other churches, the question arises why this entirely new 'stylistic feature' was adopted precisely there.[5] A more acceptable explanation of the gallery is that the west gallery, in particular, was a place of honour for royalty.[6] But that does not

H. Kähler, *Die frühe Kirche: Kult und Kultraum* (Frankfurt a.M., Berlin, etc., 1982), pp. 24 ff; Möbius, 'Basilikale Raumstruktur' (see n. 2), p. 20.

[4] See for example M. Aubert and S. Goubet, *Cathédrales, abbatiales, collégiales, prieurés*, Romans de France (Paris, 1965), p. 108; B. Craplet, *Auvergne romane*, La Nuit des Temps, 2 (Paris, 5th edn, 1978), pp. 45, 53, 99; A. Courtens, *Romanische Kunst in Belgien* (Vienna, 1969), 54–5, explains the gallery in the church of St Vincent in Soignies in this way; however, it is not certain that the church originally had a heavy barrel-vault.

[5] See for example R. Krautheimer, *Early Christian and Byzantine Architecture* (Harmondsworth, 4th edn, 1986), p. 336; F. Möbius and H. Möbius, *Sakrale Baukunst* (Berlin, 1963), pp. 9–10, 178.

[6] For the Carolingian west gallery see for example A. Fuchs, 'Zum Problem der Westwerke', in *Karolingische und ottonische Kunst: Werden–Wesen–Wirkung*, ed. F. Gerke *et al.* (Wiesbaden, 1957), pp. 110–12; A. Schmidt, 'Westwerke und Doppelchöre: höfische und liturgische Einflüsse auf die Kirchenbauten des frühen Mittelalters', *Westfälische Zeitschrift*, 106 (1956), 347–438, at pp. 393–4. For Mistra

explain why, in the German Empire, the gallery is encountered in women's convents in the first place.

Galleries are already found in some of the eastern churches established by Constantine the Great; after that period they occur, rather abruptly, at various times and places, mostly in small groups. A fruitful basis for research on this phenomenon is its socio-historical background, by which I mean the patrons who commissioned the buildings concerned and their intentions, assuming that the gallery is a vehicle of significance (*Bedeutungsträger*): a symbol of sacred, universal emperorship.

I tried to find an identical historical situation in each period in which galleries were built, and to find an explanation for the appearance of galleries in various times and places.

A brief description of the origins and development of galleries in the fourth–sixth centuries in the Roman-Byzantine Empire is given in the first sections of this article; the subsequent sections deal with Theophano and her contribution to gallery-building in the German Empire and the influence she may have exerted on gallery-building in the new kingdom that came into being in France.

The construction of galleries by Constantine the Great and his successors

Constantine the Great became universal ruler of the Mediterranean world only after the conquest of the Roman Empire in 324. The imperial triumphs were won in the Sign of the Cross and went hand in hand with the victory and spread of Christianity. It was not until 324 that Constantine and his family began to build churches with galleries, and then only in prestigious cities in eastern Roman territory. These bases of support for his spiritual and political power were Jerusalem (church of the Holy Sepulchre), Antioch (the Golden Octagon) and Constantinople (the first Hagia Sophia).

As a Christian emperor, Constantine could no longer condone the unlimited veneration of himself as a god. As the representative

and Trebizond see A. Bryer, 'Une église "à la demande du client" à Trébizonde', *Proche-Orient Chrétien*, 32 (1982), 217–32; C. Delvoye, 'Considérations sur l'emploi des tribunes dans l'église de la Vierge Hodigitria à Mistra', in *Actes du XIIe Congrès international des études byzantines*, III (Belgrade, 1964); W. Löhneysen, *Mistra, Griechenlands Schicksal im Mittelalter* (Munich, 1977), *passim*.

of Christ on earth, however, he was honoured with such titles and protocol that there was little detectable difference in this respect from the earlier deified emperors. The homage paid to Constantine increased considerably after 324, probably owing to closer contacts with the Hellenistic royal courts. To enumerate a few aspects of this homage: the double-edged diadem; the coins on which Constantine appears as *a deo coronato* (crowned by God); the exalted titles for him, as well as for his wife, Fausta, and his mother, Helena; and the appointment of *silentiarioi*, whose task it was to secure a devout silence around the divine emperor. In contrast to the pagan emperors, Constantine as the first Christian emperor had to distinguish himself above all within his basic sphere of power, the church.

In this connection it would not be surprising if he did establish a sign of his holy emperorship, sanctified by Christ, precisely within the church. This is how we should see the gallery. The motif of an elevated loge with an arcade was always firmly associated with an emperor. Imperial market halls were sometimes encircled with two levels of colonnades, and raised loggias or galleries were also found on the exteriors of palaces and gateways. These galleries were maintained as a sign of honour on the exterior of royal houses until the tenth century.[7] Since Christian worship, in contrast to pagan gatherings, took place inside, all attention in the early Christian basilicas was focused on the interior. The decoration and marks of honour, such as the *fastigium*, were transferred to the inside. This may also have been the

[7] For imperial basilicas see G. Egger, 'Römischer Kaiserkult und konstantinischer Kirchenbau', *Jahreshefte des Österreichischen Archäologischen Institutes in Wien*, 43 (1958), *Hauptblatt*, pp. 120–32, at p. 128; R. Krautheimer, 'The Constantinian basilica', *DOP*, 21 (1967), 117–40, at p. 137; J.F. Merriman, *Aristocratic and Imperial Patronage of the Decorative Arts in Rome and Constantinople A.D. 337–395* (Ann Arbor, 1980), p. 156. For exterior galleries see A. Boëthius, 'The reception halls of the Roman emperors', *British School at Athens: Annual*, 46 (1951), 28; K.G. Holum and G. Vikan, 'The Trier ivory, adventus ceremonial and the relics of St Stephen', *DOP*, 33 (1979), 115–33, at p. 125, n. 62; E.B. Smith, *Architectural Symbolism of Imperial Rome and the Middle Ages* (Princeton, 1956), pp. 31–7, 150; A. Stange, *Basiliken, Kuppelkirchen, Kathedralen: das himmlische Jerusalem in der Sicht der Jahrhunderte* (Ratisbon, 1964), pp. 73–4; K.M. Swoboda, *Römische und Romanische Paläste* (Vienna, 3rd edn, 1969), p. 276 and illustration. For the relationship of the throne-room with heaven and with the church see I. Lavin, 'The House of the Lord: aspects of the role of palace triclinia in the architecture of late Antiquity and the early Middle Ages', *The Art Bulletin*, 44 (1962), 1–27, at pp. 16–17; Stange, *Basiliken*, pp. 73–4; U. Süsenbach, *Christuskult und kaiserliche Baupolitik bei Konstantin* (Bonn, 1977), p. 57; L. Völkl, 'Die konstantinischen Kirchenbauten nach Eusebius', *Rivista di Archeologia Christiana*, 29 (1953), 49–66; 187–206, at pp. 191–9.

case with galleries. The imperial family left its own mark on each of the three churches mentioned above, using a form that was so taken for granted, that it attracted no special attention.

Constantine never visited the church of the Holy Sepulchre and the galleries could not have been intended for him as a sitting area. In modern literature on this topic the galleries are still described as a place for women, although, at that time, they were referred to by the neutral term '*hyperoa*' meaning 'elevated areas'.[8] Nothing indicates that the women sat here, separated from the men, in conjunction with the separation of the sexes.

One of the most important early sources bearing on this question is St John Chrysostom (*c.* 400). When he preached about the separation of the sexes – probably in the Golden Octagon at Antioch – he pointed at the wooden partitions, and not at the galleries, although they clearly existed.[9] In another sermon given in the first Hagia Sophia in Constantinople, St John Chrysostom speaks disapprovingly of the women *above*, but careful reading of the text reveals that he speaks of the women adorned with gold and pearls.[10] He evidently had in mind the empress and her

8 In Antiquity and in the fourth century the gallery was referred to by neutral terms such as *hyperoa* or *stoa diple*, which means 'upper floor' or 'double portico'. See for example the description of the Holy Sepulchre and the Golden Octagon by Eusebios, *Vita Constantini*, 3, 37 and 3, 50 (*Eusebius Werke*, I, 1, *Über das Leben des Kaisers Konstantin*, ed. F. Winkelmann, GCS (Berlin, 1975), pp. 100, 104–5). Not until the sixth century did words appear that link the galleries to women: Paul Silentiarios, *Descriptio ecclesiae sanctae Sophiae*, vv. 389, 587; Prokopios of Caesarea (*De aedificiis*, I, 1, 58, in *Opera omnia*, ed. J. Haury and G. Wirth, I, Bibliotheca scriptorum Graecorum et Romanorum Teubneriana (Leipzig, 1964), p. 14), also uses words such as *gynaikonitis*, 'women's place'; Chorikios of Gaza uses similar words in *Laudes Marciani episcopi*, II, 47 (in *Opera*, ed. R. Foerster and E. Richtsteig, Bibliotheca scriptorum Graecorum et Romanorum Teubneriana (Leipzig, 1929), p. 40). In the seventh century the word *katechoumenon*, 'place for catechumens', for gallery came into use. It is often used by Constantine Porphyrogennetos in his book *De ceremoniis*.

9 John Chrysostom in Mt. Hom. 73–4, 3, PG 55, 507. Quoted and explained by van de Paverd, *Zur Geschichte* (see n. 2), p. 26. Van de Paverd bases his opinion that Chrysostom preached this sermon in a church without galleries on this fact, for otherwise Chrysostom would have pointed to the galleries. There is no reason to believe that Chrysostom preached in a church other than the Golden Octagon (with galleries) for he was a cleric in that church. Only exceptionally did Chrysostom serve in another church, for instance when the Golden Octagon was being repaired. See C. Baur, *Der heilige Johannes Chrysostomus und seine Zeit*, 2 vols. (Munich, 1929–30), I, p. 22. In my opinion this sermon gives proof that common women were separated from men by screens.

10 John Chrysostom in Ps. 48, 17 Hom. 5, PG 55, 507; quoted and explained by van de Paverd, *Zur Geschichte* (see n. 2), p. 420.

imperial household, which would conform to St John's critical attitude towards the luxury of the reigning empress Eudoxia, wife of Arkadios (395–408).

The exalted symbolism with regard to the gallery may derive from the custom that the empress and her retinue sat in the gallery of the court churches.

Churches with galleries in the late fourth and fifth centuries

The galleries in the three eastern churches of Constantine the Great are not only remarkable in themselves, but it is also noteworthy that they are found in various types of churches. The Holy Sepulchre complex consisted of two parts, a basilican church with galleries and the central rotunda of the Anastasis, probably also with galleries: the Golden Octagon had a central form, too.[11]

In the West both plans, central and basilican, were adopted by the Roman emperors. The emperor Gratian (367–83) had galleries added to the basilican part of the court church at his imperial residence in Trier.[12] In 374 Gratian, born of humble status, married Constantine the Great's granddaughter, who came from Constantinople. Gratian's deliberate addition of galleries to an existing church suggests his need to attune for her his detailed imperial ceremonial to that of Constantinople, where the gallery of the first Hagia Sophia most probably was reserved for the empress and her retinue.

The only other church known to have galleries in the western territory is S. Lorenzo in Milan. This church has a central plan and can be regarded as an imperial foundation. All the signs point to Theodosios I (378–95) having founded it during his stay in Milan

[11] We do not know the form of the first Hagia Sophia, a church with galleries. The arguments adduced by R.J. Mainstone, *Hagia Sophia: Architecture, Structure and Liturgy of Justinian's Great Church* (London, 1988), pp. 133 ff, and T.F. Mathews, *The Early Churches of Constantinople: Architecture and Liturgy* (London, 1971), pp. 12 ff, in support of a basilican form are not very convincing. Some fragments of the west part of the second Hagia Sophia have been excavated by Schneider. This church was consecrated *c.* 415 during Pulcheria's reign (413–53). See for example Mainstone, *Hagia Sophia*, p. 135, and A.M. Schneider, 'Die Grabung im Westhof der Sophienkirche', in Mainstone, *Sophienkirche zu Konstantinopel*, Istanbuler Forschungen, 12 (Berlin, 1941), pp. 7–22, who emphasize the similar situation of the entry-sides of the Holy Sepulchre and of the second Hagia Sophia.

[12] This is the existing cathedral in Trier. Krautheimer, *Early Christian* (see n. 5), p. 85; Stange, *Basiliken* (see n. 7), p. 110.

(388–91).[13] For centuries after *c.* 400 no more gallery-churches were built by rulers in western Roman territory.

The building and development of this type of church continued in the East where the sacrality of universal emperorship was maintained. It is noteworthy that here initially the basilican form was chosen. The first basilicas with galleries in Constantinople were established by royal women.[14] An outstanding role in this was notably played by the powerful Pulcheria (414–53), who dominated her weak brother, Theodosios II (408–50).

Why did these royal women, in contrast to the emperors of the West, choose the basilican form, which had been 'out of fashion' for almost a century? Why did these very women use the basilica of the Holy Sepulchre as an example? This question can be answered, when we consider the historical context and sources of this period dealing with its reputed foundress, Helena, Constantine the Great's mother. According to Eusebios, the church of the Holy Sepulchre was commissioned by Constantine the Great.[15] In the fifth century, however, more voices could be heard saying that Helena was the foundress. These utterances are likely to have originated mainly from the circle of distinguished women surrounding the emperor. Helena's cult had already strongly developed at the court of Theodosios I, where women were portrayed with all the virtues (faith, philanthropy, concern for the dynasty) which Helena had also possessed. In much the same manner, for example, Theodosios' wife played an important role in the realization of the imperial propaganda. St Ambrose of Milan († 397), an influential person in court circles, was the first person to attribute the discovery of the 'True Cross' to Helena in his funeral oration for Theodosios I.

[13] D. Kinney, 'The evidence for the dating of S. Lorenzo in Milan', *Journal of the Society of Architectural Historians*, 31 (1972), 92–107, at pp. 105–7, and R. Krautheimer, *Three Christian Capitals: Topography and Politics* (Berkeley, 1983), pp. 88 ff, attribute the church to another ruler, but I fully subscribe to the view of S. Lewis, 'San Lorenzo revisited: a Theodosian palace church at Milan', *Journal of the Society of Architectural Historians*, 32 (1973), 197–222, at pp. 203–22. See author's forthcoming dissertation for further arguments in favour of this view.

[14] Two galleried basilicas were dedicated to Mary in the Blachernai and in the Chalkoprateia quarters by Pulcheria. The other churches were the church of St Polyeuktos founded by Anicia Juliana and the basilica of the Stoudios monastery. It is unclear whether John Stoudios really was the founder; see H. Delehaye, 'Stoudion-Stoudios', *Analecta Bollandiana*, 52 (1934), 64–5.

[15] Eusebios, *Vita Constantini* (see n. 8), 3, 37.

In Ambrose's eyes Helena was the second Mary. Just as Mary had overcome evil by giving birth to Jesus, so had Helena by finding the Cross.[16] St Ambrose may have got the information for his oration from the distinguished women of that time. In imitation of Helena these pious women, for example Egeria in *c.* 394 and the two Melanias (grandmother 342–409 and granddaughter 383–439), went on pilgrimages. These wealthy, noble women may have functioned as intermediates between Italy and Constantinople for the veneration of Helena. During their many travels they made contact with leading clerics and with the empresses Pulcheria and Eudokia, sister and wife of Theodosios II grandson of Theodosios I, respectively.[17]

At that time, Helena was named as the foundress of the Holy Sepulchre basilica by a number of writers.[18] It is striking that Rufinus was the first of these authors. This cleric kept intense contact with Melania the Elder. He accompanied her on a pilgrimage and worked together with her in Jerusalem for eighteen years. After him, other authors orientated towards Constantinople also ascribed the pious founding of the basilica to Helena. In this connection it is not important whether Helena actually dictated the building plan for the basilica or not; crucial is the question what people believed or wanted to believe. It was at this same time that the basilicas with galleries appeared in Constantinople. In my opinion, it was Pulcheria who instigated their building in imitation of Helena. Pulcheria, who used every opportunity to emphasize her virginity, had every reason to put herself on a line with Helena, and consequently with Mary. Who else could she use as an example in her position? As a woman she could hardly identify with Christ.[19]

By instituting herself as a New Helena/Mary, by having basilicas with galleries erected, she found a sacred legitimacy for her illegitimate position of authority. At the council of Chalcedon,

[16] I owe this information to the excellent books of J.W. Drijvers, *Helena Augusta, the Mother of Constantine the Great and the Legend of her Finding of the True Cross* (Leiden, New York, etc., 1992), pp. 117, 123, and Holum, *Theodosian Empresses* (see n. 2), pp. 34 ff.

[17] Holum, *ibid.*, p. 183, E.D. Hunt, *Holy Land Pilgrimage in the Later Roman Empire A.D. 312–460* (Oxford, 1982), pp. 224, 231.

[18] Egeria, *Peregrinatio*, 25, 9: 'sub matris praesentia suae'; Rufinus, *Historia ecclesiastica*, X, 7, 8; Socrates, *Historia ecclesiastica*, I, 17; Theodoret of Cyrrhus, *Historia ecclesiastica*, I, 17; texts in Drijvers, *Helena Augusta* (see n. 16), pp. 247 ff.

[19] Holum, *Theodosian Empresses* (see n. 2), pp. 139–43, 145.

when Mary was once again proclaimed the Mother of God, Pulcheria allowed herself to be honoured as a New Helena.[20]

The basilicas with galleries in Constantinople were, however, not the only churches with galleries. They also appeared in important cities in Greece.[21] When we review the historical background of the establishment of these churches, there always seems to have been a reason for the emperor or empress to use the founding of a gallery-church as a power symbol within the given political situation.[22]

The construction of galleries during the Justinianic dynasty, 518–610

Justinian I (518–65) certainly was the most powerful emperor of the Byzantine Empire. Through his many conquests, including those in the West, the reality of a universal emperorship came once again within reach. By means of his clever politics in relation to the pope, he was able to exercise his will over the church as well.[23] With an abundance of symbols in ceremonial and in architecture, Justinian could clearly demonstrate that he acted as God's representative, that he himself was nearly a god.

Churches with galleries continued to be built, but during Justinian's reign new words for galleries indicated that they were linked with women. Besides, the fact that in Hagia Sophia, for example, the galleries were connected to the palace by a passage shows that the women of the court had a regular place there, so that galleries not only had a symbolic meaning, but also a clearly functional purpose.

To accentuate the lustre of his divine emperorship in the church

[20] See for example Drijvers, *Helena Augusta* (see n. 16), p. 151, and Holum, *Theodosian Empresses* (see n. 2), p. 216.

[21] For example in Thessalonike, Lechaion/Corinth, Philippi and Stobi.

[22] However, it is also plausible that bishops and other dignitaries adopted the galleried church in order to show their allegiance to the emperor in Constantinople. These churches, associated with women, may have been suitable for non-imperial authorities in particular. In this way they had their own power-symbol without being pretentious. This article is too short to deal with all the fifth-century churches in this connection. In the author's dissertation, Asia Minor, Syria/Palestine and Egypt are also dealt with.

[23] See for example R.A. Markus, 'Carthage–Prima Justiniana–Ravenna: an aspect of Justinian's *Kirchenpolitik*', *Byzantion*, 49 (1979), 277–302; O.G. von Simson, *Sacred Fortress: Byzantine Art and Statecraft in Ravenna* (Princeton, 2nd edn, 1987), pp. 11–13.

building itself, Justinian needed another stronger symbol, one that was not 'spoiled' by practical usage. He found this, I believe, in the dome, where possible, combined with a centralized plan. In the East, the dome was of old the symbol of the cosmos, for example in depictions of royalty under a baldachin. In palaces, domes were built as a divine cosmic motif.[24] Justinian began with the construction of domes immediately after his coronation in 527; where he was not hindered by the basilican model of a venerable predecessor, he combined the dome with a centralized plan. Especially in areas where Justinian wanted to establish or consolidate his power, galleries were added to existing churches, or churches were built with domes, using a central plan, where possible.[25]

Under Justinian's powerless successors imperial ceremonial in the great churches was increasingly resisted and finally transferred to the palace. Court ceremonial in the time of Justin II (565–73) received a strong religious tone.[26] The icon, to which miraculous powers were ascribed, played an ever increasing role as an intermediary between the sacred and the profane, and this to the detriment of the intermediary role of the emperor and the ceremonial function of the basilica.[27] For centuries after the sixth century, no basilicas with galleries were built.

Still, the motif would be used anew as a status symbol by young, upcoming noble families.[28] This also occurred in the

[24] H. Sedlmayr, 'Das erste mittelalterliche Architektursystem', in Sedlmayr, *Epochen und Werke: gesammelte Schriften zur Kunstgeschichte*, I (Vienna and Munich, 1959), pp. 80–139; E.B. Smith, *The Dome: A Study in the History of Ideas* (Princeton, 1950), *passim*.

[25] There were galleries in some churches in North Africa, domes in Ephesus, a domed octagonal church in Ravenna. For the latter see von Simson, *Sacred Fortress* (see n. 23) and some additional information in the author's thesis.

[26] Averil Cameron, 'The Empress Sophia', *Byzantion*, 45 (1975), 5–21, at p. 8; 'Images of authority: elites and icons in late sixth century Byzantium', *Past and Present*, 84 (1979), 3–35, at pp. 4, 11, 13, 17; 'The artistic patronage of Justin II', *Byzantion*, 50 (1980), 62–84, at p. 76; E. Kitzinger, 'The cult of images in the age before Iconoclasm', *DOP*, 8 (1954), 83–150, at p. 126; Lavin, 'The House' (see n. 7), pp. 22–3.

[27] P. Brown, 'A dark-age crisis: aspects of the iconoclastic controversy', *The English Historical Review*, 88 (1973), 1–34, at pp. 10–14; Kitzinger, 'The cult' (see n. 26), pp. 95, 100, 125–6.

[28] Already in the early seventh century the motif of the galleries was used by the Ghassanids in the Hauran (South of Syria), possibly as a princely symbol. The tsars of the Bulgarian Empire followed suit. These families and their buildings are treated in detail in the author's thesis.

German Empire, where the new family of Saxon emperors needed this sacral symbol to emphasize its imperial dignity.

In the next paragraph we will see how Theophano adhered to the already prevailing ambitions of Otto I (936–73) and Otto II (973–83) and how she left a personal mark on church building in Gernrode.

The introduction of the gallery into the German Empire by Theophano?

Not until the second half of the tenth century did the first basilica with west and side galleries appear in a women's convent, in Gernrode, close to Quedlinburg, where the ancestral castle of the Saxon imperial family was located. This basilica is unique for this time and this place.[29]

The *patrocinium* of St Cyriacus, which was added rather suddenly to the church in Gernrode, is unique as well, and cannot be explained at first sight. To begin with, let us consider the documents and facts available to clarify these curious facts.[30] In a document (961), stating that Otto I (936–73) took this convent, founded by the margrave Gero, under his special protection, it is written that at that time the convent was still dedicated to Peter and Mary. Suddenly and completely Peter and Mary were replaced by St Cyriacus.

Thietmar of Merseberg (*c*. 1016), the only person offering an 'explanation' for this change, reports the following: the founder, Gero, went to Rome, where he received a relic of St Cyriacus after the death of his son, Siegfried, in 959. Then he founded the convent in Gernrode where Siegfried's widow, Hathui, became the abbess. From a document (963) from Gero himself, however, it becomes evident that he went to Rome *after* the founding of the convent in order to place the convent under papal authority. He does not mention the *patrocinium* of St Cyriacus here, which is surprising as he would just have received the relic of this saint. The pious, but not entirely correct, version of Thietmar is perhaps an

[29] If there were galleries in the church of SS Peter and Servatius and in St Mary's Church *auf dem Münzenberg* in Quedlinburg, which is still uncertain, they were presumably added for the same reasons as those in Gernrode.

[30] All relevant documents are gathered in K. Voigtländer, *Die Stiftskirche zu Gernrode und ihre Restaurierung 1858–1872* (Berlin, 1980), pp. 19–20, 53, 135 ff; see also H.K. Schulze, *Das Stift Gernrode* (Graz, 1965), pp. 2 ff.

explanation after the fact for the uncommon patron-saint of the convent.[31]

The first abbess, Gero's daughter-in-law Hathui, was Otto I's cousin and as such she belonged to the group of high-ranking women of this Saxon family. She knew so little about the new patron that she commissioned a certain Nadda to write a *Vita* of him. The rather bizarre result shows that the writer was also at a loss.[32] Clearly, Hathui did not choose the *patrocinium* of St Cyriacus deliberately.

The construction of the church (begun *c.* 961) was perhaps temporarily interrupted. On the plan a bend is visible between the short easterly transept and the nave with galleries. Differences in the foundations of the two sections have also been noted.[33] During the construction Theophano, as the wife of emperor Otto II (973–83), came to the neighbouring Quedlinburg, where she resided until 978. So far the acknowledged facts.

The socio-historical background may provide an explanation for the construction of the galleries in the church.[34] Both Otto I and Otto II had sweeping imperial ambitions. They therefore imitated several customs of the Byzantine court. A marriage to a 'princess' from Constantinople fitted in with their striving for prestige. In Italy they were considered formidable rivals of the Byzantine emperor and Otto II himself used the significant title 'Emperor of the Romans', by which he claimed for himself universal emperorship.[35] If Theophano had any influence on the building of the galleries, she adhered to the already prevailing aspirations of Otto I and II.

Questions, however, still remain: 1. Why were the galleries built especially in a convent? 2. Why was the basilican form

[31] Documents from pope Leo IX (1049), in which the convent is still named after SS Peter and Mary, show the *patrocinium* of St Cyriacus to be either unknown or unaccepted in Rome.

[32] N. Fickermann, 'Eine hagiographische Fälschung ottonischer Zeit aus Gernrode', in *Corona Quernea: Festgabe für Karl Strecker* (Leipzig, 1941), pp. 150–67.

[33] Voigtländer, *Die Stiftskirche* (see n. 30), p. 54.

[34] The only one, who – to my knowledge – connects the building of this galleried church with political facts is H.L. Nickel, 'Byzanzbezüge in der Architektur der Stiftskirche zu Gernrode', in *Byzantinischer Kunstexport: seine gesellschaftliche und künstlerische Bedeutung für die Länder Mittel- und Osteuropas*, ed. H.L. Nickel (Halle and Wittenberg, 1978).

[35] F. Dölger, 'Die Ottonenkaiser und Byzanz', in *Karolingische und ottonische Kunst* (see n. 6), p. 52; W. Ohnsorge, 'Byzanz und das Abendland im 9. und 10. Jahrhundert: zur Entwicklung des Kaiserbegriffes und der Staatsideologie', *Saeculum*, 5 (1954), 194–220, at p. 216.

adopted? 3. Why was the *patrocinium* of SS Mary and Peter so suddenly superseded by the exceptional *patrocinium* of St Cyriacus? Further research into the historical background of this question can be useful and illuminating.

1. In old Saxony, convents were very popular. They functioned as retreats for ladies and marriageable girls from aristocratic families. They were built as family convents. Because these convents were especially built as an advanced post in a half-subdued and pagan area they could develop into an expression of power of the ruling family. The 'heroes' of the family were buried there. Through their daily contact with their family tree the residents who took care of the intercessional prayer for them and for the necrology were extremely conscious of their position and their family. The family convent became the calling-card and extension of the family.[36] No strict rule was enforced. The ladies were permitted to keep their possessions, such as houses and personnel. They could take long holidays and were able to leave in order to marry. How is it then that there are galleries in this nunnery?

Hathui, as an important relative of the Saxon emperors, represented the Saxon royal family with this symbol in her 'family convent'. The galleries in her church were built as a sign of their sacred emperorship. It is doubtful whether these galleries functioned as seating places, considering that the parapets along the side-galleries were very high in relationship to the height of the women in those days, and because the accesses to the galleries led through narrow, dark spiral staircases.[37]

2. The fact that the basilican model was chosen, precisely in a convent, is noteworthy if we suppose that Theophano's influence had only to do with the latest fashion in Constantinople. Why then was the choice not made for a current cruciform church, which was in vogue in Constantinople, or for the imperial centralized church? I believe that it was exactly in the choice of an 'old-fashioned' basilica that the influence of Theophano can be

[36] W. Kohl, 'Bemerkungen zur Typologie sächsischer Frauenklöster in karolingischer Zeit', in *Untersuchungen zu Kloster und Stift*, Veröffentlichungen des Max-Planck-Institutes für Geschichte, 68 (Göttingen, 1980), pp. 112–39, at pp. 113, 125–6, 136; M. Last, 'Zur Einrichtung geistlicher Konvente in Sachsen während des frühen Mittelalters', *Frühmittelalterliche Studien*, 4 (1970), 341–7, at p. 344; M. Parisse, 'Les chanoinesses dans l'Empire germanique (IXe–XIe s.)', *Francia*, 6 (1978), 107–26.

[37] Voigtländer, *Die Stiftskirche* (see n. 30), pp. 57–8, 60.

detected. In Gernrode there is specific reference to the wide galleried basilicas of the empresses of the fifth century. Theophano expressly placed herself and the royal women of her husband's dynasty within the tradition of the Byzantine empresses, who, as we have seen, in their turn had derived their prestige from Helena/Mary. In the course of time this notion was kept alive by the women of royalty in Constantinople. The wife of Basil I (867–86) still honoured herself with the name 'The New Helena'. In her new fatherland, Theophano also sought to align herself with Helena, that shining example of pious imperial women.

3. Why was the Rome-orientated *patrocinium* of Mary and Peter so suddenly replaced by that of St Cyriacus? Now this problem can also be solved. In the legend of the finding of the True Cross, St Cyriacus was the at first unwilling Jew, who was later converted, and in the end helped Helena in finding the True Cross and the nails. A later version of this legend, in which St Cyriacus played a much more important role than in the original story, was extremely popular, especially in Western Europe.[38] Through the choice of St Cyriacus as patron of the 'Helena basilica' the entire context of Jerusalem/church of the Holy Sepulchre/Helena/Finding of the True Cross/Cross was completed in a dignified manner. This, in my opinion, is the most important and meaningful contribution of Theophano to the architecture and the naming of the church of Gernrode.

Not until more than half a century later, and in an entirely different situation, did the basilica with galleries appear again, this time in Rheims. In the German Empire they were not to be found for almost two centuries.

The west gallery, above all in convents, was, however, maintained. In Constantinople the same development could be discovered; but in Western Europe, especially in old Lorraine, an adaptation of the Carolingian tradition may have taken place. With Carolingian churches an especially strong accent was placed on the massive westwork, including a gallery. Theophano adopted this tradition in her burial church, St Pantaleon at Cologne, where she erected an impressive west front with a gallery.[39]

[38] Drijvers, *Helena Augusta* (see n. 16), pp. 165–71, 175.

[39] Her daughters and granddaughters are also known as abbesses and builders of churches with west galleries: the 'Stiftskirche' in Essen, St Mary on the Capitol in Cologne and the church of St Gertrude in Nivelles.

Other distinguished ladies followed suit in their family cloisters, even when they were not related to the imperial families. The noble abbess with her retinue may have sat here on special holy days, not because she was a woman, but because she represented the family.

Churches with galleries in France

In about 1040 the first churches with galleries make their appearance in France and especially in the sovereign lands of the Capets. Unfortunately many of the churches in monasteries and bishoprics of the Capet kings are difficult to reconstruct, therefore we will direct our attention to a clear example preserved in Rheims, the church of St Remi.[40]

The bishopric of Rheims played a large role in the rise of the house of Capet, which would rule France for centuries. The first three kings, Hugh Capet (987–96), Robert the Pious (996–1031) and Henry I (1031–60), are important for our subject. When the Carolingian royal house died out, the kingship over the West Franks was, as it were, offered to Hugh Capet by two prelates from Rheims, archbishop Adalbero (968–89) and his secretary, Gerbert of Aurillac (940–1003). This was an unlawful act, because there was still an ascendant from the Carolingian house as a rightful successor alive in Lorraine. We can certainly ascertain that the illegitimate election and crowning of Hugh in 987 was prepared and set in motion by Adalbero and Gerbert. This was done not so much out of sympathy for the Capet family but it was primarily the realization of the very clear ideas Adalbero and especially Gerbert had about a unified universal Christian empire. They saw this unity seriously threatened by the weak Carolingians in western Francia and Lorraine. They had resolutely sided with the regent, Theophano, who was residing in Aachen, when the Carolingians attacked her position in Lorraine. They saw in Hugh a better, and perhaps a more submissive successor. With these two men, who supported Ottonian politics through thick

[40] In Rheims and its environs a concentration of the gallery motif is noticeable; besides the church of St Remi in Rheims, there is also the church of St Etienne in Vignory and the church of Notre Dame in Montier-en-Der. Galleries are supposed to have existed in Tours, Orléans, Fleury-sur-Loire, Le Mans and Dijon which no longer stand, but the written and archaeological sources are incomplete.

and thin, Rheims became an advanced post of the German Empire in France.[41]

From Aachen Theophano watched neutrally, perhaps benevolently, the rise of Hugh Capet, whose mother was Otto I's sister, probably hoping that the young and inexperienced ruler would be easier to control than a member of the old Carolingian house that traditionally coveted Lorraine.

Not only was Rheims important as a power base for Capet kings who, with tenacious persistency, worked in the interest of their dynasty, but it was also important because of the many reminders of the old kingly power over the Franks. In the church of St Remi was preserved the holy baptismal oil from Clovis with which the French king would later be anointed. Therefore, the Capets fought a stubborn fight against the counts of Blois/Champagne in order to add the bishopric of Rheims to their many religious holdings. In *c.*1040 this ideal was accomplished with the dissolution of the last monastery of the count of Blois/Champagne. Rheims then was, in contrast to fifty years before, an advanced post of the 'French' Capets in the direction of the German Empire.[42]

It is not surprising then that the church of St Remi was rebuilt with galleries. They were constructed not only on the west and on both sides, but also in the transept. These prominently demonstrated the symbol of royalty, and justifiably so. With the reign of Henry I (1031–60) the dynasty was strongly established in western Francia and Rheims.

But now the question arises, why did the Capets prefer the basilican model with its many galleries? For the Capets, who had unjustly forced the Carolingians aside, it was not desirable to revert to an important Carolingian example such as the Palatine Chapel in Aachen or an extensive westwork. They had to add to this 'victory church', consecrated in 1049 by pope Leo IX, other prestigious royal elements.

It is not clear why the choice was made precisely for these motifs and where they came from. Perhaps further research on the construction, which took place in several phases, will yield more

[41] E. Pognon, *Hugues Capet, Roi de France* (Paris, 1966), pp. 106, 119, 124, 127; B. Schneidmüller *Karolingische Tradition und frühes französisches Königtum* (Wiesbaden, 1979), p. 66; L. Theis, *L'avènement d'Hugues Capet* (Paris, 1984), pp. 13, 135, 154, 190.

[42] M. Bur, *Formation du Comté de Champagne* (Nancy, 1977), pp. 176, 179, 203, 205–6; Schneidmüller, *Karolingische* (see n. 41), pp. 49–50.

information. The account of the consecration by Leo IX, written by Anselm of St Remi, is a good source for this. According to Anselm the church was begun by abbot Airard (1007–35), but his successor Theodoric (1035–46) tore down the existing walls, preserving, however, the foundations of Airard's construction for his new church. He did this after he had consulted old, wise men in Rheims. The reason Anselm gives was that Airard's first construction became too large;[43] but if Theodoric used the same foundations his construction would not have been much smaller. Is it not possible that Theodoric's building was based on a new plan, a plan in which galleries were integrated as royal symbols? Could it have been that this consultation with the old, wise men, who perhaps had been students and contemporaries of Gerbert, led to the construction of galleries?

Gerbert of Aurillac had fairly frequent contacts with Theophano and her court. He was one of the few persons who knew Greek and he was probably present already at her wedding in 972. During a later stay in Italy in 980–3 and in the years after Otto II's death, when Theophano lived in Aachen and Gerbert in Rheims, they wrote and spoke to each other.[44] At that time, as we have seen, Adalbero and Gerbert were pawns of the German Empire in Rheims. Gerbert headed a famous school there, where the future king Robert the Pious and many of his clerical collaborators were students. It is possible that Gerbert, who had a wide range of interests, had outspoken ideas as to the manifestation of the French kingship in the church building itself in addition to his ideas about a universal sacred emperorship. Just as he gave the royal Capets titles different from those of the imperial Ottonians,[45] Gerbert may have adopted the view that the symbolism in the church of the French king had to be of a different nature from the Ottonian churches of those days.

Gerbert's contacts with Theophano's court may have played a part in the introduction of churches with their symbolic side galleries. If this is so, Theophano contributed to the building of this type of church in France as well.

[43] A. Prache, *Saint Rémy de Rheims* (Paris, 1978), see p. 15 for the text.

[44] F. Trystam, *Le Coq et la louve: histoire de Gerbert et l'an mille* (Paris, 1982), pp. 48, 58.

[45] Schneidmüller, *Karolingische* (see n. 41), pp. 68–9.

16

The human and economic context*

L.F. GENICOT

In contrast to the other chapters in this volume, this chapter deals with problems of a material nature. The past, however, should be considered as a whole: economy, demographic fluctuations, the flourishing periods and the periods of depression, etc. have a strong impact on religion, philosophy and the arts. The turn of the first millennium is a time surrounded with controversy and uncertainty concerning the rural economy. In this article I shall confine myself to a survey of the complex problems and the various answers to these problems – which are explored in greater detail in my book on the *Rural Communities in the Medieval West*[1] – without pretending to develop solutions myself. Ever since the beginning of this century, with the exception of K. Lamprecht,[2] most historians of the medieval economy have treated only the urban economy. Yet 90% of the people lived in the country. This article does something to redress the balance.

The economic evolution in its entirety should be taken into account to judge the demographic evolution. A starting-point about the middle of the tenth century obliges us at the outset to address the question of continuity, the *Kontinuitätsfrage*, the transition from Antiquity to the Middle Ages, but also from the

* Dr Andrew Palmer was so kind as to adapt and translate the French text of this article for publication in this volume.

[1] L. Genicot, *Rural Communities in the Medieval West* (Baltimore, 1990).

[2] K. Lamprecht, *Deutsches Wirtschaftsleben im Mittelalter: Untersuchungen über die Entwicklung der materiellen Kultur des platten Landes auf Grund der Quellen, zunächst des Mosellandes*, 3 vols. (Leipzig, 1886).

Merovingian to the Carolingian period. H. Nuber[3] and W. Janssen[4] have recently shown that the transition to the Carolingian period was much more complex and varied according to region, more than had been thought possible. Nuber finds continuity a very relative concept when applied to the Gallo-Roman and Merovingian inhabitants of Sontheim and Brenz, in southern Germany. In the same volume, H. Steuer[5] observes hardly any change in zones of habitation and burial-grounds in Alemannic lands during the high Middle Ages. As for the economy during the Carolingian period, there are two opposing schools. A. Verhulst described them clearly in 1990:[6] it was a period of depression, according to some scholars, especially the French (e.g. G. Duby and R. Fossier), and a period of stability and even progress according to other specialists, especially those from the North. The question remains unresolved.

A greater degree of consensus has been achieved with regard to the demographic curve as the barometer of the economy. Marc Bloch, whose authority on this subject in its entirety was weighty for a long time, has situated the beginning of a new rise around 1050, at the start of what he has called 'the second age of feudalism'. But recent research has pushed this date back to 950, although the concrete evidence is less abundant than one might wish. J. Russell,[7] for example, and G. Fourquin[8] concur in this position, which is defended by A. Verhulst in his contribution to the *New Cambridge Medieval History*, ed. R. McKitterick. Verhulst gave a survey of his views in an interview:[9] a period of

[3] H.U. Nuber, 'Sontheim und Brenz in frühgeschichtlicher Zeit', in *Person und Gemeinschaft im Mittelalter: Karl Schmid zum fünfundsechzigsten Geburtstag*, ed. G. Althoff (Sigmaringen, 1988), pp.3–24.

[4] W. Janssen, 'Siedlungsgeschichtliche und siedlungsarchäologische Beobachtungen zum Haus- und Reichsgut der Salier', in *Siedlungen und Landesausbau zur Salierzeit*, ed. H.W. Böhme, 2 vols. (Sigmaringen, 1991), II, pp. 7–13.

[5] H. Steuer, 'Standortverschiebungen früher Siedlungen – von der vorrömischen Eisenzeit bis zum frühen Mittelalter', in *Person und Gemeinschaft* (see n. 3), pp. 25–59.

[6] A. Verhulst, *Précis d'histoire rurale de la Belgique* (Brussels, 1990).

[7] J.C. Russell, 'Population in Europe 500–1500', in *The Fontana Economic History of Europe*, I, *The Middle Ages 900–1500*, ed. C.M. Cipolla (London and Glasgow, 1972), pp. 25–70.

[8] G. Fourquin, 'Le temps de la croissance', in *Histoire de la France rurale*, ed. G. Duby and A. Wallon, I (Paris, 1975), pp. 397–400.

[9] M. Hanepen, B. van den Hoven and H. Roozenbeek, 'Tegenwoordig moet het allemaal *l'An mil* zijn: een interview met prof. dr. A. Verhulst', *Leidschrift: Historisch Tijdschrift*, 7 (1990/1), 69–79.

progress until about 800 followed by a period of stagnation due to famines; a recovery of the economy in the tenth century and a population explosion towards the year 1000. W. Janssen[10] expresses the same view in his conclusion that the Salians increased their material base from the earlier eleventh century onwards, thanks to the active participation of *ministeriales* in cultivation: they thus gave an opportunity to those people in society who had previously been discontented with their position.

The population growth appears to have led to a transformation in the form of living: people started to live together in villages in the tenth to eleventh centuries. R. Fossier calls this phenomenon *encellulement* and the Italians *inquadramento* (or *inorbamento* in connection with towns and cities). M. Bouri-Derruau[11] would place the origin of the village in the mid-tenth century, the preparatory phase between 950 and 1070, consolidation between 1070 and 1170 and the organization of the community and the development of the consulate in the thirteenth century.

How was the family, in particular the noble family, affected by these developments? This question is the theme of a series of fine studies which have appeared over the past twenty years. The book edited by G. Duby and J. Le Goff on families in the medieval West,[12] the study by P. Tourbert[13] on the Carolingian family and H. Hanawalt's work on peasant families in medieval England[14] deserve special mention in this respect. It becomes clear that the noble family anchors itself in a *château à motte* (a mostly timber tower on an artificial hill) or a castle (this means the beginning of the phenomenon *Verherrschaftlichung*), and *seigneuries* begin to stretch their roots out into the soil; princedoms were soon to be founded. From the point of view of the country people this development meant peace, from the point of view of the lords of the *bannum*, more favourable political and economic conditions for effective exploitation: these, broadly speaking, are the motives

[10] Janssen, 'Siedlungsgeschichtliche' (see n. 4); see also W. Janssen, 'Methodische Probleme archäologischer Wüstungsforschung', in *Nachrichten der Akademie der Wissenschaften in Göttingen*, phil.-hist. Klasse, 1968, no. 2 (Göttingen, 1968).

[11] M. Bouri-Derruau, *Villages médiévaux en Bas Languedoc: genèse d'une sociabilité, Xe–XIVe siècles*, 2 vols. (Paris, 1987).

[12] G. Duby and J. Le Goff, *Famille et parenté dans l'Occident médiéval*, Collection de l'Ecole française de Rome, 30 (Rome, 1977).

[13] P. Tourbert, 'La famille carolingienne', in *L'histoire de la famille*, ed. A. Burguière *et al.* (Paris, 1986).

[14] H.A. Hanawalt, *The Ties that Bound Peasant Families* (New York and Oxford, 1986).

on either side for the concentration in particular areas. This is confirmed by a passage in the *Gesta* by Sigebert of Gembloux, where it is said that in 1123, on the order of the abbey of the region, the relics of the saint were transported to the Mont-Saint-Guibert, where they built a church, and that many people came to live there in peace and harmony and that they built houses there for themselves.[15]

The concentration in villages did not entail major shifts of population. English scholars, especially experts on the Anglo-Saxon period, proved that from the beginning of the Middle Ages sedentarization had been combined with narrowly circumscribed peregrination dictated by the exhaustion of the soil. A whole series of monographs, collated by the writer in a book,[16] suggest one conclusion, supported by palynology and archaeology.

The increase in population density may have brought about or at least accompanied certain changes in the distribution of land and in agricultural technology. As so often in the study of phenomena concerning the collective which are not easy to date, it is difficult to decide which is the cause and which the effect. Was it demographic pressure which, requiring more efficient production, led to improved techniques? Or, on the contrary, did greater productivity permit the growth of the population in the first place? As yet there is no authoritative answer. Nor is this the only question which is unresolved. Suffice it to mention the following: the structure of the domain; the origin, the geographical spread and the chronological decline of the 'classical' bi-party domain, which was less common and less solid than was thought; the rhythm of cultivation before 1050 and between 1150 and 1250 or 1300; more data to be gathered through palynology than we have at our disposal now; the management of the territory and the reorganizations in land-distribution (some scholars are inclined to place its application only in the thirteenth century); the related application of crop rotation. For a discussion of these and more problems, see Flaran (1988).[17]

[15] Sigebert of Gembloux, *Gesta*, MGH SS VIII, pp. 552–3: 'Cum propter pacis et concordiae unitatem multi illuc convenirent et ad habitandum sibi domos construerent, iterum habito consilio cum amicis meis et cum supra dicto abbate et familia aecclesiae, decrevi ut locus ille cum oppido Gemblacensi ius legale et consuetudinarium habebet unum.'

[16] J. Genicot, *Economie rurale namuroise au bas moyen âge*, 3 vols. (Louvain and Namur, 1943–82) (vol. IV is forthcoming).

[17] *La croissance agricole du haut moyen âge: chronologie, modalités, géographie* (international conference on history at the Centre culturel de l'Abbaye de Flaran, 1988).

The demographic rise affected urban conglomerations, too. This is not the place to investigate the origins of the cities and the question of urban continuity. Besides, why should historians be so fixated on the question of origins of cities and towns in the Middle Ages and on the origins of the nobility, when every phenomenon is a continuous creation? H. Steuer recently made the same reproach to medievalists.[18] Whether you look at Dinant or at Liège or at Cologne or elsewhere, you see in the years preceding the millennium reinvigorated cities. The evidence is plain to see in E. Ennen's classic work on the medieval European city[19] and in the urban case-studies concerning the period before the year 1000, assembled in the proceedings of the fourteenth international colloquium of Spa, 1988; these are convincing.[20] J.P. Devroey and C. Devroey-Zoller, more recently, have underlined the proliferation of little markets in the tenth century;[21] and W. Bleiber has done the same for the ninth century.[22] J.L. Kupper's contribution to the debate has the added merit of putting the role of individuals in relief.[23]

Was it in the cities or in the countryside that the economy began to bloom? Our difficulty in answering this question lies in the inexactitude of the chronology, which is crucial when establishing 'the cause and the effect'. One thing can be taken as certain and that is the symbiosis of country and town. G. Despy has used hagiography, perhaps the most important source for the period, to demonstrate this.[24] D. Nicholas discovered that urban wealth

18 H. Steuer, 'Bestandsaufnamen der archäologischen Forschungsergebnisse zur Stadt des Mittelalters und ihren Ursprüngen', *Siedlungsforschung: Archäologie, Geschichte, Geographie*, 4 (1986), 225–37.

19 E. Ennen, *Die europäische Stadt des Mittelalters* (Göttingen, 4th edn, 1987).

20 See the collection of essays, 'Etudes de cas', in *La genèse et les premiers siècles des villes médiévales dans les Pays-Bas méridionaux: un problème archéologique et historique*, Actes du 14e colloque international du Comité d'Histoire du Centre du Crédit Communal de Belgique, Spa, 6–8 September 1988 (Brussels, 1990).

21 J.P. Devroey and C. Devroey-Zoller, 'Villes, campagnes, croissance agraire dans le pays mosan avant l'an mille', in *Villes et campagnes au moyen âge: mélanges G. Despy*, ed. C. Billen *et al.* (Liège, 1991), pp. 223–60.

22 W. Bleiber, 'Grundherrschaft und Markt zwischen Loire und Rhein während des 9. Jahrhunderts', *Jahrbuch für Wirtschaftsgeschichte* (1982–3), 105–31.

23 J.L. Kupper, '*Episcopus, ingenuus, cives et rustici*: La Chronique d'Anselme et la vie économique du pays mosan aux Xe–XIe siècles', in *Villes et campagnes au moyen âge* (see n. 21), and 'L'occident entre 800 et l'an mil: sous-développement ou croissance économique', *Bulletin de la Classe des Lettres de l'Académie Royale de Belgique*, 74 (1988), 325–7.

24 G. Despy, 'Villes et campagnes aux IXe et Xe siècles: l'exemple du pays mosan', *Revue du Nord*, 50 (1968), 145–68.

began its growth in the food-trade and was invested in industry after that.[25]

The demographic boom and the development of exchange had important repercussions on political and social structures. The most important of these was perhaps (in combination with difficulties concerning the power in many regions) the confirmation of the authority of the nobility by the very exploitation of the *bannum*. Whether by hereditary right, by virtue of *immunitas* or *vicecomitatus* or *centena*, by the concession of the fief or by usurpation, the *dominus* added greatly to the burden imposed on individuals from the end of the tenth century, or in other cases from the beginning or the middle of the eleventh century onwards. He superimposed on the net of landed *seigneuries* that of the feudal or *banal seigneuries*; and the burdens imposed by the latter, *pravae consuetudines* ('bad customs') as they were called, were heavier than those imposed by the former, and they were imposed on all.

This development either created or consolidated the cohesion of the rural communities and gave them their sense of corporate identity. Such units might coincide with *villae*, but more usually they included several *villae*; although very occasionally a fraction of a *villa* could have its own corporate identity.

The nobility wished now to have its *château à motte* (R. Fossier has detected fifty of these in Poitou, sixty in Lorraine and twelve in Picardy dating back to before the year 1000[26]) and at least its *donjon* while waiting for its castle. Ideally there would be a 'pantheon' in an abbey or, failing that, a more modest priory; which brings me to the way the religious orders were transformed. The parish network was enriched, new spiritual families were founded.

What then was the effect of such economic phenomena on the culture of Europe? This effect cannot be denied and was of no little importance. The leisure to think is dependent on a certain superfluity of resources. Little Belgium has alone preserved seventy-five narrative works from the tenth century, chronicles, saints' Lives, tracts, homilies composed by thirty-five different authors, all of whom are listed in A. Stainier's *Index*.[27] Cathedral

[25] D. Nicholas, 'Structures de peuplement, fonctions urbaines et formation du capital dans la Flandre médiévale', *Annales: Economies, Sociétés, Civilisations*, 33 (1978), 501–27.

[26] R. Fossier, *Paysans d'Occident* (Paris, 1984), p. 198.

[27] *Index scriptorum operumque latino-belgicorum Medii Aevi*, ed. A. Stainier *et al.*, I (Louvain, 1973).

scriptoria not only produced such books but also illuminated them. Architecture was enriched with the building of palaces and castles; inventories and analyses give us some impression of their number and importance.[28] The cloisters of this period form a beautiful continuation of the architecture from the Carolingian Renaissance towards the magnificence and size of the Romanesque. A great many village churches were built, worthy of more attention than specialists have paid to them.[29] Art is not only to be seen in exceptional monuments and works of individual and original merit. The importance of craftsmanship should not be denied; the connection between art and craft should never be forgotten. In this connection, the work of X. Barral i Altet and his collaborators is exemplary.[30]

Enough has been said to show that the demographic and economic boom which underlay the cultural, social and political transformations of Theophano's time is a vibrant area of scholarship, where much remains to be done.

[28] I. Bodsch, *Burg und Herrschaft der Erzbischöfe von Trier im Hochmittelalter bis zum Tod Dieters von Nassau (1307)* (Boppard, 1989).

[29] L.F. Genicot, *Les églises mosanes du XIe siècle*, I, *Architecture et société* (Louvain, 1972).

[30] *Artistes, artisans et productions artistiques au moyen âge*, I, *Hommes*, II, *Commande et travail*, III, *Fabrication et consommation de l'œuvre*, ed. X. Barral i Altet *et al.* (Paris, 1988–90).

17

The palace and the monastery in Byzantine spiritual life *c.* 1000

A.J. VAN DER AALST

If we accept the chronology of the lives of Theophano (955–91) and Symeon the New Theologian (949–1022) as probably right, then they must have lived in the same town when they were young, and so may well have met in the imperial palace. Both were involved in the political and religious life of the capital, in which the relations between the palace and the monastery played an important role. In order to elucidate an aspect of Byzantine spirituality in this period, a general survey of the background will be given before proceeding to discuss the more personal experience of Symeon.*

The palace and the monastery

Around the year 1000 Constantinople was the major city in the Byzantine Empire. For a long time the capital had outshone cities like Alexandria and Antioch; these had been in the hands of the

* For the works by and on Symeon the New Theologian the following abbreviations are used:
Cat.: *Catéchèses*, 3 vols., ed. B. Krivochéine, trans. J. Paramelle, SC 96, 104 and 113 (Paris, 1963–5).
Chap.: *Chapitres théologiques, gnostiques et pratiques*, ed. and trans. J. Darrouzès, SC 51 bis (Paris, 1980).
Epist.: *Epistula de confessione*, in K. Holl, *Enthusiasmus und Bussgewalt beim griechischen Mönchtum* (Leipzig, 1898, reprinted in Hildesheim, 1969), pp. 110–27.
Hym.: *Hymnes*, I, ed. J. Koder, trans. J. Paramelle, SC 156 (Paris, 1969); II, ed. J. Koder, trans. L. Neyrand, SC 174 (Paris, 1971); III, ed. J. Koder, trans. J. Paramelle and L. Neyrand, SC 196 (Paris, 1973).
TE: *Traités théologiques et éthiques*, 2 vols., ed. and trans. J. Darrouzès, SC 122, 129 (Paris, 1966–7).
Vita: Niketas Stethatos, *Vie de Syméon le Nouveau Théologien*, ed. I. Hausherr and P. Horn, Orientalia Christiana, 12 (Rome, 1928).

Muslims for centuries. Constantinople was the centre of both the empire and the national church, where power, wealth and culture were concentrated. If the city appealed to the 'barbarians', it also had a great attraction for its own people. Rich families sent their sons to the city to be educated there and to gain promotion in the official aristocracy which was closely linked to the central power. This was the case with the historian Leo the Deacon, with Michael Maleinos and with Symeon the New Theologian, the last two of whom became monks. Homesickness for 'the City' is a motive that often occurs in tenth-century letters. People felt like outcasts if they had to live in the country. For them barbarism began just outside the city walls. From his army camp Nikephoros Ouranos, who – as a general – served both on the western front (Bulgaria) and on the eastern front (Syria, Armenia), wrote letters to the bishop's *synkellos*, Stephen of Nikomedeia, who was staying in Constantinople. The elderly general Nikephoros was now fed up with campaigns and camp life. He complains of sleepless nights: *en route* or in the camp he cannot sleep a wink owing to the fifes and other noises. He complains of the food – the bread is so hard, it breaks your teeth – and of the lack of wine. But all these discomforts are nothing compared to the intense yearning for the capital, and for friends with whom he could have a good talk. Bishops liked to come to Constantinople, where they would stay for a long time, with or without a good reason. Leo, metropolitan of Synada in Phrygia, was proud to have been to Rome and Aachen as an ambassador of the emperor. He was in favour of holding synods in the capital. He complained of his life in the country, where no oil or wine was pressed and where fires had to be fed with dried cattle-dung owing to the lack of wood. He envied cattle, donkeys, pigs and sheep, which were sent from the country to the capital to be slaughtered. The animals at least see the capital before they are skinned, while he stays behind in boredom.[1]

In Constantinople the imperial palace was the centre of power and wealth. Around the year 1000 there were several palaces. The Great Palace (*Mega Palation*, started in the fourth century) had grown into an agglomerate of various buildings, imperial residences, churches and barracks surrounded by parks and sports-

[1] J. Darrouzès, *Epistoliers byzantins du Xe siècle* (Paris, 1960), pp. 198, 208; *The Correspondence of Leo Metropolitan of Synada and Syncellus*, ed. M.P. Vinson (Washington, DC, 1985).

fields, with the whole compound surrounded by a wall for reasons of safety. The emperor Romanos II and his wife Theophano liked to stay at the Mangana Palace, which, under Basil I, had been enlarged and was now a magnificent crown property. To the south of the Great Palace, Nikephoros II Phokas had the Boukaleon Palace erected, which, for the sake of safety, was provided with a jetty with steps leading down to the Sea of Marmara. That was to be the very place where the sailors would land in 969 to kill the emperor in a gruesome way. Between his campaigns Basil II loved to retire in the Hebdomon Palace, in a suburb of the city, where he also had the monastery church of St John the Baptist renovated, the church where he was to be buried.

The meaning of the palace at that time as a mystical symbol for the entanglement of politics and religion, of church and state, is revealed clearly in *The Book of Ceremonies*, compiled by Constantine VII. It is a collection of texts, 'picked like flowers in the field', to serve as 'the glorification of imperial rule'. The idea underlying all ceremonies and rites at celebrations, processions and audiences is that the emperor represented divine authority. His realm was a mirror-image of God's realm, or even a participation in it. Several details help to portray the mystic bond between worldly and heavenly power; the palace is 'sacred', and a sacred silence should be kept there; the preservation of this silence was the duty of a special officer, the *silentiarios*. The emperor is literally served hand and foot. The hierarchical character of imperial power is emphasized in everything: the layout of the palace, the throne on a dais beneath a canopy, partitioned off by a *velum* or veil, and the imperial attributes, the crown, the purple clothing, the insignia, the chants and acclamations. The aesthetic show was intended to inspire the awe of authority in everyone. For those who believed in it, it was a sublime manifestation of some higher power; for the masses who could see the emperor and his pomp at celebrations, games and processions, it was an awe-inspiring display. To the outsider who was not really involved the spectacle might have seemed an absurd piece of theatre, complete with props and *mise-en-scène*; and this is how it is depicted by Liutprand of Cremona. In front of the imperial throne, there was a tree of gilded bronze with gilded birds in its branches. The huge throne was guarded by gilded lions. It was a 'high-tech' show: as the emperor advanced towards the throne, the lions opened their mouths wide, beat the ground with their tails, and – with quivering tongues – gave a roar, while the birds in the trees started to twitter. After a threefold *proskynesis*, Liutprand suddenly saw the emperor high above, almost against the ceiling. He assumed that this elevation, called *prokypsis* by the Byzantines, was brought about by a pulley. During this audience the emperor did not converse personally with Liutprand; the distance between them would have made such conversation rather silly. But the emperor instructed his minister to inquire after the health of Berengar, whose envoy Liutprand was. The envoy gave a suitable answer, and, at a nod from the interpreter, was led away to the guest-rooms by two eunuchs who held him by the shoulders.[2]

But this display of power was not merely symbolic. The empire was at its largest since the seventh century, extending from the Euphrates to the Danube, from Armenia to Calabria. Within the period 963–1025, we find three emperors who were at the same time major generals: Nikephoros II Phokas, John Tzimiskes and Basil II. They exercised power within the empire by control of the military aristocracy, from whose families new usurpers continually arose, and along its borders, where the Arabs and the Bulgarians needed to be held in check. When the rebel Bardas Skleros had been defeated, the emperor Basil II asked him how best to secure power in the realm. The defeated rebel gave him a Machiavellian piece of advice: the emperor should prevent the generals from becoming rich by unjust taxes; he should not introduce women into the palace, nor be at anyone's disposal; or consult too many people when taking decisions.[3] The cruelty of the imperial power can be surmised from the gruesome story taken down by John Skylitzes. Emperor Basil II, who was called 'Bulgar-Slayer' (*Bulgaroktonos*) as early as the eleventh century, had punished his enemies harshly. In 1014 he blinded 14,000 prisoners of war, allowing one man in a hundred to retain one eye, so that this one-eyed man could lead his fellow-victims home.[4]

It has been observed that in this period military saints, such as St George, St Merkourios and St Demetrios, become popular in

[2] A. Vogt, *Le Livre des cérémonies*, 2 vols. (Paris, 1935–40); O. Treitinger, *Die oströmische Kaiser- und Reichsidee nach ihrer Gestaltung im höfischen Zeremoniell* (Darmstadt, 1969); Liutprand of Cremona, *Antapodosis*, 6, 5, PL, 136, 895; J. Koder and Th. Weber, *Liutprand von Kremona in Konstantinopel* (Vienna, 1980), pp. 71–99.

[3] Michael Psellos, *Chronographie*, I, ed. E. Renauld (Paris, 1926), p. 28.

[4] John Skylitzes, *Synopsis historiarum*, ed. J. Thurn, Corpus fontium historiae Byzantinae, 5, Series Berolinensis (Berlin and New York, 1973), p. 349.

iconography. These martial saints inspired the soldiers more than the petty ascetic figures from the same period.[5] Patriarch Polyeuktos opposed the emperor Nikephoros, because he wanted to 'canonize' the fallen soldiers as holy martyrs.[6] It has also been observed that, in the Menologion of Basil II (Vat. gr. 1613, the most lavishly illustrated of all Byzantine liturgical MSS), the vast majority of the scenes 'are scenes of martyrdom and torture, astonishing as much for their level of refinement, as for their extreme refinement of execution and the absence of caricature'.[7]

Unrestricted power was also apparent in the relationship between the emperor and the church. The patriarchs of that period were mainly docile instruments in imperial hands. Some only mildly protested when the possessions of a church or a monastery were threatened, the exception being patriarch Polyeuktos (956–70), who repeatedly dared to oppose the emperor and who, after Nikephoros II had been murdered, took authoritative action against his guilty successor, John Tzimiskes.[8] During his long-lasting reign, the emperor Basil II kept the patriarch's seat vacant for about eight years, because he himself was absent from the capital owing to his campaigns, and therefore did not have, or did not choose to find, time to appoint someone. He claimed an authoritative say in the appointments of the patriarchs of Antioch and Jerusalem, which had fallen into Muslim hands. And when Bulgaria had been conquered, the organization of the church was taken up; the thirty bishoprics under Ohrid were under direct Byzantine imperial rule.[9] The Christianization of Russia and the marriage of Basil II's sister Anna to prince Vladimir was an act of state and church politics at the same time.[10] The authority of the patriarch was controlled by a *synkellos*, who had been appointed by the emperor. He was a slightly ambiguous figure, both an

[5] K. Weitzmann, *The Icon: Holy Images Sixth to Fourteenth Centuries* (London, 1978), pp. 14–15; J. Walter, *Studies in Byzantine Iconography* (London, 1979), V, p. 175.
[6] See 'Peace and War', in *ODB*, p. 1611.
[7] See 'Menologion of Basil II', in *ODB*, p. 1341.
[8] R. Jenkins, *Byzantium: The Imperial Centuries AD 610–1071* (London, 1966), pp. 270–99.
[9] J. Darrouzès, *Notitiae episcopatuum ecclesiae Constantinopolitanae* (Paris, 1981), pp. 113–14; A. Michel, 'Die Kaisermacht in der Ostkirche 843–1204', *Ostkirchliche Studien*, 2 (1953), 89–109, at p. 99.
[10] A.P. Vlasto, *The Entry of the Slavs into Christendom* (Cambridge, 1970), pp. 259, 396.

imperial civil servant and a counsellor to the patriarch, who could act as a sort of 'ecclesiastical spy'.[11]

Around the year 1000 the most important monastic centres had moved to the west. Egypt, Palestine and Syria had been the cradle of a multifarious monasticism, which had spread meanwhile all over the Byzantine Empire and beyond. It is estimated that about a thousand different monasteries are mentioned in Byzantine sources. The data may give a distorted image because of the nature of the information given.[12] The ascetics or monks had a predilection for mountains and caves. Little is known about the persons who lived in Cappadocia around Göreme in rock-cut monasteries. More to the west the monasteries on Mount Olympos in Bithynia were of importance. The general Nikephoros Phokas was a religious ascetic man, who was interested in monastic life. Even before he became emperor he supported the foundation of a monastery at Olympos by his uncle Michael Maleinos, who had left the imperial court. Somewhat later the monastery of Hosios Loukas was founded in Phokis in Greece, renowned for its beautiful mosaics. Further to the west we find monasteries in Calabria. In the neighbourhood of Seminara, there lived Elias the cave-dweller (Speleotes, † 960), who warned the rebel Byzalon that his revolt against the emperor meant resistance against the divine order. A famous man from that region was Neilos from Rossano († 1004), who was to impress the empress Theophano's son, Otto III, and who, shortly before his death, established the monastery of St Mary of Kryptopherre, 18 km southeast of Rome, which was to continue as the abbey of Grottaferrata.[13]

In Rome itself most of the Greek monasteries had disappeared; only the monastery of St Athanasios was to survive.[14] From this period also dates the Pečerskaja Lavra (the cave monastery), which developed from the caves on the Dnieper, where Feodosij organized community life according to the rule and the example of Theodore of Stoudios.

There were many monasteries in and around Constantinople. H.-G. Beck estimates that on the Asian side of the Bosporos, in

[11] E.A. Sophocles, *Greek Lexicon of the Roman and Byzantine Periods* (New York, s.d.), II, pp. 1020; cf. V. Grumel, 'Les métropolites syncelles', *Etudes Byzantines*, 3 (1945), 92–114.

[12] See 'Monastery', in *ODB*, p. 1391.

[13] See 'Elias Speleotes', in *ODB*, p. 686, and 'Neilos of Rossano', in *ODB*, p. 1451.

[14] J.-M. Sansterre, *Les Moines grecs et orientaux à Rome aux époques byzantine et carolingienne*, 2 vols. (Brussels, 1982), I, pp. 48–9.

the theme of Opsikion, there were about a hundred monasteries containing thousands of monks.[15] Southeast of Chalcedon the monasteries of Rouphinianai and of Mount Auxentios had known a long history of decline and recovery. In the capital itself there were many monasteries, the largest and most famous one being the monastery of Stoudios, founded as early as the fifth century. It had become famous during Iconoclasm through its superior Theodore Stoudites, who had restored community life there. At one time this large monastery numbered 700 monks, a number of whom lived in small subordinate monastic establishments (*metochia*). Besides manual labour there was some intellectual activity in *scriptoria* where manuscripts were copied, and where monks were engaged in hymnography. The monastery received imperial donations, and we find some superiors who became patriarchs in this period, for example Antony III (974–9) and Alexios (1025–43), who both earned themselves the epithet Stoudites. Symeon the New Theologian stayed there for some time, and then moved to the smaller Mamas monastery. This had been founded in the seventh century as a mausoleum for the emperor Mauritius' family. It had declined, but Symeon the New Theologian, who was *hegoumenos* there for twenty-five years, had had it restored. The most important monastic foundations in which the emperors were closely involved were on Mount Athos. The monk Athanasios went from Bithynia to Athos to start a new monastery there with the assistance of Nikephoros Phokas. He had even reserved a place on Athos for Nikephoros, but when Nikephoros became emperor in 963 he could not take his monastic vows. To the dismay of his friend Athanasios, he followed the advice of his counsellors, monks too, to give up his ascetic life and to marry. Monks had already settled on the Athos peninsula, living as hermits in small groups, in order to protect themselves against wild animals and the Saracens, who sometimes attacked them from their base on Crete. As soon as Nikephoros II Phokas had conquered Crete in 961, he financed the building of the Great Lavra – which he himself had designed – with the loot from the Saracens. The building was started in 963.[16]

[15] H.-G. Beck, *Kirche und theologische Literatur im byzantinischen Reich*, Byzantinisches Handbuch, II, I (Munich, 1959), pp. 208–9.

[16] The year 1963 saw the commemoration of the millennium. On this occasion I. Doens, a monk at Chevetogne, compiled a bibliography on Mount Athos, containing 2634 titles: *Le Millénaire du Mont Athos 963–1963: études et mélanges*, 2 vols. (Venice and Chevetogne, 1964), II, pp. 337–483.

The Great Lavra (*Megisti Lavra*) was to be a *koinobion*, with a community of eighty monks, in the tradition of Basil the Great and Theodore Stoudites, bound to a life of strict obedience and compulsory labour.[17] The lavish donation of Nikephoros for the foundation was in sharp contrast to the prohibition issued by the same Nikephoros a year later. In his *novella* of 964 Nikephoros laid down that new monastic foundations were not allowed. He says that private institutions have done laudable work and have really contributed to the welfare of the people, but that now foundations are motivated by the vanity of the benefactors, who wish a church or monastery in their name. Instead of keeping in good repair existing, decaying monasteries, the founders prefer to establish their own new ones. Monasteries often have land, but lack means to till it well. It is advisable to invest money in existing institutions, to make better use of the soil and to increase livestock. Nikephoros does not want any new monasteries, but the consolidation of small huts (*kellia*) into a larger monastery (*lavra*).[18]

Nikephoros II Phokas was brutally murdered on 10 December 969. It is assumed that another general, John Tzimiskes, was responsible. At first, patriarch Polyeuktos resisted John as Nikephoros' successor; but after John had shown remorse and had removed from the palace Theophano, the wife of both Romanos II and Nikephoros II, who had been an accessory to the murder, he could be recognized as emperor. Perhaps out of repentance and to do penance for his crime, the emperor John Tzimiskes later showered Athanasios on Mount Athos with gifts, gold, precious stones and rich cloths, thus supporting the Great Lavra. In the meantime on Mount Athos envy was increasing of Athanasios and his Great Lavra, which enjoyed a privileged position. An insoluble problem was the discrepancy between community life and the more individualized form of monastic life, the *idiorrhythmia*. The building of a rich monastery which was favoured by the emperor prompted the resentment of the hermits: it would open Athos to the outside world and it would gain the advocate of a rigid organization, Athanasios, prestige, and at the same time be detrimental to the freedom of the hermits.

A number of monks protested to the emperor. The latter

[17] E.A. de Mendieta, *Le Mont Athos: la presqu'île des caloyers* (s.l., 1955), p. 14.

[18] *Novella de monasteriis*, in K.E. Zacharias von Lingenthal, *Jus graecoromanum* (Leipzig, 1856–84), III, pp. 292–6; cf. J.P. Thomas, *Private Religious Foundations in the Byzantine Empire* (Washington, DC, 1987), pp. 150–3.

commanded that they remain in conference until they reached a compromise. This was attested by the *typikon* of 972, a charter bearing the golden *bulla* (*chrysobull*), which is called *Tragos* (goat), because the text is written on a goat's skin. The original, written in red ink, signed by John Tzimiskes, is the oldest preserved document with an imperial signature, a goat-skin parchment more than 3 m long, which is kept with the utmost care on Athos, at Karyes, in a case with several locks.[19] Athanasios contributed to the drawing up of the Tragos, and fifty monks signed it. In it rules are laid down for the complicated organization of Athos, the control of the properties, and the life of the monks, especially the relationship between the community and the hermits. Eremitism was only permitted for a few monks, and the superior could not impose a task on them.

Athanasios was successful: he attracted many monks and started building two more monasteries, Vatopedi and Iviron next to the Great Lavra, which are under the Megisti Lavra in order of importance. A number of assimilated Armenians and Georgians lived at Constantinople in the service of the emperor. A certain John the Iberian and his son Euthymios entered the Great Lavra as monks. Shortly after there was a monk John Tornikios, of noble Georgian birth, who, when serving Basil II, had had a share in subduing the rebel Bardas Skleros. Just as Nikephoros II Phokas could finance the building of the Great Lavra with rich loot after the recapture of Crete, so Basil II could support the Great Lavra with the loot from the east of Anatolia and thank the monk John Tornikios in a special manner for services rendered. John was given the nearby monastery of Kolobou that came into the possession of the Iviron Monastery, which was being founded for the Georgians. A *scriptorium* was established there to translate and copy Greek and Georgian texts.[20] Even monks from Calabria and Amalfi settled there. Thus the Holy Mountain was internationalized, which led to separate monasteries for Bulgarians, Serbs, Rumanians and Russians.

Basil II's attitude towards the military or civil aristocracy, the church, the patriarchs, the bishoprics and monasteries showed the characteristics of an autocrat. The link between religion and politics remained a matter of course. Basil was convinced that the

[19] P. Meyer, *Die Haupturkunden für die Geschichte der Athosklöster* (Leipzig, 1894), pp. 102–22.

[20] Thomas, *Private Religious Foundations* (see n.18), pp. 47–8; cf. 'Tornikios', in *ODB*, pp. 2096–7.

prayers of the monks contributed to his eventual victory over the barbarians and he donated considerable sums of money to the Great Lavra on Athos. The texts which give us some information on the emperor's attitude towards the monastery deal with the right of ownership and taxes. The usual *charistikion*, the system of giving monasteries to private persons, often caused abuse and controversy. The rich were inclined constantly to increase their possessions by acquiring monasteries and land. To keep the rich (*dynatoi*) in check Basil II issued new laws: those causing poverty through large estates had to contribute towards paying off the tax arrears of the poor. Political rather than social motives inspired Basil to take these measures. First and foremost they were designed to keep under control the powerful aristocracy, from which usurpers often arose, and to raise the necessary funds for his continual campaigns, and not to help the poor peasants. In 996 the law *Peri ton dynaton* was issued to restrict large-scale landownership, and in 1002 the *allelengyon* was introduced, a sort of communal tax liability. The rich had to pay more taxes to spare the poor.[21] This law also affected church and monastery property. The patriarchs Sisinios and Sergios II protested in vain. The laws remained valid until after the death of Basil II. That the emperor could take a hard line is confirmed by Michael Psellos. The emperor had a rich monastery in town razed to the ground; it was a prestige object built by his detested uncle and guardian. On this occasion he is said to have jested that he would turn a meditation centre (*phrontisterion*) into a source of unrest.[22] Thus, the emperors Nikephoros, John Tzimiskes and Basil II contributed to the establishment of monasteries by gifts and privileges, and kept their number under control by laws. Their attitude especially favoured the Athos monasteries, which became autonomous and independent of patriarchs, bishops and laymen. Mount Athos could develop into a 'monastic republic' within the Byzantine Empire.

The monk, Symeon the New Theologian, on palace life and the court

Symeon the Theologian is regarded by many as the greatest mystic of Greek spirituality. Nobody ever wrote so personally

[21] Thomas, *Private Religious Foundations*, pp. 160–4.
[22] Psellos, *Chronographie* (see n. 3), I, p. 20.

and in such great detail about his own intense experiences.[23] From his youth he lived in the City: he was a real city-dweller. In his work, life in the country remains sketchy and his mysticism hardly knows any cosmic dimension. Symeon went back to the region where he was born a couple of times, and referred to life in the country in his work, but then he rather dealt with the life of the landowners, who built luxurious rural mansions, with gardens and swimming-pools, fenced off against unwanted intruders, than with the life of peasants and farm-hands.[24] The images drawn from urban culture outnumber those from the countryside and agriculture and they refer to his immediate vicinity; they concern workmen who have to labour constantly and who hardly earn enough to provide for themselves and their families, or the rich of the upper classes, governors (*archontes*), the magnates (*megistanoi*) and the illustrious (*endoxoi*).[25] The monasteries in which Symeon lived, the Stoudios and Mamas monasteries, were situated in Constantinople; his spiritual father, Symeon Eulabes, guided his spiritual 'children' there from the Stoudios monastery. When, in 1009, Symeon was banished from the 'great and illustrious City' across the Bosporos, his adherents in Constantinople had him rehabilitated, and he was granted the monastery of St Marina, land and money, gardens and vineyards by certain wealthy city-dwellers.[26]

In Constantinople Symeon was familiar with palace life and the court and in contact with patricians and courtiers. A. Kazhdan noticed that his imagery and metaphors are dominated by the palace and the court.[27] The palace was not only the centre of power and riches, but also a place of luxurious and loose life. Byzantine historiographers only rarely criticize the system, but

23 W. Völker, *Praxis und Theoria bei Symeon dem Neuen Theologen: ein Beitrag zur byzantinischen Mystik* (Wiesbaden, 1974); B. Krivochéine, *Dans la lumière du Christ: Saint Syméon le Nouveau Théologien* (Chevetogne, 1980); B. Fraigneau-Julien, *Les Sens spirituels et la vision de Dieu selon Syméon le Nouveau Théologien*, Théologie historique, 67 (Paris, 1985); H.J.M. Turner, *St Symeon the New Theologian and Spiritual Fatherhood*, Byzantina Neerlandica, 2 (Leiden, New York, etc., 1990).

24 *TE*, 1, 1, SC 122, p. 180, 92–106.

25 *TE*, 7, SC 129, p. 166, 155–9.

26 *Epist.*, 16, p. 127, 3 ff; *Cat.*, 4, SC 96, p. 312, 5 ff; *Vita*, 93–4, p. 128, 104, pp. 142 f, 109–10, pp. 150 ff.

27 A. Kazhdan, 'Das System der Bilder und Metaphern in den Werken Symeons des Neuen Theologen', in *Unser ganzes Leben Christus unserm Gott überantworten: F. von Lilienfeld zum 65. Geburtstag*, ed. P. Hauptmann (Göttingen, 1982), pp. 221–39.

they are not afraid to mention the immoral life of various figures. The emperor Romanos II was married to the daughter of a merchant, called Anastaso, who took the name of Theophano at marriage. (She may have been the god-mother of the western empress Theophano, Otto II's wife and Otto III's mother.) She was a beauty and a *femme fatale*, and as such portrayed in the portrait gallery by Ch. Diehl.[28] John Skylitzes describes the death of the emperor Constantine VII, Romanos II's father. A servant had to pass him a poisoned cup which stood in front of the Holy Icon. He tripped by accident or on purpose, so that the wine poured from the cup and the remaining quantity of poison was not sufficient for instant death. According to Leo the Deacon, emperor Romanos was a good man, but he passionately enjoyed the pleasures of youth. This attracted young people of bad taste and loose life, who surrounded the emperor with cunning and flattery.[29] After the untimely death of Romanos the competent general Nikephoros Phokas became emperor. The monks advised him to give up his ascetic life and to marry, or else, according to Leo the Deacon, they feared that he would lead a frivolous life, which usually happens when lords and masters (*autodespotes kai autonomos*) accede to power.[30] He married the young, widowed empress Theophano. In December 969, he was gruesomely killed in his bedroom by the henchman of another general, John Tzimiskes, Theophano's lover.[31] John Tzimiskes succeeded Nikephoros as emperor and ruled until 976. Under these two emperors, who might be called guardian-emperors, the children of Romanos II and Theophano grew up. After the death of Tzimiskes, their eldest son, Basil II, succeeded to the throne (976–1025). We are informed about Basil's youth by Michael Psellos. Openly, the young Basil organized parties at which they sacrificed to Bacchus and Venus, but, as an adult, he was stern with himself and others. He remained unmarried, and he defeated the rebels in the empire and the enemies on the borders.[32]

During this period (*c.* 964–76) the future monk Symeon lived in courtly circles. It is a common *topos*, almost a cliché, for a monk to call himself unworthy, humble (*tapeinos*) or a sinner (*hamarto-*

[28] Ch. Diehl, *Figures byzantines*, I (Paris, 1908), pp. 217–43.

[29] John Skylitzes, *Synopsis* (see n. 4), p. 246; Leo the Deacon, *Historiae libri decem*, ed. C.B. Hase (Bonn, 1828), p. 6, 8–10.

[30] Leo the Deacon, *Historiae*, p. 49, 19.

[31] *Ibid.*, pp. 87–9.

[32] Psellos, *Chronographie* (see n. 3), I, p. 4.

los). But in his self-accusation Symeon went to great lengths. He is frank and open in his work, and suggests that he himself participated in the frivolous life at court. He calls himself a murderer, an adulterer in his heart, lewd in desires and deeds, given to orgies of eating and drinking, a magician, a pederast, a perjurer, a liar, a money-grubber, an impudent lover and a lecher. And he concludes this list of vices with the assurance that all this was not invented, but was the actual truth.[33]

Symeon was about eleven years old when he went to Constantinople. His parents, Basil and Theophano, were wealthy and had an estate in Paphlagonia. In the capital Symeon stayed with his highly esteemed family. His uncle was lord-in-waiting (*koubikoularios*), a function mostly fulfilled by eunuchs.[34] A lord-in-waiting was in a position of confidence and, against payment, he passed on requests to the emperor. In those days a eunuch from the region where Symeon was born, a Joseph Bringas, was very powerful in the empire. Symeon's uncle had free access (*parrhesia*) to the palace and introduced his nephew to the court, who became *spatharios-koubikoularios*, sword-bearer and a member of the senate.[35] A real sword-bearer/lord-in-waiting was a member of the emperor's bodyguard and a eunuch. It is often said that, in his youth, Symeon was a handsome fellow. He himself informs us that he was good-looking when he was about twenty years old and that his dress and manners were so refined that some people distrusted him. Such was his appearance, that even the good avoided him. His biographer, Niketas Stethatos, confirms this when he tells that Symeon's uncle wanted to introduce him to the emperor because of his physical beauty and the fact that he surpassed others in elegance.[36]

One wonders if Symeon was not involved in the murder of Nikephoros Phokas in 969, because he himself suggests that he was a murderer (*phoneus*). He was twenty years old at that time. Leo the Deacon insinuates that lords-in-waiting, who had to

[33] *Hym.*, 24, SC 174, p. 232, 70–83; 25, p. 264, 122; 20, p. 120, 120; 54, SC 196, p. 244, 101; *Cat.*, 17, SC 104, p. 256, 18.

[34] R. Guilland, 'Fonctions et dignités des eunuques', *Etudes Byzantines*, 2 (1944–5), 195; P.A. Yannopoulos, *La Société profane dans l'empire des VIIe, VIIIe et IXe siècles* (Louvain, 1975), p. 36.

[35] Perhaps 'bearer of the sword/lord in waiting' was only an honorary title. The membership of the senate was only an honorary function; it was in fact a 'ceremonial or court senate' (*sénat d'apparat*). Cf. N. Oekonomides, *Les Listes de préséance byzantines des IXe et Xe siècles* (Paris, 1972), pp. 295, 300.

[36] *Cat.*, 22, SC 104, p. 366, 25; *Hym.*, 20, SC 174, p. 118, 118; *Vita*, 3, pp. 4 f.

guard the emperor at night, were accomplices in the cowardly murder.[37] Other texts contain suggestions about homosexual relationships. According to his biographer, after his death Symeon appeared unto a certain Philotheos as a 'white-haired, handsome, venerable eunuch'.[38] The eunuchs were not held in high esteem. They were recognizable by the absence of a beard. Because of the risk of homosexuality they were not allowed in most monasteries, including Athos; for that matter, all beardless youngsters were barred from the Holy Mountain. Certain outpourings in the hymns suggest that Symeon fought against his inclination towards homosexuality.[39] Homosexuality may also have played a part in his relationship with Symeon Eulabes and his conviction. After a long period of struggle and uncertainty God had mercy upon Symeon the New Theologian. He was converted particularly through his spiritual father, Symeon Eulabes, monk at the renowned Stoudios monastery. In 977, when he was about twenty-seven years old, Symeon entered this monastery as a novice. The special relationship between the two Symeons resulted in a conflict with the superior of the monastery, Peter, who had Symeon removed from the monastery within a year.[40] Then Symeon entered the nearby monastery of St Mamas, where he was ordained a priest in 980 and appointed superior of the community. He was to fulfil this function until his conviction and banishment in 1009. Symeon the New Theologian was grateful for the rest of his life for the change that had been brought about by the elder Symeon, who had become his father on earth, his guide, his guard, a prop and stay to him. He was like Moses who led away the righteous from sinful Egypt; like Christ who in a vision appeared unto Paul on his way to Damascus.[41] This ardent veneration did not come to an end when Symeon Eulabes died in 986/7. In honour of his spiritual father, Symeon junior composed hymns and lauds and wrote a *Vita*. Moreover, he had an icon painted of Symeon Eulabes and commemorated him yearly. All went well for some time. The patriarch gave his permission for the commemoration and even wished to be informed about the time of the feast, so that he could send candles and incense to pay

[37] Leo the Deacon, *Historiae* (see n. 29), pp. 85–6. [38] *Vita*, 147, pp. 216 ff.

[39] *Hym.*, 24, SC 174, p. 232, 74; cf. Turner, *St Symeon* (see n. 23), pp. 28–9, 43.

[40] *Vita*, 11–16, pp. 18 ff.

[41] *Hym.*, 2, SC 156, p. 180, 47; 56, SC 196, p. 272, 14; 7, SC 156, p. 208, 7; 18, SC 174, p. 86, 139; *Cat.*, 20, SC 104, p. 334, 60.

honour to the holy man. But from 1003 until the conviction in 1009, the *synkellos* Stephen of Nikomedeia incessantly brought charges against him to the patriarch and the synod. The conflict between Stephen of Nikomedeia and Symeon the Theologian was, in fact, a conflict about theological as well as personal matters.

Relatively little is known about Stephen of Nikomedeia, but we get a vague impression of him from stray notes. He was metropolitan of Nikomedeia (nowadays Izmit) but he had been promoted to the rank of *synkellos* by the emperor; he was highly esteemed at court and enjoyed the confidence of the emperor, who even asked him for an explanation when in 975 a comet in the shape of a cypress of fire appeared above the city at night. In 976 he was entrusted with a confidential task by the emperor; he was sent to change the mind of the rebellious general Bardos Skleros.[42] From a letter of the old general Nikephoros Ouranos it can be concluded that Stephen was a highly respected person in the upper circles of the capital and from a letter which he himself wrote to a colleague, the metropolitan of Synada, it turns out that he was proud of his honourable position at court.[43] The period under discussion used to be called the Macedonian Renaissance, but later the term Encyclopedism was introduced to replace it.[44] The collection and systematization of the available information from times past, rather than creativity, were emphasized during this period. Constantine VII and his courtiers had compiled *De thematibus*, *De administrando imperio*, and *De ceremoniis*. Compilations were also made of Roman law, agriculture and military matters. Nikephoros Ouranos mentioned above was a pious layman, patron of the Great Lavra on Athos. He had compiled a manual on military strategy, and he was also involved in the compilation of the *Menologion*, a collection of Saints' Lives, arranged according to the date (month (*men*) and day) of each saint's celebration.[45] Stephen of Nikomedeia wrote a number of minor works on the soul as composed of three parts and on the Holy Trinity, which have not yet been published. On the basis of the nature of the titles of these works, which are described as

[42] Leo the Deacon, *Historiae* (see n. 29), p. 169; George Kedrenos, *Compendium Historiarum*, PG 122, 153.

[43] Darrouzès, *Epistoliers* (see n. 1), p. 34.

[44] 'Encyclopedism', in *ODB*, pp. 696–7.

[45] G. Karlson, *Idéologie et cérémonial dans l'épistolographie byzantine* (Uppsala, 1962), p. 53; A. Dain, *La 'Tactique' de Nicéphore Ouranos* (Paris, 1937).

summaries (*syntomos*, *synopsis*), I. Hausherr assumes that Stephen was a clear-headed, practical theologian, who could put doctrine into clear-cut words.[46] In Byzantine theology G. Podskalsky distinguishes the philosophical, rational movement and the charismatic, ascetic movement, the representatives of which were often on bad terms with one another.[47] Stephen's theology belongs to the former movement, which was accepted in official circles. Elsewhere G. Podskalsky calls him a 'court theologian'.[48]

Symeon the New Theologian's theology or spirituality belongs to the charismatic ascetic movement, which is dominated by the experience of the Spirit. This experience of the Spirit is the basis of doctrine, the hierarchy and the sacraments. In this context all authorities, emperors, patriarchs, bishops, priests, spiritual leaders and theologians are judged. The principle that a person could only take authoritative action when he is inspired by the Spirit applied to all. From this position Symeon launches his hostile attacks against Stephen and his theology. His twenty-first hymn is a spontaneous tirade against his main adversary and his vain words, fallacies and pseudo-knowledge. Someone who does not have the Spirit within him should not discuss spiritual matters, the mysteries of the faith.[49] The differences between the theological approaches of Stephen and Symeon were intensified by their strained relationship, in which envy played a part. They could both rely on certain followers in Constantinople. The flame of envy announced the fire, is the opinion of Symeon's biographer. Stephen was the first one to be blamed for Symeon's suffering and conviction, the contriver of the drama (*dramatourgos*).[50] At the synod of 3 January, Symeon was convicted and banished across the Bosporos.

Formally Symeon was accused of unlawful, public worship of Symeon Eulabes as a saint, but the real cause was a different one.[51] To Symeon the New Theologian his spiritual father was a saint

[46] *Vita*, Introduction, p. LIV.

[47] G. Podskalsky, *Theologie und Philosophie in Byzanz*, Byzantinisches Archiv, 15 (Munich, 1977), p. 34.

[48] G. Podskalsky, 'Religion und religiöses Leben im Byzanz des 11. Jahrhunderts', *Orientalia Christiana Periodica*, 57 (1991), 371–97, at p. 388.

[49] *Hym.*, 21, SC 174, pp. 134–6, 54–90. Cf. *Vita*, 2, p. 4, 24; 72, p. 98, 13; 130, p. 186, 10; *TE*, 1, 12, SC 122, p. 294, 306; 2, 2, SC 122, p. 334, 132; 9, SC 129, p. 238, 252; 11, p. 354, 356.

[50] *Vita*, 83–94, pp. 112–29.

[51] 'Doch mögen die Gründe tiefer liegen', A. Kabylis, *Symeon Neos Theologos: Hymnen* (Berlin, 1976), Prolegomena, XVIII.

who was misunderstood and persecuted, a martyr. But he was glorified by the Spirit and showed himself to be a saint (*hagios*) and free of emotions (*apathes*).[52] Perhaps the compilation of the *Menologion* which was completed at that time played a part in this. The *Menologion* may have been an attempt by Stephen to keep the spontaneous growth of veneration of saints under control. But the point really was the controversial holiness of the deceased Symeon and not so much the veneration of saints in general. Stephen gave orders that the words 'the holy' on the icon which was shown at the synod be scratched out.[53] To the *synkellos* Stephen, Symeon was not at all a saint.

The virtue most admired by Symeon the New Theologian in his spiritual father was his freedom from emotion (*apatheia*). *Apatheia* means the absence of desires and sinful passions, the control of the body and the independence of the spirit, developed after the victory over passions. Since Evagrios, *apatheia* is the conclusion of ascesis and the entrance to true knowledge and vision. It implies being free of sexual passion and desire. Attitudes were sometimes ambivalent towards the concept, the more so because Messalians or Euchitai had been accused of explaining *apatheia* as the absence of sins or even the possibility of sin. To test their *apatheia* some ascetics went as far as venturing into scandalous and infamous situations.[54] Symeon junior had an unshakable faith in his spiritual father, who had reached the highest point of *apatheia* (*akra apatheia*). He could keep his natural movement under control and showed as much emotion as a corpse.[55] This *apatheia* also involves sexual indifference towards women.[56] According to some monks Symeon Eulabes had taken dangerous risks. Symeon the New Theologian defended his spiritual father: those that lack *apatheia* are not able to judge. Even if you see a person with *apatheia* do something indecent you should not believe your own eyes, but you should realize that it is a dead body you see in action.[57]

Symeon could discuss vision in high-flown words, but he could also be banal and rude. This certainly goes for the fifteenth hymn,

[52] *Cat.*, 6, SC 104, p. 36, 259–70. [53] *Vita*, 88–91, pp. 120–6.

[54] Cf. L. Rydén, *Das Leben des heiligen Narren Symeon von Leontios* (Stockholm, 1963), pp. 145–8; G. Da Costa-Louillet, 'Saints de Constantinople aux VIIIe, IXe et Xe siècles', in *Byzantion*, 24 (1954), 179–263, at pp. 201–2.

[55] *Vita*, 4, p. 6, 4; 81, p. 110, 3.

[56] *TE*, 6, SC 129, p. 120, 1–10; 6, p. 122, 44.

[57] *Cat.*, 20, SC 104, pp. 336–7, 80–7; *Hym.*, 9, SC 156, p. 226, 25.

which is called 'the most peculiar of his hymns', 'la pièce choquante'.[58] Physical love is described in detail, and subsequently applied to the mystical body of Christ. Someone without *apatheia* is not in a position to criticize Symeon Eulabes, for he was really a saint, who was not ashamed of seeing people naked or of being seen naked himself, for he was fully Christ and remained motionless, unharmed and imperturbable (*apathes*).[59] These pieces of information make it probable that the controversial holiness of Symeon senior was also at stake during the synodal legal proceedings. To Symeon the New Theologian his spiritual father was a chosen instrument of the Spirit, gifted with the highest knowledge of God. To the learned *synkellos* Stephen of Nikomedeia he was a charlatan, a spiritual bungler, who, without knowledge and not being a priest, pretended to guide his spiritual children in the capital and who, because of his annoying behaviour, was certainly not liable to be regarded as a saint.

On 3 January 1009, the case was put to the vote at the synod. Symeon was convicted and banished; on a cold winter's day he was taken across the Bosporos. A number of wealthy and important men from the capital turned to the patriarch for the rehabilitation of Symeon. The patriarch felt ill at ease with this large, illustrious delegation, fearing that this affair might eventually be taken to the emperor and that he might end up being officially convicted.[60] He rehabilitated Symeon and even offered him a bishopric, but Symeon preferred to stay in the monastery of St Marina, where he was to be active for almost thirteen years until his death.

Symeon's conviction and banishment and their background shed some light on the contrast between the more official theology and monastic spirituality, between office and charisma, between hierarchy and the monastery. It turns out that the monks had less to fear from the patriarch than from the emperor's *synkellos*. But the latter, Stephen of Nikomedeia, needed a very long time to have his point of view accepted by the patriarch and the synod, and, for fear of the mighty ones in the city and of the emperor himself, Symeon's conviction was soon followed by his rehabilitation. The synodal proceedings elucidate the relationship

[58] 'Der eigenartigste des Hymnencorpus', Kabylis, *Symeon* (see n. 51), XXVII; cf. note J. Koder, *Hym.*, 15, SC 156, pp. 276–7.
[59] *Hym.*, 15, SC 156, pp. 290–2, 158–74; *ibid.*, p. 294, 205–20.
[60] *Vita*, 102, pp. 140–2.

between the palace and the monastery, but there are also numerous texts by Symeon himself that inform us about palace life and the court.

As has been mentioned above, A. Kazhdan states that the images and metaphors in Symeon's work referring to the imperial palace outnumber others, and that they are, in fact, the essence of his imagery.[61] I suspect that the images taken from the symbolism of light are even more frequent. But it should be admitted that the images deriving from court life, dress, throne, crown, banquet, riches and imperial power occur very frequently. Two sorts of texts can be distinguished: comparisons and direct texts. The comparisons with the emperor and those with many details on the palace and the court primarily serve to illustrate the contact between the monk and God. In those days the emperor should constantly be on the alert for possible insurrections and conspiracies. Basil II successfully defeated two rebellious generals, Bardas Phokas and Bardas Skleros. Symeon informs us of the punishments and pardons. If a conspiracy against the emperor is discovered, the house of the conspirator is surrounded and he himself is punished severely. Likewise the Last Judgement will judge all those that are not invested with Christ. Or 'the emperor of the Christians' grants pardon to the rebels that repent. The pardon he grants is elaborated very sentimentally with allusions to the parable of the prodigal son. 'The emperor raises the prostrated rebel, embraces him and showers him with kisses; he gives him his own robe, a crown and purple footwear. At night he is cuddled, put in the emperor's bed, who tucks him in and embraces him.'[62]

Those who serve the heavenly Emperor are confidants and friends of God, just as the officers who have fought bravely become friends of the emperor. A blacksmith, a goldsmith or a carpenter can come to the palace to do odd jobs, but after their work they are paid and sent away, without having seen the emperor. But the soldiers who have shown themselves brave during the war are admitted to the emperor.[63] Those that surround the earthly emperor consider this to be a great honour; they are proud of it and the others envy them. How much more shall the monks be pleased who enlisted for the heavenly Emperor?[64] One whom the emperor has raised from deepest poverty to the

[61] Kazhdan, 'Das System' (see n. 27), p. 230; cf. Turner, *St Symeon* (see n. 23), p. 21.
[62] *TE*, 10, SC 129, pp. 276–8, 235–73.
[63] *TE*, 7, SC 129, p. 166, 133–56.
[64] *Cat.*, 10, SC 104, p. 138, 6–14.

greatest wealth, who is given splendid official robes that befit his illustrious dignity, who is given the assignment to stand in the sight of the emperor, will look up to him with love and affection. So shall the monk, called to keep the commands of Christ and admitted to the highest worship, be grateful for the favour, the grace of the Holy Ghost, which surrounds him like royal purple.[65]

Elsewhere the emperor acts as supreme commander. He assembles the army, he positions it for battle, he decides what weapons to use, he posts sentries, he sends out scouts. Likewise penitence, the queen of all virtues, should position the virtues for battle to parry the attack of the enemy.[66] In such comparisons Symeon seems to follow the current concept of emperorship, which is to the people a source of power and riches. But sometimes he is critical and expresses his more personal views. An earthly king and the prominent people around him do not pay attention to the poor and are not pleased with their presence. But God, whose majesty no-one can bear, deigned to become father, friend and brother to the poor.[67] And the perfect monk sees the vanity of it all. He who is 'free of emotions' (*apathes*) looks at the world with a different eye. He is not impressed by the splendour of the imperial surroundings, but only minds lasting things. Gold to him is just a piece of dust, gems just trivial stones, silk robes just a caterpillar's droppings. This pomp and circumstance and the people's cheers are to him a ridiculous display.[68] His criticism is even harsher in certain passages, where the emperor is addressed directly. Hymn fifty-eight is a reproaching appeal addressed by God (and Symeon) to all people: to emperors, bishops, monks and laymen. The emperors had better, Symeon says, wage war against the heathens (*ethne*). But, in doing so, they should not take over the inclination of the heathens and do as they do, and renounce God the King. They had better heed God's words, carry out His commands and live a simple life in poverty, mentioned by Him in the Beatitudes, than free the world of death and temporary slavery and in doing so become slaves of passions and demons themselves. All works done for God or out of compassion are good works. But the first and foremost of all works is having compassion with oneself by showing real remorse. If not, one is worse than a heathen.[69]

[65] *Chap.*, 2, 8, SC 5 bis, p. 106, 7–22.
[66] *Cat.*, 4, SC 96, p. 352, 470.
[67] *Cat.*, 2, SC 96, p. 250, 110.
[68] *TE*, 6, SC 129, p. 136, 220–36.
[69] *Hym.*, 58, SC 196, pp. 280–2, 34–63.

The fifth *Catechesis*, the longest of all, is another admonition of God (and of Symeon) to the emperor. Symeon holds David's contrition up as an example.

> But you, unhappy, mortal, perishable people, you wish to be absolute monarchs and rulers of the world (*kosmokratores*). If someone in another country does not want to submit to your authority, you will not be able to bear his insubordination. Though you are not more than he is, you treat him as a slave. You do not wish to submit to Me, your Creator and Master. You retaliate for evil inflicted on you by your enemy. But what about your own sins against Me? Do you think that no-one will ask you to justify the blood of innocent people? Or that no-one will see what you have done covertly? Have you forgotten Me, and have you imagined that there is no-one above you? Have not you heard Me say over and over again that whoever wants to be the first will be the last of all and the servant and slave of all?

The essence of all reproaches is that the emperors and princes, unlike David, have not left the punishment to God and did not do penance for their sins.[70]

Symeon must be the most outspoken representative of the ascetic-charismatic movement of Byzantine spirituality. The 'world' he left is coloured by his experience in the capital and at court. Once he has experienced the Spirit, inspired by his spiritual father, that 'world' has become vanity and illusion to him. He seems to look down on it, as it were from a different world. He repeatedly mentions two worlds.[71] By withdrawing from the world, he leaves ruling to others, which does have its consequences for the mystic's political and social ideas.[72]

His attitude towards the emperors is ambivalent. When he uses images deriving from the emperor, the palace or the court as his starting point for the comparison with the relationship with God, Symeon is in line with the ideas of the people. The people have no authority whatsoever over imperial power. They may gape in admiration at the pomp and circumstance surrounding and

[70] *Cat.*, 5, SC 96, pp. 426–30, 595–636.

[71] *Chap.*, 2, SC 51 bis, pp. 114–18, 22–4; *Hym.*, 28, SC 174, p. 296, 28; 57, SC 196, p. 276, 7. There are two worlds, two suns, two lights, two kinds of blindness and death.

[72] A.J. van der Aalst, 'Symeon de Nieuwe Theoloog 949–1022: politieke en sociale ideeën van een mysticus', *Het Christelijk Oosten*, 37 (1985), 229–47; 38 (1986), 3–22.

symbolizing power, but they cannot really have a share in it. The emperor was a superpowerful autocrat and the abyss between him and his subject was deep and wide. The idea that power could reside with the people was absurd to the Byzantines. 'If', says Symeon, 'in this large and crowded city, a person were asked for the function of grand chamberlain (*praepositus*) or of first keeper of the emperor's wardrobe (*protovestiarios*), or to go to the palace with a request, no-one would accept this and the person would call the people that asked him insane.'[73]

Symeon does not take the dignity, the power and the authority of the emperors as seriously as many a Byzantine theologian or canonist does. He does not allude to the divine mission of the emperors, nor to high-flown titles emphasizing his majesty. In his more personal approach Symeon shows himself unimpressed by all sorts of authorities, and he sometimes speaks disparagingly of the emperors and their entourage. His criticism stems from a sort of proud humbleness which is often found with monks; monks should be humble, they should consider themselves the least of all people, but they think their own world far above that of the emperor. For a monk has control over himself, is master of himself, while the emperor only controls other people and is no master over his passions. This contrast was elaborated upon as early as the fourth century by John Chrysostom, after Plato's comparison of the philosopher and the tyrant.[74] The monk is the true wise man, the world he has chosen is far above the 'vanity fair' on earth. By the end of the eleventh century a popular story was circulating, an Indian Mirror of Princes, translated into Greek, in which it is laid down that for a noble person only two dwelling-places are fitting, the king's court and the ascetic's tent.[75] Symeon clearly chose the latter.

This was the world Theophano lived in before she became empress in the West. She must have lived a rather protected life, unaware for the most part of the things we have now reconstructed, waiting for the time she would be given in marriage in 972. Once she was at the western court, her influence mingled with that of Saxon and Roman families. Both Theophano and

[73] *Cat.*, 18, SC 104, pp. 284–6, 247–60. Cf. A. Kazhdan and G. Constable, *People and Power in Byzantium* (Washington, DC, 1982), p. 35.

[74] John Chrysostom, *Comparatio regis et monachi*, PG, 47, 387–92.

[75] L.O. Sjöberg, *Stephanitis und Ichnilates* (Uppsala, 1962); 'Seth, Symeon', in *ODB*, pp. 1882–3.

her son Otto III were used to a certain luxury as well as to asceticism. Two of her daughters, Adelheid and Sophia, entered the convent and became abbesses.[76] She wanted to be buried in the monastic church of St Pantaleon in Cologne, with her hair cut off and dressed in a Benedictine's habit. And her son, Otto III, who died early in 1002, managed to combine Byzantine luxury with his admiration of the Greek monks whom he had met in southern Italy.

[76] G. Wolf, 'Nochmals zur Frage: Wer war Theophano', *BZ*, 8 (1988), 272–83.

Index

Index

Index

Lightning Source UK Ltd.
Milton Keynes UK
17 March 2011

169397UK00001B/112/A

9 780521 524674